Americans from Africa

Volume 1

Americans from Africa

Slavery and Its Aftermath

Peter I. Rose, editor

With a new preface by the editor

Transaction Publishers
New Brunswick (U.S.A.) and London (U.K.)

Library of Congress Catalog Number: 2006047989
ISBN: 978-1-4128-6328-5
eBook: 978-1-4128-6360-5
Printed in the United States of America

Library of Congress Cataloging-in-Publication Data

Slavery and its aftermath / Peter I. Rose, editor
    p. cm.
Originally published in 2 v. as Americans from Africa. New York:
    Atherton Press, 1970.
 Includes bibliographical references and index.
 ISBN 978-0-202-30941-5 (alk. paper)
 1. African Americans. 2. African Americans—Social conditions. 3. African Americans—Civil rights. 4. African Americans—Race identity. 5. United States—Race relations. 6. Slavery—United States—History. I. Rose, Peter Isaac, 1933- II. Title.
 E185.A475 2007
 305.896'073—dc22

                                                    2006047989

Contents

Preface to the Transaction Edition

The Past as Prologue

"Black Power." Two electrifying words.

It was 1964. The couplet and what it seemed to portend caught many politicians and the pundits and not a few in the civil rights movement itself by surprise. The catalytic slogan of consciousness-raising among African Americans and many other minority groups—stimulating the rise of Brown Power and Yellow Power and Red Power and a new militancy among feminists—was like a fire bell in the night, awakening a whole nation to the depth of the divisions still pervading the society. The new assertions of political power and related demands that echoed and re-echoed in government offices, urban centers, and on university campuses signaled a new phase in America's long history of identity politics. As more and more African-American "brothers" and "sisters" joined the cause, their leaders not only protested policies of which they disapproved and sought equal treatment for those they represented, but also began to speak much more forcefully about group rights, often making categorical claims to those in public and private positions of power.

Among the most vocal advocates of *group* recognition and *group* rights were a number of black leaders, including many long-time civil rights advocates who had grown impatient with the strategy of non-violent civil disobedience and were becoming increasingly dismayed with the slow pace of change in the decade "since Brown" (a reference to the 1954 Supreme Court decision that declared that "separate could never be equal") and subsequent acts that were thought to—and in many cases did—portend significant gains in a number of spheres of social and political life but, apparently, not nearly enough to eradicate the roots of racism. At the same time, some who had fought for years for integration began to have second thoughts about what a total victory might mean. In the face of programs that spoke of their people as "disadvantaged" and "culturally deprived," they began to wonder if integration could only be achieved through assimilation, by "turning white," figuratively if not literally. None was more eloquent on the subject than James Farmer, one of the founders of the decidedly bi-racial Congress of Racial Equality (CORE). Farmer stated his concern with an eloquent simplicity: "We learned that America simply couldn't *be* color-blind, it would have to *become* color-blind and that it would *become* color-blind only when we gave up our color." Then, he explained, "The white man, who presumably has no color, would have to give up only his prejudices. We would have to give up our identities. Thus, we would usher in the Great Day with an act of complete self-denial and self-abasement."

Many African Americans and many other non-whites agreed with Farmer's sentiments, expressing their disillusionment even more forcefully, directing their anger not only at the white establishment but at what many felt was a patronizing attitude of some of their own leaders as well as their liberal allies.

It wasn't just talk, Black Power was at once political and cultural, a call to action but also to introspection about the true meaning of being black in predominately white America.

While monumental in its implications, not everyone was caught off guard by the events or the reactions. There were many within the African American community and some long-time students of race relations and social class who had tried to give fair warning about the increasing polarization and to suggest ways of addressing it. They based their concerns and predictions on three phenomena: first, a familiarity with the history of slavery and the struggles that followed in the century after Emancipation; second, the growing depth of frustration at the slowness of change and its attendant alienation, reflected in many parts of the black community; and, third, the widespread lack of knowledge in white communities about the African-American experience in all its manifestations: historical, institutional, organizational and cultural, including its complex relationships with the dominant groups and the dominant culture. The pattern was and remained in many ways asymmetrical.

While rife with their own ethnocentricies, like members of minority groups everywhere, African Americans have always had to live and to function in two worlds, their own and that of those who dominated almost every sector of society, those "others" whose rules they had to know well in order to survive. It is important not only to note that asymmetry but to indicate that, as important as it might be for blacks to have a deeper understanding of any number of matters that confront them, it is even more important that white people learn about the culture and character of their fellow Americans and the challenges they face within and beyond the confines of their often restricted communities.

In the wake of the upheaval of the mid-1960s, it seemed critically apparent that it was necessary to find ways of discussing the nature of slavery and its legacy, to teach about the origins of the protests against discrimination, and to stimulate pride in self and community and a range of related issues that effected both black and white Americans.

I was one of many moved to address these and other matters in a new and challenging way. My first attempt had begun on the eve of what many would soon define as a new era in race relations.

In the late summer of 1963, several days before the great March on Washington at which Martin Luther King, Jr., spoke of his dream, I mailed the manuscript for a small book on racial and ethnic relations in the United States to my publisher. Its title, *They and We*, spoke to the dichotomy that to me had long been clearly evident in our society. The book was published by Random House a year later.*

In the year-long hiatus between delivering the manuscript and its publication a sea change in the relationship between blacks and whites had erupted. It may have been triggered by the assassination of John F. Kennedy on November 22, 1963, just three months after the historic March. It may have been related to disappointment with the promises and early actions of JFK's successor, Lyndon Johnson, as his wont to greatly expand responses to the widely feared takeover of Vietnam by the communists took precedence over his major domestic and very Rooseveltian initiative, the War on Poverty. And it was doubtlessly connected to the frustration of long-suffering campaigners for social justice throughout the country, especially in the South.

The dream of full equality could no longer be deferred. Although long in coming, the upheaval burst forth like Langston Hughes' "festering sore." "Black Power" became a battle cry for some and a haunting

---

* *They and We: Racial and Ethnic Relations in the United States* (Random House, 1964).

specter for others. "We Shall Overcome" was taking on a whole new meaning.**

I immediately thought of preparing a companion volume to under-score some of the matters discussed in *They and We* "in their own words," that is, in the powerful voices of those activists and academics who were or had long been trying to come to terms with the multiple meanings of being black in this society. I wanted readers to hear the varied viewpoints on the "they vs. we" phenomenon and to feel the tensions between blacks and whites among various actors in sectors of both groups. Furthermore, in my mind, such an anthology should be formatted, shaped and edited in a way that, as readers read each essay they would be quickly drawn into the writer's argument, hopefully becoming convinced of its logic or its veracity and would hold to that view *until they read the very next one in the section.*

To do what I thought needed to be done was a huge and expensive project. It turned out to be too big and too risky for Random House and, while saying it was a good idea, several editors suggested that I take to a university press.

While thinking of doing that, I learned that Charles D. Lieber, the senior editor who had brought me to Random House in the early 1960s, was leaving it to start his own publishing house. In a way he took me with him, especially when he gave me carte blanche to do the very book I had envisioned. In 1970, Lieber's new Atherton Press published the two-volume book of controversies, *Americans from Africa.* That book is this book, now reissued for a second time (the first reissue was in 2007) without alteration by Transaction Publishers, the company that had taken over what had become Atherton/Aldine Press.

When recently contacted by representatives of Transaction to con-sider having it once again reprint and reissue this two-volume collec-tion, now mainly to be found only in libraries and used book stores, I asked why they wanted to do it, and do it without emendations. The president of the company, Mary E. Curtis, said "because it is a classic."

Aside from making me feel like a fossil, it pleased me immensely that she and her colleagues felt, as I have felt for so long, that the issues

---

** I first wrote about my own concerns in a Letter to the Editor of the *New York* Times, published on July 27, 1964, addressing the explosions of pent up frustration and urban riot that had just taken place in an area but a few blocks from where my mother was raised and my grandmother still lived. That letter, which included the line "But as a social scientist, I am not at all surprised by what is happening," headed by the words "Reaping the Whirlwind," is now reprinted on the very first page of the 50th anniversary edition of *They and We* (Paradigm/Routledge, 2014).

addressed a half century ago still remain part and parcel—some might say the bedrock—of the continuing assessment of the African-American experience and essential to understanding it.

At a time when the latest controversy has a new slogan—"Black Lives Matter," an echo of the plaintive words "White man, listen!" penned by Richard Wright many years ago, and a quick review of the issues that generated its appeal, it is apparent that the they/we dichotomy persists in America and there is still a long way to go to make ours "a more perfect union."

About These Volumes

Americans from Africa was and remains a two-volume book of eight controversies, four in Volume I, *Slavery and Its Aftermath* and four in Volume II, *Old Memories, New Moods*.

Here, in Volume I, differing views on four seminal questions or sets of questions are grouped under singular headings. The first one, sometimes called "The Herskovits-Frazier Debate," asks how much of African cultural patterns and social relations were retained by blacks in the African Diaspora. The second, known today as "The Elkins Controversy" (named for the late historian Stanley Elkins, author of *Slavery*, a landmark study that is still the subject of learned papers and heated disputes), deals with several scholars' judgments on the impact of slavery on the personality of those who endured it. The next set of papers addresses the broader question of how similar and different were the manners and mores, attitudes, and especially the experiences of African Americans who remained in the south after the Civil War to those who moved north in the late nineteenth and early twentieth century. It includes essays and commentaries by Charles S. Johnson, Hylan Lewis, Claude Brown, Charles Keil, and Ulf Hannerz, the Swedish anthropologist and author of the book *Soulside*. The last part of *Slavery and Its Aftermath* also touches on several other issues, all variations on three themes: community, class and family life. Included there is the full text of Daniel Patrick Moynihan's controversial report on "The Negro Family" and several critical reviews of it.

As I noted in the original introductions to the two volumes, *the first volume considers how black Africans became American Negroes; the second is about how those Negroes became African–Americans.*

The debates in Volume II are in some ways even more politically charged than those in Volume I. *Old Memories, New Moods* begins with a question that is not entirely rhetorical, "Who *Was* Nat Turner?"

It considers the roots of protest and Black Nationalism. In addition to the full text of the original "confessions" of Nat Turner there is a discussion of William Styron's novel on the same subject and others' responses to it. Two sections follow these, both in one way or other on politics: the politics of liberal pluralism and, using Milton Gordon's apt phrase, the politics of corporate pluralism. The first of these offers commentaries on and critiques of the civil rights movement and the call for "Freedom Now!;" the second is on the meaning and future of "Black Power" for its advocates and followers and for those in the wider society. It begins with Stokely Carmichael's statement "What We Want" and ends with Martin Luther King, Jr.'s question "Where Do We Go From Here?" Lastly, there is a section called "Negroes Nevermore." It is about being black in American society, circa 1970—but, in many ways, is about being black in the second decade of the twenty-first century!

Most of the essays in each of the volumes are presentations of arguments in the words of their originators: writers, activists, historians, anthropologists, psychiatrists, sociologists, and policy planners. Becoming vicariously immersed in their debates may be seen as the grounding for understanding some of the more recent controversies, not only those about fairness and justice before the law, but about race and class and gender and the relations between black and white Americans as well as those between blacks and other non-white minorities, including many newcomers to the country who often seem to move in, up, and over blacks as they seek their own American Dream.

Many of the issues raised in the very first section of Volume I about "the retention of Africanisms" are being reheard in the sometimes thoughtful, sometimes vitriolic and always challenging exchanges on the meaning and challenge of Afrocentrism today. The matter of role-playing and the internalization of disgrace, both considered in "The Elkins Debate," is still a hot topic, as is the meaning of the move to the North—and, of late, the reverse migration of increasing numbers of African Americans. Few can even consider debates about the role of class in the African American world without addressing arguments offered in the last part of the first volume.

Such parallels may be drawn with each section of the second volume. New considerations of slave revolts and the rise of "Black Power," for example, must be set in the context of the earlier ones. New views of the civil rights movement cannot be understood without knowing about its origins, the principal subject of the second part of *Old Mem-*

ories, New Moods. Likewise, new approaches to nationalism and its effectiveness and the ultimate meaning of membership in a cohort or ethnic entity—a link back to the very first topic, are best understood if put into historical context.

New readers should note that most contributors—black and white—whose works are published in this book used the then-common word "Negroes" instead of the now-favored "African Americans" in their writing. The term was de rigueur prior to 1970 and it would be inappropriate to change it in this book of essays written "In their [and my] words."

All told, immersion in the debates of the not-so-distant past provides a useful prologue to understanding continuing concerns about the hardly monolithic cultures, characters, communities and identities of Americans from Africa.

Peter I. Rose
January, 2016

Acknowledgments

In a front pages of the original edition of *Americans from Africa*, a compendium of mostly previously published essays, reports, and critiques, I indicated that, at my invitation, August Meier and Elliott Rudwick, Gerald W. Mullin, and Mina Davis Caulfield prepared original essays for these two volumes of controversies. These pieces added much to the assessment of the challenging attempt to give grounding to a number of issues relating to the Black Experience in the United States. Their contributions were gratefully acknowledged; so, of course, were those of the other authors whose work was edited and reprinted in these pages. My gratitude for having been granted permission to include the seminal works of all the contributors remains. Now, with the reissuing of *Americans from Africa*, new generations of readers can study their thought-provoking and often conflicting opinions on the eight issues addressed.

Like to many authors and editors, I remain grateful for the advice and counsel from those behind the scenes. Among those who were particularly helpful on various aspects of the initial project as it was taking shape were my friends Ely Chinoy and David Riesman, my assistant Deborah Keehn Black, a number of specialists on the history and politics of intergroup relations, several members of civil rights organizations, and many students and colleagues at Smith, Wesleyan, the University of Colorado, and UCLA. No less important were Charles D. Lieber, Marlene Mandel, and the staff of Atherton Press for their many helpful suggestions and constant support in the preparation, design, and distribution of *Americans from Africa*, first published by Atherton in 1970.

To these heartfelt encomiums I wish to add a special note of thanks to Mary E. Curtis, president of Transaction Publishers, which had absorbed what had become Aldine/Atherton Press into her company in 2007. Mary's interest and involvement, has, as it did when the book was re-released by Transaction that same year, once again given new life to this vintage collection.

Peter I. Rose

Contributors

CLAUDE BROWN is a writer. His most famous work is *Manchild in the Promised Land.*

LAURA CARPER has been actively engaged in the movement for human rights. She is a member of the Michigan Civil Rights Commission.

MINA DAVIS CAULFIELD, who once worked as a semi-skilled stitcher in Boston's garment district and lived in the South End and Roxbury ghettos, is now completing graduate work in psychological anthropology at the University of California, Berkeley.

KENNETH B. CLARK is Professor of Psychology at the City College of the City University of New York. He is the author of *Prejudice and Your Children* and *Dark Ghetto* and the editor of *The Negro Protest.*

C. FRANKLIN EDWARDS is Chairman of the Department of Sociology at Howard University and author of *The Negro Professional Class.*

STANLEY M. ELKINS is Sydenham Clark Parsons Professor of History at Smith College. He is the author of *Slavery: A Problem in American Institutional and Intellectual Life.*

E. FRANKLIN FRAZIER was Chairman of the Department of Sociology at Howard University at the time of his death. A former president of the American Sociological Association, Frazier was the author of *Black Bourgeoisie, The Negro Family,* and *The Negro in the United States.*

EUGENE D. GENOVESE, author of *The Political Economy of Slavery*, is Chairman of the Department of History at the University of Rochester.

ULF HANNERZ is an anthropologist at the Institute of Ethnography at the University of Stockholm, Sweden. He has conducted field research in Africa and in the United States, and is the author of *Soulside: Inquiries into Ghetto Culture and Community.*

MELVILLE J. HERSKOVITS, an anthropologist, was Director of the African Studies Program at Northwestern University at the time of his death. His books include *The American Negro: A Study of Racial Crossing* and *The Myth of the Negro Past.*

CHARLES S. JOHNSON, a sociologist, was President of Fisk University from 1946 until 1956. He wrote many books, including *The Negro in American Civilization, Preface to Racial Understanding, Growing Up in the Black Belt, Patterns of Negro Segregation,* and *Education and the Cultural Crisis.*

LEROI JONES, poet, playwright, and teacher of literature, is the author of the plays *Dutchman* and *The Slave,* the study *Blues People,* and other works on black and white America.

WINTHROP D. JORDAN teaches history at the University of California, Berkeley. He is the author of *White Over Black: Attitudes Toward the Negro, 1550–1812.*

CHARLES KEIL, an authority on ethnomusicology, is the author of *Urban Blues.*

HYLAN LEWIS is Professor of Sociology at Brooklyn College of the City University of New York. His published work includes the study *The Blackways of Kent.*

DANIEL P. MOYNIHAN is special assistant on domestic affairs to the President of the United States. Former head of the Joint Center for Urban Studies at Harvard and M.I.T., he is the author of *Maximum Feasible Misunderstanding* and the coauthor of *Beyond the Melting Pot.*

BENJAMIN F. PAYTON, formerly a teacher at Howard University, is Director of the Office of Church and Race of the Protestant Council of the City of New York.

ULRICH BONNELL PHILLIPS. Between 1901 and his death in 1934, Professor Phillips wrote many books on the American South, including *Georgia and States' Rights*, *American Negro Slavery*, *Life and Labor in the Old South*, and *The Course of the South to Secession*.

PETER I. ROSE, the editor, is Sophia Smith Professor Emeritus of Sociology and Anthropology and senior fellow of the Kahn Institute at Smith College and a visiting fellow at Stanford. His other books include *They and We*, *The Subject is Race*, *Strangers in Their Midst*, *The Ghetto and Beyond*, *Through Different Eyes*, *Mainstream and Margins*, *Working with Refugees*, *Tempest-Tost*, and *The Dispossessed*.

KENNETH M. STAMPP is Professor of History at the University of California, Berkeley. His many books include *And the War Came*, *The Peculiar Institution: Slavery in the Antebellum South*, and *The Era of Reconstruction*.

EARLE E. THORPE is Professor of History at North Carolina College. His books include *Negro Historians in the U.S.*, *The Desertion of Man: A Critique of the Philosophy of History*, and *The Mind of the Negro: An Intellectual History*.

MELVIN M. TUMIN is Professor of Sociology and Anthropology at Princeton University. Among his many books are *Caste in a Peasant Society*, *Social Class and Social Change in Puerto Rico*, *Desegregation*, and *Social Stratification: The Forms and Functions of Inequality*.

BERNARD WOLFE, a novelist and short story writer, is the author of *Really the Blues*, *Magic of Their Singing*, *Come on Out Daddy*, and *Move Up, Dress Up, Drink Up, Burn Up*.

Introduction

Red, White, Blue—and Black

History is often written in terms of the images people wish to project. American history, for example, was long recounted as if the English, Scottish, Irish, Welsh Protestants—and a few Dutchmen—were the only ones to have had an impact on the growth and development of the country.

Early books and classroom lectures dealt almost exclusively with the "Anglo-American Tradition" or "Our Christian Heritage." Throughout most of the eighteenth and nineteenth centuries, newcomers from northwestern Europe (whom Fletcher Knebel has recently named the "out-WASPs") were encouraged to forget about the customs of Germany or Scandinavia and to adapt themselves to those eminently superior *American* lifeways. Other immigrants were most often considered beyond the pale of social acceptance. In story and song Irish Catholics, Poles, Italians, and Russian Jews—to say nothing about those who came from China or Japan—were referred to as "unassimilable aliens." Many politicians expressed serious doubts about whether such immigrants would ever have the makings of real Americans. Many noted social scientists went so far as to endorse the Dillingham Commission Reports and the restrictive legislation of the 1920s.

In time, most scholars changed their views, and their histories changed as well. Pluralism became *en vogue* and school children and college students began to be told that "our differences make us strong," that "America is a multiplicity in a unity," or, as John Dewey once said, in this country "the hyphen connects instead of separates." It even became fashionable to teach about the "Judaeo-Christian Heritage" and to consider Catholics Christians, too. Indeed, as if to bear public witness to such a revisionist view, the single Protestant preacher who had always intoned opening prayers at official gatherings was supplanted by an ubiquitous triumvirate: minister, priest, and rabbi, representatives of "our three great religions." (Sociologists even gave expression to this new phenomenon and America became known, at least in the parlance of the classroom, as a "triple melting pot.")

And now it is time to include yet another figure on the dais—and to add another "culture" to the heritage. Behavior rises to meet expectations, and the behavior of academic historians, sociologists, and other intellectuals seems no exception. Today the bookstores are flooded with a thousand volumes on the "Negro problem." The problem isn't new. It is as old as America. But, worried about the future, we have once again begun to look at—and, to some extent, rewrite—the past.

The textbooks being prepared for the 1970s will indicate that there is much more to "black history" than the slave block, the Old Plantation, Emancipation and the grateful darkies, Freedmen's Bureaus, the Hayes-Tilden Compromise, *Plessy* v. *Ferguson*, Booker T. Washington, race riots during the two world wars, Marian Anderson, Jackie Robinson, Ralph Bunche, Thurgood Marshall, and the Supreme Court decision of 1954. Rather, to judge by the advertising copy, the books already under preparation will dwell on the role played by black Americans who, "under the most adverse conditions, fought and died to gain their own freedom" and who (paradoxically, it seems) "were enlisted in every major battle to save this Republic."

The new texts will continue to tell a story of life in the antebellum South, but the readers will learn that things were not so tranquil beneath the mimosa trees, that not all Negroes sought to emulate the ways of their masters, and that none ever had good relations with them ("no matter what the romantics say"). They will also learn that black men didn't really move "north to freedom" but exchanged one kind of hell for another.

As more and more new histories appear, a far different picture of black Americans will emerge. And it will not be limited to the celebration of the martyrdom of Crispus Attucks (the Negroes' Colin Kelly) or, say, to the achievements of George Washington Carver (the black Jonas Salk). The new books will include discussions of black soldiers who fought in the Union Army; they will tell of black politicians in the turbulent days of Reconstruction; they will praise the black cowboys who helped to open the West, the black troopers who rode with Teddy Roosevelt, the black workers who toiled along the railbeds and in the factories and on the farms. Some will go farther, extolling the virtues of blackness and the solidarity of "soul" and exposing the pallid character of "white culture" in contrast to "black."

The motivation for this latest attempt at re-examining American history and giving the Negro an honored place along with other "minorities" has come about as a consequence of the civil rights movement and the campaign to eliminate segregation. The demand for an entirely new view of the "Afro-American" is, however, an offshoot of that larger struggle.

Feeling that many of the hard-won victories of the 1950s and 1960s have not made very much difference, angry black spokesmen have begun to challenge a number of basic assumptions of the reform-minded civil rights advocates. First, they argue, liberal white leaders (whatever they wanted personally) could rarely offer much more than palliatives that, often as not, were viewed as programs to keep "their" cities from erupting rather than being expressly designed to help poor blacks. Second, they say that traditional Negro leaders have never been much better. They were either out of touch with the people for whom they claimed to speak (as many felt about the late Dr. Martin Luther King) or were too willing to play the "Establishment game" (as has often been said of Roy Wilkins). Arguing that their people have always been deluded by whites who had taken up the "burden" and Negroes who were trying to lighten it, the new militants wanted to turn them "blackwards," wanted them to have an identity truly their own. They began their campaign by singing a litany of curses against white liberals, "Uncle Toms," and, especially, "honkie society." They are carrying it forward with appeals to black nationalism. They may end by making (and, in some cases, making up) history itself.

Of course, since no group has a monopoly on ethnocentrism, it should not be surprising to find that many of the new views of black history will be similar to most paeans to the past: compilations of vague memories which have become legends, of vague legends which have become memories, isolated incidents swelled to monumental significance, and a good deal of hard evidence of what actually happened and, for any number of reasons, has been overlooked or purposely ignored. The history of "Afro-Americans," like that of European immigrants, is almost by necessity going to turn out to be a potpourri of fancy and fact. What makes it different is that it has to serve a double function of helping to strengthen communal ties among blacks while, simultaneously, teaching other Americans that those who came from Africa also had a noble past and are a proud people.

To tell it like it really was is a difficult and frustrating task. It is difficult because there are so few data that are untainted by the biases and romanticisms of those who captured the oral tradition or the written record; it is frustrating because even the sketchy story that does emerge is so terribly ambiguous, ambiguous not in terms of the patterns of oppression so much as their effects upon the oppressed. But one thing is fairly clear: much of the old heritage was replaced by a new orientation. Western ways and southern values were absorbed and for good or ill, countless thousands of black Africans became Negroes.

W. E. B. DuBois once suggested, "There is nothing so indigenous, so made in America, as me." And yet, as is too well known, few Negroes came to enjoy the freedoms that other Americans take for granted. Few ever got away from the stigma attached to the color of their skins. As DuBois and others repeatedly pointed out, every Negro child has always asked, "Who am I?" "What am I?"

Self, Segregation, and "Soul"

Not very long ago, James Baldwin wrote an essay entitled "Nobody Knows My Name." In a sense, it deals with only half the problem. White people don't know what to call him and *he doesn't know himself* (or didn't know until quite recently). Baldwin's people—variously called blacks, coloreds, Negroes, and blacks again—had little to look forward to and even less to look back upon, or so it seemed.

Still, saying they had little is not to say they had nothing. There is such a thing as Afro-American culture and every black person in this country knows it. Like all cultures it is made up of many things—memories and moods and myths galore. What makes it different is that the memories and moods and even the myths "remembered" are unique: slavery and its aftermath, spiritual uplift and over-Jordan imagery, continued subjugation by those who claimed and repeatedly tried to prove that "white" was always right.

Against (and, in some ways, in response to) these debilitating aspects there was resilience, richness, and romance. The Negro world was, for its embattled members, open and not closed, free and expressive rather than uptight and instrumental, full of hot rage and cool sound. It had (and has) its cuisine (now called "soul food"), its old-time religion, its rules of conduct, its lingo, its forms of artistic expression. Those who now study the black experience in America contend that it has left Negroes with different conceptions of time and space and property—and life. (Today it is even fashionable in certain liberal circles to celebrate the unique characteristics of Negro people in this country. A mere five years ago such contentions, traditionally made by many segregationists, would have been called "racist" by the very same liberals—and by many Negro leaders, too.)

Resistance was another matter. Being frozen into the rigidity of a caste system and unable to become full partners in the society from which so many of their own customs, beliefs, and values were derived, black people often lacked the opportunity to develop the kind of organizational apparatus characteristic of that possessed by other ethnic groups in America—the very groups to which black Americans have long been compared and, perhaps more significantly, to which they have often compared themselves. For years they talked about organizing and fighting their tormentors but, faced with retribution from large institutions and powerful men, they usually had no recourse but to adapt themselves to the system that kept them in servitude.

Segregation kept the Negro humble, and sometimes his own leaders in their innocence aided and abetted the Man. Both spoke of their children, both tended their "flocks." (Of course, not all white men and not all leaders of Negroes acted in such a manner. But the point is that *these* were the most significant role models available for the vast majority of black people, especially in the Old South.)

There is an obvious parallel to be drawn between the plight of Negroes in this country and that of mental patients. Some psychiatrists have recently reintroduced the notion of reality therapy. Crudely described, reality therapy is a technique used to shock patients into the realization that, yes, the world is cruel and if they are going to make it, they are going to have to do more than play out the sick role that "enlightened doctrine" has ascribed to them and that, quite understandably, they have internalized. For years now few well-educated people have said that blacks are innately inferior; they know better. Rather, the conventional wisdom sounds strikingly like that of the old planters and ministers of God. Saying "only we know what's good for them," many social workers and schoolteachers have held to this view to the present day. Disadvantaged black people are viewed and treated as victims or patients or some sort of unfortunates in need of care and succor. In turn, many Negroes, like the inmates of one asylum after another, have long been internalizing the roles ascribed to them and have acted accordingly.

This is not to say that most Negroes are (or perhaps ever were) simple "Sambos." But many did and continue to learn to act out the stereotypes others have held of them and many, even in putting the white man down by seeming to play along, came to believe—in spite of themselves—that they are in fact inferior. Malcolm X understood; he said, "the worst crime the white man has committed is teaching us to hate ourselves."

Perhaps one can understand the bitterness of those who now claim to speak for the Negro, those who say there has really been no progress, only expanded "welfare colonialism." And one should be able to understand why young black radicals choke on that noblest of all words in the lexicon of human relationists: brotherhood. To too many brotherhood has meant: when you become like me, brother, then we'll be as one. They have a point. Time and again Negroes have found there was always one more river to cross; white people would offer the boats if the black rowers didn't rock them too hard.

What a choice for a potential leader—tell your people to remain supplicants in the hope that someday the white man will overcome his prejudices and other personal hang-ups and welcome you into his big *white* house, or become a firebrand in the hope that you might force his capitulation. And once having made the decision, where were you usually left? Dead on the inside or dead all around.

It is no wonder that the civil rights movement itself was always whitewardly oriented—no matter what is being said about it today. To solve the dilemma of supplication vs. rebellion, most efforts to redress the grievances of the past have been channeled into campaigns for integration (not quite supplication and not quite rebellion). Most black people, it seems, wanted to give the impression (and many actually wanted to believe) that, someday, somehow, color would really be overlooked. And those the angriest black spokesmen hold in contempt today—the white liberals—helped perpetuate this myth without, for the most part, realizing what they were doing and without having very much personal contact with those they claimed to accept as equals.

Attention has been focused on "most" Negroes, and "many" Negroes, but not all. There are those who have made it: some by the very same techniques used by other members of minority groups, including the exploitation of those whose identity they share; some by becoming athletes and soul singers and jazz musicians performing for both their own and the "wider" community; some—undoubtedly the largest group—by sheer determination to overcome the barriers of segregation, often by entering government service as postmen and clerks, teachers and soldiers, and working their way up. Together, these members of what have come to be called the "black bourgeoisie" and the "colored entertainers" and the "Negro respectables" represent to white folks (especially middle class whites) living evidence that black people can make it if they try hard enough and are willing to thicken their skins (often fairly light skins) against whatever abuses the "system" and its agents mete out. Perhaps. It is true that many such people have prided themselves on their progress and, for all their difficulties, seemed quite stable, even happy, in American society. They have belied the claim that Negroes are characteristically lazy or ignorant or walking phallic symbols and even seemed to be the essence of middle class respectability: friendly, hardworking, religious, and community-minded.

Many of their children who are now in college think differently. They, and not just the poor people in Watts, know what Ron Karenga means when he decries, "There are only three kinds of people in this country: white people, black people, and Negroes. Negroes? They are black people that act like white people."

The message isn't lost. Those Negro college students, particularly at northern schools and the larger southern ones, know that part of the rhetoric is addressed to them and concerns their parents. ("Which side are *you* on?") Those who have suffered least from the stigma of color are beginning to suffer the most. Many are reacting by forming Afro-American organizations on the campus and by going "home" to Harlem or Hattiesburg to work and teach and organize. Some, to resolve their race/class schizophrenia, have begun to join the ranks of the most militant members of the black community and to provide the copy for the spokesmen and the plans for the revolution. Stressing both poverty and race, the disorganized "black lumpen" have become their cause. With the poor, one can put to use some of the direct and fringe benefits of a college education. And for them one can try to offer a new and different view of those Americans whose ancestors came from Africa.

Historical Perspectives and Sociological Interpretations

This volume concentrates on four of the most controversial aspects of the black experience in the United States: the extent to which the African heritage was retained (or was able to be retained) by those who came in bondage; the impact of slavery on personality and on social structure; the nature of life in the South and in the North for those who were black and referred to as "Negroes"; and, finally, the realities of community and family life, particularly in the black ghettos of the urban centers.

Taken together, the articles and essays and notes contained in each of these sections should provide the reader with some insight into how black Africans became Negro Americans—and what this has meant. It should be readily apparent that several of the selections could have been placed in a different part of the volume (or even in Volume II, which deals with the new moods and movements in the black communities), for they deal with overlapping matters. The decision of where to put them was, in such cases, quite arbitrary.

Withal it is the editor's intention to let each author—and there are twenty-two in this volume alone—speak for himself. The reader is left the difficult task of unraveling the sometimes conflicting assessments of the same subject. He must, for example, consider the question of the retention of "Africanisms" after reading what anthropologist Melville Herskovits, sociologist E. Franklin Frazier, historians Kenneth Stampp and Eugene D. Genovese, and playwright LeRoi Jones have to say about the matter. He will find five rather different points of view.

In like manner, the reader will find different opinions about the impact of slavery. Following a description and a discussion of slavery by Winthrop D. Jordan and Ulrich Phillips, respectively, Stanley M. Elkins' controversial essay is presented. Elkins, a historian, puts forth his argument that slavery imposed an indelible imprint on the slave's personality and that the roles he played reflected this. Since it was originally published in 1958, Elkins' work has provoked a lively debate and much serious criticism. Two of his critics, Earle E. Thorpe and Mina Davis Caulfield, offer their views at the end of the second section. Thorpe zeroes in on Elkins' suggestion that black enslavement may be seen as analogous to the plight of Jews during the Nazi regime. Caulfield goes further, calling into question the basic premises upon which Elkins builds his entire psychosocial theory.

The relationship between social structure and personality is an important one for students of the black experience. They continue to ask what it was like to grow up as a slave or as an emancipated but still segregated Negro in the "Black Belt" of America. To illustrate the complexity of the situation the distinguished sociologist Charles S. Johnson once presented ten personality profiles. These are reprinted in the third section. To put Johnson's work in its proper context, one should first read Hylan Lewis' description of the "Blackways of Kent," a southern community, and Bernard Wolfe's interpretative essay "Uncle Remus and the Malevolent Rabbit."

Half of America's black people now live north of the Mason-Dixon line. For many of them, the South remains "down home." For others, however, it is more than miles away, it is a world apart. Claude Brown, for example, is a *northern* Negro, according to his own description "a manchild in the promised land." Part of his autobiography is presented in "Harlem, My Harlem." Another view of city life, with a special focus on cultural expression and urban blues, is offered by Charles Keil. Finally, Ulf Hannerz, a Swedish ethnologist who has done research in an urban ghetto, offers his own observations on segregation and the "rhetoric of soul."

Sociologist G. Franklin Edwards is noted for his seminal work on the Negro in America. The last section begins with his description of the impact of segregation. His article is followed by four others, each dealing with the structure and character of family life among black people in this country, especially in the inner city. The first, by Kenneth Clark, describes "The Psychology of the Ghetto." This is followed by the controversial "Moynihan Report" (which is reprinted in its entirety), and two reactions to it. The first is by Laura Carper, the second by Benjamin F. Payton. There is one more article presented here, Melvin M. Tumin's assessment of the social consequences of research on race relations, including the sort of studies conducted by G. Franklin Edwards, Kenneth Clark, and Daniel P. Moynihan.

It should be noted that the volume ends where it began, asking questions about the interpretation of history and social structure. Many who read these pages may feel they have come full circle, particularly if they are still confused. It is to be hoped that the difference between then and now will be that the queries will be based on direct exposure to some of the critical issues toward which scholars have been turning (and will increasingly turn) their attention in their attempts to "tell it like it is"—and was.

I

The African as Slave

Africa and the New Americans

When black people got to this country, they were Africans, a foreign people. Their customs, attitudes, desires, were shaped to a different place, a radically different life. What a weird and unbelievably cruel destiny for those people who were first brought here. Not just the mere fact of being sold into slavery—that in itself was common practice among the tribes of West Africa, and the economic system in which these new slaves were to form so integral a part was not so strange either. . . . But to be brought to a country, a culture, a society, that was, and is, in terms of purely philosophical correlatives, the complete antithesis of one's own version of man's life on earth—that is the cruelest aspect of this particular enslavement.

Le Roi Jones

What aspects of African life, if any, survived enslavement, the brutal "middle passage," the auction block, and plantation life in the entirely new world? Scholars of the black experience have sought answers to this question for many years.

While there was never any doubt about the retention of "Africanisms" in the West Indies and Latin America, a debate has ensued about such survivals here. The foremost advocate of the "carry-over" theory was the late Melville J. Herskovits, author of The Myth of the Negro Past *and numerous other works that linked the so-called Negro American to his African heritage. The following essay offers an introduction to Herskovits' work—and to our study of Americans from Africa.*

1

Africanisms in Secular Life

Melville J. Herskovits

Our analysis of African survivals may begin with a consideration of how certain isolated African traits have held over in American Negro behavior, most often in uninstitutionalized form. That more examples of carry-overs falling in this category are not found in the literature is probably due to the lack of acquaintance of observers with related New World Negro cultures and the African background, so that such points of significance are not reported. From a larger point of view, however, these instances, in the aggregate, contribute to no slight degree to the total pattern of Negro behavior and, because of their African character, help to distinguish it from the behavior of other elements in the population.

The retention of Africanisms in motor habits presents a vast field for study. Methodological difficulties in the way of such research are

Abridgment of pp. 145–155, 157–163, 166–172, 174–182 in *The Myth of the Negro Past* by Melville J. Herskovits, New York: Harper and Brothers, 1941. Copyright 1941 by Melville J. Herskovits. Reprinted by permission of Harper & Row, Publishers.

appreciable, since results having scientific validity can be obtained only by analyzing motion pictures of such routine activities as walking, speaking, laughing, sitting postures, or of dancing, singing, burden carrying, hoeing, and movements made in various industrial techniques. Yet on the basis of uncontrolled observation, it is a commonplace that many American Negro forms of dancing are essentially African; and this is confirmed by motion pictures taken of the Kwaside rites for the ancestors of the chief of the Ashanti village of Asokore, which include a perfect example of the Charleston, or by the resemblance to other styles of Negro dancing well known in this country included in films taken in Dahomey and among the Yoruba.

In another less well-known field, it may be indicated that the precise method of planting photographed in Dahomey and in Haiti was observed by Bascom in the Gulla Islands in the summer of 1939.[1] This method, already described and illustrated for these other two regions,[2] is to work down and back each pair of rows in a field. A container of seed is held under the left arm, and the right or left heel, as the case may be, is used to make a shallow depression in the soil. The seeds are dropped in this hole, and dirt to cover them pushed over it with the toes; this foot is then placed ahead of the sower, and the same movements performed in the opposite row with the other foot. Whether this method is used elsewhere in the United States cannot be stated, but where it does occur it constitutes a direct survival of a West African motor habit.

The description given of a Sea Island woman of the Civil War period may be cited as another instance of the survival of motor behavior:

> It was not an unusual thing to meet a woman coming from the field, where she had been hoeing cotton, with a small bucket or cup on her head, and a hoe over her shoulder, contentedly smoking a pipe and briskly knitting as she strode along. I have seen, added to all these, a baby strapped to her back.[3]

The habit of carrying burdens on the head, so widespread in tropical countries, is favored in West Africa and the West Indies. To what extent it has survived in the United States cannot be said, but that the practice has had an important influence on walking style is apparent. Whether or not it is the factor that has given the Negro his distinctive walk is for future research to determine, but the point must be kept in mind as at least a somewhat more tenable hypothesis than that advanced by one Freudian disciple, who held the Negro "slouch" to be the manifestation of a castration complex! The ways in which southern rural Negro women habitually carry their infants do not today ordinarily include the method depicted in the quotation above; as described, however, it corresponds exactly to one manner in which infants are transported in West Africa. The other method, still commonly to be seen among persons of the lower socio-economic strata of Negro rural society in this country, is to use one arm to hold the child as it straddles the hip of its carrier.

The retention of certain industrial habits is hinted in the following passage:

> Broughton was a rice island, and the garnered rice was carried from the fields to the flats, then towed to the mill, where it was threshed and loaded on ships to be carried to the city. The rice was not husked at the plantation mills. This was done in the city, as rice was not considered good in those days unless freshly beaten. On the plantation it was beaten fresh for dinner every day. For this purpose pestles and mortars, hewn from the trunks of trees, were used, these becoming smooth and shining like metal from constant use. Two boys or two women would seize the pestles together in the middle, raising and letting them fall so quickly and evenly that the beating of rice was not considered a difficult task. The children often tried it, but never succeeded, as the motion required a knack they did not possess. After the rice was loosened from the husks, it was placed in flat-bottomed baskets called fanners, held high, and allowed to fall into baskets placed on the ground, the wind blowing the chaff away. This process, which was called "fanning the rice," was repeated until the rice was perfectly clean.[4]

This technique is still employed in the islands, but the use of mortar and pestle elsewhere in the South has not been reported. Mortars and pestles of the type included in the collection from the Sea Islands at Northwestern University and woven trays used in winnowing the rice[5] are entirely African. Their use to shell cereals of one kind and another is ubiquitous throughout Africa, though of course not con-fined to that continent. The way in which these are used, however, shows a further retention of motor habit, especially in the tendency to work as rhythmically as possible; in the West Indies, Guiana, and West Africa, it takes some experience for the visitor to learn to dis-tinguish the alternate strokes of two pestles in the mortar from the beat of a drum. The woven trays used in the Sea Islands are made with the sewing technique called coiling, which is paramount in West Africa; more interesting is the fact that, as in Africa, the coils, in all instances examined, are laid on in a clockwise direction. This is an excellent example of the way in which the determinants of behav-ior lying beneath the conscious level may be continued where the manipulation of materials is involved. And this point is of the utmost importance in assessing carry-overs in personal habits which, lying beyond the attention of those to whose advantage it was during slavery to mold Negro behavior, continued undisturbed until today, to be numbered among those intangibles which give to the expression of Negro motor habits their distinctive form.

The ways in which the hair of some Negro women, but particularly of small Negro girls, is dressed is so distinctive that only mention of this convention is necessary to bring it to mind. As far as is known, the one attempt to give a derivation for these styles of hair-dressing has been made by Puckett:

> In Africa, decoration of the hair reaches a high point, often consisting in mixing some plastic material with the hair and shaping the whole into a highly fantastic coiffure. With the Negro woman of the South the hair is still a prime object of decoration as evidenced by the many elaborate coiffures and by the "Hair Dresser" signs on many a lowly Negro cabin; although there is a decided tendency to remove the kink, by odoriferous unguents of all kinds in imitation of the straight hair of the whites.[6]

. . . The correspondences to be found in hairdressing are, however, far more specific and definite than those mentioned in the preceding passage. Unfortunately, we do not know whether definite names are given the many patterns into which the hair of Negro women and children is braided, nor have the actual braid designs been systematically described. Yet the multiplicity of these is the outstanding feature of the hair-braiding pattern; unbroken parts running the length of the head, lengthwise parts broken by lateral lines, and many other combinations emphasize the contrasts between the whiteness of the scalp and the blackness of the hair, while the units into which the hair is gathered for braiding are frequently so small that one wonders how the braids can be achieved. These modes of hair-dressing are ubiquitous in West Africa, while everywhere in the West Indies Negro girls and women dress their hair in a similar manner, with similar designs based on the whiteness of the lines when the scalp shows between the numerous parts. In Dutch Guiana, these designs are frequently given names; among the Bush Negroes of that country men as well as women part and braid their hair in this fashion. This, however, is a local elaboration, since in West Africa and the rest of the New World men customarily cut the hair close and wear it unparted, in the manner to be seen among the rural Negroes in this country.

"Wrapping" the hair is part of the head-dressing complex as is the wearing of kerchiefs. This wrapping has been recorded both in the Sea Islands and farther west. Parsons has remarked the custom in the former locality:

> Women, old and young, quite commonly wear kerchiefs around the head and tied at the back. Underneath, the hair is likely to be "wrapped." You "wrap um" (i.e., wrap strings around wisps of hair), beginning at the roots of the hair, and winding to the ends, "to make um grow." [7]

Again, from Missouri, the existence of this custom during a somewhat earlier period is vouchsafed:

> There was nothing Aunt Mymee desired less than a "head-handker-chief," as she wore her hair (except on Sundays, when it was carded out in a great black fleece), in little wads the length and thickness of her finger, each wad being tightly wrapped with white cord. [8]

Concerning the wearing of headkerchiefs in the United States, another Africanism, we have but little knowledge. The headkerchief was common enough so that it came to be accepted as an integral part of the conventional portrait of the Negro "mammy," and a pre-emancipation passage hints at reasons for this earlier importance:

> Precedence and rank were respected among the slaves. In Charleston Ferguson noted that the married women were distinguished by a peculiarly-tied kerchief they wore upon their heads. [9]

In recent decades the wearing of headkerchiefs has greatly decreased in the United States, but they are to be seen everywhere in the West Indies, while, as we move southward to Guiana, they are found to function importantly in the everyday life of women through the varying significance of the names given kerchief designs and styles of tying. [10] A West African distribution cannot be given on the basis of our present knowledge, but that a considerable number—over fifty—proverb-names for styles of tying kerchiefs could be recorded among the Ashanti of the Gold Coast is to be regarded as of some significance. Informants there maintained that the custom was one of long standing. In Haiti a white headkerchief marks the *mambo*, or woman officiant in the *vodun* cult, and elderly people in general, men as well as women, often wear kerchiefs bound about their heads.

Etiquette

Outstanding among the intangible values of Negro life in the United States is strict adherence to codes of polite behavior. Comments on the etiquette of Negro slaves are numerous, and some of these may be cited as illustrating the point. Botume, who worked among the Negroes released by Union troops on the Sea Islands, gives one aspect of the code:

> Before I had gone far I discovered that as I had begun to make calls, I must not omit one house, nor fail to speak to a single person, from the oldest grandparent to the youngest child. Their social rights were inexorable. My guide said, "All them people waits to say how d'ye to you," so I went on. [11]

Doyle, whose discussion is primarily concerned with the canons of interracial behavior, quotes a contemporary statement which shows how readily the pattern of politeness among whites was taken over by the slaves who accompanied their masters to the health resort at White Sulphur Springs:

> If you would take your stand near the spring where they come down after pitchers of water you would witness practical politeness. The courtesy of Samuel, coachman of Dr. W——to Mary, the maid of Mrs. Colonel——. . . The polite salaams of Jacob to Rachel, the dressing woman, and of Isaac, the footman, to Rebecca, the nursery maid, would charm you. [12]

That this behavior did not merely imitate that of the whites, but had a solid foundation in the mores of the slaves themselves is to be seen from the following, wherein Douglass tells how politeness was exacted in the cabins:

> These mechanics were called "uncles" by all the younger slaves, not because they really sustained that relationship to any, but according to plantation *etiquette*, as a mark of respect, due from the younger to the older slaves. Strange, and even ridiculous as it may seem, among a people so uncultivated, and with so many stern trials to look in the face, there is not to be found, among any people, a more rigid enforcement of the law of respect to elders, than they maintain. I set this down as partly constitutional with my race, and partly conventional. There is no better material in the world for making a gentleman, than is furnished in the African. He shows to others, and exacts for himself, all the tokens of respect which he is compelled to manifest toward his master. A young slave must approach the company of the older with hat in hand, and woe betide him, if he fails to acknowledge a favor, of any sort, with the accustomed "tank'ee," etc. So uniformly are good manners enforced among slaves, that I can easily detect a "bogus" fugitive by his manners. [13]

This strict ordering of conduct is by no means a matter that began with slavery nor has ended with it. Puckett in several passages comments on Negro etiquette, attempting to account for it in a number of ways, among which is the importance of taking adequate precautions against magic:

> Many of these taboos have to do with matters of etiquette and seem to be in reality a linking of unpleasant results with uncouth manners in an attempt to frighten the young into a quicker acquisition of American good-breeding.[14]

As will be seen shortly, however, the elements in the Negro code differ somewhat from patterns followed by the American majority, so that an explanation in terms of drives to acquire these new modes of conduct is not entirely satisfactory. Puckett's analysis of the respect accorded elderly folk is more to the point. Here he notes "the practice of calling all old people 'Uncle' and 'Aunty' whether they are relatives or not,"[15] and in the following passage, which affords testimony of how viable has been the custom noted for a preceding generation by Douglass, he says:

> it is considered bad luck to . . . "sass" the old folks. This latter idea may have at one time had a real meaning, since the old folks were "almost ghosts," and hence worthy of good treatment lest their spirits avenge the disrespect and actually cause bad luck to the offender.[16]

The validity of this explanation is best indicated by referring the assertion that "old folks" are "almost ghosts" to the tenets of the ancestral cult which, as one of the most tenacious Africanisms, has left many traces in New World Negro customs. For, as has been shown, the belief in the power of the ancestors to help or harm their descendants is a fundamental sanction of African relationship groupings, and this has influenced the retention of Africanisms in many aspects of Negro life in the New World.

Another specific survival of African etiquette is the matter of turning the head when laughing (sometimes with the hand over the mouth), or in speaking to elders or other respected persons of averting the eyes and perhaps the face. The clue to this correspondence came when working with a native of the Kru tribe of Liberia, who, while demonstrating his language to a university class, performed what was thought to be this characteristically American Negro gesture as the group before him laughed at a joke he had made. On inquiry the nature of this as a form of politeness was made clear, the theory behind it being that it is rude to laugh in the face of another. This convention was later found general in other portions of West Africa; unfortunately, the literature does not deal with minor

11

matters of personal conduct such as this, and other comparative data are therefore lacking.

In Guiana, not only does one not laugh in the face of another, but a young man does not even look at the elder to whom he is speaking. Moreover, he speaks in a low voice, and introduces a conventionalized stammer into his speech. How this pattern has carried over into Negro behavior in this country is to be seen from the experience of a colored principal in a northern school, where many children, recent migrants from the South, had to be dealt with. It was only when this officer learned that to turn the head is a mark of respect and not a sign of inattention, that the injustice that had been done to a number of those southern Negro children sent to the school office for discipline was realized.

The manner in which, in many Negro churches, the sermon forms a kind of litany between preacher and congregation represents the reworking of still another form of African polite behavior. In these discourses, it will be recalled, the words of the preacher are constantly interspersed with such expressions as "Yes, Lord," or "Oh, Jesus," and those other numerous phrases that have come to be standard in such rituals. Insight into the African nature of this convention came during field work in the interior of Dutch Guiana, where a running series of assents to what is being said by a man of rank or age punctuates his speech, the responses being the more frequent and fervent the more important the person speaking, and the greater the respect to which he is entitled. "Yes, friend," "So it is," "*Ya-hai*," "True, true," are some of the expressions which are as standardized as are the interpolations of Negro worshipers during the sermons of their ministers.[17] The same trait marks West Indian Negro churches, while in the Caribbean there is also a tendency to interject stylized assents into what is often no more than give-and-take between two acquaintances. And, completing the sequence, it may be noted that the same rule of polite conduct characterizes the African scene, both as regards the responses made by common persons to those of rank and between persons of equal position, it being explicitly stated there that to listen passively to the words of another is to be guilty of rudeness.

A different kind of carry-over from an earlier tradition is found in such an intangible as the concept of time held by Negroes. By this is not meant the disregard for punctuality so often made the occasion for joking when reference is made to such an hour as "eight o'clock C. P. T." signifying that, since this is "Colored Peoples' Time," an hour or two later than the one named is actually meant. Disregard for punctuality is to be expected wherever timekeeping devices are lacking; which is to say that approximations of time rather than punctuality mark the life of most human beings. What is meant here is the way in which the day is divided, and the special significance for Negroes of terms such as "evening" and "morning." The point can be made by a quotation from Dollard which illustrates "the initial appearance of strangeness" he experienced in the manners of the Negro community he was to study:

> I took my laundry one day to a Negro laundress . . . and asked her when it would be ready. She said, "Oh, tomorrow evening." After supper the next day I went back. She reproached me on the ground that it had been done for five or six hours and I could have had it earlier: "I expected you to come around about two o'clock this evening." Morning is from when you get up until around two, and evening is from then on. At first I thought only Negroes used the word in this way, but later found that white people do too.[18]

The same linguistic conception of time divisions is to be encountered throughout the West Indies, while the prevalence of a similar usage throughout West Africa traces them to their source.

At this point we may consider in some detail manifestations in the United States of the ability of the Negro to adjust to his situation by adapting himself to the requirements of the moment, a point that has been referred to several times before. Ordinarily, this is held to indicate the quickness of members of this underprivileged group to comprehend and acquiesce in the wishes of those over them, especially manifest in their circumspectness in handling whites. Some of the comments that have been made on Negro reticence and pliability may be indicated. Doyle analyzes the common reaction:

> The Negro . . . "gets along" because, when in doubt as to what is expected of him, he will ask what is customary—not what is the law. He seems subconsciously to feel that custom is more powerful than law. And yet there are instances where no one can tell him just what is the custom or what will be accepted. In this case he falls back on old habits. If these habits are not accepted, the Negro merely "turns on his personality" and, by apology, ingratiation, or laughter, will be able to turn even this hard corner.[19]

How one element in this technique was employed during slavery is recounted by this same writer in the following passage:

> A slave, on occasion, might be impudent if he supported his impudence with a quotation from the Scriptures. A slave trader was

unloading a carload of Negroes at a station in Georgia. As he stepped on the platform he asked if all the Negroes were there. Thereupon one slave replied: "Yes, massa, we's all heah." "Do dyself no harm, foh we's all heah," added another, quoting Saint Peter. . . . On other occasions slaves would improvise songs which were positively impudent, but which, clothed in the right forms, would pass unnoticed, or even provoke a smile or laughter.

We raise de wheat, dey gib us de corn;
We bake de bread, dey gib us de cruss;
We sif' de meal, dey gib us de huss;
We peal de meat, dey gib us de skin;
And dat's de way dey takes us in.
We skims de pot, dey gib us de liquor,
An' say, "Dat's good enough fer a nigger."[20]

Puckett feels that perhaps "the opportunity of poking fun at the white race in an indirect way is the basis of the many Irishman jokes, so widespread among the Southern Negro," and indicates the form which such satisfactions take in the following passage:

> the Negro does love to laugh at the mishaps of his white master, as evidenced by such stories as that of the new field hand who did not understand the meaning of the dinner bell. His master found him in the field still working after the bell had rung, and angrily commanded him to "drop whatever he had in his hands" and run for the table whenever he heard it ring. Next day at noon he was carrying his master, taken sick in the fields, across a foot-log over the creek when the bell rang. He "dropped" the white man in the water and nothing was done to him for he had only done what the master had commanded.[21]

This complex of indirection, of compensation by ridicule, of evasion, and of feigned stupidity has obviously been important in permitting the Negro to get on in the different situations of everyday life he has constantly encountered. How this operated during the days of slavery has been summarized as follows:

> the Negroes are scrupulous on one point; they make common cause, as servants, in concealing their faults from their owners. Inquiry elicits no information; no one feels at liberty to disclose the transgressor; all are profoundly ignorant; the matter assumes the sacredness of a "professional secret": for they remember that they may hereafter require the same concealment of their own transgressions from their fellow servants, and if they tell upon them now, they may have the like favor returned them; besides, in the meantime, having their names cast out as evil from among their brethren, and being subjected to scorn, and perhaps personal violence or pecuniary injury.[22]

... Numerous examples of the operation of the rule of indirection in West Africa could be given, but its institutionalized forms best demonstrate how congenial is the principle to the thought of the people. An outstanding instance is the role it played in the taxation systems of the various monarchies. These systems have been described in detail, both for the Ashanti of the Gold Coast and for the kingdom of Dahomey, and hence need only be outlined here.[23] Among the former people, the throne did not exact inheritance taxes except at several times removed from the original levy. When an ordinary man died, the local chief took control of the government's share, and retained this during his lifetime. The duties on the estate of such a local chief went to his superior, the district head; and it was only on the death of such a high official that the inheritance taxes of those under him who had died during his lifetime finally reached the central power. In Dahomey, the entire system of census enumeration and the taking of vital statistics, on which taxation was based, postulated the acquisition of the requisite information without the knowledge of those being counted. The identical principle operated in levying the taxes themselves, for necessary counting of resources and goods was similarly achieved by such devious ways that one can well believe the statement of members of the native royal family that the people rarely realized when or by whom the count was taken.

This was but a part of an entire system of control. Each official, through whose hands flowed the stream of wealth directed toward the royal palace, was "controlled" by a "wife" of the king who, as a member of the inner bureaucracy, was charged with seeing to it that not even the word of the highest officials was taken without independent validation. The attitude of the natives toward the straightforwardness of the European is revealed by current comment on the methods of the French colonial officials in administering taxation. The French have imposed a head tax which, like the taxes of the native kingdom, is based on census enumeration. Unlike native practice, however, the French query each compound head directly as to the number of people in his compound. It is well understood that the more truthful a man is, the more he will have to pay; the comment on the technique was: "Our ancestors may have had no guns and had to fight with hoe handles, but they were wiser than to ask directly that a man tell them something to his disadvantage!"

As has been stated, many other instances of the principle of indirection as this operates among Negroes might be given from the West Indies and West Africa no less than from the United States, such as the oblique references in the "songs of allusion" that play an appreciable role in regulating social life. Certainly this principle is everywhere given clear expression as a guide to overt behavior. That as life is lived, it is a worth-while principle to speak with reserve, to hold back something of what one knows, to reveal no more than one must, can be immediately recognized; in the most ordinary dealings, the principle that one keep one's counsel and, as a minimum, offer only such information as may be requested, has been found to be not unprofitable. To ask a question such as Puckett poses, "May not the organized hypocrisy of the Southern Negro also be an adaptation forced upon the Negro by conditions of life?" shows how misinterpretation can easily arise where the force of traditional sanctions has gone unrecognized. For diplomacy, tact, and mature reserve are not necessarily hypocrisy; and while the situation of the Negro in all the New World, past and present, has been such as to force discretion upon him as a survival technique, it is also true that he came on to the scene equipped with the technique rather than with other procedures that had to be unlearned before this one could be worked out.

The principle of indirection, then, must be looked on as immediately descended from the African scene. The implications of this fact in giving form to Negro behavior, like other intangibles such as canons of etiquette and concepts of time also considered in this section, cannot be overlooked if a true picture of Negro life is to be had, either for scientific analysis or to help understand the present-day interracial situation.

Associations

We now move from less overt aspects of culture to more institutionalized forms, and consider first those elements in the organization of Negro society that are not dependent on relationship ties. The question at this point reduces itself essentially to what vestiges of African "associations," if any, are to be discerned—the extent to which such nonpolitical organizations as cooperative groupings of various kinds and secret or nonsecret societies have survived the experience of slavery.

It would be strange if African political forms had continued in any degree of purity except where successful escape from slavery rendered necessary some administrative arrangement to care for the affairs of the runaway group. In such cases as those of Brazil, Dutch Guiana, and Jamaica, African political organizations were set up.

But for other parts of the New World, little information of the controls that operate within Negro communities is to be had. Colonial administration, or the organization of national governments on the republican model, as in Haiti, effectively mask any extralegal institutions which may exist among the Negroes. In Trinidad, among such a group as the followers of the Shango cult, or in the "shouting" Baptist churches, little recourse is had to governmental instruments for the settling of disputes or for administering other measures of control. The leader and elders are entirely capable of handling such situations as arise within the community, and their decrees are followed by common consent. This is probably similar to what is found in more tenuous form among the Negroes of the southern part of the United States, where similar extralegal devices operate. These may perhaps represent a response to the conviction that justice is not to be found in the white man's courts and that it is therefore the part of wisdom to submit disputes to the arbitration of an impartial member of the group.[24]

Yet the question remains whether any survivals of African legal institutions are to be found beyond these informal methods of caring for situations that might otherwise fall into the hands of the law. Aimes has given the matter the most careful study of any student to date, but has found few clues except in the early history of the period of slavery.[25] The Negroes of New England, particularly of Connecticut, appear to have elected a headman or "governor." A record exists of a gravestone in the burial ground of Norwich, Connecticut, inscribed "In memory of Boston Trowtrow, Governor of the African tribe in this Town, who died 1772, aged 66."[26] Steiner, who takes it for granted that the election of such an official by the Negroes "showed the usual imitation of . . . white masters"—which Aimes disputes—quotes a description of this officer:

> The negroes, "of course, made their election to a large extent deputatively, as all could not be present, but uniformly yielded to it their assent. . . . The person they selected for the office was usually one of much note among themselves, of imposing presence, strength, firmness, and volubility, who was quick to decide, ready to command, and able to flog. If he was inclined to be arbitrary, belonged to a master of distinction, and was ready to pay freely for diversions—these were circumstances in his favor. Still it was necessary he should be an honest negro, and be, or appear to be, wise above his fellows." What his powers were was probably not well defined, but he most likely "settled all grave disputes in the last resort, questioned conduct, and imposed penalties and punishments sometimes for vice and misconduct."[27]

It is understandable how the institutions Negroes set up to control their own affairs eventually came into conflict with the need for centralization of authority in the North; in the South, any toleration of such types of organization was unlikely. Aimes' findings confirm such an a priori judgment:

> Considerable research has failed to reveal any very satisfactory material relating to these institutions in the South. The laws repressing meetings of negroes appear to have been severe. The following account of an African "wizard" is interesting and important, but the fact that he is said to have operated "many years ago" may detract somewhat from its value. An old Guinea negro, a horse-trainer and hanger-on of sporting contests, "claimed to be a conjurer, professing to have derived the art from the Indians after his arrival from Africa." The only use he made of this valuable accomplishment was "in controlling riotous gatherings" of negroes, and "in causing runaway slaves to return, foretelling the time they would appear and give themselves up." He would get the masters and overseers to pardon their erring slaves. This shows a powerful control in this man over his fellows, and one that could be put to good use if properly directed. The basis of his power undoubtedly lay in some combination of the mores of the negroes themselves. Traces of this individual power seem to be present in the Gabriel revolt in Virginia in 1800, and in the Nat Turner revolt at a later date. It is not to be supposed that the negroes would have submitted to a form of conjuration derived from Indians.[28]

It is thus understandable why few institutionalized survivals of the political systems of West Africa are to be encountered in this country. It is rather a tradition of discipline and organization that is found, a "feel" for the political maneuver apparent in operations marking the attainment of control within Negro organizations, or the shrewdness with which participation of Negro groups in the larger political scene is directed by Negro politicians so as to get the most out of the truncated situation.[29] Yet because in the main we find African sanctions rather than African political institutions does not mean that within the Negro group more specific manifestations of the African pattern of organized directed effort are lacking. In West Africa, these nonrelationship groupings have their most important manifestation in cooperative endeavor. It is therefore to various kinds of cooperative and mutual-aid effort among Negroes of this country that we must look for the survivals of the African tradition of discipline and control based on acquiescence and directed toward the furtherance of community needs.

The tradition of cooperation in the field of economic endeavor is outstanding in Negro cultures everywhere. It will be recalled that this cooperation is fundamental in West African agriculture, and in other industries where group labor is required, and has been reported from several parts of the slaving area.[30] This tradition, carried over into the New World, is manifest in the tree-felling parties of the Suriname Bush Negroes, the *combites* of the Haitian peasant, and in various forms of group labor in agriculture, fishing, house-raising, and the like encountered in Jamaica, Trinidad, the French West Indies, and elsewhere. This African tradition found a congenial counterpart in the plantation system; and when freedom came, its original form of voluntary cooperation was reestablished. It is said to have reappeared in the Sea Islands immediately after the Civil War,[31] but its outstanding present form is gang labor. It is the essence of this system that work is carried on cooperatively under responsible direction; by use of the precise formula under which cooperative work is carried on in all those offer parts of the New World, and in Africa, where it has been reported.

Such instances of cooperative labor among Negroes of the United States as have been noticed have been dismissed as something borrowed from such forms in European tradition as the "bee." That these types of cooperation were important in frontier life is self-evident; it does not follow, however, that cooperation among Negroes is merely a reflection of these white manifestations of organized aid. The "bee," characteristic of white America, was, as a matter of fact, not current to any considerable degree in those parts of the country where Negroes were most to be found. The phenomenon characterized the northern and northwestern states rather than the southern; in a plantation slave economy, the necessity of calling in neighbors to help in doing work slaves could perform was obviated. This is especially true since the neighbors, themselves presumably slave-owners, had no great competence in the manual arts. It is thus much simpler to assume that resemblances existed between European and African patterns which tended to reinforce each other.

Cooperation among the Negroes of this country is principally found in such institutions as lodges and other benevolent societies, which in themselves are directly in line with the tradition underlying similar African organizations. The role of the secret societies in the parts of Africa from which the slaves were derived is well known, but has been stressed in favor of the large number of less sensational, but no less important, nonsecret associations. It is these more prosaic organizations, however, that in time of need assure their members access to resources greater than those of any individual, which give this type of society an especially significant part in assuring stability to African social structure. That in this country Negro assurance societies, especially burial societies, take on the form of lodges in so many cases, and that Negro lodges of various types represent such an exuberant development of the common American lodge, is to be explained in two ways. In the first case, the coalescence of the cooperative assurance and secret society traditions may be considered as developing out of a tendency, under acculturation, to blur distinctions which prior to contact were quite clear. Secondly, the psychological device of compensation through overdevelopment, so often encountered among underprivileged groups forced to adhere to majority patterns, and the failure of white lodges to accept their Negro counterparts brought it about that the initial stimulus was diverted from the channels it followed among the donor group and emphasized for the Negro lodge its distinctive traits.

Whatever the derivation of such organizations, their importance has long been recognized. Citations such as the following are typical of earlier studies:

> Perhaps no phase of negro life is so characteristic of the race and has developed so rapidly as that which centers around secret societies and fraternal orders. . . . Scores of different orders are represented in Southern towns, with hundreds of local chapters. A special feature of the colored organizations is found in the local character of their orders. The majority have their home offices in the state in which they do business. Few extend over much greater territory.[32]

Continuing, this account becomes somewhat more specific:

> Investigations show that other societies are in operation in Mississippi besides those chartered and recorded on the official lists. Some of these operate under secret rules and assess members according to their own agreement. The total number of such organizations, including the many little ephemeral societies operated wherever groups of negroes are found, would run into the hundreds. Sometimes they continue for a year, sometimes only for one or two meetings. . . .A study of the names of the societies . . . will reveal much of their nature. . . . They pay burial expenses, sick benefits, and small amounts to beneficiaries of deceased members. Such amounts are in many cases determined entirely by the number of members, the assessment plan being the most common and most practical one. Members are admitted variously according to a flexible constitution made to meet the demands of the largest number of people. There are non-paying members who receive only the advantages coming from the fraternal society; there are those who take insurance for sick benefits only, while others wish burial

expenses also. Still others take life insurance, while some combine all benefits, thus paying the larger assessments and dues.[33]

Though couched in language not commonly employed at the present time by students of the Negro, the following further observations of this same student are to the point:

> Some evidences of the higher forms of sympathy may be seen in the working of the fraternal societies in ministering to the sick, the widows and the orphans, and in paying off benefits. While the obligation of the society upon its members seems in every case to be the direct cause of a service, sympathy often grows out of the deed, and the members of such societies grow enthusiastic in their advocacy of the cause, giving these deeds of service as evidence. So it happens that the leaders of the various societies have come to feel, in addition to the personal gratification of succeeding in rivalry, an eager interest in their work.[34]

This explanation of how sympathy is aroused in this people may be dismissed as aside from the point; what is important for our purpose is the variety of ends which these societies fulfill in exercising their cooperative function. . . .

The lodge itself, aside from its insurance features, is another expression of the Africanlike flair for organization. Granting the elementary fact that Negroes in the United States, like all other persons here, tend to adapt their behavior to prevailing patterns, yet the divergences from the patterns that are found in the case of these lodges are especially cogent. For while it is true that many Negro fraternal organizations are the counterparts of white groups having similar names, rituals, and paraphernalia, yet the numbers of Negro lodges, including those which have no counterparts among the whites, and their role in everyday Negro life, which far transcends their importance for the vast majority of white lodge members, makes them distinctive in the American scene.

This is relevant to the fact that numerous other societies exist in Africa, taking forms and having objectives that resemble the aims of Negro lodges in the United States far more than is recognized. Not only do many of these societies have some religious basis, but many of them are essentially religious organizations. In one instance, groupings considered secret societies were found to be actually cult groups, whose secrets are religious secrets, whose initiatory rites are education in the ways of the gods, and whose public appearances in regalia are made on those occasions when the deities are worshiped. This recalls the structure and functioning of various New World Christian religious "orders" among Negroes, notably the Trinidad

Baptist groups. While a direct relationship between this and the religious preoccupations of Negro societies of various sorts, either secret or economic, is difficult to envisage, it is yet entirely possible that something of the strong nonsecular bent of the Negro lodges in this country is a partial survival of this tradition. For again, it is the importance laid on this aspect of the "work" in the Negro lodges that in one respect differentiates them—in degree, it must be emphasized, not in kind—from societies having white membership.[35]

Family

It is well recognized that Negro family structure in the United States is different from the family organization of the white majority. Outstanding are its higher illegitimacy rate and the particular role played by the mother. Certain other elements in Negro social organization also make it distinctive, and these will be considered later; but for the moment the more prominent characteristics must be treated in terms of the cognate African sanctions which make them normal, rather than abnormal, and go far in aiding us to comprehend what must otherwise, after the conventional manner, be regarded as aberrant aspects of the family institution.

At the outset, it is necessary to dismiss the legal implications of the term "illegitimate" and to recognize the sociological reality underlying an operational definition of the family as a socially sanctioned mating. In this case, illegitimacy is restricted to those births which are held outside the limits of accepted practice. The situation in the West Indies, projected against the African background of marriage rites and family structure, will here as elsewhere make for clarity. In West Africa, it will be remembered, preliminaries to marriage include negotiations between the families of the two contracting parties to assure all concerned that the young man and woman are ready for marriage, that they are competent to assume their obligations under it, and that no taboos in terms of closeness of actual or putative relationship stand in the way of the match. This done, the young man (and in some tribes the young woman) assumes certain obligations toward his prospective father- and mother-in-law, which in many instances continue after marriage. In all this area, it is further to be recalled, the family is marked by its polygynous character, and the manner of its extension into such larger kinship groupings as the extended family and the sib.

In the New World, these forms when brought into contact with

European patterns of monogamy and the absence of wider social structures based on relationship have resulted in institutions which, however, though differing considerably from one region to another, have nonetheless become stabilized in their new manifestations. Thus the elaborateness of the betrothal mechanism has in several regions been translated into ceremonies which even when European in form are essentially African in feeling. The Haitian *lettre de demande*[36] and its counterpart in the British West Indian islands are, in their form and mode of presentation, entirely in the tradition of Africa. The survival of the polygynous marriage pattern is likewise found in Haiti in the distinction made between marriage and what is termed *plaçage*, a system whereby a woman is given a man by her father but without legal or church sanction. The similar means whereby a man and woman in the British West Indies may form regularly constituted unions without the approval of church or government is seen in the institution of the "keeper." . . .

Another aspect of West African social organization having important implications for the study of New World Negro kinship groupings concerns the place of women in the family. By its very nature, a polygynous system brings about a different relation between mother and children than a monogamous type—a relationship that goes far in bringing about an understanding of the so-called "matriarchal" form of the Negro family in the United States, the West Indies, and South America. The question most often raised in accounting for any African derivation of this type of family, wherein, unlike most white groups, the importance of the mother transcends that of the father, is whether this may not reflect African unilateral canons of sib descent. But while this fact may enter into the traditional residue, it is not to be regarded as playing any considerable role. In West Africa, descent is counted more often on the father's than on the mother's side and, as in other portions of the continent, the parent socially unrelated to the child is as important from a personal and sentimental point of view as is the one to whose family the child legally belongs.

What is much more important for an understanding of the sanctions underlying this "matriarchal" Negro family type is the fact that in a polygynous society a child shares his mother only with his "true" brothers and sisters—everywhere recognized as those who have the same father and the same mother—as against the fact that in the day-to-day situations of home life he shares his father with the children of other women. This means that the attachments between a mother and her child are in the main closer than those between father and children; from the point of view of the parent, it means that the responsibilities of upbringing, discipline, and supervision are much more the province of the mother than of the father. In most parts of the African areas which furnished New World slaves, the conventions of inheritance are such that a man may, and often does make an arbitrary selection of his heir from among his sons. Because of this, there is a constant jockeying for position among his wives, who are concerned each with placing her children in the most favorable light before the common husband. The psychological realities of life within such a polygynous household have yet to be studied in detail; but that the purely human situation is such as to make the relationship between a mother and her children more intimate than that between the family head, and any but perhaps one or two of the offspring of the various wives who share this common husband and father, is a point which cannot be overestimated.

Against this background the patterns of marriage and family organization prevalent in the Negro communities of the United States may be projected, so as to indicate the points in the available literature at which the influence of African tradition can be discerned. The following summary statement as concerns mating and the family in the southern county studied by C. S. Johnson is to the point:

> The postponement of marriage in the section . . . does not preclude courtship, but accentuates it, and gives rise to other social adjustments based on this obvious economic necessity. The active passions of youth and late adolescence are present but without the usual formal restraints. Social behavior rooted in this situation, even when its consequences are understood, is lightly censured or excused entirely. Conditions are favorable to a great amount of sex experimentation. It cannot always be determined whether this experimentation is a phase of courtship, or love-making without the immediate intention of marriage, or recreation and diversion. Whether or not sexual intercourse is accepted as a part of courtship it is certain no one is surprised when it occurs. When pregnancy follows pressure is not strong enough to compel the father either to marry the mother or to support the child. The girl does not lose status, nor are her chances for marrying seriously threatened. An incidental compensation for this lack of censuring public opinion is the freedom for the children thus born from warping social condemnation. There is, in a sense, no such thing as illegitimacy in this community.[37]

In studying a community such as this, we are therefore faced with a situation where acculturation has brought on disintegration—disintegration due to slavery, to the present economic background of life, and to those psychological reactions which are the concomitants of life without security. Reinterpretation of earlier, pre-American patterns has occurred, but readjustment to normal conditions of life has been inhibited. We thus must recognize that the elasticity of the marriage concept among Negroes derives in a measure, largely unrecognized, from the need to adjust a polygynous family form to patterns based on a convention of monogamy, in a situation where this has been made the more difficult by economic and psychological complications resulting from the nature of the historical situation.

A rich documentation exists in the way of indices which point the aspects of Negro social organization that differ strikingly from white patterns. It is only necessary to turn to the general study of the problem by Frazier[38] or such a specialized analysis as that of Reed[39] to realize to what an extent the incidence of productive matings without legal status is out of line with white practices. Yet when the emphasis laid on the proper type of marriage proposal in the Sea Islands, where there is some measure of stability in Negro society,[40] is compared with Frazier's statement that 30 per cent of the births on that island are illegitimate, it is apparent that here, at least, sanctions other than those of the European type are operative. Johnson's summary of the various forms of union found among the Negroes of Macon County, Georgia, provides further illustrative material:

> Children of common-law relationships are not illegitimate, from the point of view of the community or of their stability, for many of these unions are as stable as legally sanctioned unions. They hold together for twenty or thirty years, in some cases, and lack only the sense of guilt. Again, there are competent, self-sufficient women who not only desire children but need them as later aids in the struggle for survival when their strength begins to wane, but who want neither the restriction of formal marriage nor the constant association with a husband. They get their children not so much through weakness as through their own deliberate selection of a father. Sexual unions for pleasure frequently result in children. There is a term for children born under the two latter circumstances. They are called "stolen children." "Stolen children," observed one mother, "is the best." A woman with children and who has been married though later separated from her husband may add other children to her family without benefit of formal sanctions. These are "children by the way." The youthful sex experimentation, which is in part related to the late marriages, often results in children. These are normally taken into the home of the girl's parents and treated without distinction as additions to the original family. Finally, there are the children who result from the deliberate

philandering of the young men who "make foolments" on young girls. They are universally condemned. These children, as circumstances direct, may be placed with the parents of the mother or father of the child, an uncle, sister, or grandmother. They are accepted easily into the families on the simple basis of life and eventually are indistinguishable from any of the other children. Even if there were severe condemnation of true "illegitimates," confusion as to origin would tend both to mitigate some of the offenses and to obscure them all from specific condemnation.[41]

What is recognizably African in all this? The "common-law relationship" is merely a phrase for the recognition of the fact that matings not legally sanctioned may achieve enough stability to receive equal recognition with regularly performed marriages. In Africa, and in the West Indies where Africanisms persist, marriage is not a matter requiring approval of the state or of any religious body. Only consent of the families concerned is needed, while marriage rites depart from the secular only to the extent that they are directed toward obtaining the benevolent oversight of the ancestors. Therefore Negro common-law marriages in the United States conflict in no wise with earlier practices, while in so far as they require the approval of the families of the principals, they are, indeed, directly in line with African custom.

The "competent, self-sufficient women" who wish to have no husbands are of especial interest. The social and economic position of women in West Africa is such that on occasion a woman may refuse to relinquish the customary control of her children in favor of her husband, and this gives rise to special types of matings that are recognized in Dahomey and among the Yoruba, and may represent a pattern having a far wider distribution. The phenomenon of a woman "marrying" a woman,[42] which has been reported from various parts of the African continent and is a part of this same complex, testifies to the importance of a family type which might well have had the vitality necessary to make of it a basis for the kind of behavior outlined in the case of the "self-sufficient" woman who, in the United States, desires children but declines to share them with a husband. The same traditional basis exists for "children by the way," those offspring of women, once married, by men other than their husbands. . . .

Of the several classifications of Negro family types which take the position of the woman into account, two may be cited. The first concerns the family as it exists at the present time among the Negro urban workers:

The status of husband and wife in the black worker's family assumes roughly three patterns. Naturally, among the relatively large percentage of families with women heads, the woman occupies a dominant position. But, because of the traditional role of the black wife as a contributor to the support of the family, she continues to occupy a position of authority and is not completely subordinate to masculine authority even in those families where the man is present. . . . The entrance of the black worker in industry where he has earned comparatively good wages has enabled the black worker's wife to remain at home. Therefore, the authority of the father in the family has been strengthened, and the wife has lost some of her authority in family matters. . . . Wives as well as children are completely subject to the will of the male head. However, especially in southern cities, the black worker's authority in his family may be challenged by his mother-in-law.[43]

Johnson has differentiated family types in the rural region studied by him into another set of categories. Noting the fact that in terms of the commonly accepted pattern wherein the father is head of the family, "the families of this area are, . . . considerably atypical," since, "in the first place, the role of the mother is of much greater importance than in the more familiar American group," he goes on to distinguish three kinds of families. First come those "which are fairly stable" and are "sensitive to certain patterns of respectability"; then there are those termed "artificial quasi-families" that "have the semblance of a normal and natural family, and function as one," except that "the members of the group are drawn into it by various circumstances rather than being a product of the original union"; and finally the form is found where "the male head remains constant while other types of relationship, including a succession of wives and their children by him, shift around him."[44] In addition to these, however, are the families headed by women:

The numbers of households with old women as heads and large numbers of children, although of irregular structure, is sufficiently important to be classed as a type. . . . The oldest generation is the least mobile, the children of these in the active ages move about freely and often find their own immediate offspring, while young, a burden, as they move between plantations. Marriages and remarriages bring increasing numbers of children who may be a burden to the new husband or a hindrance to the mother if she must become a wage-earner. The simplest expedient is to leave them with an older parent to rear. This is usually intended as a temporary measure, but it most often ends in the establishment of a permanent household as direct parental support dwindles down. The responsibility is accepted as a matter of course by the older woman and she thereafter employs her wits to keep the artificial family going.[45]

Powdermaker likewise notes the elasticity of families headed by women, and indicates how congenial this pattern is to Negroes living in various social and environmental settings:

> The personnel of these matriarchal families is variable and even casual. Step-children, illegitimate children, adopted children, mingle with the children of the house. No matter how small or crowded the home is, there is always room for a stray child, an elderly grandmother, an indigent aunt, a homeless friend. . . . The pattern of flexibility, however, expanding and contracting the household according to need is not restricted to the poorer and more crowded homes. A typical family of the upper middle class is headed by a prosperous widow, who in her early twenties married a man over sixty years old. He was considered very wealthy and had been married several times before. The household now includes his widow's eleven-year-old daughter (an illegitimate child born before she met her husband), the dead husband's granddaughter by one of his early marriages, and the granddaughter's two children, two and three years old. The granddaughter was married but is divorced from her husband. Everyone in the household carries the same family name.[46]

It is evident that this so-called "maternal" family of the Negro is a marked deviant from what is regarded as conventional by the white majority. Yet it must not be forgotten that the economic and social role of the man in Negro society is of the utmost significance in rounding out the picture of Negro social life. Though important from the point of view of the search for Africanisms, interest in the position of women in the family must not obscure perspective so as to preclude the incidence and role of those families wherein the common American pattern is followed. Despite the place of women in the West African family, the unit holds a prominent place for the husband and father who, as head of the polygynous group, is the final authority over its members, sharing fully in all those obligations which the family must meet if it is to survive and hold its place in the stable society of which it forms a part.

With this point in mind, certain further special characteristics of the Negro family may be considered before the causes which may best account for its place in Negro life are analyzed. Outstanding among these is the fact that an older woman frequently gives the group its unity and coherence. Frazier indicates the following sanctions in explaining the place of such elderly females in Negro families:

The Negro grandmother's importance is due to the fact not only that she has been the "oldest head" in a maternal family organization but also to her position as "granny" or midwife among a simple peasant folk. As the repository of folk wisdom concerning the inscrutable ways of nature, the grandmother has been depended upon by mothers to ease the pains of childbirth and ward off the dangers of ill luck. Children acknowledge their indebtedness to her for assuring them, during the crisis of birth, a safe entrance into the world. Even grown men and women refer to her as a second mother and sometimes show the same deference and respect for her that they accord their own mothers.[47] . . .

One of the most popular explanations of the aberrant forms taken by the Negro family is by reference to the experience of slavery. A less extreme example of this position, conventionally phrased, is to be found in Johnson's work. Noting that the role of the mother is of "much greater importance than that in the more familiar American group," he goes on to state:

This has some explanation in the slave origins of these families. Children usually remained with the mother; the father was incidental and could very easily be sold away. The role of mother could be extended to that of "mammy" for the children of white families.[48]

Frazier has presented this point of view at greater length. One statement reads:

We have spoken of the mother as the mistress of the cabin and as the head of the family. . . . Not only did she have a more fundamental interest in her children than the father but, as a worker and a free agent, except where the master's will was concerned, she developed a spirit of independence and a keen sense of her personal rights.[49]

"In spite of the numerous separations," it is stated, "the slave mother and her children, especially those under ten, were treated as a group";[50] while, "because of the dependence of the children upon the mother it appears that the mother and smaller children were sold together."[51] To make the point, slave advertisements such as the following are cited:

A Wench, complete cook, washer and ironer, and her four children—a Boy 12, another 9, a Girl 5 that sews; and a Girl about 4 years old. Another family—a Wench, complete washer and ironer, and her Daughter, 14 years old, accustomed to the house.[52]

These citations are not made to suggest that due attention has not been paid to the place of the father in the slave family, though it is undoubtedly true that he has received less study than has the mother in research into the derivation of present-day family types among the Negroes. The fact of the matter, however, is that the roles of both parents were individually determined, varying not only from region to region and plantation to plantation, but also being affected by the reactions of individual personalities on one another. Not only was the father a significant factor during slaving, but a reading of the documents will reveal how the selling of children—even very young children—away from their mothers is stressed again and again as one of the most anguishing aspects of the slave trade. Whether in the case of newly arrived Negroes sold from the slave ships or of slaves born in this country and sold from the plantations, there was not the slightest guarantee that a mother would not be separated from her children. The impression obtained from the contemporary accounts, indeed, is that the chances were perhaps more than even that separation would occur. This means, therefore, that, though the mechanism ordinarily envisaged in establishing this "maternal" family was operative to some degree, the role of slavery cannot be considered as having been quite as important as has been assumed.

The total economic situation of the Negro was another active force in establishing and maintaining the "maternal" family type. No considerable amount of data are available as to the inner economic organization of Negro families, but the forms of Negro family life themselves suggest that the female members of such families, and especially the elderly women, exercise appreciable control over economic resources. That the economic role of the women not only makes of them managers but also contributors whose earnings are important assets is likewise apparent. This economic aspect of their position is described by Johnson in the following terms:

> The situation of economic dependence of women in cities is reversed in this community, and is reflected rather strikingly in the economic independence on the part of the Negro women in the country. Their earning power is not very much less than that of the men, and for those who do not plan independent work there is greater security in their own family organization where many hands contribute to the raising of cotton and of food than there is for them alone with a young and inexperienced husband.[53]

In Mississippi the following obtains in plantation families:

> In many cases the woman is the sole breadwinner. Often there is no man in the household at all. In a number of instances, elderly women in their seventies and their middle-aged daughters with or without

children and often without husbands, form one household with the old woman as head.[54]

It is to be expected that such a situation will be reflected in property ownership:

> In this town of a little more than three thousand inhabitants, . . . 202 colored people own property. The assessed value for the majority of these holdings ranges from $300 to $600. Of the 202 owners, 100 are men, owning property valued at $61,250, and 93 are women, with holdings valued at $57,460. Nine men and women own jointly property totaling $3280 in value. Among the Whites also, about half the owners are women. When White women are owners, it usually means that a man has put his property in his wife's name so that it cannot be touched if he gets into difficulty. Among the Negroes, many women bought the property themselves, with their own earnings.[55]

Of the high proportion of holdings by men in the more favored socio-economic group of Negroes, it is stated, "if more property were owned by Negroes in the lower strata, there would probably be a higher percentage of female ownership." Yet as it is, the percentage would seem to be sufficiently high in terms of current American economic patterns, especially since, as stated, Negro women actually bought and hold their property for themselves rather than for their husbands, as is the common case among the whites.

The absence of any reference to African background in the citations concerning Negro families headed by women is merely another instance of the tendency to overlook the fact that the Negro was the carrier of a preslavery tradition. It is in the writings dealing with this aspect of Negro life that we find truncated history in its most positive expression, since in this field the existence of an African past has been recognized only in terms of such denials of its vitality as were cited in the opening pages of this work. Yet the aspects of Negro family which diverge most strikingly from patterns of the white majority are seen to deviate in the direction of resemblances to West African family life.

It cannot be regarded only as coincidence that such specialized features of Negro family life in the United States as the role of women in focusing the sentiment that gives the family unit its psychological coherence, or their place in maintaining the economic stability essential to survival, correspond closely to similar facets of West African social structure. And this becomes the more apparent when we investigate the inner aspects of the family structure of Negroes in the New World outside the United States. Though everywhere the father has his place, the tradition of paternal control and the function of the father as sole or principal provider essential to the European pattern is deviated from. In the coastal region of the Guianas, for example, the mother and grandmother are essentially the mainstays of the primary relationship group. A man obtains his soul from his father, but his affections and his place in society are derived from his mother; a person's home is his mother's, and though matings often endure, a man's primary affiliation is to the maternal line. In Trinidad, Jamaica, the Virgin Islands, or elsewhere in the Caribbean, should parents separate, the children characteristically remain with their mother, visiting their father from time to time if they stay on good terms with him.

The woman here is likewise an important factor in the economic scene. The open-air market is the effective agent in the retail distributive process, and business, as in West Africa, is principally in the hands of women. It is customary for them to handle the family resources, and their economic independence as traders makes for their personal independence, something which, within the family, gives them power such as is denied to women who, in accordance with the prevalent European custom, are dependent upon their husbands for support. In both West Africa and the West Indies the women, holding their economic destinies in their own hands, are fully capable of going their own ways if their husbands displease them; not being hampered by any conception of marriage as an ultimate commitment, separation is easily effected and a consequent fluidity in family personnel such as has been noted in the preceding pages of this section results. Now if to this complex is added the tradition of a sentimental attachment to the mother, derived from the situation within the polygynous households of West Africa, ample justification appears for holding that the derivations given for Negro family life by most students of the Negro family in the United States present serious gaps.

As in the case of most other aspects of Negro life, the problem becomes one of evaluating multiple forces rather than placing reliance on simpler explanations. From the point of view of the search for Africanisms, the status of the Negro family at present is thus to be regarded as the result of the play of various forces in the New World experience of the Negro, projected against a background of aboriginal tradition. Slavery did not cause the "maternal" family; but it tended to continue certain elements in the cultural endowment brought to the New World by the Negroes. The feeling between mother and children was reinforced when the father was sold away from the rest of the family; where he was not, he continued life in a way that tended to consolidate the obligations assumed by him in the integrated societies of Africa as these obligations were reshaped to fit the monogamic, paternalistic pattern of the white masters. That the plantation system did not differentiate between the sexes in exploiting slave labor tended, again, to reinforce the tradition of the part played by women in the tribal economics.

Furthermore, these African sanctions have been encouraged by the position of the Negro since freedom. As underprivileged members of society, it has been necessary for Negroes to continue calling on all the labor resources in their families if the group was to survive; and this strengthened woman's economic independence. In a society fashioned like that of the United States, economic independence for women means sexual independence, as is evidenced by the personal lives of white women from the upper socio-economic levels of society. This convention thus fed back into the tradition of the family organized about and headed by women, continuing and reinforcing it as time went on. And it is for these reasons that those aspects of Negro family life that depart from majority patterns are to be regarded as residues of African custom. Families of this kind are not African, it is true; they are, however, important as comprehending certain African survivals. For they not only illustrate the tenacity of the traditions of Africa under the changed conditions of New World life, but also in larger perspective indicate how, in the acculturative situation, elements new to aboriginal custom can reinforce old traditions, while at the same time helping to accommodate a people to a setting far different from that of their original milieu. . . .

Notes

1. W. R. Bascom, "Acculturation among the Gullah Negroes," *Amer. Anth.,* 43: 43–50, 1941.
2. Herskovits, *Dahomey,* Vol. I, pp. 32 f., Plate 3, and *Life in a Haitian Valley,* p. 254, plate opposite p. 100.
3. Botume, *First Days amongst the Contrabands,* p. 53.
4. Caroline Couper Lovell, *The Golden Isles of Georgia,* Boston, 1932, pp. 187 f.
5. The former collected by W. R. Bascom; the latter by M. J. Herskovits.
6. *Folk Beliefs of the Southern Negro,* p. 27.
7. *Folk-Lore of the Sea Islands, South Carolina,* Cambridge, 1923, p. 204.
8. Mary A. Owen, *Old Rabbit the Voodoo and Other Sorcerers,* London, 1893, pp. 10 f.
9. Doyle, *The Etiquette of Race Relations in the South,* p. 76, quoting William Ferguson, *America by River and Rail,* London, 1856, p. 149.
10. M. J. and F. S. Herskovits, *Suriname Folk-Lore,* pp. 4 ff.
11. *First Days amongst the Contrabands,* p. 59.

12. *The Etiquette of Race Relations in the South*, p. 76.
13. *My Bondage and My Freedom*, pp. 69 f.
14. *Folk Beliefs of the Southern Negro*, p. 393.
15. *Ibid.*, p. 23.
16. *Ibid.*, p. 394.
17. For illustrations of this and other instances of how elaborate the rules of etiquette can be in a Negro tribe, see M. J. and F. S. Herskovits, *Rebel Destiny*, various passages indicated under "Etiquette" in the index.
18. *Caste and Class in a Southern Town*, p. 6.
19. *The Etiquette of Race Relations in the South*, p. 161.
20. *Ibid.*, pp. 79 f. The first illustration is given as from Olmsted, *The Cotton Kingdom: a Traveler's Observations on Cotton and Slavery in the American Southern States*, New York, 1861, Vol. II, pp. 1 f.; the second from Douglass, *My Bondage and My Freedom*, pp. 252 f.
21. *Folk Beliefs of the Southern Negro*, p. 50.
22. Charles C. Jones, *The Religious Instruction of the Negroes*, Savannah, 1842, pp. 130 f.
23. Rattray, *Ashanti Law and Constitution*, pp. 107 ff., and Herskovits, *Dahomey*, Vol. I, pp. 106 ff., Vol. II, pp. 72 ff.
24. Powdermaker, *After Freedom*, p. 126.
25. "African Institutions in America," *Journal of American Folklore*, 18:15–32, 1905; see also Bernard C. Steiner, "History of Slavery in Connecticut," *Johns Hopkins Univ. Stud. in Hist. and Pol. Sci.*, 11th Ser., September-October, 1893.
26. Aimes, *ibid.*, p. 16; Steiner, *ibid.*, p. 78.
27. Steiner, *op. cit.*, pp. 78 f.; see also Aimes, *op. cit.*, p. 16.
28. *Ibid.*, p. 19.
29. Paul Lewinson, *Race, Class, and Party; a History of Negro Suffrage and White Politics in the South*, New York, 1932, *passim*.
30. Cf. among others Forde, "Land and Labour in a Cross River Village"; René Maunier, "La Construction Collective de la Maison en Kabylie," *Tr. et Mèm., Inst. d'Eth.*, Vol. III, Paris, 1926; Herskovits, *Dahomey*, Vol. I, pp. 75 f.
31. W. R. Bascom, "Acculturation among the Gullah Negroes," *Amer. Anth.*, 43: 44–46, 1941.
32. H. W. Odum, *Social and Mental Traits of the American Negro*, New York, 1910, pp. 98 f.
33. *Ibid.*, pp. 104 f.
34. *Ibid.*, p. 249.
35. Cf. Gist, Noel, "Secret Societies: A Cultural Study of Fraternalism in the United States," *Univ. Missouri Studies*, 15:1–184, 1940.
36. Herskovits, *Life in a Haitian Valley*, pp. 107 ff., 258 ff.
37. *Shadow of the Plantation*, p. 49.
38. *The Negro Family in the United States*, pp. 109 f., 343 ff., 620 ff.
39. *Negro Illegitimacy in New York City*, New York, 1926, *passim*.
40. As indicated, for example, by Parsons, *Folk-Lore of the Sea Islands, South Carolina*, p. 206.
41. *Shadow of the Plantation*, pp. 66 f.
42. M. J. Herskovits, "A Note on 'Woman Marriage' in Dahomey," *Africa*, 10: 335–341, 1937.
43. *The Negro Family in the United States*, pp. 461 f.

44.   *Shadow of the Plantation*, pp. 29, 32 f., 39 f.
45.   *Ibid.*, p. 37.
46.   *After Freedom*, pp. 146 f.
47.   *The Negro Family in the United States*, p. 153.
48.   *Shadow of the Plantation*, p. 29.
49.   The Negro Family in the United States, pp. 57 f.
50.   *Ibid.*, p. 55.
51.   "*The Negro Slave Family*," *loc. cit.*, p. 234.
52.   *Ibid.*
53.   *Shadow of the Plantation*, pp. 48 f.
54.   Powdermaker, *After Freedom*, p. 146.
55.   *Ibid.*, p. 127.

E. Franklin Frazier agreed with Herskovits that there were African survivals in the culture and character of North American slaves. However, Frazier was more impressed with what was lost when Africans were forced to adapt to their new environment. The best evidence of their differing points of view is to be found in the famous debates about family structure.

Herskovits argued that the slave family was a modified version of the African one. Frazier contended that it was a product of the exigencies of life in an economic setting where the only binding ties were between mother and child. Frazier's argument is presented below.

2

The Significance of the African Background

E. Franklin Frazier

Among the "twenty Negers" who were brought in "a dutch man of warre" to Virginia in 1619, there were some whose names indicated that they had been baptized by the Spaniards.[1] But to what extent baptism and a new name were an indication that these slaves had lost their African cultural heritage or had acquired Spanish culture, the records do not inform us. Baptism and the acquisition of a Spanish name might have been artificial ceremonies, as they often were, when at the port of embarkation in Africa three or four hundred slaves were baptized and given a slip of paper in order that they might not forget their Spanish names.[2]

The manner in which young slaves were captured and sold on slave markets and confined in the slave pens in African ports had a more important effect upon the integrity of their cultural heritage. Such experiences, however, as well as the ordeal of the journey to the

From *The Negro in the United States* by E. Franklin Frazier, pp. 3–21. Copyright 1949 by the Macmillan Company. Reprinted by permission of the Macmillan Company.

West Indies—the "middle passage"—did not destroy completely their African heritage. Individual slaves brought to America memories of their homeland and certain patterns of behavior and attitudes toward their fellow men and the physical world. It was in the New World, particularly in what became the United States, that new conditions of life destroyed the significance of their African heritage and caused new habits and attitudes to develop to meet new situations. Despite fresh importations from Africa, the process of sloughing off African culture continued. Since Emancipation this process has been so thoroughgoing that at the present time only in certain isolated areas can one discover what might be justly called African cultural survivals.[3]

Our Knowledge Concerning African Backgrounds

Only recently have we begun to secure sufficiently exact Knowledge of the origin of the slaves brought to America to be in a position to identify African survivals. In the West Indies, the planters had some knowledge of the tribal backgrounds of the slaves; while in Brazil terms were used by the planters to indicate vaguely the area in Africa from which the slaves came. Recent investigations by Brazilian scholars have shown that "three great Negro peoples entered Brazil." "At the beginning of the slave trade," as pointed out by Ramos, "the largest number of those imported into Brazil were from Angola, the Congo and Guinea. When more active communication began with Bahia, the leading source of supply was Guinea and the western Sudan. There began a remarkable influx of Yorubas, Minas from the Gold Coast, Dahomans and various Islamized tribes such as the Hausas, Tapas, Mandingos, and Fulahs."[4] In the United States it has generally been assumed by scholars that throughout the slave trade slaves were drawn from far in the interior of Africa.[5] This assumption has been challenged recently by Herskovits who has studied the documents bearing on the slave trade, especially those collected and analyzed by Miss Donnan.[6] By analyzing the data found "in manifests recorded from Virginia between the years 1710 and 1769" he was able to determine the specific areas from which came approximately 25,000 of the 45,000 slaves imported directly from Africa. The areas that figured most prominently were Guinea, "which means the west coast of Africa from the Ivory Coast to western Nigeria, Calabar, which represents the Niger Delta region, Angola, or the area about the lower Congo, and the Gambia."[7] As in the case of slaves imported into other states, only a few of these slaves—1,011 out of a total of 52,504—were from Madagascar. During the last half of the eighteenth century, the vast majority of the slaves imported into the American colonies came from the areas described above; but toward the close of the century the number of slave ships coming from the Congo increased.[8] In the nineteenth century when efforts were made by the United States, England, and France to outlaw the slave trade in those parts of Africa under the control of the latter two powers, the Congo, which was under Portuguese control, became the chief source of slaves for the illegal trade to the United States as well as to Brazil.

This more precise knowledge of the areas from which the slaves came has not, however, enabled investigators to refer African survivals in the United States to a specific tribe or a definite area.[9] In fact, students of the Negro are agreed that there were fewer African survivals in the United States than in other areas of the New World.[10] This was due, first, to differences in the character of slavery and the plantation system in the United States and in other parts of the New World. In the West Indies and Brazil, large numbers of African slaves were concentrated on vast plantations for the production of sugar. Under such conditions it was possible for the slaves to reestablish their African ways of life and keep alive their traditions. But in the United States the slaves were scattered in relatively small numbers on plantations and farms over a large area. In 1860 in the South as a whole, three-fourths of the farms and plantations had less than fifty slaves.[11] Even in the lower South, where the slaveholdings were larger on the average, two-thirds of the holdings were less than fifty slaves. Only in Arkansas, Georgia, Louisiana, Mississippi, and South Carolina were there holdings with more than 500 slaves and such holdings constituted less than one per cent of the holdings in all these states except South Carolina.

Size of Plantation and African Survivals

The size of the slaveholdings on the farms and plantations significantly influenced both the extent and nature of the contacts between the slaves and the whites. There was little contact between the great body of field slaves and the whites on the large sugar and cotton plantations in the southern states, as was true also on the large sugar plantations in Brazil and in the West Indies. Concerning the situation in South Carolina, Mrs. Johnson writes: "On St. Helena Island, where there were some two thousand slaves to little more than two hundred whites, the Negroes learned very slowly the ways of the whites. Their mastery of English was far less advanced than that of the Piedmont slaves."[12] However, the majority of the slaves in the United States were on small farms and plantations. In some of the upland cotton regions of Alabama, Mississippi, Louisiana, and Arkansas the median number of slaves per holding did not reach twenty; while in regions of general farming based mainly upon slave labor in Kentucky, Maryland, Missouri, North Carolina, South Carolina, and Tennessee the median holdings were even less.[13] In some of these latter regions the close contacts between the slaves and whites extended to working together on the smaller farms.

Slaves freshly imported from Africa usually had to be "broken in" to the plantation regime. A traveler in Louisiana described the process as follows:

> Negroes bought from the importers and carried home by the pur-chasers are ordinarily treated differently from the old ones. They are only gradually accustomed to work. They are made to bathe often, to take walks from time to time, and especially to dance; they are distributed in small numbers among old slaves in order to dispose them better to acquire their habits. These attentions are not usually due to sentiments of humanity. Interest requires them. It happens too often that poor masters, who have not other slaves, or are too greedy, require hard labor of these fresh negroes, exhaust them quickly, lose them by sickness and more often by grief. Often they hasten their own death; some wound themselves, others stifle themselves by drawing in the tongue so as to close the breathing passage, others take poison, or flee and perish of misery and hunger.[14]

It is likely that these new slaves with their African ways and memories of Africa had to face the disdain, if not the hostility, of Negroes who had become accommodated to the slave regime and had acquired a new conception of themselves.[15] They were most likely to meet such an atti-tude on the part of the household slaves, who because of their intimate association with the whites had taken over the culture of the latter.[16]

Adjustment of Slaves to New Environment

Because of the fact that the manner of the Negro's enslavement tended to destroy so completely his African culture, some scholars have been inclined to dismiss the influence of the African culture on the Negro's behavior. They have recognized, to be sure, that the speech of the Negro folk as well as their religious practices and family life differ from the behavior and customs of the whites; but these differences have been attributed to their isolation and incomplete assimilation.[17] On the other hand, there has been much speculation on the influence of African culture as a cause of these differences. In some instances this speculation has betrayed an ignorance of African cultures or has simply reflected popular prejudices in regard to "primitive" people or so-called "savages." But there has also been speculation of a nature that has led to fantastic conclusions concerning the influence of African survivals on the behavior of Negroes in the United States.[18] Only recently have competent scholars with a knowledge of the culture of the African areas from which the Negroes came attempted to identify definite African survivals.[19]

The first adjustment which the transported Negroes had to make in their new environment was to acquire some knowledge of the language of the whites for communication. Where the slaves, sometimes from childhood, were in close contacts with the whites, they took over completely the speech and language of their masters. On the other hand, the great masses of isolated slaves, as in the case of the slaves on St. Helena Island, acquired the speech and language of the whites more slowly. The peculiar speech of Negroes in such isolated places has generally been attributed to their isolation, their lack of appreciation of grammatical rules, or to the fact that they had preserved the characteristics of English as spoken at an earlier period. But Lorenzo D. Turner has discovered approximately four thousand words of West African origin in the Gullah vocabulary of Negroes on the coast of South Carolina and Georgia.[20] Moreover, he found numerous African given names and African phrases that had been translated into English. In view of Turner's researches, the current notion that African words have completely disappeared from the vocabulary of Negroes in all sections of the United States must be modified.[21]

Destruction of African Family

In contrast to such concrete data on linguistic survivals, there is scarcely any evidence that recognizable elements of the African social organization have survived in the United States. This has been especially true in regard to those phases of the African social organization which had a political character.[22] A rare instance of such a survival may be found in the early history of New England, where it was customary for the Negroes to elect a "governor," who exercised an almost despotic discipline over local groups of slaves.[23] In regard to the African family organization there have been from time to time reports of survivals.[24] For example, in the autobiography of an exslave the following incident is related:

> I assisted her and her husband to inter the infant—which was a little boy—and its father buried with it, a small bow and several arrows; a little bag of parched meal; a miniature canoe, about a foot long, and a little paddle (with which he said it would cross the ocean to his own country), a small stick, with an iron nail, sharpened, and fastened into one end of it; and a piece of white muslin, with several curious and strange figures painted on it in blue and red, by which, he said, his relations and countrymen would know the infant to be his son, and would receive it accordingly, on its arrival amongst them. . . . He cut a lock of hair from his head, threw it upon the dead infant, and closed the grave with his own hands. He then told us the God of his country was looking at him, and was pleased with what he had done.[25]

If we can rely on the account of an old Negro woman that "a slave who married a girl from a group of native Africans just received on the plantation" was required "to obtain the consent of every member of the girl's group before he was allowed to marry her,"[26] we have what might be an instance of the continued control of the extended family or clan organization. In his researches concerning linguistic survivals, Turner found that in isolated areas on the coast of Georgia and South Carolina, the Gullahs who often confine the use of African words to the intimate circle of the family reveal the influence of African traditions in the naming of their children. He writes:

> Even though the Gullahs may not know the meaning of many African words they use for proper names, in their use of English words they follow a custom common in West Africa of giving their children names which suggest the time of birth, or the conditions surrounding it, or the temperament or appearance of the child. All twelve months of the year and the seven days of the week are used freely. In some cases the name indicates the time of day at which the birth occurs.[27]

These rare and isolated instances of survivals associated with the Negro family only indicate how completely the African social organization was wiped out by slavery.

Although Herskovits agrees with other students of the Negro that the plantation system destroyed African family types as well as their underlying moral and supernatural sanctions, he nevertheless thinks that a diluted form of the African family continued to exist.[28] A diluted form of the African family may be recognized, he thinks, in the so-called common-law marriages among Negroes. "We . . . must recognize," he writes, "that the elasticity of the marriage concept among Negroes derives in a measure, largely unrecognized, from the need to adjust a polygynous family form to patterns based on a convention of monogamy, in a situation where this has been made the more difficult by economic and psychological complications resulting from the nature of the historical situation."[29] Likewise, he sees in the so-called "matriarchal" or "maternal" family among Negroes, in which the mother and grandmother play important rôles, evidence of the continuation in a diluted form of African traditions. "It cannot be regarded only as coincidence," he maintains, "that such specialized features of Negro family life in the United States as the rôle of women in focusing the sentiment that gives the family unit its psychological coherence, or their place in maintaining the economic stability essential to survival, correspond closely to similar facets of West African social structure."[30]

These statements concerning the continuation in a diluted form of the African family in the United States are not based upon any data showing continuity between African traditions and the familial behavior of American Negroes. They are only an ingenious attempt to show similarity between certain customs and practices of Negroes in the United States and in Africa in regard to sex and family behavior. However, the supposed similarities in attitudes and behavior are not real similarities in a cultural sense. When loose and unregulated sex behavior is encountered among American Negroes, it is not the same as the polygynous customs and practices of African Negroes. The latter are regulated by custom and tradition while the former lack the sanction of traditions and customs. Although in some areas "common-law" matings occur on a large scale among certain classes of Negroes, such behavior can be explained in terms of practices which sometimes have become customary as the result of social and economic forces in the American environment.[31] Moreover, such behavior is often recognized as being in conflict with the mores of the larger society.

The same fallacies appear in the attempt to explain illegitimacy among Negroes and the important position of the woman in the Negro family as a diluted form of African cultural survival. The argument that the impulsive and uncontrolled sex behavior of foot-loose Negro women which often results in illegitimacy has a basis in African traditions may be dismissed simply as unwarranted speculation.

On the other hand, the statement concerning the survival of African customs in regard to the woman's place in the family deserves some consideration. It is probably true that the situation under the slave regime might have given support to those African traditions supporting the woman's important position in the family. But African traditions supporting male dominance were just as likely to survive in the New World. For example, even today it appears that the African pattern of family life is perpetuated in the patriarchal family organization of the West Indian Negroes.[32]

In the United States it is neither possible nor is it necessary to seek an explanation of the dominance of the male or the female in the family organization of Negroes in supposed survivals of the African social organization. The important position of the mother in the Negro family in the United States has developed out of the exigencies of life in the new environment. In the absence of institutional controls, the relationship between mother and child has become the essential social bond in the family and the woman's economic position has developed in her those qualities which are associated with a "matriarchal" organization. On the other hand, the Negro family has developed as a patriarchal organization or similar to the American family as the male has acquired property and an interest in his family and as the assimilation of American attitudes and patterns of behavior has been accelerated by the breaking down of social isolation, sometimes through physical amalgamation,[33] Herskovits sees even in such well integrated patriarchal families, with a secure economic basis and traditions extending over several generations, evidence of the survival of the African ancestral cult in their family reunions when they praise the accomplishments of their ancestors or visit the family burying ground. Yet he admits that the overt manifestations of the ancestral cult have been obliterated and European religious beliefs have been taken over, and that only the "spirit" of ancestral culture has remained.[34] This simply means that the existence of such survivals cannot be validated on scientific grounds.

African Religious Survivals

There can be no question about the survival of African religious ceremonies and rituals in some parts of the New World. In Brazil at the present time African religious survivals are easily recognized in the religious cults of the Negroes and people of Negro descent. The *macumbas* of the Negroes in the region about Rio de Janeiro are true African religious survivals that have become greatly "adulterated in contact with an elaborate and complicated urban civilization."[35] On the other hand, such religious cults as the *candomblés* of Bahia and some of the *shangôs* of the northeast have preserved many African elements. In these religious cults, formerly concealed from the whites, the worship of Yoruban deities was carried on for centuries; but at the present time African deities are becoming identified with Catholic saints and beliefs are becoming fused with spiritualism.[36] Likewise, in Haiti one may find African survivals in the religious beliefs and rituals of the peasantry.[37]

In the United States it has been more difficult to discover African survivals in the religious behavior of the Negroes. During slavery there were reports of the dancing and singing of the slaves which indicated that African religious ceremonies had been carried over. Moreover, there were reports of slaves praying in a manner that indicated that they had been converted to Mohammedanism.[38] Since the emancipation of the slaves, we have had accounts of authentic religious practices which were undoubtedly of African origin.[39] Then, too, on the Sea Islands, where the isolated unmixed Negroes speak a distinct dialect, the "praise house" probably represents a fusion of African culture traits and Christian practices.[40] However, except for such instances, generally occurring among isolated groups of Negroes, it has been difficult to identify religious traits that could correctly be called African survivals.

Despite the general absence of African beliefs and rituals in the religious behavior of the Negroes in the United States, there has been some speculation on the existence of less obvious African survivals. For example, the fact that the majority of the Negroes in the United States are affiliated with the Baptist churches seems to Herskovits to be due primarily to certain features in the Negro's African heritage. His first statement of this viewpoint was that

> The importance of baptism in the ritual practices of Negro Christians has often been commented upon. It is not unreasonable to relate the strength of adherence to this practice to the great importance of the river-cults in West Africa, particularly in view of the fact that, as has been observed, river-cult priests were sold into slavery in great numbers.[41]

Evidently after Herskovits became acquainted with the "aggressive proselytizing activities of Protestantism" and the fact that white Baptists emphasized total immersion, he revised the statement of his position so as to include these facts.[42] He, nevertheless, maintains his position with reference to the rôle of priests of river-cults who were sold to rich Dahomean "conquerors of troublesome leaders." His most recent statement is as follows:

> In the New World, where the aggressive proselytizing activities of Protestantism made the retention of the inner forms of African religion as difficult as its outer manifestations, the most logical adaptation for the slaves to make to the new situation, and the simplest, was to give their adherence to that Christian sect which in its ritualism most resembled the types of worship known to them. As we have seen, the Baptist churches had an autonomous organization that was in line with the tradition of local self-direction congenial to African practice. In these churches the slaves were also permitted less restrained behavior than in the more sedate denominations. And such factors only tended to reinforce an initial predisposition of these Africans toward a cult which, in emphasizing baptism by total immersion, made possible the worship of the new supernatural powers in ways that at least contained elements not entirely unfamiliar.[43]

The proselytizing activities of the Baptists and Methodists provide an adequate explanation of the fact that the majority of the Negroes are members of the Baptist church. Moreover, they provide an adequate explanation of the fact that about a third of the Negroes are members of Methodist churches, which do not practice baptism by immersion, a fact which the speculation about the influence of African river-cults fails to explain. The Negro slaves seemingly from the beginning of their residence in the United States took over the religious beliefs and rituals to which they were exposed. During the eighteenth century the Society for the Propagation of the Gospel in Foreign Parts operating through the ministers of the Established Church of England converted many slaves to Christianity. For example, in the Goose Creek Parish in South Carolina in 1705, a Reverend Samuel Thomas had given religious instruction to a thousand slaves, "many of whom could read the Bible distinctly and great numbers of them were engaged in learning the scriptures."[44]

Then came the revivals during the latter half of the eighteenth century which drew vast numbers of the slaves into the Methodist and Baptist churches. Around the opening of the nineteenth century appeared the camp meeting revivals that tended to revive and enforce the effects of the religious awakening of the preceding century.[45] The Methodist and Baptist preachers carried the "gospel of salvation" to the black slave as well as to the poor and ignorant white.[46] In King William County, Virginia, in 1789 the sheriff appealed to the Governor because the Baptists and Methodists were meeting with slaves several times a week and had ejected the patrollers from their meetings.[47] In fact, when the Methodists and Baptists began their proselyting among the slaves and poor whites they were outspoken against slavery. When they ceased to oppose slavery openly, they continued to present Christianity as an escape for the enslaved blacks from their earthly condition.

Although the Methodists made the same appeal as the Baptists, there were certain features in the Baptist church organization and in their policy with reference to the Negroes that caused the latter to enter the Baptist organization more freely than the Methodist church. The Baptists encouraged a form of local self-government that favored the growth of Negro congregations. Then, too, they permitted and encouraged Negroes to become preachers, at first to whites as well as Negroes, and later as leaders of Negro congregations. Because of these features of the Baptist church policy, the enslaved and free Negro was given an opportunity for self-expression not provided by the Methodist church.[48] Under the Methodist church organization he was not only subject to the control emanating from the bishops but he was generally under white leadership in churches.[49]

One may reasonably assume that among the Negroes who received the "call to preach," there were some who had been influenced by African traditions and that others cherishing memories of their African background found in the emotionalism and the ecstatic form of worship that characterized the Methodist and Baptist revivals an opportunity for self-expression. But such assumptions provide no proof for Herskovits' assertion that the emotionalism and ecstatic behavior that characterized the Great Awakening and the camp meetings were largely due to African influences and that contrary to usual accounts the whites took over the behavior of the Negroes.[50] In support of this view he cites Davenport's observation on the difference between the automatisms of the Kentucky and the Ulster revivalists, the former, he thinks, having been influenced by the Negroes.[51] This reasoning is in line with Herskovits' general belief in the "toughness of culture," which enables it to survive under the most unfavorable conditions. However, such an argument fails to take into account the rôle of spontaneous impulses in human behavior, which probably account for the differences between the behavior of the Kentucky revivalists and those in Ulster. Likewise, much of the behavior of the Negroes was spontaneous and expressive and was not rigidly controlled by traditional patterns of behavior. It is significant that their religious behavior in the United States is similar to that of whites, while it differs markedly from that of Brazilian Negroes who have preserved African rituals and beliefs in their religious organizations.[52]

Other Phases of Culture

Herskovits' belief in the "toughness of culture" has led him to speculate upon the influence of African traditions upon various phases of Negro life. He thinks that economic cooperation among Negroes in the United States has been influenced by African traditions. Of the cooperation found in the lodges he writes:

> Cooperation among the Negroes of this country is principally found in such institutions as lodges and other benevolent societies, which in themselves are directly in line with the tradition underlying similar African organizations.[53]

Even in the fraternal organization among Negroes in cities, he sees "deep-seated drives in Negro life; drives so strong, indeed, that it is difficult, if not impossible, to account for them satisfactorily except in terms of a tradition which reaches further than merely to the period of slavery."[54] In regard to such speculation, one can only say that historical data concerning the leadership, the needs of an isolated group laboring under economic disadvantages, and the manner in which these organizations developed provide an adequate explanation of such phenomena. The "deep-seated" drives, which are referred to, are strong because they represent general human needs and, as we shall see in a later chapter, they are provided for in a manner consistent with the resources and the experiences of the people involved.

In some of the magic and folk beliefs of the rural Negroes in the United States, some African elements have probably been retained. But it is recognized by even Herskovits that "magic and other types of folk belief" originating in Africa and Europe have become amalgamated.[55] Therefore, the problem of the student seeking African survivals is to disentangle African from other elements in such beliefs and practices. On the basis of his knowledge of African cultures, Herskovits has attempted to show that unsuspected African elements have survived.[56] Puckett, who has devoted himself to the same task, concludes that the Negro has taken "over English practices in regard to the direct maintenance and perpetuation of life, while in things relating to pleasure, his customs seemingly have more of an African turn."[57] However, he adds that the African influence has been least where the Negro has had the most contact with the whites and that there are beliefs among Negroes "which seem to have no direct European or African parallels, and may represent independent Afro-American developments."[58]

The latter statement by Puckett concerning the appearance of new ways of thinking and acting applies to all aspects of Negro life in the United States. African patterns of thought and behavior could survive only where the Negroes were isolated and where there was sufficient common understanding among them to give significance to African survivals. But the isolation of the Negro from the whites was always limited by the fact that the majority of the slaves were scattered over a vast territory on small farms and plantations. Their isolation was further broken down by the organization of slave labor and the internal slave trade which created some mobility among the slave population. More important still was the fact that the African family system, the chief means of cultural transmission, was destroyed. Under such circumstances African languages were lost and the African social organization could not be reconstituted in the new environment. Consequently, Negroes acquired new habits and modes of thought, and whatever elements of African culture were retained lost their original meaning in becoming fused with their experiences in the New World. Beginning with emancipation Negroes have from time to time been uprooted from their customary ways of life and have gradually escaped from their isolation. As they have emerged from the world of the folk, they have been affected by the modes of thought and behavior characteristic of civilized or urbanized societies. This has constantly resulted in considerable social disorganization; but at the same time it has led to reorganization of life, at least among certain elements, on a pattern consistent with civilized modes of behavior. During this process of adjusting themselves to American civilization, the majority of the Negroes have sloughed off completely the African heritage.

Notes

1. Helen T. Catterall (ed.), *Judicial Cases Concerning American Slavery and the Negro* (Washington, D.C., 1926), Vol. I, pp. 55–56.
2. Enrique de Gandia, *Francisco de Alfaro y la Condicion Social de los Indios* (Buenos Aires, 1939). p. 38.
3. The most comprehensive and systematic study of the problem of African cultural survivals is to be found in Melville J. Herskovits, *The Myth of the Negro Past* (New York, 1942). Throughout this chapter there will be occasion to refer to this work, though our discussion will often be in disagreement with the conclusions of Herskovits, who attempts to show that African survivals

can be discovered in practically every phase of Negro life in the United States.

4. *The Negro* in *Brazil,* by Arthur Ramos, p. 11. Copyright 1939 by The Associated Publishers, Inc.

5. See for example U. B. Phillips, *American Negro Slavery* (New York, 1936). p. 31; Robert E. Park, "The Conflict and Fusion of Cultures," *Journal of Negro History,* Vol. IV, p. 117; and Edward Byron Reuter, *The American Race Problem* (New York, 1938), p. 123.

6. Herskovits, *The Myth of the Negro Past,* pp. 35–53. See also Elizabeth Donnan, *Documents Illustrative of the Slave Trade to America,* Vols. I-IV (Washington, D.C., 1930–1935).

7. *The Myth of the Negro Past,* by Melville J. Herskovits, p. 41. Copyright 1941 by Harper & Brothers.

8. *Ibid.,* pp. 52–53. According to Herskovits' analysis of Miss Donnan's sources, approximately 22,000 of the 65,466 slaves imported into South Carolina between 1733 and 1738 came from Angola and the Congo. *Ibid.,* p. 48.

9. ". . . one can set off the United States from the rest of the New World as a region where departure from African modes of life was greatest, and where such Africanisms as persisted were carried through in generalized form, almost never directly referable to a specific tribe or a definite area." *Ibid.,* p. 122.

10. See *ibid.,* p. 16, where Herskovits arranges areas of Negro concentration in the New World on a scale according to the intensity of African survivals. The area of most intensive survivals is in Suriname (the Bush Negroes) while next to the last group at the other end of the scale appear isolated groups of Negroes on the coast of Georgia and South Carolina. "Finally," writes Herskovits, "we should come to a group where, to all intents and purposes, there is nothing of the African tradition left, and which consists of people of varying degrees of Negroid physical type, who only differ from their white neighbors in the fact that they have more pigmentation in their skins." *Ibid.,* p. 16.

11. Lewis C. Gray, *History of Agriculture in the Southern United States to 1860* (New York, 1941), Vol. I, p. 529.

12. Reprinted from *A Social History of the Sea Islands,* by Guion Griffis Johnson, p. 127, by permission of The University of North Carolina Press. Copyright 1930 by The University of North Carolina Press.

13. Gray, *op. cit.,* Vol. I, pp. 534–35.

14. "Voyages . . . de la Louisiane," vol iii, 169–70, by C. C. Robin, from *Plantation and Frontier: Documents: 1649–1863.* Vol. II. p. 31, by Ulrich B. Phillips. Copyright 1909 by A. H. Clark Company.

15. The following newspaper account of the reception of four native Africans on a Georgia plantation, except for the inferred detail concerning the delight of the newcomers, is probably indicative of the general attitude of the slaves toward their African background: "Our common darkies treat them with sovereign contempt walking around them with a decided aristocratic air. But the Africans are docile and very industrious and are represented as being perfectly delighted with new homes and improved conditions. The stories that they are brutes and savages is all stuff and nonsense. It was put in the papers by men who do not know what they are talking about. As to their corrupting our common negroes, we venture the assertion would come nearer the truth if stated the other way." *Atlanta* (Ga.) *Daily Intelligencer,* March 9, 1859, from Phillips, *op. cit.,* 54–55.

16. See Chapter 111 [of *The Negro in the United States*].

17. See Reuter, *op. cit.*, pp. 129–31; and Park, *op. cit.*, pp. 115–17.

18. For example, see Woodson, *The African Background Outlined or Handbook for the Study of the Negro*, pp. 168–75, where the author, among other equally untenable conjectures, states: "The industry of the Negro in the United States may be partly explained as an African survival. The Negro is born a worker. In the African social order work is well organized. Everybody is supposed to make some contribution to the production of food and clothing necessary for the whole community" (*The African Background Outlined or Handbook for the Study of the Negro* by Carter G. Woodson, p. 171. Copyright 1936 by Association for the Study of Negro Life and History. Reprinted by permission of The Associated Publishers, Inc.). The claim of a social worker (Corinne Sherman, "Racial Factors in Desertion," *Family*, III, 224) that she was not able to understand "the conjugal habits of colored clients" until she had gained a knowledge of African customs shows to what fantastic conclusions speculations about African survivals in America may lead one.

19. See pp. 4 ff. [of *The Negro in the United States*].

20. See Herskovits, *op. cit.*, pp. 276–79.

21. In the West Indies and Suriname, it has been easier to trace many words in the language of the Negroes to their African sources. See Melville J. Herskovits, "On the Provenience of New World Negroes," *Social Forces*, XII, 252–59. In Brazil, the Islamized Negroes who maintained connections with Africa not only continued to speak Arabic but also conducted schools. Among the non-Islamized Negroes, Yoruba was the chief means of communication, this language being preserved today in the religious practices of Brazilian Negroes about Bahia. See Arthur Ramos, *O Negro Brasileiro* (Rio de Janeiro, 1940) and Nina Rodrigues, *Os Africanos* (2a Edição, São Paulo, 1935).

22. In the West Indies and in Brazil, there were numerous instances where free Negroes and especially slaves that had revolted or escaped revived features of the traditional African political organization. See Chapter V [of *The Negro in the United States*].

23. H. S. Aimes, "African Institutions in America," *Journal of American Folklore*, Vol. XVIII, pp. 15–17.

24. W. E. B. DuBois, who believed that careful research would reveal traces, but traces only, "of the African family in America" since "the effectiveness of the slave system meant the practically complete crushing out of the African clan and family life," nevertheless gives as an example of survival the case of a Negro country wedding in Lowndes County, Alabama, in 1892, in which the bride was chased "after the ceremony in a manner very similar to the Zulu ceremony." *The Negro Family* (Atlanta, 1908), p. 21.

25. Charles Ball, *Slavery in the United States: A Narrative of the Life and Adventures of Charles Ball, A Black Man* (Lewistown, Pa., 1836), pp. 203–5.

26. Newbell Niles Puckett, *Folk Beliefs of the Southern Negro* (The University of North Carolina Press, 1926), p. 24.

27. Melville J. Herskovits, *The Myth of the Negro Past*, Harper & Brothers, 1941, p. 192.

28. "It goes without saying," writes Herskovits, "that the plantation system rendered the survival of African family types impossible, as it did their underlying moral and supernatural sanctions, except in dilute form." *Ibid.*, p. 139.

29. Melville J. Herskovits, *The Myth of the Negro Past*, p. 170.

30. *Ibid.*, p. 180.

31. See E. Franklin Frazier, *The Negro Family in the United States* (Chicago, 1939), Part II, "The House of the Mother."

32. Martha W. Beckwith, *Black Roadways: A Study of Jamaican Folk Life* (Chapel Hill, 1929), p. 54. In the following observations of a visitor to the French West Indies about the year 1700 we have, doubtless, an example of this patriarchal authority which had its roots in Africa. Labat says: "I have often taken pleasure in watching a negro carpenter at Guadaloupe when he ate his meals. His wife and children gathered around him, and served him with as much respect as the best drilled domestics serve their masters; and if it was a fete day or Sunday, his sons-in-law and daughters did not fail to be present, and bring him some small gifts. They formed a circle about him, and conversed with him while he was eating. When he had finished, his pipe was brought to him, and then he bade them eat. They paid him their reverences, and passed into another room, where they all eat together with their mother." Pere Labat, *Voyage aux isles francoises*, 11, 54, cited in Aimes, *op. cit.*, pp. 24–25.

33. See Frazier, *op. cit.*, Part III, "In the House of the Father."

34. See Herskovits, *op. cit.*, p. 199.

35. Arthur Ramos, *The Negro in Brazil*, p. 81.

36. *Ibid.*, pp. 82–93. See also Arthur Ramos, *O Negro Brasileiro;* Nina Rodrigues, *Os Africanos;* and Edison Carneiro, *Religioes Negras* (Rio de Janeiro, 1936).

37. See Melville J. Herskovits, *Life in a Haitian Valley* (New York, 1937), pp. 139–248.

38. See, for example, Ball, *op. cit.*, p. 127, where he tells of a slave "who prayed five times every day, always turning his face to the east."

39. See George W. Cable, "Creole Slave Songs," *Century Magazine*, Vol. XXI, pp. 807–27.

40. Guion G. Johnson, *A Social History of the Sea Islands* (Chapel Hill, 1930), pp. 147–53.

41. Melville J. Herskovits, "Social History of the Negro," in Carl Murchison, *A Handbook of Social Psychology* (Worcester, 1935), pp. 256–57.

42. The backwoods preacher, Peter Cartwright, wrote as follows concerning the activities of the white Baptist preachers in Tennessee during the early years of the nineteenth century: ". . . indeed, they made so much ado about baptism by immersion, that the uninformed would suppose that heaven was an island, and that there was no way to get there but by diving or swimming." *Autobiography of Peter Cartwright*, edited by W. P. Strickland (New York, 1857), p. 134.

43. Herskovits, *The Myth of the Negro Past*, p. 233.

44. Carter G. Woodson. *The History of the Negro Church*, The Associated Publishers, Inc., 1921, p. 7.

45. See Frederick M. Davenport, *Primitive Traits in Religious Revivals* (New York, 1917), pp. 60 ff.

46. The Presbyterian revivalists were also active at this time among the slaves.

47. Luther P. Jackson, "Religious Development of the Negro in Virginia from 1760 to 1860," *The Journal of Negro History*, Vol. XVI, pp. 172–73.

48. See Chapter XIII [of *The Negroes in the United States*].

49. See Jackson, *op. cit.*, p. 147.

50. Herskovits, *op. cit.*, pp. 227–32.

51. Herskovits gives the following quotation from Davenport, *op. cit.*, p. 92: "I wish in closing to call attention to the difference in type of the automatisms of Kentucky and Ulster. In Kentucky the motor automatisms, the voluntary muscles in violent action, were the prevailing type, although there were many of the sensory. On the other hand, in Ulster the sensory automatisms, trance, vision, the physical disability and the sinking of muscular energy were the prevailing type, although there were many of the motor. I do not mean that I can explain it. It may be that as the Charcot and Nancy schools of hypnosis brought out by chance, each in its own field, different kinds of hypnotic phenomena which, when known, spread by imitation in the respective localities and under the respective influences, so in Kentucky and the north of Ireland by chance there appeared different types of physical manifestation which were then imitated in the respective countries." Melville J. Herskovits, *The Myth of the Negro Past*, pp. 230–31.

52. This statement is based upon the writer's uncontrolled observations as well as the accounts of others. See, for example, Arthur Ramos, *O Negro Brasileiro*, passim.

53. Melville J. Herskovits, *The Myth of the Negro Past*, p. 161.

54. *Ibid.*, p, 164.

55. *Ibid.*, p. 235.

56. *Ibid.*, pp. 235–51.

57. Newbell Niles Puckett, *Folk Beliefs of the Southern Negro*, p. 78.

58. *Ibid.*

The controversy continues. Here historian Kenneth Stampp discusses the view that, while certain Africanisms were retained (particularly in story and song), the slaves increasingly found their "reference group" in the "host" society on which they were hapless parasites. This was obviously not a satisfactory arrangement. As Stampp says, "so far from slavery acting as a civilizing force, it merely took away from the African his native culture and gave him, in exchange, little more than vocational training."

The slave was, in reality, a marginal man, caught between two vastly different and antagonistic social worlds. His salvation was the creation of a marginal culture marked by its own codes and life styles. Stampp briefly discusses this phenomenon, which is also examined in succeeding selections.

3

Between Two Cultures

Kenneth M. Stampp

What else was there in the lives of slaves besides work, sleep, and procreation? What filled their idle hours? What occupied their minds? What distinguished them from domestic animals? Much will never be known, for surviving records provide only brief glimpses into the private life of the slave quarters. But much can be learned from Negro songs and folklore, from the recollections of former slaves, and from the observations of the more perceptive and sensitive whites.

I

The average bondsman, it would appear, lived more or less aimlessly in a bleak and narrow world. He lived in a world without schools,

From *The Peculiar Institution* by Kenneth M. Stampp, New York: Vintage, 1964, pp. 361–382. Copyright © 1956 by Kenneth M. Stampp. Reprinted by permission of Alfred A. Knopf, Inc.

without books, without learned men; he knew less of the fine arts and of aesthetic values than he had known in Africa; and he found few ways to break the montonous sameness of all his days. His world was the few square miles of earth surrounding his cabin—a familiar island beyond which were strange places (up North where people like him were not slaves), frightening places ("down the river" where overseers were devils), and dead places (across the ocean where his ancestors had lived and where he had no desire to go). His world was full of mysteries which he could not solve, full of forces which he could not control. And so he tended to be a fatalist and futilitarian, for nothing else could reconcile him to his life.

When they left Africa the Negroes carried with them a knowledge of their own complex cultures. Some elements of their cultures—or at least some adaptations or variations of them—they planted somewhat insecurely in America. These surviving "Africanisms" were evident in their speech, in their dances, in their music, in their folklore, and in their religion. The amount of their African heritage that remained varied with time and place. More of it was evident in the eighteenth century when a large proportion of the slaves were native Africans, than in the mid-nineteenth century when the great majority were second- and third-generation Americans. Field-hands living on large plantations in isolated areas, such as the South Carolina and Georgia sea islands, doubtless preserved more "Africanisms" than slaves who were widely dispersed in relatively small holdings or who lived in their master's houses as domestics. How substantial and how durable the African heritage was is a question over which students of the American Negro have long disagreed.[1]

But the disagreement has been over the size of what was admittedly a fragment; few would deny that by the ante-bellum period slaves everywhere in the South had lost most of their African culture. In bondage, the Negroes lacked cultural autonomy—the authority to apply rigorous sanctions against those who violated or repudiated their own traditions. Instead, they were exposed to considerable pressure to learn and accept whichever of the white man's customs would help them to exist with a minimum of friction in a biracial society. Before the Civil War, American Negroes developed no cultural nationalism, no conscious pride in African ways. At most they unconsciously preserved some of their old culture when it had a direct relevance to their new lives, or they fused it with things taken from the whites.

If anything, most ante-bellum slaves showed a desire to forget their African past and to embrace as much of white civilization as they could. They often looked with contemptuous amusement upon newly imported Africans. When a Tennesseean attempted to teach a group of slaves a dance he had witnessed on the Guinea coast, he was astonished by their lack of aptitude and lack of interest. In fact, the feelings of these slaves were "hurt by the insinuation which his effort conveyed."[2] Thus the "Africanisms" of the slaves—even of the Gullah Negroes of the South Carolina sea islands—were mere vestiges of their old cultures. For example, a few African words remained in their speech; the rest was the crude and ungrammatical English of an illiterate folk.

There was an element of tragedy in this. The slaves, having lost the bulk of their African heritage, were prevented from sharing in much of the best of southern white culture. There were exceptions, of course. Occasionally a gifted slave overcame all obstacles and without formal education became a brilliant mathematician or a remarkable linguist. A few showed artistic talents of a high order. Others learned to read and write, or, in the case of house servants, manifested polite breeding which matched—and sometimes surpassed—that of their masters. But the life of the generality of slaves, as a visitor to South Carolina observed, was "far removed from [white] civilization"; it was "mere animal existence, passed in physical exertion or enjoyment." Fanny Kemble saw grown slaves "rolling, tumbling, kicking, and wallowing in the dust, regardless alike of decency, and incapable of any more rational amusement; or lolling, with half-closed eyes, like so many cats and dogs, against a wall, or upon a bank in the sun, dozing away their short leisure hour."[3]

This was essentially the way it had to be as long as the Negro was held in bondage. So far from slavery acting as a civilizing force, it merely took away from the African his native culture and gave him, in exchange, little more than vocational training. So far from the plantation serving as a school to educate a "backward" people, its prime function in this respect was to train each new generation of slaves. In slavery the Negro existed in a kind of cultural void. He lived in a twilight zone between two ways of life and was unable to obtain from either many of the attributes which distinguish man from beast. Olmsted noted that slaves acquired, by example or compulsion, some of the external forms of white civilization; but this was poor compensation for "the systematic withdrawal from them of all the usual influences which tend to nourish the moral nature and develop the intellectual faculties, in savages as well as in civilized free men."[4]

What, then, filled the leisure hours of the slaves? The answer, in part, is that these culturally rootless people devoted much of this time to the sheer pleasure of being idle. Such activities as they did engage in were the simple diversions of a poor, untutored folk—activities that gave them physical pleasure or emotional release.

Slaves probably found it more difficult to find satisfying amusements on the small farms where they had few comrades, than in the cities and on the plantations where they could mix freely with their own people.

"I have no desire to represent the life of slavery as an experience of nothing but misery," wrote a former bondsman. In addition to the unpleasant things, he also remembered "jolly Christmas times, dances before old massa's door for the first drink of egg-nog, extra meat at holiday times, midnight visits to apple orchards, broiling stray chickens, and first-rate tricks to dodge work." Feasting, as this account suggested, was one of the slave's chief pleasures, one of his "principle sources of comfort." The feast was what he looked forward to not only at Christmas but when crops were laid by, when there was a wedding, or when the master gave a reward for good behavior. "Only the slave who has lived all the year on his scanty allowance of meal and bacon, can appreciate such suppers," recalled another ex-bondsman. Then his problems were forgotten as he gave himself up "to the intoxication of pleasurable amusements." Indeed he might when, for example, a Tennesee master provided a feast such as this: "They Barbecue *half* a small Beef and two fat shoats and some Chickens—have peach pies—Chicken pies, beets [,] Roasting Ears and potatoes in profusion."[5]

Occasions such as Christmas or a corn-shucking were times not only for feasting but also for visiting with slaves on nearby establishments. In Virginia a visitor observed that many bondsmen spent Sundays "strolling about the fields and streets" finding joy in their relative freedom of movement. They dressed in bright-colored holiday clothes, which contrasted pleasantly with their drab everyday apparel. The slaves seemed to welcome each holiday with great fervor, for they found in it an enormous relief from the boredom of their daily lives. "All are brushing up, putting on their best rigging, and with boisterous joy hailing the approach of the Holy days," noted an Arkansas master at the start of the Christmas season.[6]

Dancing was one of the favorite pastimes of the slaves, not only on special holidays but on Saturday nights as well. A few pious masters prohibited this diversion, as did a Virginian who was shocked when neighborhood slaves attended a dancing party: "God forbid that one of my Family either white or colored should ever be caught at such an abominable wicked and adulterous place." But most masters, too wise to enforce a regime so austere, permitted a shuffle at least occasionally. "This is Saturday night," wrote a Louisianian, "and I hear the fiddle going in the Quarter. We have two parties here among the Negroes. One is a dancing party and the other a Praying party. The dancers have it tonight, and the other party will hold forth tomorrow."[7]

The kinds of jigs and double shuffles that slaves indulged in were once described as "dancing all over"; they revealed an apparent capacity to "agitate every part of the body at the same time." Such dances were physical and emotional orgies. Fanny Kemble found it impossible to describe "all the contortions, and springs, and flings, and kicks, and capers" the slaves accomplished as they danced "Jim Crow." A visitor at a "shake-down" in a Louisiana sugar house found the dancers in a "thumping ecstasy, with loose elbows, pendulous paws, angulated knees, heads thrown back, and backs arched inwards—a glazed eye, intense solemnity of mien."[8] Slaves danced to the music of the fiddle or banjo, or they beat out their rhythm with sticks on tin pans or by clapping their hands or tapping their feet. These ancestors of twentieth-century "jitterbugs" developed their own peculiar jargon too. In Virginia a skilled dancer could "put his foot good"; he was a "ring-clipper," a "snow-belcher," and a "drag-out"; he was no "bug-eater," for he could "carry a broad row," "hoe de corn," and "dig de taters."[9]

Other holiday amusements included hunting, trapping, and fishing. In spite of legal interdictions, slaves gambled with each other and with "dissolute" whites. But some found both pleasure and profit in using their leisure to pursue a handicraft; they made brooms, mats, horse collars, baskets, boats, and canoes. These "sober, thinking and industrious" bondsmen scorned those who wasted time in frivolities or picked up the white man's vices.[10]

A few things in the lives of slaves belonged to them in a more intimate and personal way; these were things which illustrated peculiarly well the blending of African traditions with new experiences in America. For instance, folklore was important to them as it has always been to illiterate people. Some of it preserved legends of their own past; some explained natural phenomena or described a world of the spirits; and some told with charming symbolism the story of the endless warfare between black and white men. The tales of Br'er Rabbit, in all their variations, made virtues of such qualities as wit, strategy, and deceit—the weapons of the weak in their battles with the strong. Br'er Bear had great physical power but was a hapless bumbler; Br'er Fox was shrewd and crafty as well as strong but, nonetheless, was never quite a match for Br'er Rabbit. This was a scheme of things which the slave found delightful to contemplate.[11]

The bondsmen had ceremonial occasions of their own, and they devised special ways of commemorating the white man's holidays. At Christmas in eastern North Carolina, they begged pennies from the whites as they went "John Canoeing" (or "John Cunering") along the roads, wearing masks and outlandish costumes, blowing horns, tinkling tambourines, dancing, and chanting

Hah! Low! Here we go!
Hah! Low! Here we go!
Hah! Low! Here we go!
Kuners come from Denby!

Virginia slaves had persimmon parties where they interspersed dancing with draughts of persimmon beer and slices of persimmon bread. At one of these parties the banjo player sat in a chair on the beer barrel: "A long white cowtail, queued with red ribbon ornamented his head, and hung gracefully down his back; over this he wore a three-cocked hat, decorated with peacock feathers, a rose cockade, a bunch of ripe persimmons, and . . . three pods of red pepper as a top-knot." On some Louisiana sugar plantations, when the cutters reached the last row of cane they left the tallest cane standing and tied a blue ribbon to it. In a ceremony which marked the end of the harvest, one of the laborers waved his cane knife in the air, "sang to the cane as if it were a person, and danced around it several times before cutting it." Then the workers mounted their carts and triumphantly carried the last cane to the master's house where they were given a drink.[12]

Rarely did a contemporary write about slaves without mentioning their music, for this was their most splendid vehicle of self-expression. Slave music was a unique blend of "Africanisms," of Protestant hymns and revival songs, and of the feelings and emotions that were a part of life in servitude.[13] The Negroes had a repertory of songs for almost every occasion, and they not only sang them with innumerable variations but constantly improvised new ones besides. They sang spirituals which revealed their conceptions of Christianity and professed their religious faith. They sang work songs (usually slow in tempo) to break the monotony of toil in the tobacco factories, in the sugar houses, on the river boats, and in the fields. They sang whimsical songs which told little stories or ridiculed human frailties. They sang nonsense songs, such as "Who-zen-John, Who-za" sung by a group of Virginia slaves as they "clapped juber" to a dance:

Old black bull come down de hollow,
He shake hi' tail, you hear him bellow;
When he bellow he jar de river,
He paw de yearth, he make it quiver.
Who-zen-John, who-za.[14]

Above all, they sang plaintive songs about the sorrows and the yearnings which they dared not, or could not, more than half express. Music of this kind could hardly have come from an altogether care-free and contented people. "The singing of a man cast away on a desolate island," wrote Frederick Douglass, "might be as appropriately considered an evidence of his contentment and happiness, as the singing of a slave. Sorrow and desolation have their songs, as well as joy and peace."[15] In their somber and mournful moods the bondsmen voiced sentiments such as these: "O Lord, O my Lord! O my good Lord keep me from sinking down"; "Got nowhere to lay my weary head"; "My trouble is hard"; "Nobody knows the trouble I've seen"; and "Lawd, I can't help from cryin' sometime." The Gullah Negroes of South Carolina sang:

> I know moon-rise, I know star-rise,
>   Lay dis body down.
> I walk in de moonlight, I walk in de starlight,
>   To lay dis body down.
> I'll walk in de graveyard, I'll walk through de graveyard,
>   To lay dis body down.
> I'll lie in de grave and stretch out my arms;
>   Lay dis body down;
> I go to de judgment in de evenin' of de day,
>   When I lay dis body down;
> And my soul and your soul will meet in de day
>   When I lay dis body down.[16]

One final ingredient helped to make pleasant the leisure hours of numerous slave men and women: alcohol in its crudest but cheapest and most concentrated forms. To be sure, these bibulous bondsmen merely indulged in a common vice of an age of hard liquor and heavy drinkers; but they, more than their masters, made the periodic solace of the bottle a necessity of life. In preparing for Christmas, slaves somehow managed to smuggle "fresh bottles of rum or whisky into their cabins," for many thought of each holiday as a time for a bacchanalian spree. Indeed, recalled a former bondsman, to be sober during the holidays was "disgraceful; and he was esteemed a lazy and improvident man, who could not afford to drink whisky during Christmas."[17] No law, no threat of the master, ever kept liquor out of the hands of slaves or stopped the illicit trade between them and "unscrupulous" whites. Some masters themselves furnished a supply of whisky for holiday occasions, or winked at violations of state laws and of their own rules.

There was little truth in the abolitionist charge that masters gave liquor to their slaves in order to befuddle their minds and keep them in bondage. On the other hand, many bondsmen used intoxicants for a good deal more than an occasional pleasant stimulant, a mere conviviality of festive occasions. They found that liquor provided their only satisfactory escape from the indignities, the frustrations, the emptiness, the oppressive boredom of slavery. Hence, when they had the chance, they resorted to places that catered to the Negro trade or found sanctuaries where they could tipple undisturbed. What filled their alcoholic dreams one can only guess, for the dreams at least were theirs alone.

II

Most slaves took their religion seriously, though by the standards of white Christians they sinned mightily. In Africa the Negro's world was inhabited by petulant spirits whose demands had to be gratified; his relationship to these spirits was regulated by the rituals and dogmas of his pagan faith. Some of this was in the corpus of "Africanisms" brought to America. But most of it was lost within a generation, not only because of the general decay of Negro culture but also because new problems and experiences created an urgent need for a new kind of religious expression and a new set of beliefs. What the slave needed now was a spiritual life in which he could participate vigorously, which transported him from the dull routine of bondage and which promised him that a better time was within his reach. Hence, he embraced evangelical Protestantism eagerly, because it so admirably satisfied all these needs.

"The doctrine of the Savior comes to the negro slaves as their most inward need, and as the accomplishment of the wishes of their souls," explained a visitor to the South. "They themselves enunciate it with the purest joy. . . . Their prayers burst forth into flame as they ascend to heaven." On many plantations religious exercises were almost "the only habitual recreation not purely sensual," Olmsted noted; hence slaves poured all their emotions into them "with an intensity and vehemence almost terrible to witness." A former slave recalled the ecstasy he felt when he learned that there was a salvation *"for every man"* and that God loved black men as well as white. "I seemed to see a glorious being, in a cloud of splendor, smiling down from on high," ready to "welcome me to the skies."[18]

Like the whites, many slaves alternated outbursts of intense religious excitement with intervals of religious calm or indifference, for both races participated in the revivals that periodically swept rural America. At the emotional height of a revival, most of the slaves in a neighborhood might renounce worldly pleasures and live austere lives without the fiddle, without dancing, and without whisky. But this could not last forever, and gradually they drifted back to their sinful ways.[19] And their masters often drifted with them; for although many used religion as a means of control, many others neglected it between revivals.

Of the Protestant sects, the Baptists and Methodists proselytized among the slaves most vigorously and counted among their members the great majority of those who joined churches. The decorous Episcopalians were ineffectual in their missionary work; even masters who adhered to this sect seldom managed to convert their own slaves. The Presbyterians had greater success than the Episcopalians but far less than the Baptists or Methodists. Indeed, Presbyterian clergymen who preached to the slaves were advised to write out their sermons in advance and to discourage "exclamations," "outcries," and "boisterous singing." As a result, explained a Methodist, while the Presbyterian parson was composing his sermon the Methodist itinerant traveled forty miles and gave "hell and damnation to his unrepentant hearers." According to an ex-slave, the Methodists "preached in a manner so plain that the way-faring man, though a fool, could not err therein."[20] So did the Baptists—and, in addition, their practice of baptism by immersion gave them a special appeal.

In the North, Negroes organized their own independent churches; in the South, except in a few border cities, the laws against slave assemblies prevented them from doing this before the Civil War. Many slaves attended the white-controlled churches or were preached to by white ministers at special services. This inhibited them and limited both the spiritual and emotional value of their religious experience, because there was an enormous gap between a congregation of slaves and even the most sympathetic white clergyman. As one missionary confessed, "The pastor will meet with some rough and barren spots, and encounter tardiness, indifference, heaviness of eyes and inattention—yea, many things to depress and discourage."[21]

Yet it was from white preachers that the slaves first received their Christian indoctrination. To many bondsmen affiliation with a white church was a matter of considerable importance, and they did not take lightly the penalty of being "excluded from the fellowship" for immorality or "heathenism." Some white clergymen preached to them with great success. Nor was it uncommon to see whites and slaves "around the same altar . . . mingling their cries for mercy" and together finding "the pearl of great price."[22]

Even so, most bondsmen received infinitely greater satisfaction from their own unsupervised religious meetings which they held secretly or which their masters tolerated in disregard of the law. In these gatherings slaves could express themselves freely and interpret the Christian faith to their own satisfaction, even though some educated whites believed that their interpretation contained more heathen superstition than Christianity. The slaves, observed Olmsted, were "subject to intense excitements; often really maniacal," which they considered to be religious; but "I cannot see that they indicate anything but a miserable system of superstition, the more painful that it employs some forms and words ordinarily connected with true Christianity."[23]

Not only the practice of voodooism which survived among a few slaves in southern Louisiana, but the widespread belief in charms and spirits stemmed in part from the African past. Frederick Douglass learned from an old African (who had "magic powers") that if a slave wore the root of a certain herb on his right side, no white man could ever whip him. Slave conjurers accomplished wondrous feats with "root work" and put frightful curses upon their enemies. A Louisiana master once had to punish a slave because of "a phial which was found in his possession containing two ground puppies as they are called. The negroes were under some apprehension that he intended to do mischief."[24]

But slave superstitions did not all originate in Africa, and it would even be difficult to prove that most did. For the slaves picked up plenty of them from "the good Puritans, Baptists, Methodists, and other religious sects who first obtained possession of their ancestors." (Indeed, more than likely Negroes and whites made a generous exchange of superstitions.) There is no need to trace back to Africa the slave's fear of beginning to plant a crop on Friday, his dread of witches, ghosts, and hobgoblins, his confidence in good-luck charms, his alarm at evil omens, his belief in dreams, and his reluctance to visit burying grounds after dark. These superstitions were all firmly rooted in Anglo-Saxon folklore. From the whites some slaves learned that it was possible to communicate with the world of spirits: "It is not at all uncommon to hear them refer to conversations which they allege, and apparently believe themselves to have had with Christ, the apostles, or the prophets of old, or to account for some of their actions by attributing them to the direct influence of the Holy Spirit, or of the devil." During the 1840's, many slaves heard about Millerism and waited in terror for the end of the world.[25] The identification of superstition is, of course, a highly subjective process; and southern whites tended to condemn as superstition whatever elements of slave belief they did not happen to share—as they condemned each other's sectarian beliefs.

The influence of Africa could sometimes be detected in the manner in which slaves conducted themselves at their private religious services. In the sea islands, for example, a prayer meeting at the "praise house" was followed by a "shout," which was an invigorating group ceremony. The participants "begin first walking and by-and-by shuffling around, one after the other, in a ring. The foot is hardly taken from the floor, and the progression is mainly due to a jerking, hitching motion, which agitates the entire shouter, and soon brings out streams of perspiration. Sometimes they dance silently, sometimes as they shuffle they sing the chorus of the spiritual, and sometimes the song itself is sung by the dancers." This, a white witness believed, was "certainly the remains of some old idol worship." Olmsted reported that in social worship the slaves "work themselves up to a great pitch of excitement, in which they yell and cry aloud, and, finally, shriek and leap up, clapping their hands and dancing, as it is done at heathen festivals."[26]

But again it is not easy to tell how much of their "heathenism" the slaves learned in the white churches and at white revival meetings. One Sunday morning, in Accomac County, Virginia, a visitor attended a Methodist church where the slaves were permitted to hold their own services before the whites occupied the building. "Such a medley of sounds, I never heard before. They exhorted, prayed, sung, shouted, cryed, grunted and growled. Poor Souls! They knew no better, for I found that when the other services began the sounds were similar, which the white folks made; and the Negroes only imitated them and shouted a little louder."[27]

A camp meeting in South Carolina provided an equally striking illustration of this point. When the services began, a great crowd assembled around a wooden platform, the Negroes on one side and the whites on the other. On the platform stood four preachers, and between the singing of hymns two of them exhorted the Negroes and two the whites, "calling on the sinners . . . to come to the Savior, to escape eternal damnation!" Soon some of the white people came forward and threw themselves, "as if overcome," before the platform where the ministers received their confessions and consoled them. Around a white girl, who had fallen into a trance, stood a dozen women singing hymns of the resurrection. "In the camp of the blacks is heard a great tumult and a loud cry. Men roar and bawl out; women screech like pigs about to be killed; many, having fallen into convulsions, leap and strike about them, so that they are obliged to be held down." The Negroes made more noise and were more animated than the whites, but the behavior of the two races did not differ in any fundamental way. Except for condemning a "holy dance" which some Negro women engaged in for a new convert, the whites did not appear to think that the Negroes acted in an outrageous or unchristian fashion.[28]

In short, the religion of the slaves was, in essence, strikingly similar to that of the poor, illiterate white men of the ante-bellum South.

III

Since the masters kept diaries and wrote letters, books, and essays, it is relatively easy to discover their various attitudes toward slaves. What the slaves thought of their masters (and of white people generally) is just as important to know but infinitely more difficult to find. Not only did slaves and ex-slaves write a good deal less but most of them seemed determined that no white man should ever know their thoughts. As Olmsted observed, the average slave possessed considerable "cunning, shrewdness, [and] reticence."[29]

Several points, however, are clear: (1) slaves did not have one uniform attitude toward whites, but a whole range of attitudes; (2) they gave much attention to the problem of their relationship with whites; and (3) they found the "management of whites" as complex a matter as their masters found the "management of Negroes." Every slave became conscious of the "white problem" sometime in early childhood; for in a society dominated by whites, Negro children have always had to learn, more or less painfully, the meaning of caste and somehow come to terms with it.[30] In bondage, they also had to learn what it meant to be property.

During the first half dozen years of their lives neither caste nor bondage had meaning to the children of either race, and blacks and whites often played together without consciousness of color. But it was not long before the black child, in some way, began to discover his peculiar position. Perhaps his mother or father explained his status to him and told him how to behave around the master and other whites. ("My father always advised me to be tractable, and get along with the white people in the best manner I could," recalled a former slave.)[31] Perhaps the slave child saw the white child begin to assume an attitude of superiority prior to their separation. Perhaps he first encountered reality when the master or overseer began to supersede parental authority—or, in a more shocking way, when he saw the master or overseer administer a reprimand or corporal punishment to one of his parents. Thus the young slave became conscious of the "white problem," conscious that the white man was a formidable figure with pretensions of omniscience and omnipotence. As he became involved with white men, the slave gradually developed an emotional attitude toward them.

His attitude, while perhaps seldom one of complete confidence, was frequently one of amiable regard, sometimes of deep affection. A slave who lived close to a warm, generous, and affectionate master often could not help but reciprocate these feelings, for the barriers of bondage and caste could not prevent decent human beings from showing sympathy and compassion for one another—slave for master as well as master for slave. The domestic's proverbial love for the white family was by no means altogether a myth. But it should be remembered that a slave's love for the good white people he knew was not necessarily a love of servitude, that a slave could wish to be free without hating the man who kept him in chains. A Negro woman who escaped from bondage in Missouri remembered fondly her master and many other whites she had known.[32]

Some slaves, in dealing with whites, seemed to be coldly opportunistic; they evidently had concluded that it was most practical to use the arts of diplomacy, to "keep on the right side" of their masters, in order to enjoy the maximum privileges and comforts available to them in bondage. So they flattered the whites, affected complete subservience, and behaved like buffoons. When Olmsted was introduced to a slave preacher he shook the Negro's hand and greeted him respectfully; but the latter "seemed to take this for a joke and laughed heartily." The master explained in a "slightly humorous" tone that the preacher was also the driver, that he drove the field-hands at the cotton all week and at the Gospel on Sunday. At this remark the preacher "began to laugh again, and reeled off like a drunken man—entirely overcome with merriment." Thus, remarked Olmsted, having concluded that the purpose of the interview was to make fun of him, the preacher "generously" assumed "a merry humor."[33] This slave, like many others, seemed willing enough to barter his self-respect for the privileges and prestige of his high offices.

Other slaves exhibited toward whites no strong emotion either of affection or hatred, but rather an attitude of deep suspicion. Many contemporaries commented upon their "habitual distrust of the white race" and noted that they were "always suspicious." When this was the Negro's basic attitude, the resulting relationship was an amoral one which resembled an unending civil war; the slave then seemed to think that he was entitled to use every tactic of deception and chicanery he could devise. Many ex-slaves who spoke of their former masters without bitterness still recalled with particular pleasure the times when they had outwitted or beguiled them ("'cause us had to lie").[34]

To a few slaves this civil war was an intense and serious business, because they felt for their masters (sometimes for all whites) an abiding animosity. In speaking of the whites, such bondsmen used "the language of hatred and revenge"; on one plantation the slaves in their private conversations contemptuously called their master "Old Hogjaw." Externally these slaves wore an air of sullenness. "You need only look in their faces to see they are not happy," exclaimed a traveler; instead, they were "depressed" or "gloomy." Field-hands often gave no visible sign of pleasure when their master approached; some made clumsy bows, but others ignored him entirely.[35]

The poor whites were the one group in the superior caste for whom the slaves dared openly express their contempt, and the slaves did so in picturesque terms. Masters often tolerated this and were even amused by it. However, it is likely that some slaves were thereby expressing their opinion of the whole white race. A transparent example of the malice that a portion of the slaves bore the whites occurred in St. Louis when a mob tarred and feathered a white man. "One feature of the scene I could not help remarking," wrote a witness: "the negroes all appeared in high glee, and many of them actually danced with joy."[36]

But the predominant and overpowering emotion that whites aroused in the majority of slaves was neither love nor hate but fear. "We were always uneasy," an ex-slave recalled; when "a white man spoke to me, I would feel frightened," another confessed. In Alabama, a visitor who lost his pocketbook noted that the slave who found it "was afraid of being whipped for theft and had given it to the first white man he saw, and at first was afraid to pick it up." A fugitive who was taken into the home of an Ohio Quaker found it impossible to overcome his timidity and apprehension. "I had never had a white man to treat me as an equal, and the idea of a white lady waiting on me at the table was still worse! . . . I thought if I could only be allowed the privilege of eating in the kitchen, I should be more than satisfied."[37]

The masters themselves provided the most vivid evidence of the frightening image that white men assumed in the minds of many slaves. When they advertised for runaways, the owners frequently revealed a distressing relationship between the two races, a relationship that must have been for these slaves an emotional nightmare. In their advertisements no descriptive phrases were more common than these: "stutters very much when spoken to"; "speaks softly and has a downcast look"; "has an uneasy appearance when spoken to"; "speaks quickly, and with an anxious expression of countenance"; "a very down look, and easily confused when spoken to"; "stammers very much so as to be scarcely understood."

"I feel lighter,—the dread is gone," affirmed a Negro woman who had escaped to Canada. "It is a great heaviness on a person's mind to be a slave."[38]

Notes

1. The literature on this subject is vast, but for the two points of view see Robert E. Park, "The Conflict and Fusion of Cultures with Special Reference to the Negro," *Journal of Negro History*, IV (1919), pp. 111–33; Melville J. Herskovits, "On the Provenience of New World Negroes," *Social Forces*, XII (1933). pp. 247–62.

2. Ingraham (ed.,), Sunny *South*, pp. 146–47.

3. Harrison, *Gospel Among the Slaves*, p. 245; [Ingraham], *South-West*, II, p. 194, Kemble, *Journal*, p. 66.

4. Olmsted, *Back Country*, pp. 70–71.

5. Henson, *Story*, pp. 19–20, 56; Northup, *Twelve Years a Slave*, pp. 213–16; Steward, *Twenty-Two Years a Slave*, pp. 28–31; Bills Diary, entry for July 24, 1858.

6. Emerson Journal, entry for September 19, 1841; John W. Brown Diary, entry for December 25, 1853.

7. Walker Diary, entry for February 13, 1841; H. W. Poynor to William G. Harding, March 22, 1850, Harding-Jackson Papers.

8. *De Bow's Review*, XI (1851), p. 66; Kemble, *Journal*, pp. 96–97; Russell, *Diary*, pp. 258–59.

9. *Farmer's Register*, VI (1838), pp. 59–61.

10. Johnson, *Ante-Bellum North Carolina*, pp. 555–57; Douglass, *My Bondage*, pp. 251–52

11. Crum, *Gullah*, p. 120; Benjamin A. Botkin (ed.), *Lay My Burden Down*, p. 2.

12. Johnson, *Ante-Bellum North Carolina*, p. 553; *Farmers' Register*, VI (1838), pp. 59–61; Moody, "Slavery on Louisiana Sugar Plantations," *op. cit.*, p. 277 n.

13. The most recent collection of slave songs is Miles Mark Fisher, *Negro Slave Songs in the United States* (Ithaca, 1953).

14. *Farmers' Register*, VI (1838), pp. 59–61.

15. Douglass, *My Bondage*, pp. 99–100.

16. Thomas Wentworth Higginson, *Army Life in a Black Regiment* (Boston, 1870), p. 209.

17. Hundley, *Social Relations*, pp. 359–60; Olmsted, *Seaboard*, pp. 75, 101–102; Adams Diary, entry for December 29, 1857; Douglass, *My Bondage*, pp. 251–52.

18. Bremer, *Homes of the New World*, II, p. 155; Olmsted, *Back Country*, p. 106; Henson, *Story*, pp. 28–29.

19. Smedes, *Memorials*, pp. 161–62, Henry Watson, Jr., to his mother, July 7, 1846, Watson Papers.

20. Jones, *Suggestions on the Religious Instruction of the Negroes*, pp. 14–15; Carter G. Woodson, *The History of the Negro Church* (Washington, D.C., 1921), pp. 97–98, Thompson, *Life*, p. 18.

21. Jones, *Suggestions on the Religious Instruction of the Negroes*, p. 17.

22. Flat River Church Records (Person County, North Carolina); Harrison, *Gospel Among the Slaves*, pp. 199–201.

23. Olmsted, *Seaboard*, p. 114.

24. Sitterson, *Sugar Country*, p. 102; Douglass, *My Bondage*, p. 238; Hammond Diary, entry for October 16. 1835; Marston Diary, entry for November 25, 1825.

25. Olmsted. *Back Country*, p. 105, Davis (ed.), *Diary of Bennet H. Barrow*, pp. 283–85.

26. Johnson, *Sea Islands*, pp. 149–51; Olmsted, *Seaboard*, pp. 449–50.

27. Emerson Journal, entry for September 26, 1841.

28. Bremer, *Homes of the New World*, I, pp. 306–315.

29. Olmsted, *Back Country*, p. 384.

30. Cf. E. Franklin Frazier, *Negro Youth at the Crossways* (Washington, D.C., 1940), *passim.*

31. Drew, *The Refugee*, p. 358.

32. *Ibid.,* pp. 299–300.

33. Olmsted. *Seaboard*, p. 451.

34. Olmsted, Back Country, p. 114; Bremer, Homes of the New World, I, p. 292, Botkin, *Lay My Burden Down, passim.*

35. Northup, *Twelve Years a Slave*, pp. 62–63, 197; Russell, *Diary*, pp. 133, 146–47. 258, 262; Stirling, *Letters*, p. 49; Buckingham, *Slave States*, I, pp. 62–63.

36. Drew, *The Refugee*, pp. 156–57; Benwell, *Travels*, p. 99.

37. Drew, *The Refugee*, pp. 30, 86; Watson Diary, entry for January 1, 1831; Brown, *Narrative*, pp. 102–103.

38. Drew, *The Refugee*, p. 179.

In recent years historians and other social scientists have turned their attention to the economics of slavery in Africa as well as in the New World. Eugene D. Genovese, author of The Political Economy of Slavery, *offers his views on the debilitating and devastating character of the American plantation system, which depended upon Africans who were wrenched from their home settings, defined as categorically inferior ("Negroes") by racial criteria, and then used as human beasts of burden.*

4

The Negro Laborer in Africa and the Slave South

Eugene D. Genovese

Kenneth M. Stampp's *The Peculiar Institution* challenges effectively the traditional view that enslavement in America raised the Negro from savagery to civilization.[1] Drawing upon anthropological data, he shows that Africans brought to the United States as slaves had been removed from societies far more advanced than most of our historians have appreciated. Unfortunately, he pays only passing attention to that aspect of the traditional view bearing most directly on the economies of slavery in general and the productivity of black labor in particular.

The Negro slave worked badly, according to some leading historians, not because he was a slave but because he was a Negro. This argument has taken two forms: (1) the Negro has certain unfortunate biological traits, such as a migratory instinct or an easygoing indolence;[2] and (2) the Negro came from a lower culture in Africa

From Eugene D. Genovese, *The Political Economy of Slavery,* New York: Pantheon (Random House) 1965, pp. 70–84. This article originally appeared in *Phylon,* the Atlanta University Review of Race and Culture.

and had to be disciplined to labor.[3] The first argument does not require refutation here; the negative findings of genetics and anthropology are conclusive and well known.[4] The second argument raises serious economic and social questions. In the words of Lewis C. Gray:

> The great body of Negroes came to America ignorant savages. Care was requisite to prevent them from injuring themselves with the implements employed. It was necessary to teach them the simplest operations with hand tools and to instruct them in the elementary methods of living—how to cook, put on their clothing and care for their houses. . . . Under competent supervision the Negro acquired peculiar skill in picking and hoeing cotton and other simple routine operations of field labor.[5]

Ulrich B. Phillips defends slavery as a historically progressive institution that assembled the working population in a more productive pattern than had existed previously. He then implies that enslavement in America civilized the Negro and disciplined him to labor. Probably, ancient slavery often did play the role Phillips suggests, but to accept that generalization by no means commits one to the corollary drawn for American Negro slavery. Phillips gives no evidence but refers to the views of the sociologist Gabriel Tarde, who, we are told, "elaborated" on Thomas R. Dew's idea that enslavement domesticated men much as animals had been domesticated previously.[6]

An examination of Tarde's discussion shows that it offers little support to Phillips. The idea of reducing men to slavery, Tarde suggests, probably arose after the successful domestication of animals, and in both cases the subjected were tamed, transformed into beasts of burden, and made productive for others. Tarde's ideas should be considered within the context of his theory of imitation, according to which an enslaved people learns from its conquerors, whereas the latter do not deign to absorb the ways of their victims.[7] This idea is in itself dubious—how much richer is Hegel's analysis of "Lordship and Bondage" in his *Phenomenology of Mind,* in which the interaction of master and slave is so brilliantly explored—but if it has any relevance to the problem at hand, it merely suggests that the Negro in America came into contact with a higher culture. Who, outside the ranks of the most dogmatic cultural relativists, would argue with such a generalization? On the central question of labor productivity Tarde's thesis is valid only if we assume that the Negro had to be brought to America to acquire the habit of systematic agricultural labor. Phillips never puts the matter quite that baldly, but his analysis rests on this proposition.

Phillips' interpretation of African life has had a profound effect upon students of American Negro slavery, but it depends on the now discredited work of Joseph Alexander Tillinghast and Jerome Dowd. According to Tillinghast, African Negroes were "savages," subject to the "unfathomable . . . mysterious force" of heredity. The West African population before the European conquest supposedly had no cereals and survived on a bare subsistence of vegetable roots. Tillinghast, Dowd, and others upon whose work Phillips draws have applied untenable methods, made dubious assumptions, and produced work that anthropologists today consider of little or no value.[8] One might be inclined to pardon Phillips and those who have followed him for trusting the judgment of anthropologists were it not that the arguments contain hopeless contradictions, and were it not that even during the nineteenth century some scholars were perceptive enough to warn that anthropologists and other social scientists often fell victim to the racial prejudices permeating European and American life.[9] By the time of Phillips' death and during the period in which Craven and Gray were writing, impressive new work on African society was coming off the presses.

The first contradiction in the Tillinghast-Phillips interpretation is the fact of importation, for if the African had not been disciplined to agricultural labor why was he brought here at all? The "domestication" of savages is no easy matter, and only a small percentage of the enslaved usually survive. Europeans first brought Negroes from Africa because they were accustomed to agricultural labor, whereas many of the previously enslaved Indians were not and tended to collapse under the pressure.[10]

Second, in order to show that Africans were backward, Tillinghast and Phillips say that slavery was common among them. And so it was![11] There is no better proof that African society had "domesticated" its own population before the white man volunteered to assume responsibility. West African peoples like the Ashanti and Dahomey had, in addition to successful labor systems, elaborate military structures, legal arrangements, and commercial relations.[12] A re-examination of the economic structure of West Africa and of its implications for American slavery is therefore in order.

There are other objections to Phillips' argument. He assumes that the Negro, once brought here, retained many African traits, which hampered his productivity. So prominent an anthropologist as Melville J. Herskovits, who certainly does not share Phillips' biases or general conclusions, attempts to prove that the Negro has preserved a large part of his African heritage to the present day.[13] This contention has come under heavy and successful fire from E. Franklin Frazier, who shows that Herskovits' evidence illuminates Brazilian rather than North American experience. American Negroes had contempt for newly imported Africans and set out to "Americanize" them forthwith. As Frazier says, the array of isolated instances of African survivals only indicates how thoroughly American slavery wiped out African social organization, habits, and ways of thought.[14] If we are to avoid baseless racist and mystical assumptions, we shall have to know just what traits the Negro supposedly brought from Africa and kept for generations and just how they affected his productivity. We have received no such data, and nothing in Herskovits' work, which deals with a different set of problems, lends support to the Phillips-Gray-Craven school. We must conclude, therefore, that the assertion of special traits does nothing more than to restate the original notion of a Negro undisciplined to agricultural labor until brought here.

Phillips has to assume that the poor work habits of slaves amounted to mere negligence or even stupidity, but they often reflected an awareness of economic value and a penchant for sabotage. Side by side with ordinary loafing and mindless labor went deliberate wastefulness, slowdowns, feigned illnesses, self-inflicted injuries, and the well-known abuse of livestock and equipment, which itself probably arose within a complex psychological framework.[15] Viewed as such, Phillips' easy notion of ignorant savages making a mess of things falls to the ground.

Most Negroes brought from Africa to North America doubtless came from the West Coast. The Dahomey, famous as slave raiders, rarely went more than two hundred miles inland, and most of their victims lived much closer to the coast.[16] The West African peoples undoubtedly had mature systems of agriculture. The Dahomey even had a plantation system; all these peoples—Dahomey, Ashanti, Yoruba, to mention a few of the outstanding—had significant division of labor. They carried on and carefully regulated a system of trade; craft guilds existed widely; and a class structure had begun to emerge.[17]

The Yoruba, Nupe, and Fulani had absorbed Moslem culture, and when the Fulani overran northern Nigeria, they carried Moslem scholars with them. Before the Fulani conquest, the Nupe of Nigeria had developed an urban civilization partly under Moslem influence.[18] This influence undoubtedly had a positive effect on Negro technical and economic life, but most of the indigenous peoples did not need outsiders to teach them the fundamentals of agrarian life. "West African societies," writes the outstanding authority on Islam in Africa, "had already achieved fully developed techniques and economic organization before Islam made its appearance. Its influence was most evident in the commercial sphere which in the Sudan belt was wholly taken over by Moslems."[19]

The development of mining provides some clues to the economic level of West Africa. Gold and iron mining flourished at least as early as the fourteenth century, and the Arabs drew upon the area for gold. The tales of wonderful metals and metalwork attracted the Portuguese and led to their initial explorations. The peoples of Ghana and Nigeria used iron hoes and other agricultural implements, and the Yoruba of southern Nigeria enjoyed a reputation for fine work in copper and tin.[20] Diamond writes: "Iron hoes were, of course, essential to the Dahomean economy, and were perhaps the most important products manufactured in the young state. Therefore, the blacksmiths were revered by the people, as were all craftsmen who did good work."[21]

In contrast to Tillinghast's picture of indolent, berry-picking natives, the proverbs, aphorisms, and customs of the West African peoples indicate that they were accustomed to hard work. Sayings included: "Poverty is the elder of laziness"; "He who stays in bed when he is able to work will have to get up when he cannot"; and "Dust on the feet is better than dust on the behind."[22] Prestige accrued to those who worked hard, fast, and well and was therefore a powerful motivating force. These facts, now taken for granted by anthropologists, are not so surprising when one considers that even in the most primitive societies there is hard work to do. One works, as Herskovits says, because everyone works, because one must work to live, and because it is the tradition to work. The Dahomey, who were among the more advanced of the African peoples, had a reputation for industriousness, held hard work praiseworthy, and practiced crop rotation and agricultural diversification.[23]

The most puzzling aspect of Phillips' position is his awareness of slavery among the West Africans. He remarks that slavery was "generally prevalent" and adds that, according to Mungo Park, the slaves in the Niger Valley outnumbered the free men by three to one at the end of the eighteenth century.[24] Phillips never seems to realize that the existence of African slavery shatters his insistence that the Negroes had not been habituated to agricultural labor. Tillinghast and Dowd, for their part, set the bad example, for in the same books in which they assure us that the Negroes were the laziest of food gatherers they announce that these same Negroes had slaves, debt peons, and private property.[25]

The Dahomey had large crown-owned plantations worked by slave gangs under the direction of overseers whose business was to maximize output. Debt peonage was a well-established institution.[26] Among the Nupe, slaves did a great deal of agricultural labor and reportedly numbered in the thousands by the time of the British conquest. The more primitive tribes of northern Nigeria had been conquered and enslaved by the Nupe before the beginning of the nineteenth century.[27] The Ashanti had an elaborate system of family land ownership and imposed a light *corvée* on those of low status. The tribes of the Ashanti hinterland practiced slavery, debt peonage, and systematic agriculture. The Ashanti defeated one of these tribes, the Dagomba, at the end of the seventeenth century and obligated it to produce two thousand slaves annually.[28] The Ibo of southeastern Nigeria, slave traders as well as a source of slaves, produced several important crops with servile labor.[29] During the eighteenth and early nineteenth centuries the great West African peoples—the Yoruba, Dahomey, and Fulani—fought continually for control of southwestern Nigeria, and each in turn enslaved thousands during the wars.[30]

African slavery was far removed from New World slavery in many respects and perhaps ought not to be considered under the same rubric. The Ashanti economy in which slaves participated strove, for example, toward autarky. The system of land tenure placed a brake on individual accumulation of land, and status therefore rested primarily on political and social rather than economic criteria. However surprisingly, masters had no power over the economic surplus produced by their slaves, who worked for themselves. In the words of A. Norman Klein:

> The productivity of "slave" labor was never applied to the process of economic accumulation. Nor could it be. To be a slaveowner was not to be a member of a special group deriving its income from the outputs of the chattel. There simply was no mechanism for accumulation from slave labor. The only stratum in Ashanti society which stood to gain from the productivity of "slave" labor was the slave stratum itself. By assuring, in Ashanti law, that the general rule for personal property applied to its "slaves" it nipped in the bud the formation of any such vested interests. That rule of personal property may be stated: No individual may be deprived of the results of his own economic endeavor. The primary function of "slavery" in Ashanti society was not in production but in social status.

Of the slaves in this strange system, Klein writes:

> His main liabilities stemmed from his being non-kin and unaffiliated. This meant that the *odonko* stood outside and was isolated from the closed network of matrilineally derived rights and obligations. His humanity was valued less than that of a lineage member. To be someone's personal property entailed becoming thingified, depersonalized,

> treated as a commodity. This last was, in fact, his hallmark. . . . His
> gravest concern arose from the possibility of being ritually dispatched
> at the next funeral service.[31]

The term "slavery" applied to West African societies could easily mislead us, for the slaves held therein functioned in the economy without special disadvantage. Apart from the gloomy possibility of ritual execution, the worst a slave suffered was to have to endure as a pariah who could be shifted from one household to another by sale. Since no mechanism for economic exploitation existed, no impassable barriers to freedom did either. The ease with which a slave might be adopted into the family as a free man varied markedly in time and place but remained noticeable. Because of certain peculiarities of property inheritance in a matrilineal society, there were even special advantages in taking a slave for a wife. Two conclusions emerge: West Africans had disciplined themselves to agricultural labor; and the transfer of a slave from an African to a European master meant a profound change in the nature and extent of his obligations.

The absence of slavery, in any form, among some of the coastal peoples does not imply that agriculture was undeveloped or that hard work was lacking. The Bobo, for example, who were probably an important source of slaves for the United States, refused to hold slaves but had a reputation for being conscientious laborers.[32]

Angola and the Congo supplied numerous slaves to South America and some to North America. These peoples, too, came from societies resting on agricultural foundations. The Bantu-speaking peoples of southwestern Africa practiced slavery, although to what extent we do not know. The more primitive and undeveloped peoples, including some cannibals, did not supply slaves from among their own but did act as slave catchers for the Europeans.[33]

For a general statement of the economic level of pre-colonial West Africa we may turn to the distinguished former premier of Senegal, whose credentials as a student of African history and culture are not in question. Writes Mamadou Dia in his essay on "L'Économie africaine avant l'intervention européenne":

> The traditional African economy does not deserve to be treated
> disdainfully as a primitive economy, based on static structures, with
> technical routines incapable of adapting themselves to new situations.
> Everything proves, on the contrary, that this agricultural economy
> showed evidence of a strong vitality with possibilities for creating or
> assimilating techniques appropriate to assure its survival.[34]

The African economy was nevertheless much less developed than that of the European world, and we may assume that the productivity of the Negro was well below that of the white man of Western Europe. We need not rush to accept the grotesque exaggerations about the level of West African society that currently are flooding the literature. Emancipation would not have suddenly accomplished the miracle of raising the productivity of the Southern Negro to the level of, say, the Northern farmer. Since the Negro was accustomed to agricultural work in Africa as well as in the South, the task of raising his productivity should not have been difficult. In a friendly society, with adequate incentives, the Negro laborer's efficiency should have improved quickly. There is no scientific basis for any other assumption.

That the Negro worked hard in African agriculture does not prove that his economic faculties did not decline once he was separated from his homeland. Frank Wesley Pitman writes that Negroes taken to the West Indies knew how to tend their own gardens and care for livestock but were totally unprepared for the work expected of them in the sugar fields.[35] By what process, it may be wondered, does a man prepare himself to be driven in a slave gang? Yet we know that even the slave plantation was known in Africa, and Herskovits has shown that American slavery represented a distorted continuation of the various forms of collective labor common to Africa.[36]

The brutality of American slavery confronted the African—even the African who had been a slave in his homeland—with something new. Under its mildest forms Southern slavery had to be much harsher than its African counterpart. With the partial exception of the Dahomey, African slavery was patriarchal. Even slaves from a conquered tribe were sometimes assimilated into the new culture. A slave might buy his freedom and become a free man in a new homeland. There was little racial antipathy, although it was by no means unknown. In the South the Negro received a series of hard blows. He worked under more stringent conditions, was torn from his culture, family life, and system of values, and found himself in a society that offered no adequate substitutes. If the Negro was "culturally" unattuned to hard work, this condition reflected not his African background but a deterioration from it.

To say that the Negro suffered from a cultural dislocation that may have affected his economic propensities is not to imply that, after all, the Negro slave proved a poor worker because he was a Negro. Enslavement itself, especially the enslavement of a people regarded as racially inferior and unassimilable, produces such dislocations. Once slavery passes from its mild, patriarchal stage, the laborer is regarded less and less as a human being and more and more as a beast of burden, particularly when he is a foreigner who can be treated as a biological inferior. Even in patriarchal societies, slavery facilitates the growth of large-scale production, which corrodes the older comradeship between master and slave. The existence of slavery lays the basis for such a development, especially where markets are opened and institutional barriers to commercialization removed. Such a course may not be inevitable, but slavery does establish a powerful tendency toward large-scale exploitation of men and resources. The rise of the plantation system in Dahomey serves as an illustration, although the economic structure was unusual and cannot be regarded as a mature, commercially oriented slave system. Thus slavery, no matter how patriarchal at first, will, if permitted to grow naturally, break out of its modest bounds and produce an economy that will rip the laborer from his culture and yet not provide him with a genuine replacement.

Even if we judge the problem of the slave South to have been the presence of a culturally dislocated labor force, we should not be justified in asserting that the difficulty lay with the Negro as a Negro. Rather, the cause of the process of dislocation and the deterioration of his work habits was slavery itself. Slavery, once it becomes a large-scale enterprise, reverses its earlier contribution to the productivity of the laborer and undermines the culture, dignity, efficiency, and even the manhood of the enslaved worker.

Notes

1. Stampp, *The Peculiar Institution*, Chap. I.
2. Alfred Holt Stone, *Studies in the American Race Problem* (New York, 1908), pp. 145, 790–93.
3. Gray, *History of Agriculture*, Vol. I, Chap. XX; Phillips, *American Negro Slavery*, pp. 278 ff, 344; and *Life and Labor in the Old South* (Boston, 1948). pp. 188 ff; Craven. *Soil Exhaustion*, p. l63.
4. See, *e.g.*, Otto Klineberg, *Race Differences* (New York, 1935). Recent work has not altered his major conclusions, which are based on psychological, genetic. and other data.
5. *History of Agriculture*, I, 467.
6. Phillips, *American Negro Slavery*, p. 344 and n.1; generally Chaps. I and XVIII.
7. Gabriel Tarde, *The Laws of Imitation*, tr. Elsie Clews Parsons (New York, 1903), pp 278 f, also p. 221 and *passim.*
8. Joseph Alexander Tillinghast, *The Negro in Africa and America* ("Publications of the American Economic Association," 3rd Series, III, No. 2; New York, 1902), pp. 2 f, 18 f; *cf.* Jerome Dowd, *The Negro Races* (New York, 1907). Vol. I. For a thorough and convincing critique of these works see Melville J.

Herskovits, *The Myth of the Negro Past* (New York, 1941), Chaps. I and II. esp. pp 55–61.

9. Consider, *e.g.*, N. G. Chernyshevsky's stinging rebuke to Western scientists in his splendid essay "An Essay on the Scientific Conception of Certain Problems of World History: Part One—Races," *Selected Philosophical Essays* (Moscow, 1953), pp. 199–220. The essay was written in 1887 and appeared in Russia a year later.

10. The experience of the Indians within the present limits of the United States is well known. Even more impressive is the evidence from Latin America, where a sustained effort to enslave Indians was successful only where they had previously developed an agricultural society. In other cases, the experience paralleled that of Bahia, Brazil, where 40,000 Indians were enslaved in 1563 but only about 3,000 survived the next twenty years. See João Dornas Filho, A *Escravidão no Brasil* (Rio de Janeiro, 1939), p. 40.

11. We know little about indigenous African slavery, but most reliable anthropological and historical works refer to its existence.

12. C. G. Seligman, *Races of Africa* (3rd ed.; London, 1957), p. 58.

13. See his *Myth of the Negro Past,* esp. p. 16.

14. E. Franklin Frazier, *The Negro in the United States* (New York, 1949), pp. 6–11. I think Frazier goes too far. Certain influences did remain. We cannot explore them here, but they would not support the Phillips thesis anyway.

15. *Cf.* Raymond and Alice Bauer, "Day to Day Resistance to Slavery," *JNH,* XXVII (Oct. 1942), 401 f. 407.

16. Herskovits, *Myth of the Negro Past,* pp. 61 f.

17. Seligman, *Races of Africa,* pp. 51–54; Melville J. Herskovits, *Economic Anthropology (New York, 1952),* esp. Chaps. VI and VIII; Rosemary Arnold, "A Port of Trade; Whydah on the Guinea Coast," Chap. VIII of Polanyi *et al., Trade and Market in the Early Empires.*

18. S. F. Nadel, *A Black Byzantium: The Kingdom of the Nupe in Nigeria* (London, 1946), pp. 76–85.

19. J. Spencer Trimingham, *Islam in West Africa* (Oxford, 1959), p. 185.

20. Walter Cline, *Mining and Metallurgy in Negro Africa* (Menasha, Wis., 1937), pp. 11–17.

21. Stanley Diamond, "Dahomey; A Proto-State in West Africa," unpublished doctoral dissertation, Columbia University, 1951, p. 52.

22. Herskovits, *Economic Anthropology,* p. 118.

23. Melville J. Herskovits, *Dahomey, An Ancient West African Kingdom* (2 vols.; New York, 1938), I, 33 f.

24. Phillips, *American Negro Slavery,* pp. 6, 27; Life *and Labor,* pp. 188 ff.

25. Tillinghast, *The Negro,* pp. 25, 38; Dowd, *The Negro Races,* I, 91–99.

26. Herskovits, *Dahomey,* I, 82 f, 99, 102; II, 97.

27. Nadel, *Black Byzantium,* pp. 85, 196 ff.

28. R. S. Rattray, *Ashanti* (Oxford, 1923), pp. 223–27; and *The Tribes of the Ashanti Hinterland* (2 vols.; Oxford, 1932), I, 261–68; II, 348 f, 402 f, 564.

29. C. K. Meek, *Law and Authority in a Nigerian Tribe* (London, 1937), pp. 5–8, 102 f, 133 f, 204.

30. Daryll Forde, *The Yoruba-Speaking Peoples of South-Western Nigeria* (London, 1951), p. 4.

31. A. Norman Klein, "Some Structural Consequences of 'Slavery' and 'Pawnage'

in Precolonial Ashanti Social and Economic Structure," unpublished draft of the first chapter of a forthcoming book on statemaking in West Africa. I am indebted to Mr. Klein for permission to quote and for allowing me to see his unfinished manuscript. When published, it will rank as our first analysis of precolonial slavery and a major contribution to the history of West Africa as well as to the problem of state formation in general.

32. H. J. Nieboer, *Slavery as an Industrial System: Ethnological Researches* (The Hague, 1900), p. 154. Phillips read and referred to this book.

33. *Ibid.*, pp. 145–49, [H. P. Smit], *The Native Tribes of South-West Africa* (Cape Town, 1928), pp. 33 f, 41; L. Marquard and T. L. Standing, *The Southern Bantu* (London, 1939), p. 50. For an introduction to the vast literature on Angola and the Congo see C. R. Boxer's chapter, "Angola—The Black Mother," in his superb *Salvador de Sá* and *the Struggle for Brazil and Angola. 1602–1686* (London, 1952).

34. Mamadou Dia, *Réflexions sur l'économie de l'Afrique noire* (nouv. ed.; Paris, 1960), p. 23.

35. "Slavery on the British West India Plantations in the Eighteenth Century," *JNH*, XI (Oct. 1926), p. 594.

36. Myth of the Negro Past, p. 161.

LeRoi Jones argues that African survivals are far more prevalent in the Caribbean and Latin America than in this country, He points out that the most vigorously suppressed aspects of culture were the various forms of political and economic activity ("two of the most profound sophistications of African culture"). Moreover, technology died as well.

What was retained, and was eventually to flourish, was that which could not be readily destroyed: religion and, especially, musical forms. To Jones, what we must study and understand is the significance of art, not artifact. According to many recent observers, such nonmaterial elements gave body to the "soul" of Afro-American culture.

5

Art Not Artifact

LeRoi Jones

The Negro as Property

It is extremely important in a "study" of any aspect of the history of the American Negro to emphasize how strange and unnatural the initial contacts with Western slavery were for the African, in order to show how the black man was set apart throughout the New World from the start. This should enable one to begin to appreciate the amazing, albeit agonizing, transformation that produced the contemporary black American from such a people as were first bound and brought to this country.

Sociologists are always making fearsome analogies between minorities regarding their *acculturation* in this country (usually when confronted by, say, statistics on how many of the total crimes committed in any given year are attributable to Negroes). They claim

From LeRoi Jones, *Blues People: Negro Music in White America,* New York: William Morrow and Company, Inc., and London: MacGibbon & Kee, 1963, pp. 11–31. Copyright © 1963 by LeRoi Jones.

that each one of the "newcomers" (a euphemism for "furriners") shows parallel development in the race toward ultimate Americanization. They say, flaunting their statistics, "See how, after such and such time, the sons and daughters of the once-despised Irish immigrants moved into genteel middle-class social respectability." So, with the Italians, they point out the decrease in crimes "directly attributable to persons of Italian extraction" after enough time had passed to enable this minority also to enter into the mainstream of American life. And certainly, there are some analogies to be made between minority groups who have, since their initial removal to this country from their homelands, edged out from their first ghetto existences into the promise and respectability of this brave New World. But no such strict analogy will serve for Afro-Americans. There are too many aspects of these "newcomers' " existence in America that will not sit still under those kinds of statistics.

First of all, we know that of all the peoples who form the heterogeneous yet almost completely homogenous mass that makes up the United States population, Negroes are the only descendants of people who were not happy to come here. The African was brought to this country in bondage and remained in bondage more than two hundred and fifty years. But most of the black people who were freed from formal slavery in 1865 *were not* Africans. They were Americans. And whether or not we choose to characterize the post-Emancipation existence of Negroes in the United States as "freedom," we must still appreciate the idea that a group of people who became familiar with the mores, attitudes, language, and other culture references of this country while being enslaved by it cannot be seen as analogous to peoples who move toward complete assimilation of these same mores by *choice*, even though these peoples are also despised by the "natives" of the country as "furriners." The African as slave was one idea, *i.e.,* these people from another country were brought to this country against their wills. But the American-born slaves offer a less easily defined situation.

The first-born of these Africans in America knew about Africa only through the stories, tales, riddles, and songs of their older relatives. But usually the children born in this country were separated from their African parents. No mother could be sure she would see her child after it was weaned. The American-born African children were much prized, and the masters had to exercise extreme care that the women didn't do away with these children to save them from the ugliness of slavery. (Many African mothers smothered their first-born American children, and the owners thought this was the result of carelessness, or callousness, characteristic of "savages.") These children also had to learn about slavery, but there were no centuries of culture to unlearn, or old long-held habits to suppress. The only way of life these children knew was the accursed thing they had been born into.

If we think about the importation of Africans into the New World as a whole, rather than strictly into the United States, the most apparent difference that can be seen is that Africans throughout the rest of the Americas were much slower to become Westernized and "acculturated." All over the New World there are still examples of pure African traditions that have survived three hundred years of slavery and four hundred years of removal from their source. "Africanisms" are still part of the lives of Negroes throughout the New World, in varying degrees, in places like Haiti, Brazil, Cuba, Guiana. Of course, attitudes and customs of the non-continental Negroes were lost or assumed other less apparent forms, but still the amount of pure Africanisms that have been retained is amazing. However, in the United States, Africanisms in American Negroes are not now readily discernible, although they certainly do exist. It was in the United States only that the slaves were, after a few generations, unable to retain any of the more obvious of African traditions. Any that were retained were usually submerged, however powerful their influence, in less recognizable manifestations. So after only a few generations in the United States an almost completely different individual could be born and be rightly called an American Negro.

Herskovits says about this phenomenon: "The contact between Negroes and whites in continental United States as compared to the West Indies and South America goes far to explain the relatively greater incidence of Africanisms in the Caribbean. In the earliest days, the number of slaves in proportion to their masters was extremely small, and though as time went on thousands and tens of thousands of slaves were brought to satisfy the demands of the southern plantations, nonetheless the Negroes lived in constant association with whites to a degree not found anywhere else in the New World. That the Sea Islands off the Carolina and Georgia coast offer the most striking retention of Africanisms to be encountered in the United States is to be regarded as but a reflection of the isolation of these Negroes when compared to those on the mainland."[1]

Some of this "constant association" between the white masters and the black slaves that took place in this country can be explained by comparing the circumstances of the slaves' "employment" in America with the circumstances of their employment in the rest of the New World. It was only in the United States that slaves were used on the smaller farms. Such a person as the "poor white" was a strictly American phenomenon. To turn again to Herskovits: "Matters were quite different in the Caribbean islands and in South America. Here racial numbers were far more disproportionate; estates where a single family ruled dozens, if not hundreds, of slaves were commonplace and the 'poor white' was found so seldom that he receives only cursory mention. . . . The white man with but a few slaves was likewise seldom encountered."[2]

But in the United States, the Utopia of the small businessman, the small farmer was the rule, rather than the exception, and these farmers could usually afford to own only a very small number of slaves.

On these small farms intimate contact between master and slave was unavoidable (I will just mention here the constant extra-curricular sexual activities that were forced on the slave women by their white masters). In 1863, Frederick Olmsted reported: "The more common sort of habitations of the white people are either of logs or loosely-boarded frame, a brick chimney running up outside, at one end; and black and white children, are commonly lying very promiscuously together, on the ground about the doors. I am struck with the close co-habitation and association of black and white—negro women are carrying black and white babies together in their arms; black and white children are playing together [not going to school together]; black and white faces constantly thrust together out of doors to see the train go by."[3] One result of this intimacy between the poorer master and his slaves was, of course, the invention of still another kind of Afro-American, the mulatto. But certainly the most significant result was the rapid acculturation of the African in this country. With no native or tribal references, except perhaps the stories of his elders and the performance of nonreligious dances and songs, the American-born slave had only the all-encompassing mores of his white master. Africa had become a foreign land, and none of the American-born slaves could ever hope to see it.

A graph could be set up to show just exactly what aspects of African culture suffered most and were most rapidly suppressed by this constant contact with Euro-American culture. It is certainly immediately apparent that all forms of political and economic thought, which were two of the most profound sophistications of African culture, were suppressed immediately. The extremely intricate political, social, and economic systems of the West Africans were, of course, done away with completely in their normal manifestations. The much praised "legal genius" that produced one of the strictest and most sophisticated legal systems known could not function, except very informally, in the cotton fields of America. The technology of the

Africans, iron-working, wood-carving, weaving, etc., died out quickly in the United States. Almost every material aspect of African culture took a new less obvious form or was wiped out altogether. (The famous wood sculpture of the Yoruba could not possibly have fallen into an area less responsive to its beauties than colonial America. The artifact was, like any other material manifestation of pure African culture, doomed. It is strange to realize that even in the realm of so-called high culture, Western highbrows have only in this century begun to think of African, Pre-Columbian, and Egyptian art, as well as the art of other pre-literate and/or "primitive" cultures, as art rather than archaeology. Of course, nowadays, it is a must in the home of any Westerner who pays homage to the arts to include in his collection of *objets d'art* at least a few African, Egyptian, and Pre-Columbian pieces.)

Only religion (and magic) and the arts were not completely submerged by Euro-American concepts Music, dance, religion, do not have *artifacts* as their end products, so they were saved. These non-material aspects of the African's culture were almost impossible to eradicate. And these are the most apparent legacies of the African past, even to the contemporary black American. But to merely point out that blues, jazz, and the Negro's adaptation of the Christian religion all rely heavily on African culture takes no great amount of original thinking. How these activities derive from that culture is what remains important.

African Slaves/American Slaves: Their Music

It is a comparatively short period of history that passes between the time, when Richard Francis Burton could say of African music that "it is monotonous to a degree, yet they delight in it," or when H. E. Krehbiel could ask (1914), "Why savages who have never developed a musical or other art should be supposed to have more refined aesthetic sensibilities than the peoples who have cultivated music for centuries, passes my poor powers of understanding . . ."[4] until the time (1920) when a great mass of white Americans are dancing a West African (Ashanti) ancestor dance they know as the "Charleston."

Jazz is commonly thought to have begun around the turn of the century, but the musics jazz derived from are much older. Blues is the parent of all legitimate jazz, and it is impossible to say exactly how old blues is—certainly no older than the presence of Negroes in the United States. It is a native American music, the product of the black man in this country: or to put it more exactly the way I have come to think about it, blues could not exist if the African captives had not become American captives.

The immediate predecessors of blues were the Afro-American/ American Negro work songs, which had their musical origins in West Africa. The religious music of the Negro also originates from the same African music. However, while the general historical developments of Negro secular and religious music can be said to be roughly parallel, *i.e.*, they follow the same general trends in their development, and in later forms are the result of the same kind of accultural processes, a Negro religious music contingent on Christianity developed later than the secular forms. An Afro-American work song could come about more quickly in slavery than any other type of song because even if the individual who sang it was no longer working for himself, most of the physical impetuses that suggested that particular type of singing were still present. However, Africans were not Christians, so their religious music and the music with which they celebrated the various cultic or ritualistic rites had to undergo a distinct and complete transfer of reference.

For the African in the United States there was little opportunity for religious syncretism (the identification of one set of religious dogma or ritual with analogous dogma or ritual in a completely alien religion). In the essentially Catholic New World cultures, the multitudes of saints were easily substituted for the many *loa* or deities in the various West African religions. But in Protestant America this was not possible.

So the music which formed the *link* between pure African music and the music which developed after the African slave in the United States had had a chance to become exposed to some degree of Euro-American culture was that which contained the greatest number of Africanisms and yet was foreign to Africa. And this was the music of the second generation of slaves, their work songs. The African slave had sung African chants and litanies in those American fields. His sons and daughters, and their children, began to use America as a reference.

As late as the nineteenth century, pure African songs could be heard and pure African dances seen in the Southern United States. Congo Square, in New Orleans, would nightly rock to the "master drums" of new African arrivals. In places like Haiti or Guiana, these drums still do remind the West that the black man came from Africa, not Howard University. But in the United States pure African sources grew scarce in a relatively short time after the great slave importations of the eighteenth century.

The work song took on its own peculiar qualities in America for a number of reasons. First, although singing to accompany one's labor was quite common in West Africa, it is obvious that working one's own field in one's own land is quite different from forced labor in a foreign land. And while the physical insistence necessary to suggest a work song was still present, the references accompanying the work changed radically. Most West Africans were farmers and, I am certain, these agricultural farm songs could have been used in the fields of the New World in the same manner as the Old. But the lyrics of a song that said, "After the planting, if the gods bring rain,/My family, my ancestors, be rich as they are beautiful," could not apply in the dreadful circumstance of slavery. Secondly, references to the gods or religions of Africa were suppressed by the white masters as soon as they realized what these were—not only because they naturally thought of any African religious customs as "barbarous" but because the whites soon learned that too constant evocation of the African gods could mean that those particular Africans were planning on leaving that plantation as soon as they could! The use of African drums was soon prevented too, as the white man learned that drums could be used to incite revolt as well as to accompany dancers.

So the work song, as it began to take shape in America, first had to be stripped of any purely African ritual and some cultural reference found for it in the New World. But this was difficult to do within the African-language songs themselves. The diverse labors of the African, which were the sources of this kind of song, had been funneled quite suddenly into one labor, the cultivation of the white man's fields. The fishing songs, the weaving songs, the hunting songs, all had lost their pertinence. But these changes were not immediate. They became the realized circumstances of a man's life after he had been exposed sufficiently to their source and catalyst—his enslavement.

And this is the basic difference between the first slaves and their offspring. The African slave continued to chant his native chants, sing his native songs, at work, even though the singing of them might be forbidden or completely out of context. But being forbidden, the songs were after a time changed into other forms that weren't forbidden in contexts that were contemporary. The African slave might have realized he was losing something, that his customs and the memory of his land were being each day drained from his life. Still there was a certain amount of forbearance. No one can simply decree that a man change the way he thinks. But the first black Americans had no native cultural references other than the slave culture. A work song about fishing when one has never fished seems meaningless, especially when one works each day in a cotton field. The context of the Africans' life had changed, but the American-born slaves never knew what the change had been.

It is impossible to find out exactly how long the slaves were in America before the African work song actually did begin to have extra-African references. First, of course, there were mere additions of the foreign words—French, Spanish or English, for the most part, after the British colonists gained power in the United States. Krehbiel lists a Creole song transcribed by Lafcadio Hearn, which contains both French (or patois) and African words (the italicized words are African):

> *Ouendé, ouendé, macaya!*
>   Mo pas barrasse, *macaya!*
> *Ouendé, ouendé, macaya!*
>   Mo bois bon divin, *macaya!*
> *Ouendé, ouendé, macaya!*
>   Mo mange bon poulet, *macaya!*
> *Ouendé, ouendé, macaya!*
>   Mo pas barrasse, *macaya!*
> *Ouendé, ouendé, macaya!*
>   *Macaya!*

Hearn's translation was:

> *Go on! go on! eat enormously!*
>   I ain't one bit ashamed—*eat outrageously!*
> *Go on! go on! eat prodigiously!*
>   I drink good wine!—*eat ferociously!*
> *Go on! go on! eat unceasingly!*
>   I eat good chicken—*gorging myself!*
> *Go on! go on!* etc.

It is interesting to note, and perhaps more than coincidence, that the portions of the song emphasizing excess are in African, which most of the white men could not understand, and the portions of the song elaborating some kind of genteel, if fanciful, existence are in the tongue of the masters. But there was to come a time when there was no black man who understood the African either, and those allusions to excess, or whatever the black man wished to keep to himself, were either in the master's tongue or meaningless, albeit rhythmical, sounds to the slave also.

Aside from the actual transfer or survival of African words in the songs and speech of the early slaves, there was also some kind of syntactical as well as rhythmical transfer since Africans and their descendants tended to speak their new languages in the same manner as they spoke their West African dialects. What is called now a "Southern accent" or "Negro speech" was once simply the accent of a foreigner trying to speak a new and unfamiliar language, although it was characteristic of the white masters to attribute the slave's "inability" to speak perfect English to the same kind of "childishness" that was used to explain the African's belief in the supernatural. The owners, when they bothered to listen, were impressed that even the songs of their native American slaves were "incomprehensible" or "unintelligible." However, as Herskovits says of early Afro-American speech:

> since grammar and idiom are the last aspects of a new language to be learned, the Negroes who reached the New World acquired as much of the vocabulary of their masters as they initially needed or was later taught to them, pronounced these words as best they were able, but organized them into aboriginal speech patterns. Thus arose the various forms of Negro-English, Negro-French, Negro-Spanish and Negro-Portuguese spoken in the New World, their "peculiarities" due to the fact that they comprise European words cast into an African grammatical mold. But this emphatically does not imply that those dialects are without grammar, or that they represent an inability to master the foreign tongue, as is so often claimed.[5]

A few of the "unintelligible" songs are not as unintelligible as their would-be interpreters would have it. For instance, Mr. Krehbiel lists as unintelligible two "corn songs"—songs sung while working the corn fields. Only a fragment of one song remains the words "Shock along, John." It seems to me incredible that Krehbiel could not see that *shock* is the word *shuck,* meaning to strip the corn of its outer covering, which is what the slaves did.

> Five can't ketch me and ten can't hold me—
>   Ho, round the corn, Sally!
> Here's your iggle-quarter and here's your count-aquils—
>   Ho, round the corn, Sally!
> I can bank, 'ginny bank, 'ginny bank the weaver—
>   Ho, round the corn, Sally!

All of the above seems obvious to me except the third and fifth lines. But *iggle* is, of course, *eagle,* and an eagle quarter was American money. It would also seem that *count* in the phrase "your countaquils" is either a reference to that money or the count of merchandise being harvested—in this instance, the corn. *Aquil* could be either an appropriation of the Spanish *aquí,* meaning *here,* or more likely an appropriation of the French word *kilo,* which is a term of measure.

Another less "obscure" song of probably an earlier period:

> Arter you lub, you lub you know, boss. You can't broke lub. Man can't broke lub. Lub stan'—he ain't gwine broke—Man heb to be very smart for broke lub. Lub is a ting stan' just like tar, arter he stick, he stick, he ain't gwine move. He can't move less dan you burn him. Hab to kill all two arter he lub fo' you broke lub.[6]

Though the above should be considered an American song, it still retains so much of the African that it might be difficult for some people to understand. Yet I think the references quite American. But now, however, by *African,* I do not mean actual surviving African words, but rather the African accent and the syntactical construction of certain West African dialects. It is relatively easy to see the connection in the syntax of this song and the literal translation into English of African phrases. For example, the literal English rendering of an Ashanti (Twi dialect) phrase meaning "to calm a person" is "cool he heart give him." (And here, I think, even the word *cool* should bear further consideration.)

African speech, African customs, and African music all changed by the American experience into a native American form. But what was a pure African music? Were there similarities between African and European music before the importation of the slaves? What strictly musical changes occurred to transform African music into American? How did this come about?

The role of African music in the formulation of Afro-American music was misunderstood for a great many years. And the most obvious misunderstanding was one that perhaps only a Westerner would make, that African music ". . . although based on the same principles of European music, suffers from the African's lack of European technical skill in the fashioning of his crude instruments. Thus the strangeness and out-of-tune quality of a great many of the played notes." Musicologists of the eighteenth and nineteenth centuries, and even some from the twentieth, would speak of the "aberration" of the diatonic scale in African music. Or a man like Krehbiel could say: "There is a significance which I cannot fathom in the circumstance that the tones which seem *rebellious* [my italics] to the negro's sense of intervallic propriety are the fourth and seventh of the diatonic major series and the fourth, sixth and seventh of the minor."[7] Why did it not occur to him that perhaps the Africans were using not a diatonic scale, but an African scale, a scale that would seem ludicrous when analyzed by the normal methods of Western musicology?

Even Ernest Borneman says: "It seems likely now that the common source of European and West African music was a simple non-hemitonic pentatone system. Although indigenous variants of the diatonic scale have been developed and preserved in Africa, modern West Africans who are not familiar with European music will tend to become uncertain when asked to sing in a tempered scale. This becomes particularly obvious when the third and seventh steps of a diatonic scale are approached. The singer almost invariably tries to skid around these steps with slides, slurs or vibrato effects so broad as to approach scalar value."[8]

These sliding and slurring effects in Afro-American music, the basic "aberrant" quality of a blues scale, are, of course, called "blueing" the notes. But why not of "scalar value?" It is my idea that this is a different scale.

Sidney Finkelstein, in *Jazz: A People's Music:*

> these deviations from the pitch familiar to concert music are not, of course, the result of an inability to sing or play in tune. They mean that the blues are a non-diatonic music. . . . Many books on jazz . . . generally describe the blues as a sequence of chords, such as the tonic, subdominant and dominant seventh. Such a definition, however, is like putting the cart before the horse. There are definite patterns of chords which have been evolved to support the blues, but these do not define the blues, and the blues can exist as a melody perfectly recognizable as the blues without them. Neither are the blues simply a use of the major scale with the "third" and "seventh" slightly blued or flattened. The fact is that both this explanation, and the chord explanation, are attempts to explain one musical system in terms of another; to describe a non-diatonic music in diatonic terms.[9]

The most apparent survivals of African music in Afro-American music are its rhythms: not only the seeming emphasis in the African music on rhythmic, rather than melodic or harmonic, qualities, but also the use of polyphonic, or contrapuntal, rhythmic effects. Because of this seeming neglect of harmony and melody, Westerners thought the music "primitive." It did not occur to them that Africans might have looked askance at a music as vapid rhythmically as the West's.

The reason for the remarkable development of the rhythmic qualities of African music can certainly be traced to the fact that Africans also used drums for communication; and not, as was once thought, merely by using the drums in a kind of primitive Morse code, but by the phonetic reproduction of the words themselves—the result being that Africans developed an extremely fine and extremely complex rhythmic sense, as well as becoming unusually responsive to timbral subtleties. Also, the elaborately developed harmonic system used in the playing of percussion instruments, *i.e.,* the use of drums or other percussion instruments of different timbres to produce harmonic contrasts, was not immediately recognizable to the Western ear; neither was the use of two and three separate rhythmic patterns to underscore the same melody a concept easily recognizable to Westerners used to less subtle musical devices.

Melodic diversity in African music came not only in the actual arrangements of notes (in terms of Western transcription) but in the singer's vocal interpretation. The "tense, slightly hoarse-sounding vocal techniques" of the work songs and the blues stem directly from West African musical tradition. (This kind of singing voice is also common to a much other non-Western music.) In African languages the meaning of a word can be changed simply by altering the *pitch* of the word, or changing its stress—basically, the way one can change the word *yeh* from simple response to stern challenge simply by moving the tongue slightly. Philologists call this "significant tone," the "combination of pitch and timbre" used to produce changes of meaning in words. This was basic to the speech and music of West Africans, and was definitely passed on to the Negroes of the New World.

Another important aspect of African music found very readily in the American Negro's music is the antiphonal singing technique. A leader sings a theme and a chorus answers him. Those answers are usually comments on the leader's theme or comments on the answers themselves in improvised verses. The amount of improvisation depends on how long the chorus wishes to continue. And improvisation, another major facet of African music, is certainly one of the strongest survivals in American Negro music. The very character of the first work songs suggests that they were largely improvised. And, of course, the very structure of jazz is the melodic statement with an arbitrary number of improvised answers or comments on the initial theme.

Just as some of the African customs survived in America in their totality, although usually given just a thin veneer of Euro-American camouflage, so pure African songs, dances, and instruments showed up on this side of the water. However, I consider this less significant because it seems to me much more important, if we speak of music, that features such as basic rhythmic, harmonic, and melodic devices were transplanted almost intact rather than isolated songs, dances, or instruments.

The very nature of slavery in America dictated the way in which African culture could be adapted. Thus, a Dahomey river gods ceremony had no chance of survival in this country at all unless it was incorporated into an analogous rite that was present in the new culture—which is what happened. The Christians of the New World called it baptism. Just as the African songs of recrimination survive as a highly competitive game called "the dozens." (As any young Harlemite can tell you, if someone says to you, "Your father's a woman," you must say, as a minimal comeback, "Your mother likes it," or a similar putdown.) And in music: where the use of the African drum was strictly forbidden, other percussive devices had to be found, like the empty oil drums that led to the development of the West Indian steel bands. Or the metal wash basin turned upside down and floated in another basin that sounds, when beaten, like an African hollow-log drum. The Negro's way in this part of the Western world was adaptation and reinterpretation. The banjo (an African word) is an African instrument, and the xylophone, used now in all Western concert orchestras, was also brought over by the Africans. But the survival of the *system* of African music is much more significant than the existence of a few isolated and finally superfluous features. The notable fact is that the only so-called popular music in this country of any real value is of African derivation.

Another important aspect of African music was the use of folk tales in song lyrics, riddles, proverbs, etc., which, even when not accompanied by music, were the African's chief method of education, the way the wisdom of the elders was passed down to the young. The use of these folk stories and legends in the songs of the American Negro was quite common, although it was not as common as the proportion of "Americanized" or American material grew. There are, however, definite survivals not only in the animal tales which have become part of this country's tradition (the Uncle Remus/Br'er Rabbit tales, for example) but in the lyrics of work songs and even later blues forms.

And just as the lyrics of the African songs were usually as important or *more* important than the music, the lyrics of the work songs and the later blues were equally important to the Negro's concept of music. In fact the "shouts" and "field hollers" were little more than highly rhythmical lyrics. Even the purely instrumental music of the American Negro contains constant reference to vocal music. Blues-playing is the closest imitation of the human voice of any music I've heard; the vocal effects that jazz musicians have delighted in from Bunk Johnson to Ornette Coleman are evidence of this. (And it seems right to conclude that the African and blues scales proceed from this concept of vocal music, which produces note values that are almost impossible to reproduce on the fixed Western tempered scale, but can nevertheless be played on Western instruments.)

If we think of African music as regards its intent, we must see that it differed from Western music in that it was a purely *functional* music. Borneman lists some basic types of songs common to West African cultures: songs used by young men to influence young women (courtship, challenge, scorn); songs used by workers to make their tasks easier; songs used by older men to prepare the adolescent boys for manhood, and so on. "Serious" Western music, except for early religious music, has been strictly an "art" music. One would not think of any particular *use* for Haydn's symphonies, except perhaps the "cultivation of the soul." "Serious music" (a term that could only have extra-religious meaning in the West) has never been an integral part of the Westerner's life; no art has been since the Renaissance. Of course, before the Renaissance, art could find its way into the lives of almost all the people because all art issued from the Church, and the Church was at the very center of Western man's life. But the discarding of the religious attitude for the "enlightened" concepts of the Renaissance also created the schism between what was art and what was life. It was, and is, inconceivable in the African culture to make a separation between music, dancing, song, the artifact, and a man's life or his worship of his gods. *Expression* issued from life, and *was* beauty. But in the West, the "triumph of the economic mind over the imaginative," as Brooks Adams said, made possible this dreadful split between life and art. Hence, a music that is an "art" music as distinguished from something someone would whistle while tilling a field.

There are still relatively cultivated Westerners who believe that before Giotto no one *could* reproduce the human figure well, or that the Egyptians painted their figures in profile because they *could not* do it any other way. The idea of progress, as it has infected all other areas of Western thought, is thus carried over into the arts as well. And so a Western listener will criticize the tonal and timbral qualities of an African or American Negro singer whose singing has a completely alien *end* as the "standard of excellence." The "hoarse, shrill" quality of African singers or of their cultural progeny, the blues singers, is thus attributed to their lack of proper vocal training, instead of to a conscious desire dictated by their own cultures to produce a prescribed and certainly calculated effect. A blues singer and, say, a Wagnerian tenor cannot be compared to one another in any way. They issue from cultures that have almost nothing in common, and the musics they make are equally alien. The

Western concept of "beauty" cannot be reconciled to African or Afro-American music (except perhaps now in the twentieth century, Afro-American music has enough of a Euro-American tradition to make it seem possible to judge it by purely Western standards. This is not quite true.) For a Westerner to say that the Wagnerian tenor's voice is "better" than the African singer's or the blues singer's is analogous to a non-Westerner disparaging Beethoven's Ninth Symphony because it wasn't improvised.

The Western concept of the cultivation of the voice is foreign to African or Afro-American music. In the West, only the artifact can be beautiful, mere expression cannot be thought to be. It is only in the twentieth century that Western art has moved away from this concept and toward the non-Western modes of art-making, but the principle of the beautiful thing as opposed to the natural thing still makes itself felt. The tendency of white jazz musicians to play "softer" or with "cleaner, rounder tones" than their Negro counterparts is, I think, an insistence on the same Western artifact. Thus an alto saxophonist like Paul Desmond, who is white, produces a sound on his instrument that can almost be called legitimate, or classical, and the finest Negro alto saxophonist, Charlie Parker, produced a sound on the same instrument that was called by some "raucous and uncultivated." But Parker's sound was *meant* to both those adjectives. Again, reference determines value. Parker also would literally imitate the human voice with his cries, swoops, squawks, and slurs, while Desmond always insists he is playing an instrument, that it is an artifact separate from himself. Parker did not admit that there was any separation between himself and the agent he had chosen as his means of self-expression.

By way of further illustration of this, another quote from Mr. Borneman:

> While the whole European tradition strives for regularity—of pitch, of time, of timbre and of vibrato—the African tradition strives precisely for the negation of these elements. In language, the African tradition aims at circumlocution rather than at exact definition. The direct statement is considered crude and unimaginative; the veiling of all contents in ever-changing paraphrases is considered the criterion of intelligence and personality. In music, the same tendency towards obliquity and ellipsis is noticeable: no note is attacked straight; the voice or instrument always approaches it from above or below, plays around the implied pitch without ever remaining any length of time, and departs from it without ever having committed itself to a single meaning. The timbre is veiled and paraphrased by constantly changing vibrato, tremolo and overtone effects. The timing and accentuation,

finally, are not *stated*, but *implied* or *suggested*. The denying or with-holding of all signposts.[10]

Notes

1. Herskovitz, M., *The Myth of the Negro Past* (New York: Harper & Row, 1941), p. 120.
2. *Ibid.*, p. 121.
3. *A Journey in the Seaboard Slave States* (New York, 1863), p. 17.
4. H. E. Krehbiel, *Afro-American Folksongs* (New York, C. Schirmer, 1914), p. 73.
5. *Op. cit.*, p. 80.
6   From Maud Cuney-Hare, *Negro Musicians and Their Music* (Washington, D.C., Associated Publishers, 1936), p. 27.
7. *Ibid.*, p. 73.
8. "The Roots of Jazz," in Nat Hentoff and Albert J. McCarthy, eds., *Jazz* (New York, Rinehart, 1959), p. 13.
9. *Jazz: A People's Music* (New York, Citadel, 1948), p. 68.
10. *Op. cit.*, pp. 23–24.

Suggested Readings

Botkin, Benjamin. *Lay My Burden Down.* Chicago: University of Chicago Press, 1945.
This is a folk history of slavery. It includes many stories said to have been derived from Africa.

Frazier, E. Franklin. *The Negro in the United States.* New York: Macmillan, 1957.
An excellent general introduction to the study of Black Americans by one of the best-known Negro sociologists.

Herskovits, Melville J. *The Myth of the Negro Past.* New York: Harper & Brothers, 1941.
The most famous of Herskovits' many examinations of the retention of Africanisms by Negroes in the United States.

Jordan, Winthrop D. *White Over Black.* Chapel Hill: University of North Carolina Press, 1968.
An historian reviews and interprets American attitudes toward the Negro from 1550–1812.

Tannenbaum, Frank. *Slave and Citizen.* New York: Alfred A. Knopf, 1946.
A brief but classic statement of the view that slavery was very different in North and South America.

Tax, Sol, editor. *Acculturation in the Americas.* New York: Cooper Square Publishers, republication 1967.
Proceedings and selected papers of the 29th International Congress of Americanists, 1952, dealing with "Africa and the Negro."

The Legacy of Slavery

Not that they starve, but starve so dreamlessly,
Not that they sow, but that they seldom reap,
Not that they serve but they have no gods to serve,
Not that they die, but that they die like sheep.

Vachel Lindsay

Like the chicken-egg controversy, the debate over slavery and prejudice has lasted for years. In this essay Winthrop D. Jordan examines the evidence offered to support the two traditional views. He concludes by contending that act and attitude were mutually reinforcing. Together they resulted in a social arrangement that left the black man degraded and debilitated.

6

Modern Tensions and the Origins of American Slavery

Winthrop D. Jordan

Thanks to John Smith we know that Negroes first came to the British continental colonies in 1619.[1] What we do not know is exactly when Negroes were first enslaved there. This question has been debated by historians for the past seventy years, the critical point being whether Negroes were enslaved almost from their first importation or whether they were at first simply servants and only later reduced to the status of slaves. The long duration and vigor of the controversy suggest that more than a simple question of dating has been involved. In fact certain current tensions in American society have complicated the historical problem and greatly heightened its significance. Dating the origins of slavery has taken on a striking modem relevance.

From *Journal of Southern History*, 28 (February 1962), 18–30. Copyright 1962 by the Southern Historical Association. Reprinted by permission of the Managing Editor. A modified and much more complete description of the origin of American slavery is in Winthrop D. Jordan, *White Over Black: American Attitudes Toward the Negro*, 1550–1812, Chapel Hill: The University of North Carolina Press, 1968.

During the nineteenth century historians assumed almost universally that the first Negroes came to Virginia as slaves. So close was their acquaintance with the problem of racial slavery that it did not occur to them that Negroes could ever have been anything but slaves. Philip A. Bruce, the first man to probe with some thoroughness into the early years of American slavery, adopted this view in 1896, although he emphasized that the original difference in treatment between white servants and Negroes was merely that Negroes served for life. Just six years later, however, came a challenge from a younger, professionally trained historian, James C. Ballagh. His *A History of Slavery* in *Virginia* appeared in the *Johns Hopkins University Studies in Historical and Political Science,* an aptly named series which was to usher in the new era of scholarly detachment in the writing of institutional history. Ballagh offered a new and different interpretation; he took the position that the first Negroes served merely as servants and that enslavement did not begin until around 1660, when statutes bearing on slavery were passed for the first time.[2]

There has since been agreement on dating the statutory establishment of slavery, and differences of opinion have centered on when enslavement began in actual practice. Fortunately there has also been general agreement on slavery's distinguishing characteristics: service for life and inheritance of like obligation by any offspring. Writing on the free Negro in Virginia for the Johns Hopkins series, John H. Russell in 1913 tackled the central question and showed that some Negroes were indeed servants but concluded that "between 1640 and 1660 slavery was fast becoming an established fact. In this twenty years the colored population was divided, part being servants and part being slaves, and some who were servants defended themselves with increasing difficulty from the encroachments of slavery."[3] Ulrich B. Phillips, though little interested in the matter, in 1918 accepted Russell's conclusion of early servitude and transition toward slavery after 1640. Helen T. Catterall took much the same position in 1926. On the other hand, in 1921 James M. Wright, discussing the free Negro in Maryland, implied that Negroes were slaves almost from the beginning, and in 1940 Susie M. Ames reviewed several cases in Virginia which seemed to indicate that genuine slavery had existed well before Ballagh's date of 1660.[4]

All this was a very small academic gale, well insulated from the outside world. Yet despite disagreement on dating enslavement, the earlier writers—Bruce, Ballagh, and Russell—shared a common assumption which, though at the time seemingly irrelevant to the main question, has since proved of considerable importance. They assumed that prejudice against the Negro was natural and almost innate in the white man. It would be surprising if they had felt otherwise in this period of segregation statutes, overseas imperialism, immigration restriction, and full-throated Anglo-Saxonism. By the 1920's, however, with the easing of these tensions, the assumption of natural prejudice was dropped unnoticed. Yet only one historian explicitly contradicted that assumption: Ulrich Phillips of Georgia, impressed with the geniality of both slavery and twentieth-century race relations, found no natural prejudice in the white man and expressed his "conviction that Southern racial asperities are mainly superficial, and that the two great elements are fundamentally in accord."[5]

Only when tensions over race relations intensified once more did the older assumption of natural prejudice crop up again. After World War II American Negroes found themselves beneficiaries of New Deal politics and reforms, wartime need for manpower, world-wide repulsion at racist excesses in Nazi Germany, and growingly successful colored anticolonialism. With new militancy Negroes mounted an attack on the citadel of separate but equal, and soon it became clear that America was in for a period of self-conscious reappraisal of its racial arrangements. Writing in this period of heightened tension (1949) a practiced and careful scholar, Wesley F. Craven, raised the old question of the Negro's original status, suggesting that Negroes had been enslaved at an early date. Craven also cautiously resuscitated the idea that white men may have had natural distaste for the Negro, an idea which fitted neatly with the suggestion of early enslavement. Original antipathy would mean rapid debasement.[6]

In the next year (1950) came a sophisticated counterstatement, which contradicted both Craven's dating and implicitly any suggestion of early prejudice. Oscar and Mary F. Handlin in "Origins of the Southern Labor System" offered a case for late enslavement, with servitude as the status of Negroes before about 1660. Originally the status of both Negroes and white servants was far short of freedom, the Handlins maintained, but Negroes failed to benefit from increased freedom for servants in mid-century and became less free rather than more.[7] Embedded in this description of diverging status were broader implications: Late and gradual enslavement undercut the possibility of natural, deep-seated antipathy toward Negroes. On the contrary, if whites and Negroes could share the same status of half freedom for forty years in the seventeenth century, why could they not share full freedom in the twentieth?

The same implications were rendered more explicit by Kenneth

M. Stampp in a major reassessment of Southern slavery published two years after the Supreme Court's 1954 school decision. Reading physiology with the eye of faith, Stampp frankly stated his assumption "that innately Negroes *are*, after all, only white men with black skin, nothing more, nothing less." [8] Closely following the Handlins' article on the origins of slavery itself, he almost directly denied any pattern of early and inherent racial antipathy: "...Negro and white servants of the seventeenth century seemed to be remarkably unconcerned about their visible physical differences." As for "the trend toward special treatment" of the Negro, "physical and cultural differences provided handy excuses to justify it."[9] Distaste for the Negro, then, was in the beginning scarcely more than an appurtenance of slavery.

These views squared nicely with the hopes of those even more directly concerned with the problem of contemporary race relations, sociologists and social psychologists. Liberal on the race question almost to a man, they tended to see slavery as the initial cause of the Negro's current degradation. The modern Negro was the unhappy victim of long association with base status. Sociologists, though uninterested in tired questions of historical evidence, could not easily assume a natural prejudice in the white man as the cause of slavery. Natural or innate prejudice would not only violate their basic assumptions concerning the dominance of culture but would undermine the power of their new Baconian science. For if prejudice was natural there would be little one could do to wipe it out. Prejudice must have followed enslavement, not vice versa, else any liberal program of action would be badly compromised. One prominent social scientist suggested in a UNESCO pamphlet that racial prejudice in the United States commenced with the cotton gin![10]

Just how closely the question of dating had become tied to the practical matter of action against racial prejudice was made apparent by the suggestions of still another historian. Carl N. Degler grappled with the dating problem in an article frankly entitled "Slavery and the Genesis of American Race Prejudice."[11] The article appeared in 1959, a time when Southern resistance to school desegregation seemed more adamant than ever and the North's hands none too clean, a period of discouragement for those hoping to end racial discrimination. Prejudice against the Negro now appeared firm and deep-seated, less easily eradicated than had been supposed in, say, 1954. It was Degler's view that enslavement began early, as a result of white settlers' prejudice or antipathy toward the first Negroes. Thus not only were the sociologists contradicted but the dating problem was now overtly and consciously tied to the broader question of whether slavery caused prejudice or prejudice caused slavery. A new self-consciousness over the American racial dilemma had snatched an arid historical controversy from the hands of an unsuspecting earlier generation and had tossed it into the arena of current debate.

Ironically there might have been no historical controversy at all if every historian dealing with the subject had exercised greater care with facts and greater restraint in interpretation. Too often the debate entered the realm of inference and assumption. For the crucial early years after 1619 there is simply not enough evidence to indicate with any certainty whether Negroes were treated like white servants or not. No historian has found anything resembling proof one way or the other. The first Negroes were sold to the English settlers, yet so were other Englishmen. It can be said, however, that Negroes were set apart from white men by the word *Negroes,* and a distinct name is not attached to a group unless it is seen as different. The earliest Virginia census reports plainly distinguished Negroes from white men, sometimes giving Negroes no personal name; and in 1629 every commander of the several plantations was ordered to "take a generall muster of all the inhabitants men woemen and Children as well *Englishe* as *Negroes.*"[12] Difference, however, might or might not involve inferiority.

The first evidence as to the actual status of Negroes does not appear until about 1640. Then it becomes clear that *some* Negroes were serving for life and some children inheriting the same obligation. Here it is necessary to suggest with some candor that the Handlins' statement to the contrary rests on unsatisfactory documentation.[13] That some Negroes were held as slaves after about 1640 is no indication, however, that American slavery popped into the world fully developed at that time. Many historians, most cogently the Handlins, have shown slavery to have been a gradual development, a process not completed until the eighteenth century. The complete deprivation of civil and personal rights, the legal conversion of the Negro into a chattel, in short slavery as Americans came to know it, was not accomplished overnight. Yet these developments practically and logically depended on the practice of hereditary lifetime service, and it is certainly possible to find in the 1640's and 1650's traces of slavery's most essential feature.[14]

The first definite trace appears in 1640 when the Virginia General Court pronounced sentence on three servants who had been retaken after running away to Maryland. Two of them, a Dutchman and a Scot, were ordered to serve their masters for one additional year and then the colony for three more, but "the third being a negro named John Punch shall serve his said master or his assigns for the time of his natural life here or else where." No white servant in America, so far as is known, ever received a like sentence.[15] Later the same month a Negro was again singled out from a group of recaptured runaways; six of the seven were assigned additional time while the Negro was given none, presumably because he was already serving for life.[16] After 1640, too, county court records began to mention Negroes, in part because there were more of them than previously—about two per cent of the Virginia population in 1649.[17] Sales for life, often including any future progeny, were recorded in unmistakable language. In 1646 Francis Pott sold a Negro woman and boy to Stephen Charlton "to the use of him . . . forever." Similarly, six years later William Whittington sold to John Pott "one Negro girle named Jowan; aged about Ten yeares and with her Issue and produce duringe her (or either of them) for their Life tyme. And their Successors forever"; and a Maryland man in 1649 deeded two Negro men and a woman "and all their issue both male and Female." The executors of a York County estate in 1647 disposed of eight Negroes—four men, two women, and two children—Captain John Chisman "to have hold occupy posesse and inioy and every one of the afforementioned Negroes forever[.]"[18] The will of Rowland Burnham of "Rapahanocke," made in 1657, dispensed his considerable number of Negroes and white servants in language which clearly differentiated between the two by specifying that the whites were to serve for their "full terme of tyme" and the Negroes "for ever."[19] Nor did anything in the will indicate that this distinction was exceptional or novel.

In addition to these clear indications that some Negroes were owned for life, there were cases of Negroes held for terms far longer than the normal five or seven years.[20] On the other hand, some Negroes served only the term usual for white servants, and others were completely free.[21] One Negro freeman, Anthony Johnson, himself owned a Negro.[22] Obviously the enslavement of some Negroes did not mean the immediate enslavement of all.

Further evidence of Negroes serving for life lies in the prices paid for them. In many instances the valuations placed on Negroes (in estate inventories and bills of sale) were far higher than for white servants, even those servants with full terms yet to serve. Since there was ordinarily no preference for Negroes as such, higher prices must have meant that Negroes were more highly valued because of their greater length of service. Negro women may have been especially prized, moreover, because their progeny could also be held perpetually. In 1645, for example, two Negro women and a boy were sold for 5,500 pounds of tobacco. Two years earlier William Burdett's inventory listed eight servants (with the time each had still to serve) at valuations ranging from 400 to 1,100 pounds, while a "very ancient" Negro was valued at 3,000 and an eight-year-old Negro girl at 2,000 pounds, with no time-remaining indicated for either. In the late 1650's an inventory of Thomas Ludlow's large estate evaluated a white servant with six years to serve at less than an elderly Negro man and only one half of a Negro woman.[23] The labor owned by James Stone in 1648 was evaluated as follows:

	lb tobo
Thomas Groves, 4 yeares to serve	1300
Francis Bomley for 6 yeares	1500
John Thackstone for 3 yeares	1300
Susan Davis for 3 yeares	1000
Emaniell a Negro man	2000
Roger Stone 3 yeares	1300
Mingo a Negro man	2000[24]

Besides setting a higher value on the two Negroes, Stone's inventory, like Burdett's, failed to indicate the number of years they had still to serve. It would seem safe to assume that the time remaining was omitted in this and similar documents simply because the Negroes were regarded as serving for an unlimited time.

The situation in Maryland was apparently the same. In 1643 Governor Leonard Calvert agreed with John Skinner, "mariner," to exchange certain estates for seventeen sound Negro "slaves," fourteen men and three women between sixteen and twenty-six years old. The total value of these was placed at 24,000 pounds of tobacco, which would work out to 1,000 pounds for the women and 1,500 for the men, prices considerably higher than those paid for white servants at the time.[25]

Wherever Negro women were involved, however, higher valuations may have reflected the fact that they could be used for field work while white women generally were not. This discrimination between Negro and white women, of course, fell short of actual enslavement. It meant merely that Negroes were set apart in a way clearly not to their advantage. Yet this is not the only evidence that Negroes were subjected to degrading distinctions not directly related to slavery. In several ways Negroes were singled out for special treatment which suggested a generalized debasing of Negroes as a group. Significantly, the first indications of debasement appeared at about the same time as the first indications of actual enslavement.

The distinction concerning field work is a case in point. It first

appeared on the written record in 1643, when Virginia pointedly recognized it in her taxation policy. Previously tithable persons had been
defined (1629) as "all those that worke in the ground of what qualitie
or condition soever." Now the law stated that all adult men and *Negro*
women were to be tithable, and this distinction was made twice again
before 1660. Maryland followed a similar course, beginning in 1654.[26]
John Hammond, in a 1656 tract defending the tobacco colonies, wrote
that servant women were not put to work in the fields but in domestic
employments, "yet som wenches that are nasty, and beastly and not fit
to be so imployed are put into the ground."[27] Since all Negro women
were taxed as working in the fields, it would seem logical to conclude
that Virginians found them "nasty" and "beastly." The essentially racial
nature of this discrimination was bared by a 1668 law at the time slavery
was crystallizing on the statute books:

> Whereas some doubts, have arisen whether negro women set free
> were still to be accompted tithable according to a former act, *It is
> declared by this grand assembly* that negro women, though permitted
> to enjoy their ffreedome yet ought not in all respects to be admitted
> to a full fruition of the exemptions and impunities of the English, and
> are still lyable to payment of taxes.[28]

Virginia law set Negroes apart in a second way by denying them
the important right and obligation to bear arms. Few restraints could
indicate more clearly the denial to Negroes of membership in the white
community. This action, in a sense the first foreshadowing of the slave
codes, came in 1640, at just the time when other indications first appear
that Negroes were subject to special treatment.[29]

Finally, an even more compelling sense of the separateness of
Negroes was revealed in early distress concerning sexual union
between the races. In 1630 a Virginia court pronounced a now famous
sentence: "Hugh Davis to be soundly whipped, before an assembly
of Negroes and others for abusing himself to the dishonor of God
and shame of Christians, by defiling his body in lying with a negro."[30]
While there were other instances of punishment for interracial
union in the ensuing years, fornication rather than miscegenation
may well have been the primary offense, though in 1651 a Maryland
man sued someone who he claimed had said "that he had a black
bastard in Virginia."[31] There may have been nothing racial about the
1640 case by which Robert Sweet was compelled "to do penance in
church according to laws of England, for getting a negroe woman with
child and the woman whipt."[32] About 1650 a white man and a Negro

woman were required to stand clad in white sheets before a congregation in Lower Norfolk County for having had relations, but this punishment was sometimes used in ordinary cases of fornication between two whites.[33]

It is certain, however, that in the early 1660's when slavery was gaining statutory recognition, the colonial assemblies legislated with feeling against miscegenation. Nor was this merely a matter of avoiding confusion of status, as was suggested by the Handlins. In 1662 Virginia declared that "if any Christian shall commit ffornication with a negro man or woman, hee or shee soe offending" should pay double the usual fine. Two years later Maryland prohibited interracial marriages:

> forasmuch as divers freeborne English women forgettfull of their free Condicön and to the disgrace of our Nation doe intermarry with Negro Slaves by which alsoe divers suites may arise touching the Issue of such woemen and a great damage doth befall the Masters of such Negros for prevention whereof for deterring such freeborne women from such shamefull Matches. . . ,

strong language indeed if the problem had only been confusion of status. A Maryland act of 1681 described marriages of white women with Negroes as, among other things, "always to the Satisfaccön of theire Lascivious & Lustfull desires, & to the disgrace not only of the English butt allso of many other Christian Nations." When Virginia finally prohibited all interracial liaisons in 1691, the assembly vigorously denounced miscegenation and its fruits as "that abominable mixture and spurious issue."[34]

One is confronted, then, with the fact that the first evidences of enslavement and of other forms of debasement appeared at about the same time. Such coincidence comports poorly with both views on the causation of prejudice and slavery. If slavery caused prejudice, then invidious distinctions concerning working in the fields, bearing arms, and sexual union should have appeared only after slavery's firm establishment. If prejudice caused slavery, then one would expect to find such lesser discriminations preceding the greater discrimination of outright enslavement.

Perhaps a third explanation of the relationship between slavery and prejudice may be offered, one that might fit the pattern of events as revealed by existing evidence. Both current views share a common starting point: They predicate two factors, prejudice and slavery, and demand a distinct order of causality. No matter how qualified by recognition that the effect may in turn react upon the cause, each approach inevitably tends to deny the validity of its opposite. But what if one were to regard both slavery and prejudice as species of a general debasement of the Negro? Both may have been equally cause and effect, constantly reacting upon each other, dynamically joining hands to hustle the Negro down the road to complete degradation. Mutual causation is, of course, a highly useful concept for describing social situations in the modern world.[35] Indeed it has been widely applied in only slightly altered fashion to the current racial situation: Racial prejudice and the Negro's lowly position are widely accepted as constantly reinforcing each other.

This way of looking at the facts might well fit better with what we know of slavery itself. Slavery was an organized pattern of human relationships. No matter what the law might say, it was of different character than cattle ownership. No matter how degrading, slavery involved human beings. No one seriously pretended otherwise. Slavery was not an isolated economic or institutional phenomenon; it was the practical facet of a general debasement without which slavery could have no rationality. (Prejudice, too, was a form of debasement, a kind of slavery in the mind.) Certainly the urgent need for labor in a virgin country guided the direction which debasement took, molded it, in fact, into an institutional framework. That economic practicalities shaped the external form of debasement should not tempt one to forget, however, that slavery was at bottom a social arrangement, a way of society's ordering its members in its own mind.

Notes

1. "About the last of August came in a dutch man of warre that sold us twenty Negars." Smith was quoting John Rolfe's account. Edward Arber and A. G. Bradley (eds.), *Travels and Works of Captain John Smith . . .* (2 vols., Edinburgh, 1910), II, 541.
2. Philip A. Bruce, *Economic History of Virginia in the Seventeen th Century* (2 vols., New York, 1896), II, 57–130; James C. Ballagh, *A History of Slavery in Virginia* (Baltimore, 1902), 28–35.
3. John H. Russell, *The Free Negro in Virginia, 1619–1865* (Baltimore, 1913), 29.
4. *Ibid.*, 23–39; Ulrich B. Phillips, *American Negro Slavery* (New York, 1918), 75–77, and *Life and Labor in the Old South* (Boston, 1929), 170; Helen T. Catterall (ed.), *Judicial Cases Concerning American Slavery and the Negro* (5 vols., Washington. 1926–1937), I, 54–55, 57–63; James M. Wright, *The Free Negro* in *Maryland, 1634–1860* (New York, 1921), 21–23; Susie M. Ames, *Studies of the Virginia Eastern Shore in the Seventeenth Century* (Richmond, 1940), 100–106. See also T. R. Davis, "Negro Servitude in the United States," *Journal of Negro History,* VIII (July 1923), 247–83, and Edgar T. Thompson, "The Natural History of Agricultural Labor in the South" in David K. Jackson

(ed.), *American Studies in Honor of William Kenneth Boyd* (Durham. N.C., 1940), 127–46.

5. Phillips, *American Negro Slavery*, viii.

6. Wesley F. Craven, *The Southern Colonies in the Seventeenth Century, 1607–1689* (Baton Rouge, 1949), 217–19, 402–403.

7. *William and Mary Quarterly*, s. 3, VII (April 1650), 199–222.

8. Kenneth M. Stampp, *The Peculiar Institution: Slavery* in *the Ante-Bellum South* (New York, 1956), vii-viii. 3–33.

9. *Ibid.*, 21–22.

10. Arnold Rose, "The Roots of Prejudice" in UNESCO, *The Race Question in Modern Science* (New York, 1956), 224. For examples of the more general view see Frederick G. Detweiler, "The Rise of Modern Race Antagonisms," *American Journal of Sociology*, XXXVII (March 1932), 743; M. F. Ashley Montagu, *Man's Most Dangerous Myth: The Fallacy of Race* (New York, 1945),10–11, 19–20; Gunnar Myrdal, *An American Dilemma: The Negro Problem and Modern Democracy* (New York, 1944), 83–89, 97; Paul Kecskemeti, "The Psychological Theory of Prejudice: Does it Underrate the Role of Social History?" *Commentary*, XVIII (October 1954), 364–66.

11. *Comparative Studies in Society and History*, II (October 1959), 49–66. See also Degler, *Out of Our Past: The Forces that shaped Modern America*, (New York, 1959), 26–39.

12. H. R. Mcllwaine (ed.), *Minutes of the Council and General Court of Colonial Virginia, 1622–1632, 1670–1676* (Richmond, 1924), 196. See the lists and musters of 1624 and 1625 in John C. Hotten (ed.), *The Original Lists of Persons of Quality . . .* (New York, 1880), 169–265.

13. "The status of Negroes was that of servants; and so they were identified and treated down to the 1660s' ("Origins" 203) The footnote to this statement reads, 'For disciplinary and revenue laws in Virginia that did not discriminate Negroes from other servants, see Hening, *Statutes*, I, 174 198 200 243 306 (1631–1645)." But pp 200 and 243 of William Waller Hening (ed.) *The Statutes at Large; Being a Collection of All the Laws of Virginia* (2nd ed. of vols. 1–4, New York, 1823), I, in fact contain nothing about either servants or Negroes, while a tax provision on p. 242 specifically discriminates against Negro women. The revenue act on p. 306 lists the number of pounds of tobacco levied on land, cattle, sheep, horses, etc., and on tithable persons and provides for collection of lists of the above so that the colony can compute its tax program; nothing else is said of servants and tithables. To say, as the Handlins did in the same note, that Negroes, English servants, and horses, etc., were listed all together in some early Virginia wills, with the implication that Negroes and English servants were regarded as alike in status, is hardly correct unless one is to assume that the horses were sharing this status as well. (For complete bibliographical information on Hening [ed.], *Statutes*, see E. C. Swem, *Virginia Historical Index* [2 vols., Roanoke, Va., 1934–1936], I, xv–xvi.)

14. Latin-American Negroes did not lose all civil and personal rights, did not become mere chattels, yet we speak of "slavery" in Latin America without hesitation See Frank Tannenbaum, *Slave and Citizen: The Negro in the Americas* (New York, 1947), and Gilberto Freyre, *The Masters and the Slaves: A Study in the Development of Brazilian Civilization* (New York, 1946)

15 "Decisions of the General Court," *Virginia Magazine of History and Biography*, V (January 1898), 236. Abbot Emerson Smith in the standard work on servitude in America, *Colonists in Bondage. White Servitude and Convict Labor in America, 1607–1776* (Chapel Hill, 1947), 171, says that "there was never any such thing as perpetual slavery for any white man in any English colony." There were instances in the seventeenth century of white men sold into "slavery," but this was when the meaning of the term was still indefinite and often equated with servitude.

16. "Decisions of the General Court," 236–37.

17. *A Perfect Description of Virginia* . . . (London, 1649), reprinted in Peter Force (ed.), *Tracts* . . . (4 vols., Washington, 1836–1846), II.

18. These four cases may be found in Northampton County Deeds, Wills &c. (Virginia State Library, Richmond), No. 4 (1651–1654), 28 (misnumbered 29), 124; *Archives of Maryland* (69 vols., Baltimore, 1883–1961), XLI, 261–62; York County Records (Virginia State Library), No. 2 (transcribed Wills & Deeds, 1645–1649), 256–57.

19. Lancaster County Loose Papers (Virginia State Library), Box of Wills, 1650–1719, Folder 1658–1659.

20. For examples running for as long as thirty-five years, see *William and Mary Quarterly*, s. 1, XX (October 1911), 148; Russell, *Free Negro in Virginia*, 26–27; Ames, *Eastern Shore*, 105. Compare the cases of a Negro and an Irish servant in *Calendar of Virginia State Papers* . . . (11 vols., Richmond, 1875-1893), I, 9–10, and *Maryland Archives*, XLI. 476–78; XLIX, 123–24.

21. Russell, *Free Negro in Virginia*, 24-41. See especially the cases in *Virginia Magazine of History and Biography*, V (July 1897), 40; York County Deeds, Wills, Orders, etc. (Virginia State Library), No. 1 (1633–1657, 1691–1694), 338–39.

22. John H. Russell, "Colored Freemen As Slave Owners in Virginia," *Journal of Negro History*, I (July 1916), 234–37.

23. York County Records, No. 2, 63; Northampton County Orders, Deeds, Wills, &c., No. 2 (1640–1645), 224; York County Deeds, Orders, Wills, &c. (1657–1662), 108–109.

24. York County Records, No. 2, 390.

25. Apparently Calvert's deal with Skinner was never consummated. *Maryland Archives*, IV, vii, 189, 320–21. For prices of white servants see *ibid.*, IV, 31, 47–48, 74, 78–79, 81, 83, 92, 98, 108–109, 184, 200, 319.

26. Hening (ed.), *Statutes*, I, 144, 242, 292, 454. The Handlins erroneously placed the "first sign of discrimination" in this matter at 1668 ("Origins," 217 *n*). For Maryland, see *Maryland Archives*, I, 342, II, 136, 399, 538–39; XIII, 538–39.

27. John Hammond, *Leah and Rachel, or, the Two Fruitfull Sisters Virginia, and Mary-land: Their Present Condition, Impartially Stated and Related* . . . (London, 1656), reprinted in Force (ed.), *Tracts*, II.

28. Hening (ed.), *Statutes*, II, 267. The distinction between white and colored women was neatly described at the turn of the century by Robert Beverley, *The History and Present State of Virginia*, Louis B. Wright, ed. (Chapel Hill, 1947), 271–72.

29. Hening (ed.), *Statutes*, I, 226, and for the same act in more detail see *William and Mary Quarterly*, s. 2, IV (July 1924), 147. The Handlins discounted this law: "Until the 1660's the statutes on the Negroes were not at all unique. Nor

did they add up to a decided trend." ("Origins," 209.) The note added to this statement reads, "That there was no trend is evident from the fluctuations in naming Negroes slaves or servants and in their right to bear arms. See Hening, *Statutes*, I, 226, 258, 292, 540; Bruce, *Institutional History*, II, 5 ff., 199 ff. For similar fluctuations with regard to Indians, see Hening, *Statutes*, I, 391, 518." But since the terms "servants" and "slaves" did not have precise meaning, as the Handlins themselves asserted, fluctuations in naming Negroes one or the other can not be taken to mean that their status itself was fluctuating. Of the pages cited in Hening, p. 258 is an act encouraging Dutch traders and contains nothing about Negroes, servants, slaves, or arms. Page 292 is an act providing that fifteen tithable persons should support one soldier; Negroes were among those tithable, but nothing was said of allowing them to arm. Page 540 refers to "any negro slaves'" and "said negro," but mentions nothing about servants or arms. In the pages dealing with Indians, p. 391 provides that no one is to employ Indian servants with guns, and p. 518 that Indians (not "Indian servants") are to be allowed to use their own guns; the two provisions are not contradictory. Philip A. Bruce, *Institutional History of Virginia in the Seventeenth Century* (2 vols., New York, 1910). II, 5 ff., indicates that Negroes were barred from arming in 1639 and offers no suggestion that there was any later fluctuation in this practice.

30. Hening (ed.), *Statutes*, I, 146. "Christianity" appears instead of "Christians" in McIlwaine (ed.), *Minutes of the Council*, 479.

31. *Maryland Archives*, X, 114–15.

32. Hening (ed.), *Statutes*, I, 552; McIlwaine, *Minutes of the Council*, 477.

33. Bruce, *Economic History of Virginia*, II, 110.

34. Hening (ed.), *Statutes*, II. 170; III, 86–87; *Maryland Archives*, I, 533–34; VII, 204. Opinion on this matter apparently was not unanimous, for a petition of several citizens to the Council in 1699 asked repeal of the intermarriage prohibition. H. R. McIlwaine (ed.), *Legislative Journals of the Council of Colonial Virginia* (3 vols., Richmond, 1918–1919), I, 262. The Handlins wrote ("Origins," 215), "Mixed marriages of free men and servants were particularly frowned upon as complicating status and therefore limited by law." Their citation for this, Hening (ed.), *Statutes*, II, 114 (1661/62), and Marcus W. Jernegan, *Laboring and Dependent Classes in Colonial America, 1607–1783* (Chicago, 1931), 55, 180, gives little backing to the statement. In Virginia secret marriage or bastardy between whites of different status got the same punishment as such between whites of the same status. A white servant might marry any white if his master consented. See Hening (ed.), *Statutes*, 1, 252–53, 438–39; II, 114–15, 167; III, 71–75, 137–40. See also James C Ballagh, *White Servitude in the Colony of Virginia* (Baltimore, 1895), 50. For Maryland, see *Maryland Archives*, I, 73, 373–74 , 441–42; II, 396–97; XIII, 501–502. The Handlins also suggested that in the 1691 Virginia law, "spurious" meant simply "illegitimate," and they cited Arthur W. Calhoun, *A Social History of the American Family from Colonial Times to the Present* (3 vols., Cleveland, O., 1917–1919), I, 42, which turns out to be one quotation from John Milton. However, "spurious" was used in colonial laws with reference only to unions between white and black, and never in bastardy laws involving whites only. Mulattoes were often labeled "spurious" offspring.

35. For example, George C. Homans, *The Human Group* (New York, 1950).

The following selection offers Ulrich B. Phillips' "benign" view of slavery, a view mentioned by Jordan in the last essay In these pages, Phillips refers to the plantation as a homestead, a school, even a "chapel of ease."

It is writing such as Phillips' that has given the impression that, bad as slavery must have been, there were many benefits accruing to those who had previously lived in the "Dark Continent." Increasingly, hard evidence is being found that belies such claims in regard to both the "benefits" of slavery and the "backwardness" of Africa.

7

Slavery in the Old South

Ulrich Bonnell Phillips

The simplicity of the social structure on the plantations facilitated Negro adjustment, the master taking the place of the accustomed chief.[1] And yet these black voyagers experienced a greater change by far than befell white immigrants. In their home lands they had lived naked, observed fetish, been bound by tribal law, and practiced primitive crafts. In America none of these things were of service or sanction. The Africans were thralls, wanted only for their brawn, required to take things as they found them and to do as they were told, coerced into self-obliterating humility, and encouraged to respond only to the teachings and preachings of their masters, and adapt themselves to the white men's ways.

In some cases transported talent embraced the new opportunity in extraordinary degree. . . . But in general, as always, the common middle course was passive acquiescence.

From *Life and Labor in the Old South* by Ulrich Bonnell Phillips, Boston: Little, Brown, 1929, pp. 194–217, by permission of Little, Brown and Company. Copyright 1929 by Little, Brown, Copyright © 1957 by Mrs. Ulrich B. Phillips.

To make adaptation the more certain, it was argued that "no Negro should be bought old; such are always sullen and unteachable, and frequently put an end to their lives."[2] And indeed planters who could afford an unproductive period were advised to select young children from the ships, "for their juvenile minds entertain no regrets for the loss of their connections. They acquire the English language with great ease, and improve daily in size, understanding and capacity for labour."[3] The proportion of children in the cargoes was great enough to permit such a policy by those who might adopt it.[4] But the fact that prices for imported Negroes, even after seasoning, ranged lower than for those to the American manner born is an evidence that the new habituation as a rule never completely superseded the old. Thanks, however, to plantation discipline and to the necessity of learning the master's language if merely to converse with fellow slaves of different linguistic stocks, African mental furnishings faded even among adult arrivals.

To the second and later generations folklore was transmitted, but for the sake of comprehension by the children an American Brer Rabbit replaced his jungle prototype. If lullabies were crooned in African phrase their memory soon lapsed, along with nearly all other African terms except a few personal names, Quash, Cuffee, Cudjoe and the like.[5] And even these may have owed such perpetuation as they had to the persistence of the maritime slave trade which long continued to bring new Quashes and Cuffees from the mother country. In short, Foulahs and Fantyns, Eboes and Angolas begat American plantation Negroes to whom a spear would be strange but a "languid hoe" familiar, the tomtom forgotten but the banjo inviting to the fingers and the thumb. Eventually it could be said that the Negroes had no memories of Africa as a home.[6] Eventually, indeed, a Virginia freedman wrote after thirteen years of residence in Liberia, "I, being a Virginian," rejoice that "the good people of my old state are about to settle a colony on the coast of Africa"; and went on to say of himself and his compatriots, "there is some of us that would not be satisfied in no other colony while ever there was one called New Virginia."[7] His very name, William Draper, is an index of his Anglo-Americanization; and a pride which he expresses that Virginia Negroes have been the founders and the chief rulers "of almost all the settlements" in Liberia proves him a true son of the Old Dominion, "the mother of states and of statesmen." But William Draper was an exceptional specimen. In the main the American Negroes ruled not even themselves. They were more or less contentedly slaves, with grievances from time to time but not ambition. With "hazy pasts and rackless futures," they lived in each moment as it flew, and left "Old Massa" to take such thought as the morrow might need.

The plantation force was a conscript army, living in barracks and on constant "fatigue." Husbands and wives were comrades in service under an authority as complete as the commanding personnel could wish. The master was captain and quartermaster combined, issuing orders and distributing rations. The overseer and the foreman, where there were such, were lieutenant and sergeant to see that orders were executed. The field hands were privates with no choice but to obey unless, like other seasoned soldiers, they could dodge the duties assigned.

But the plantation was also a homestead, isolated, permanent and peopled by a social group with a common interest in achieving and maintaining social order. Its régime was shaped by the customary human forces, interchange of ideas and coadaptation of conduct. The intermingling of white and black children in their pastimes was no more continuous or influential than the adult interplay of command and response, of protest and concession. In so far as harmony was attained—and in this the plantation mistress was a great if quiet factor—a common tradition was evolved embodying reciprocal patterns of conventional conduct.

The plantation was of course a factory, in which robust laborers were essential to profits. Its mere maintenance as a going concern required the proprietor to sustain the strength and safeguard the health of his operatives and of their children, who were also his, destined in time to take their parents' places. The basic food allowance came to be somewhat standardized at a quart of corn meal and half a pound of salt pork per day for each adult and proportionally for children, commuted or supplemented with sweet potatoes, field peas, sirup, rice, fruit and "garden sass" as locality and season might suggest. The clothing was coarse, and shoes were furnished only for winter. The housing was in huts of one or two rooms per family, commonly crude but weathertight. Fuel was abundant. The sanitation of the clustered cabins was usually a matter of systematic attention; and medical service was at least commensurate with the groping science of the time and the sparse population of the country. Many of the larger plantations had central kitchens, day nurseries, infirmaries and physicians on contract for periodic visits.[8] The aged and infirm must be cared for along with the young and able-bodied, to maintain the good will of their kinsmen among the workers, if for no other reason. Morale was no less needed than muscle if performance were to be kept above a barely tolerable minimum.

The plantation was a school. An intelligent master would consult his own interest by affording every talented slave special instruction and by inculcating into the commoner sort as much routine efficiency, regularity and responsibility as they would accept. Not only were many youths given training in the crafts, and many taught to read and write, even though the laws forbade it, but a goodly number of planters devised and applied plans to give their whole corps spontaneous incentive to relieve the need of detailed supervision. . . .

The civilizing of the Negroes was not merely a consequence of definite schooling but a fruit of plantation life itself. The white household taught perhaps less by precept than by example. It had much the effect of a "social settlement" in a modern city slum, furnishing models of speech and conduct, along with advice on occasion, which the vicinage is invited to accept. . . . The bulk of the black personnel was notoriously primitive, uncouth, improvident and inconstant, merely because they were Negroes of the time; and by their slave status they were relieved from the pressure of want and debarred from any full-force incentive of gain.

Many planters, however, sought to promote contentment, loyalty and zeal by gifts and rewards, and by sanctioning the keeping of poultry and pigs and the cultivation of little fields in off times with the privilege of selling any produce. In the cotton belt the growing of nankeen cotton was particularly encouraged, for its brownish color would betray any surreptitious addition from the master's own fields. Some indeed had definite bonus systems. A. H. Bernard of Virginia determined at the close of 1836 to replace his overseer with a slave foreman, and announced to his Negroes that in case of good service by the corps he would thereafter distribute premiums to the amount of what had been the overseer's wages. . . .

But any copious resort to profit-sharing schemes was avoided at large as being likely to cost more than it would yield in increment to the planter's own crop. The generality of planters, it would seem, considered it hopeless to make their field hands into thorough workmen or full-fledged men, and contented themselves with very moderate achievement. Tiring of endless correction and unfruitful exhortation, they relied somewhat supinely upon authority with a tone of kindly patronage and a baffled acquiescence in slack service. . . .

It has been said by a critic of the twentieth-century South: "In some ways the negro is shamefully mistreated—mistreated through leniency," which permits him as a tenant or employee to lean upon the whites in a continuous mental siesta and sponge upon them habitually, instead of requiring him to stand upon his own moral and economic legs.[9] The same censure would apply as truly in any preceding generation. The slave plantation, like other schools, was conditioned by the nature and habituations of its teachers and pupils.

Its instruction was inevitably slow; and the effect of its discipline was restricted by the fact that even its aptest pupils had no diploma in prospect which would send them forth to fend for themselves.

The plantation was a parish, or perhaps a chapel of ease. Some planters assumed the functions of lay readers when ordained ministers were not available, or joined the congregation even when Negro preachers preached.[10] Bishop Leonidas Polk was chief chaplain on his own estate, and is said to have suffered none of his slaves to be other than Episcopalian;[11] but the generality of masters gave full freedom as to church connection.

The legislature of Barbados, when urged by the governor in 1681 to promote the Christianization of slaves on that island, replied, "their savage brutishness renders them wholly incapable. Many have endeavored it without success."[12] But on the continent such sentiments had small echo; and as decades passed masters and churches concerned themselves increasingly in the premises. A black preacher might meet rebuke and even run a risk of being lynched if he harped too loudly upon the liberation of the Hebrews from Egyptian bondage;[13] but a moderate supervision would prevent such indiscretions. The Sermon on the Mount would be harmless despite its suggestion of an earthly inheritance for the meek; the Decalogue was utterly sound; and "servants obey your masters," "render unto Caesar the things that are Caesar's," and "well done, thou good and faithful servant" were invaluable texts for homilies. The Methodists and Baptists were inclined to invite ecstasy from free and slave alike. Episcopalians and Presbyterians, and the Catholics likewise, deprecating exuberance, dealt rather in quiet precept than in fervid exhortation—with far smaller statistical results.[14]

The plantation was a pageant and a variety show in alternation. The procession of plowmen at evening, slouched crosswise on their mules; the dance in the new sugarhouse, preceded by prayer; the bonfire in the quarter with contests in clogs, cakewalks and Charlestons whose fascinations were as yet undiscovered by the great world; the work songs in solo and refrain, with not too fast a rhythm; the baptizing in the creek, with lively demonstrations from the "sisters" as they came dripping out; the torchlight pursuit of 'possum and 'coon, with full-voiced halloo to baying houn' dawg and yelping cur; the rabbit hunt, the log-rolling, the house-raising, the husking bee, the quilting party, the wedding, the cock fight, the crap game, the children's play, all punctuated plantation life—and most of them were highly vocal.[15] A funeral now and then of some prominent slave

121

would bring festive sorrowing, or the death of a beloved master an outburst of emotion.[16]

The plantation was a matrimonial bureau, something of a harem perhaps, a copious nursery, and a divorce court. John Brickell wrote of colonial North Carolina: "It frequently happens, when these women have no Children by the first Husband, after being a year or two cohabiting together, the Planters oblige them to take a second, third, fourth, fifth, or more Husbands or Bedfellows; a fruitful Woman amongst them being very much valued by the Planters, and a numerous Issue esteemed the greatest Riches in this Country."[17] By running on to five or more husbands for a constantly barren woman Brickell discredits his own statement. Yet it may have had a kernel of truth, and it is quite possible that something of such a policy persisted throughout the generations. These things do not readily get into the records. I have myself heard a stalwart Negro express a humorous regret that he was free, for said he in substance: "If I had lived in slavery times my master would have given me half a dozen wives and taken care of all the children." This may perhaps voice a tradition among slave descendants, and the tradition may in turn derive from an actual sanction of polygamy by some of the masters. A planter doubtless described a practice not unique when he said "that he interfered as little as possible with their domestic habits except in matters of police. 'We don't care what they do when their tasks are over—we lose sight of them till next day. Their morals and manners are in their own keeping. The men may have, for instance, as many wives as they please, so long as they do not quarrel about such matters.'"[18] But another was surely no less representative when he instructed his overseer: "Marriages shall be performed in every instance of a nuptial contract, and the parties settled off to themselves without encumbering other houses to give discontent. No slave shall be allowed to cohabit with two or more wives or husbands at the same time; doing so shall subject them to a strict trial and severe punishment."[19]

Life was without doubt monogamous in general; and some of the matings were by order,[20] though the generality were pretty surely spontaneous. . . .

In the number of their children the Negro women rivaled the remarkable fecundity of their mistresses. One phenomenal slave mother bore forty-one children, mostly of course as twins;[21] and the records of many others ran well above a dozen each. As a rule, perhaps, babies were even more welcome to slave women than to free; for childbearing brought lightened work during pregnancy and suckling, and a lack of ambition conspired with a freedom from economic anxiety to clear the path of maternal impulse.

Concubinage of Negro women to planters and their sons and overseers is evidenced by the census enumeration of mulattoes and by other data.[22] It was flagrantly prevalent in the Creole section of Louisiana, and was at least sporadic from New England to Texas. The régime of slavery facilitated concubinage not merely by making black women subject to white men's wills but by promoting intimacy and weakening racial antipathy. The children, of whatever shade or paternity, were alike the property of the mother's owner and were nourished on the plantation. Not a few mulattoes, however, were manumitted by their fathers and vested with property.

Slave marriages, not being legal contracts, might be dissolved without recourse to public tribunals. Only the master's consent was required, and this was doubtless not hard to get. On one plantation systematic provision was made in the standing regulations; "When sufficient cause can be shewn on either side, a marriage may be annulled; but the offending party must be severely punished. Where both are in the wrong, both must be punished, and if they insist on separating must have a hundred lashes apiece. After such a separation, neither can marry again for three years."[23] If such a system were in general effect in our time it would lessen the volume of divorce in American society. But it may be presumed that most plantation rules were not so stringent.

The home of a planter or of a well-to-do townsman was likely to be a "magnificent negro boarding-house," at which and from which an indefinite number of servants and their dependents and friends were fed.[24] In town the tribe might increase to the point of embarrassment....

Each plantation had a hierarchy. Not only were the master and his family exalted to a degree beyond the reach of slave aspiration, but among the Negroes themselves there were pronounced gradations of rank, privilege and esteem. An absent master wrote: "I wish to be remembered to all the servants, distinguishing Andrew as the head man and Katy as the mother of the tribe. Not forgetting Charlotte as the head of the culinary department nor Marcus as the Tubal Cain of the community, hoping that they will continue to set a good example and that the young ones will walk in their footsteps."[25] The foreman, the miller and the smith were men of position and pride. The butler, the maid and the children's nurse were in continuous contact with the white household, enjoying the best opportunity to acquire its manners along with its discarded clothing. The field hands were at the foot of the scale, with a minimum of white contact and privileged only to plod, so to say, as brethren to the ox.

At all times in the South as a whole perhaps half of the slaves were owned or hired in units of twenty or less, which were too small for the full plantation order, and perhaps half of this half were on mere farms or in town employment, rather as "help" than as a distinct laboring force. Many small planters' sons and virtually all the farmers in person worked alongside any field hands they might possess; and indoor tasks were parceled among the women and girls white and black. . . .

However the case may have been as to relative severity on farms and plantations, there can be no doubt that the farmers' slaves of all sorts were likely to share somewhat intimately such lives as their masters led[26] and to appropriate a considerable part of such culture as they possessed—to be more or less genteel with their gentility or crude with their crudity, to think similar thoughts and speak much the same language. On the other hand, the one instance of wide divergence in dialect between the whites and the Negroes prevailed in the single district in which the scheme of life was that of large plantations from the time when Africans were copiously imported. On the seaboard of South Carolina and Georgia most of the blacks (and they were very black) still speak Gullah, a dialect so distinct that unfamiliar visitors may barely understand it. And dialect, there as elsewhere, is an index to culture in general.

The life of slaves, whether in large groups or small, was not without grievous episodes. A planter's son wrote to his father upon a discovery of mislaid equipment: "The bridle and martingal which you whipped Amy so much for stealing was by some inattention of Robert's left in Mr. Clark's stable." Again, an overseer, exasperated by the sluggishness of his cook, set her to field work as discipline, only to have her demonstrate by dying that her protestations of illness had been true.

Grievances reinforced ennui to promote slacking, absence without leave, desertion and mutiny The advertising columns of the newspapers bristled with notices of runaways; and no detailed plantation record which has come to my hand is without mention of them. . . .

Certain slaves were persistent absconders, and the chronic discontent of others created special problems for their masters. . . .

By one means or another good will and affection were often evoked. When his crop was beset with grass and the work strenuous, a Mississippian wrote of his corps as being "true as steel."[27] A Georgian after escaping shipwreck on his way to Congress in 1794 wrote: "I have ever since been thinking of an expression of Old

Qua's in Savannah a few days before I sailed. The rascal had the impudence to tell me to stay at home & not fret myself about Publick —'What Publick care for you, Massa? God! ye get drowned bye & bye, Qua tell you so, and what going come of he Family den?' "[28] An Alabama preacher while defending slavery as divinely ordained said of the Negro: "He is of all races the most gentle and kind. The *man*, the most submissive; the *woman*, the most affectionate. What other slaves would love their masters better than themselves?"[29] And a British traveler wrote from his observation of slaves and masters; "There is an hereditary regard and often attachment on both sides, more like that formerly existing between lords and their retainers in the old feudal times of Europe, than anything now to be found in America."[30]

On some estates the whip was as regularly in evidence as the spur on a horseman's heel.[31] That cruelties occurred is never to be denied. Mrs. Stowe exploited them in *Uncle Tom's Cabin* and validated her implications to her own satisfaction in its *Key*. Theodore D. Weld had already assembled a thousand more or less authentic instances of whippings and fetters, of croppings and brandings, of bloodhound pursuits and the break-up of families.[32] Manuscript discoveries continue to swell the record. . . .

Most of the travelers who sought evidence of asperity in the plantation realm found it as a rule not before their eyes but beyond the horizon. Charles Eliot Norton while at Charleston in 1855 wrote home to Boston. "The slaves do not go about looking unhappy, and are with difficulty, I fancy, persuaded to feel so. Whips and chains, oaths and brutality, are as common, for all that one sees, in the free as the slave states. We have come thus far, and might have gone ten times as far, I dare say, without seeing the first sign of Negro misery or white tyranny."[33] Andrew P. Peabody wrote of the slaves of his host at Savannah: "They were well lodged and fed, and could have been worked no harder than was necessary for exercise and digestion."[34] Louis F. Tasistro remarked of the slaves on a plantation at the old battle field below New Orleans: "To say that they are underworked and overfed, and far happier than the labourers of Great Britain would hardly convey a sufficiently clear notion of their actual condition. They put me much more in mind of a community of grown-up children, spoiled by too much kindness, than a body of dependants, much less a company of slaves."[35] Frederika Bremer had virtually nothing but praise for the slave quarters which she visited or their savory food which she tasted.[36] Welby, Faux, Lyell, Basil Hall, Marshall Hall, Robert Russell, William Bussell, Olmsted[37] and sundry others concur in their surprise at finding slavery unsevere, though some of them kept seeking evidence to the contrary without avail.

The surprise was justified, for tradition in the outer world ran squarely opposite. And the tradition was reasonable. Slavery had been erected as a crass exploitation, and the laws were as stringent as ever. No prophet in early times could have told that kindliness would grow as a flower from a soil so foul, that slaves would come to be cherished not only as property of high value but as loving if lowly friends.[38] But this unexpected change occurred in so many cases as to make benignity somewhat a matter of course. To those habituated it became no longer surprising for a planter to say that no man deserved a Coromantee who would not treat him rather as a friend than as a slave;[39] for another to give his "people" a holiday out of season because "the drouth seems to have afflicted them, and a play day may raise their spirits";[40] or for a third to give one of his hands an occasional week-end with a dollar or two each time to visit his wife in another county,[41] and send two others away for some weeks at hot springs for the relief of their rheumatism.[42]

The esteem in epitaphs, whether inscribed in diaries or on stone, was without doubt earned by their subjects and genuinely felt by their composers. . . .

On the other hand slaves in large numbers were detached from their masters, whether by sale, by lease to employers or by hire to themselves. The personal equation was often a factor in such transactions. Some slaves were sold as punishment, for effect upon the morale of their fellows. On the other hand some whose sales were impelled by financial stress were commissioned by their masters to find buyers of their own choice; some purchases were prompted by a belief that the new management would prove more congenial and fruitful than the old;[43] and still more transfers were made to unite in ownership couples who desired union in marriage.

In the hiring of slaves likewise the personal equation often bulked large, for the owner's desire for a maximum wage was modified by his concern for assured maintenance of physique and morale, and the lessee on his part wanted assurance from the slave of willing service or of acquiescence at least.[44] The hiring of slaves to the slaves themselves was a grant of industrial freedom at a wage. It was an admission that the slave concerned could produce more in self-direction than when under routine control, a virtual admission that for him slavery had no industrial justification. In many cases it was a probationary period, ended by self-purchase with earnings accumulated above the wages he had currently paid his owner.

Slave hiring and self-hire were more characteristic of town than of country. Indeed urban conditions merely tolerated slavery, never promoted it. And urban slaveholders were not complete masters, for slavery in full form required a segregation to make the master in effect a magistrate. A townsman's human chattels could not be his subjects, for he had no domain for them to inhabit. When a slave ran an errand upon the street he came under the eye of public rather than private authority; and if he were embroiled by chance in altercation with another slave the two masters were likely to find themselves champions of opposing causes in court, or partisans even against the constables, with no power in themselves either to make or apply the law.[45]

Town slaves in a sense rubbed elbows with every one, high and low, competed with free labor, white and black, and took tone more or less from all and sundry. The social hierarchy was more elaborate than on the plantations, the scheme of life more complex, and the variety wider in attainment and attitude. The obsequious grandiloquence of a barber contrasted with the caustic fluency of a fishwife. But even the city chain gang was likely to be melodious, for its members were Negroes at one or two removes from the plantation. All in all, the slave regime was a curious blend of force and concession, of arbitrary disposal by the master and self-direction by the slave, of tyranny and benevolence, of antipathy and affection.

Notes

1. *Cf.* N. S. Shaler, "The Nature of the Negro," in the *Arena*, III, 28.
2. *Gentleman's Magazine*, XXXIV, 487 (London, 1764).
3. *Practical Rules*, reprinted in *Plantation and Frontier Documents*, II, 133.
4. For example there were 102 below ten years of age among the 704 slaves brought by five ships to South Carolina between July and October, 1724.— British transcripts in the South Carolina archives, XI, 243.
5. A table of the names most common among imported Negroes, which were derived from the days of the week, is printed in Long's *Jamaica*, II, 427.
6. Charleston *Courier*, July 8, 1855.
7. Letter of William Draper, Bassa Cove, Liberia, August 17, 1837, to William Maxwell, Norfolk, Va. T. C. Thornton, *An Inquiry into the History of Slavery* (Washington, 1841), 272.
8. For example, James Hamilton, Jr., while Congressman from South Carolina, engaged Dr. Furth of Savannah to make visits on schedule to his plantation a few miles away. In 1828 he wrote from Washington to his factor at Savannah: "I have just received a letter from Mr. Prioleau, informing me that the eyes of my old and faithful Servant Peter were in a perilous condition. I will [thank] you to request Dr Furth to attend to them promptly and effectually... I will thank you to supply for my Hospital on his requisition all that may be necessary *in his opinion* to make my negroes comfortable when they are sick. I will thank you to request him to drop me a line occasionally of the

health of my people and the success of the reform I propose thro him to institute in attention to the sick. . . . Be so good as to give to Peter the value of a couple of Dollars monthly for comforts to his family." Manuscript in private possession.

On rations, quarters, work schedules and the like see [Ebenezer Starnes] *The Slave-holder Abroad* (Philadelphia, 1860), appendix; *DeBow's Review*, VIII, 381, X, 621, XI, 369; *Southern Literary Messenger*, VII, 775; and travelers' accounts at large.

9. Howard Snyder in the *Atlantic Monthly*, CXXVII, 171.

10. *E.g.*, Rev. I. E. Lowery, *Life on the Old Plantation in Ante-bellum Days* (Columbia, S.C., 1911), 71, 72. The author was an ex-slave.

11. Olmsted, *Back Country*, 107 *note*.

12. *Calendar of State Papers, Colonial*, 1681–1685, p. 25.

13. *E.g.*, letter of James Habersham, May 11, 1775, to Robert Kean in London, in the *Georgia Historical Society Collections*, VI, 243, 244.

14. Surveys of religious endeavor among the slaves: Rev. Charles C. Jones, *The Religious Instruction of the Negroes in the United States* (Savannah, 1842); C. F. Deems, ed., *Annals of Southern Methodism for 1856* (Nashville [1857]); W. P. Harrison, ed., *The Gospel among the Slaves* (Nashville, 1893).

15. Doubtless many a plantation was blessed, or cursed as the case might be, with a practical joker such as Jack Baker, who kept himself and his whole neighborhood in Richmond entertained by his talent in mimicry. "Jack's performances furnished rare fun in the dog-days, when business was dull, and his pocket was furnished by the same process," One of his private amusements was to call some other slave in the tone of his master, and vanish before the summons was answered. "His most frequent dupe was a next door neighbor, whose master, a Scotchman, took frequent trips to the country on horseback. During his absence Jack would, before retiring to bed, rap on the gate and call 'Jasper! come and take my horse.' Jasper, aroused from his nap, came, but found neither master nor horse, and well knew who quizzed him. One night the veritable master made the call, some time after Jack had given a false alarm. Jasper was out of patience, and replied in a loud voice, 'D—n you, old fellow, if you call me again I'll come out and thrash you!' After that, poor Jasper was at Jack's mercy, unless he resorted to 'thrashing.'"—*DeBow's Review*, XXVIII, 197.

16. *Cf.* Catherine Bremer, *Homes of the New World*, I, 374.

17. John Brickell, *The Natural History of North Carolina* (Dublin, 1737), 275.

18. Basil Hall, *Travels*, III, 191.

19. *Southern Agriculturist*, III, 329. These instructions continued: "All my slaves are to be supplied with sufficient land, on which I encourage and even compel them to plant and cultivate a crop, all of which I will, as I have hitherto done, purchase at a fair price from them."

20. An instance of coercive breeding is reported by Frederick Douglass, in *Narrative* (Boston, 1849), 62. For this item I am indebted to Mr. Theodore Whitfield of Johns Hopkins University.

21. Phillips, *American Negro Slavery*, 298, 299.

22. It is hinted, for example, by the exclamation point in this Virginian letter of 1831: "P. P. Burton has quit his wife, sent her to her father's and gone off

with Sandy Burton to Texas and taken a female slave along!" Manuscript in private possession.

23. Plantation manual of James H. Hammond. Manuscript in the Library of Congress.

24. A. P. Peabody, in the *Andover Review*, XVI, 156.

25. P. Carson, *Life of James Louis Pettigru* (Washington, 1920), 431. In another letter Pettigru conjured his sister: "Do not allow the little nigs to forget that their hands were given them principally for the purpose of pulling weeds."—*Ibid.*, 23.

26. *Cf.* Basil Hall, *Travels*, III, 279.

27. *Mississippi Historical Society Publications*, X, 354.

28. T. U. P. Charlton, *Life of James Jackson* (Augusta, 1809, reprint Atlanta, n. d.), 154 of the reprint.

29. Fred A. Ross, *Slavery Ordained of God* (Philadelphia, 1859), 26.

30. Sir Charles Lyell, *Second Visit*, 2d ed., I, 352.

31. *E.g.*, J. W. Monette in [J. H. Ingraham] *The South West*, II, 286–288.

32. *American Slavery as it is: Testimony of a Thousand Witnesses* (New York, 1839).

33. *Letters of Charles Eliot Norton* (Boston, 1913), I, 121.

34. *Andover Review*, XVI, 157.

35. *Random Shots and Southern Breezes* (New York, 1842), II, 13.

36. *Homes of the New World*, I, 293 et passim.

37. Some of these are quoted in Phillips, *American Negro Slavery*, 306–308.

38. A Virginia woman, talking in 1842 with a visiting preacher from the North, said that her superannuated cook was "as pious a woman, and a lady of as delicate sensibilities as I ever saw; she is one of the very best friends I have in the world." The visitor wrote on his own score: "I am more and more convinced of the injustice we do the slaveholders. Of their feelings toward their negroes I can form a better notion than formerly, by examining my own toward the slaves who wait on my wife and mind my children. It is a feeling most like that we have to near relations." And again as to the slaves: "They are unspeakably superior to our Northern free blacks, retaining a thousand African traits of kindliness and hilarity, from being together in masses. I may say with Abram [Venable, a planter whom he visited], 'I love a nigger, they are better than we.' So they are: grateful, devoted, self-sacrificing for their masters."—John Hall ed., *Forty Years' Familiar Letters of James W. Alexander, D. D.* (New York, 1860), I, 351–353.

39. Christopher Codrington, in *Calendar of State Papers, Colonial*, 1701, p. 721.

40. Diary of London Carter, in the *William and Mary College Quarterly*, XIII, 162.

41. "The Westover Journal of John A. Seldon," in *Smith College Studies*, VI, 289 *et passim.*

42. *Ibid.*, 308.

43. For a striking example see *Plantation and Frontier*, I, 337, 338.

44. For a vivid account of a tripartite negotiation see Robert Russell, *North America* (Edinburgh, 1857), 151.

45. *E.g.*, Carson, *Pettigru*, 348; Phillips, *American Negro Slavery*, 414, 415.

Few books dealing with the impact of slavery have provoked more heated debate than Stanley M. Elkins' Slavery: A Problem in American Institutional and Intellectual Life. *Most controversial is Elkins' discussion of the "Sambo" personality-type, which, he argues, was the inevitable result of accommodation to the master-servant character of the plantation status system. Elkins has been criticized both for his social-psychological views on the internalization of the role the slave was forced to play and for equating the Negro with the victims of Nazism who were sent to concentration camps and ultimately destroyed.*

Here Elkins speaks for himself on the underlying issue of "infantilization."

8

Slavery and Negro Personality

Stanley M. Elkins

Personality Types and Stereotypes

. . . It will be assumed that there were elements in the very structure of the plantation system—its "closed" character—that could sustain infantilism as a normal feature of behavior. These elements, having less to do with "cruelty" per se than simply with the sanctions of authority, were effective and pervasive enough to require that such infantilism be characterized as something much more basic than mere "accommodations." It will be assumed that the sanctions of the system were in themselves sufficient to produce a recognizable personality type.[1]

It should be understood that to identify a social type in this sense is still to generalize on a fairly crude level—and to insist for a limited purpose on the legitimacy of such generalizing is by no means to deny that, on more refined levels, a great profusion of individual types might have been observed in slave society. Nor need it be claimed that the "Sambo" type, even in the relatively crude sense employed here, was a universal type. It was, however, a plantation type, and a plantation existence embraced well over half the slave population.[2] Two kinds of material will be used in the effort to picture the mechanisms whereby this adjustment to absolute power—an adjustment whose end product included infantile features of behavior—may have been effected. One is drawn from the theoretical knowledge presently available in social psychology, and the other, in the form of an analogy, is derived from some of the data that have come out of the German concentration camps. It is recognized in most theory that social behavior is regulated in some general way by adjustment to symbols of authority—however diversely "authority" may be defined either in theory or in culture itself—and that such adjustment is closely related to the very formation of personality. A corollary would be, of course, that the more diverse those symbols of authority may be, the greater is the permissible variety of adjustment to them—and the wider the margin of individuality, consequently, in the development of the self. The question here has to do with the wideness or narrowness of that margin on the ante-bellum plantation.

The other body of material, involving an experience undergone by several million men and women in the concentration camps of our own time, contains certain items of relevance to the problem here being considered. The experience was analogous to that of slavery and was one in which wide-scale instances of infantilization were observed. The material is sufficiently detailed, and sufficiently documented by men who not only took part in the experience itself but who were versed in the use of psychological theory for analyzing it, that the advantages of drawing upon such data for purposes of analogy seem to outweigh the possible risks.

The introduction of this second body of material must to a certain extent govern the theoretical strategy itself. It has been recognized both implicitly and explicitly that the psychic impact and effects of the concentration-camp experience were not anticipated in existing theory and that consequently such theory would require some major supplementation.[3] It might be added, parenthetically, that almost any published discussion of this modern Inferno, no matter how learned, demonstrates how "theory," operating at such a level of shared human experience, tends to shed much of its technical trappings and to take on an almost literary quality. The experience showed, in any event, that infantile personality features could be induced in a relatively short time among large numbers of adult human beings coming from very diverse backgrounds. The particular strain which was thus placed upon prior theory consisted in the need to make room not only for the cultural and environmental sanctions that sustain personality (which in a sense Freudian theory already had) but also for a virtually unanticipated problem: actual change in the personality of masses of adults. It forced a reappraisal and new appreciation of how completely and effectively prior cultural sanctions for behavior and personality could be detached to make way for new and different sanctions, and of how adjustments could be made by individuals to a species of authority vastly different from any previously known. The revelation for theory was the process of detachment.

These cues, accordingly, will guide the argument on Negro slavery. Several million people were detached with a peculiar effectiveness from a great variety of cultural backgrounds in Africa—a detachment operating with infinitely more effectiveness upon those brought to North America than upon those who came to Latin America. It was achieved partly by the shock experience inherent in the very mode of procurement but more specifically by the type of authority-system to which they were introduced and to which they had to adjust for physical and psychic survival. The new adjustment, to absolute power in a closed system, involved infantilization, and the detachment was so complete that little trace of prior (and thus alternative) cultural sanctions for behavior and personality remained for the descendants of the first generation. For them, adjustment to clear and omnipresent authority could be more or less automatic—as much so, or as little, as it is for anyone whose adjustment to a social system begins at birth and to whom that system represents normality. We do not know how generally a full adjustment was made by the first generation of fresh slaves from Africa. But we do know—from a modern experience—that such an adjustment is possible, not only within the same generation but within two or three years. This proved possible for people in a full state of complex civilization, for men and women who were not black and not savages. . . .

Three Theories of Personality

The immense revelation for psychology in the concentration-camp literature has been the discovery of how elements of dramatic personality change could be brought about in masses of individuals. And yet it is not proper that the crude fact of "change" alone should dominate the conceptual image with which one emerges from this problem. "Change" per se, change that does not go beyond itself, is productive of nothing; it leaves only destruction, shock, and howling bedlam behind it unless some future basis of stability and order lies waiting to guarantee it and give it reality. So it is with the human psyche, which is apparently capable of making terms with a state other than liberty as we know it. The very dramatic features of the process just described may upset the nicety of this point. There is the related danger, moreover, of unduly stressing the individual psychology of the problem at the expense of its social psychology.

These hazards might be minimized by maintaining a conceptual distinction between two phases of the group experience. The process of detachment from prior standards of behavior and value is one of them, and is doubtless the more striking, but there must be another one. That such detachment can, by extension, involve the whole scope of an individual's culture is an implication for which the vocabulary of individual psychology was caught somewhat unawares. Fluctuations in the state of the individual psyche could formerly be dealt with, or so it seemed, while taking for granted the more or less static nature of social organization, and with a minimum of reference to its features. That such organization might itself become an important variable was therefore a possibility not highly developed in theory, focused as theory was upon individual case histories to the invariable minimization of social and cultural setting. The other phase of the experience should be considered as the "stability" side of the problem, that phase which stabilized what the "shock" phase only opened the way for. This was essentially a process of adjustment to a standard of social normality, though in this case a drastic readjustment and compressed within a very short time—a process which under typical conditions of individual and group existence is supposed to begin at birth and last a lifetime and be transmitted in many and diffuse ways from generation to generation. The adjustment is assumed to be slow and organic, and it normally is. Its numerous aspects extend much beyond psychology; those aspects have in the past been treated at great leisure within the rich provinces not only of psychology but of history, sociology, and literature as well. What rearrangement and compression of those provinces may be needed to accommodate a mass experience that not only involved profound individual shock but also required rapid assimilation to a drastically different form of social organization, can hardly be known. But perhaps the most conservative beginning may be made with existing psychological theory.

The theoretical system whose terminology was orthodox for most of the Europeans who have written about the camps was that of Freud. It was necessary for them to do a certain amount of improvising, since the scheme's existing framework provided only the narrowest leeway for dealing with such radical concepts as out-and-out change in personality. This was due to two kinds of limitations which the Freudian vocabulary places upon the notion of the "self." One is that the superego—that part of the self involved in social relationships, social values, expectations of others, and so on—is conceived as only a small and highly refined part of the "total" self. The other is the assumption that the content and character of the superego is laid down in childhood and undergoes relatively little basic alteration thereafter.[4] Yet a Freudian diagnosis of the concentration-camp inmate—whose social self, or superego, did appear to change and who seemed basically changed thereby—is, given these limitations, still possible. Elie Cohen, whose analysis is the most thorough of these, specifically states that "the superego acquired new values in a concentration camp."[5] The old values, according to Dr. Cohen, were first silenced by the shocks which produced "acute depersonalization" (the subject-object split: "It is not the real 'me' who is undergoing this"), and by the powerful drives of hunger and survival. Old values, thus set aside, could be replaced by new ones. It was a process made possible by "infantile regression"—regression to a previous condition of childlike dependency in which parental prohibitions once more became all-powerful and in which parental judgments might once more be internalized. In this way a new "father-image," personified in the SS guard, came into being. That the prisoner's identification with the SS could be so positive is explained by still another mechanism: the principle of "identification with the aggressor." "A child," as Anna Freud

writes, "interjects some characteristic of an anxiety-object and so assimilates an anxiety-experience which he has just undergone.... By impersonating the aggressor, assuming his attributes or imitating his aggression, the child transforms himself from the person threatened into the person who makes the threat."[6] In short, the child's only "defense" in the presence of a cruel, all-powerful father is the psychic defense of identification.

Now one could, still retaining the Freudian language, represent all this in somewhat less cumbersome terms by a slight modification of the metaphor. It could simply be said that under great stress the superego, like a bucket, is violently emptied of content and acquires, in a radically changed setting, new content. It would thus not be necessary to postulate a literal "regression" to childhood in order for this to occur. Something of the sort is suggested by Leo Alexander. "The psychiatrist stands in amazement," he writes, "before the thoroughness and completeness with which this perversion of essential superego values was accomplished in adults . . . [and] it may be that the decisive importance of childhood and youth in the formation of [these] values may have been overrated by psychiatrists in a society in which allegiance to these values in normal adult life was taken too much for granted because of the stability, religiousness, legality, and security of the 19th Century and early 20th Century society."[7]

A second theoretical scheme is better prepared for crisis and more closely geared to social environment than the Freudian adaptation indicated above, and it may consequently be more suitable for accommodating not only the concentration-camp experience but also the more general problem of plantation slave personality. This is the "interpersonal theory" developed by the late Harry Stack Sullivan. One may view this body of work as the response to a peculiarly American set of needs. The system of Freud, so aptly designed for a European society the stability of whose institutional and status relationships could always to a large extent be taken for granted, turns out to be less clearly adapted to the culture of the United States. The American psychiatrist has had to deal with individuals in a culture where the diffuse, shifting, and often uncertain quality of such relationships has always been more pronounced than in Europe. He has come to appreciate the extent to which these relationships actually support the individual's psychic balance—the full extent, that is, to which the self is "social" in its nature. Thus a psychology whose terms are flexible enough to permit altering social relationships to make actual differences in character structure would be a psychology especially promising for dealing with the present problem.[8]

Sullivan's great contribution was to offer a concept whereby the really critical determinants of personality might be isolated for purposes of observation. Out of the hopelessly immense totality of "influences" which in one way or another go to make up the personality, or "self," Sullivan designated one—the estimations and expectations of others —as the one promising to unlock the most secrets. He then made a second elimination: the *majority* of "others" in one's existence may for theoretical purposes be neglected; what counts is who the *significant* others are. Here, "significant others"[9] may be understood very crudely to mean those individuals who hold, or seem to hold, the keys to security in one's own personal situation, whatever its nature. Now as to the psychic processes whereby these "significant others" become an actual part of the personality, it may be said that the very sense of "self" first emerges in connection with anxiety about the attitudes of the most important persons in one's life (initially, the mother, father, and their surrogates—persons of more or less absolute authority), and automatic attempts are set in motion to adjust to these attitudes. In this way their approval, their disapproval, their estimates and appraisals, and indeed a whole range of their expectations become as it were internalized, and are reflected in one's very character. Of course as one "grows up," one acquires more and more significant others whose attitudes are diffuse and may indeed compete, and thus "significance," in Sullivan's sense, becomes subtler and less easy to define. The personality exfoliates; it takes on traits of distinction and, as we say, "individuality." The impact of particular significant others is less dramatic than in early life. But the pattern is a continuing one; new significant others do still appear, and theoretically it is conceivable that even in mature life the personality might be visibly affected by the arrival of such a one—supposing that this new significant other were vested with sufficient authority and power. In any event there are possibilities for fluidity and actual change inherent in this concept which earlier schemes have lacked.

The purest form of the process is to be observed in the development of children, not so much because of their "immaturity" as such (though their plasticity is great and the imprint of early experience goes deep), but rather because for them there are fewer significant others. For this reason —because the pattern is simpler and more easily controlled—much of Sullivan's attention was devoted to what happens in childhood. In any case let us say that unlike the adult, the child, being drastically limited in the selection of significant others, must operate in a "closed system."

Such are the elements which make for order and balance in the normal self: "significant others" plus "anxiety" in a special sense—conceived with not simply disruptive but also guiding, warning functions.[10] The structure of "interpersonal" theory thus has considerable room in it for conceptions of guided change—change for either beneficent or malevolent ends. One technique for managing such change would of course be the orthodox one of psychoanalysis; another, the actual changing of significant others.[11] Patrick Mullahy, a leading exponent of Sullivan, believes that in group therapy much is possible along these lines.[12] A demonic test of the whole hypothesis is available in the concentration camp.

Consider the camp prisoner—not the one who fell by the wayside but the one who was eventually to survive; consider the ways in which he was forced to adjust to the one significant other which he now had—the SS guard, who held absolute dominion over every aspect of his life. The very shock of his introduction was perfectly designed to dramatize this fact; he was brutally maltreated ("as by a cruel father"); the shadow of resistance would bring instant death. Daily life in the camp, with its fear and tensions, taught over and over the lesson of absolute power. It prepared the personality for a drastic shift in standards. It crushed whatever anxieties might have been drawn from prior standards; such standards had become meaningless. It focused the prisoner's attention constantly on the moods,

137

attitudes, and standards of the only man who mattered. A truly child-like situation was thus created: utter and abject dependency on one, or on a rigidly limited few, significant others. All the conditions which in normal life would give the individual leeway—which allowed him to defend himself against a new and hostile significant other, no matter how powerful—were absent in the camp. No competition of significant others was possible; the prisoner's comrades for practical purposes were helpless to assist him.[13] He had no degree of independence, no lines to the outside, in any matter. Everything, every vital concern, focused on the SS: food, warmth, security, freedom from pain, all depended on the omnipotent significant other, all had to be worked out within the closed system. Nowhere was there a shred of privacy; everything one did was subject to SS supervision. The pressure was never absent. It is thus no wonder that the prisoners should become "as children." It is no wonder that their obedience became unquestioning, that they did not revolt, that they could not "hate" their masters. Their masters' attitudes had become *internalized* as a part of their very selves; those attitudes and standards now dominated all others that they had. They had, indeed, been "changed."

There still exists a third conceptual framework within which these phenomena may be considered. It is to be found in the growing field of "role psychology." This psychology is not at all incompatible with interpersonal theory; the two might easily be fitted into the same system.[14] But it might be strategically desirable, for several reasons, to segregate them for purposes of discussion. One such reason is the extraordinary degree to which role psychology shifts the focus of attention upon the individual's cultural and institutional environment rather than upon his "self." At the same time it gives us a manageable concept—that of "role"—for mediating between the two. As a mechanism, the role enables us to isolate the unique contribution of culture and institutions toward maintaining the psychic balance of the individual. In it, we see formalized for the individual a range of choices in models of behavior and expression, each with its particular style, quality, and attributes. The relationship between the "role" and the "self," though not yet clear, is intimate; it is at least possible at certain levels of inquiry to look upon the individual as the variable and upon the roles extended him as the stable factor.[15] We thus have a potentially durable link between individual psychology and the study of culture. It might even be said, inasmuch as its key term is directly borrowed from the theater, that role psychology offers in workable form the long-awaited connection—apparently missed by Ernest Jones in his *Hamlet* study—between the insights of the classical dramatists and those of the contemporary social theorist.[16] But be that as it may, for our present problem, the concentration camp, it suggests the most flexible account of how the ex-prisoners may have succeeded in resuming their places in normal life.

Let us note certain of the leading terms.[17] A "social role" is definable in its simplest sense as the behavior expected of persons specifically located in specific social groups.[18] A distinction is kept between "expectations" and "behavior"; the expectations of a role (embodied in the "script") theoretically exist in advance and are defined by the organization, the institution, or by society at large. Behavior (the "performance") refers to the manner in which the role is played. Another distinction involves roles which are "pervasive" and those which are "limited." A pervasive role is extensive in scope ("female citizen") and not only influences but also sets bounds upon the other sorts of roles available to the individual ("mother," "nurse," but not "husband," "soldier"); a limited role ("purchaser," "patient") is transitory and intermittent. A further concept is that of "role clarity." Some roles are more specifically defined than others; their impact upon performance (and, indeed, upon the personality of the performer) depends on the clarity of their definition. Finally, it is asserted that those roles which carry with them the clearest and most automatic rewards and punishments are those which will be (as it were) most "artistically" played.

What sorts of things might this explain? It might illuminate the process whereby the child develops his personality in terms not only of the roles which his parents offer him but of those which he "picks up" elsewhere and tries on. It could show how society, in its coercive character, lays down patterns of behavior with which it expects the individual to comply. It suggests the way in which society, now turning its benevolent face to the individual, tenders him alternatives and defines for him the style appropriate to their fulfillment. It provides us with a further term for the definition of personality itself: there appears an extent to which we can say that personality is actually made up of the roles which the individual plays.[19] And here, once more assuming "change" to be possible, we have in certain ways the least cumbersome terms for plotting its course.

The application of the model to the concentration camp should be simple and obvious. What was expected of the man entering the role of camp prisoner was laid down for him upon arrival:

> Here you are not in a penitentiary or prison but in a place of instruction. Order and discipline are here the highest law. If you ever want to see freedom again, you must submit to a severe training. . . . But woe to those who do not obey our iron discipline. Our methods are thorough! Here there is no compromise and no mercy. The slightest resistance will be ruthlessly suppressed. Here we sweep with an iron broom! [20]

Expectation and performance must coincide exactly; the lines were to be read literally; the missing of a single cue meant extinction. The role was pervasive; it vetoed any other role and smashed all prior ones. "Role clarity"—the clarity here was blinding; its definition was burned into the prisoner by every detail of his existence:

> In normal life the adult enjoys a certain measure of independence; within the limits set by society he has a considerable measure of liberty. Nobody orders him when and what to eat, where to take up his residence or what to wear, neither to take his rest on Sunday nor when to have his bath, nor when to go to bed. He is not beaten during his work, he need not ask permission to go to the W.C., he is not continually kept on the run, he does not feel that the work he is doing is silly or childish, he is not confined behind barbed wire, he is not counted twice a day or more, he is not left unprotected against the actions of his fellow citizens, he looks after his family and the education of his children.
>
> How altogether different was the life of the concentration-camp prisoner! What to do during each part of the day was arranged for him, and decisions were made about him from which there was no appeal. He was impotent and suffered from bedwetting, and because of his chronic diarrhea he soiled his underwear. . . . The dependence of the prisoner on the SS . . . may be compared to the dependence of children on their parents. . . . [21]

The impact of this role, coinciding as it does in a hundred ways with that of the child, has already been observed. Its rewards were brutally simple—life rather than death; its punishments were automatic. By the survivors it was—it had to be—a role *well played.*

Nor was it simple, upon liberation, to shed the role. Many of the inmates, to be sure, did have prior roles which they could resume, former significant others to whom they might reorient themselves, a repressed superego which might once more be resurrected. To this extent they were not "lost souls." But to the extent that their entire personalities, their total selves, had been involved in this experience, to the extent that old arrangements had been disrupted, that society itself had been overturned while they had been away, a "return" was fraught with innumerable obstacles. [22]

It is hoped that the very hideousness of a special example of slavery has not disqualified it as a test for certain features of a far milder and more benevolent form of slavery. But it should still be possible to say, with regard to the individuals who lived as slaves within the respective systems, that just as on one level there is every difference between a wretched childhood and a carefree one, there are, for other purposes, limited features which the one may be said to have shared with the other.

Both were closed systems from which all standards based on prior connections had been effectively detached. A working adjustment to either
system required a childlike conformity, a limited choice of "significant
others." Cruelty per se cannot be considered the primary key to this; of far
greater importance was the simple "closedness" of the system, in which all
lines of authority descended from the master and in which alternative social
bases that might have supported alternative standards were systematically
suppressed.[23] The individual, consequently, for his very psychic security, had
to picture his master in some way as the "good father."[24] even when, as in the
concentration camp, it made no sense at all.[25] But why should it not have
made sense for many a simple plantation Negro whose master did exhibit,
in all the ways that could be expected, the features of the good father who
was really "good"? If the concentration camp could produce in two or three
years the results that it did, one wonders how much more pervasive must
have been those attitudes, expectations, and values which had, certainly, their
benevolent side and which were accepted and transmitted over generations.

For the Negro child, in particular, the plantation offered no really satisfactory father-image other than the master. The "real" father was virtually
without authority over his child, since discipline, parental responsibility,
and control of rewards and punishments all rested in other hands; the
slave father could not even protect the mother of his children except by
appealing directly to the master. Indeed, the mother's own role loomed
far larger for the slave child than did that of the father. She controlled
those few activities—household care, preparation of food, and rearing of
children—that were left to the slave family. For that matter, the very etiquette
of plantation life removed even the honorific attributes of fatherhood from
the Negro male, who was addressed as "boy"—until, when the vigorous
years of his prime were past, he was allowed to assume the title of "uncle."

From the master's viewpoint, slaves had been defined in law as property,
and the master's power over his property must be absolute. But then this
property was still human property. These slaves might never be quite as
human as *he* was, but still there were certain standards that could be laid
down for their behavior: obedience, fidelity, humility, docility, cheerfulness, and so on. Industry and diligence would of course be demanded, but
a final element in the master's situation would undoubtedly qualify that
expectation. Absolute power for him meant absolute dependency for the
slave—the dependency not of the developing child but of the perpetual
child. For the master, the role most aptly fitting such a relationship would
naturally be that of the father. As a father he could be either harsh or kind,
as he chose, but as a *wise* father he would have, we may suspect, a sense

141

of the limits of his situation. He must be ready to cope with *all* the qualities of the child, exasperating as well as ingratiating. He might conceivably have to expect in this child—besides his loyalty, docility, humility, cheerfulness, and (under supervision) his diligence—such additional qualities as irresponsibility, playfulness, silliness, laziness, and (quite possibly) tendencies to lying and stealing. Should the entire prediction prove accurate, the result would be something resembling "Sambo."

The social and psychological sanctions of role-playing may in the last analysis prove to be the most satisfactory of the several approaches to Sambo, for, without doubt, of all the roles in American life that of Sambo was by far the most pervasive. The outlines of the role might be sketched in by crude necessity, but what of the finer shades? The sanctions against overstepping it were bleak enough,[26] but the rewards—the sweet applause, as it were, for performing it with sincerity and feeling—were something to be appreciated on quite another level. The law, untuned to the deeper harmonies, could command the player to be present for the occasion, and the whip might even warn against his missing the grosser cues, but could those things really insure the performance that melted all hearts? Yet there was many and many a performance, and the audiences (whose standards were high) appear to have been for the most part well pleased. They were actually viewing their own masterpiece. Much labor had been lavished upon this chef d'oeuvre, the most genial resources of Southern society had been available for the work; touch after touch had been applied throughout the years, and the result—embodied not in the unfeeling law but in the richest layers of Southern lore—had been the product of an exquisitely rounded collective creativity. And indeed, in a sense that somehow transcended the merely ironic, it was a labor of love. "I love the simple and unadulterated slave, with his geniality, his mirth, his swagger, and his nonsense," wrote Edward Pollard. "I love to look upon his countenance shining with content and grease; I love to study his affectionate heart; I love to mark that peculiarity in him, which beneath all his buffoonery exhibits him as a creature of the tenderest sensibilities, mingling his joys and his sorrows with those of his master's home."[27] Love, even on those terms, was surely no inconsequential reward.

But what were the terms? The Negro was to be a child forever. "The Negro . . . in his true nature, is always a boy, let him be ever so old. . . ."[28] "He is . . . a dependent upon the white race; dependent for guidance and direction even to the procurement of his most indispensable necessaries. Apart from this protection he has the helplessness of a child—without foresight, without faculty of contrivance, without thrift of any kind."[29] Not only was he a child; he was a happy child. Few Southern writers failed to describe with obvious fondness the bubbling gaiety of a plantation holiday or the perpetual good humor that seemed to mark the Negro character, the good humor of an everlasting childhood.

The role, of course, must have been rather harder for the earliest generations of slaves to learn. "Accommodation," according to John Dollard, "involves the renunciation of protest or aggression against undesirable conditions of life and the organization of the character so that protest does not appear, but acceptance does. It may come to pass in the end that the unwelcome force is idealized, that one identifies with it and takes it into the personality; it sometimes even happens that what is at first resented and feared is finally loved."[30]

Might the process, on the other hand, be reversed? It is hard to imagine its being reversed overnight. The same role might still be played in the years after slavery—we are told that it was[31]—and yet it was played to more vulgar audiences with cruder standards, who paid much less for what they saw. The lines might be repeated more and more mechanically, with less and less conviction; the incentives to perfection could become hazy and blurred, and the excellent old piece could degenerate over time into low farce. There could come a point, conceivably, with the old zest gone, that it was no longer worth the candle. The day might come at last when it dawned on a man's full waking consciousness that he had really grown up, that he was, after all, only playing a part.

Mechanisms of Resistance to Absolute Power

One might say a great deal more than has been said here about mass behavior and mass manifestations of personality, and the picture would still amount to little more than a grotesque cartoon of humanity were not some recognition given to the ineffable difference made in any social system by men and women possessing what is recognized, anywhere and at any time, simply as character. With that, one arrives at something too qualitatively fine to come very much within the crude categories of the present discussion; but although it is impossible to generalize with any proper justice about the incidence of "character" in its moral, irreducible, individual sense, it may still be possible to conclude with a note or two on the social conditions, the breadth or narrowness of their compass, within which character can find expression.

Why should it be, turning once more to Latin America, that there one finds no Sambo, no social tradition, that is, in which slaves were defined by virtually complete consensus as children incapable of being trusted with the full privileges of freedom and adulthood? There, the system surely had its brutalities. The slaves arriving there from Africa had also undergone the capture, the sale, the Middle Passage. They too had been uprooted from a prior culture, from a life very different from the one in which they now found themselves. There, however, the system was not closed.

Here again the concentration camp, paradoxically enough, can be instructive. There were in the camps a very small minority of the survivors who had undergone an experience different in crucial ways from that of the others, an experience which protected them from the full impact of the closed system. These people, mainly by virtue of wretched little jobs in the camp administration which offered them a minute measure of privilege, were able to carry on "underground" activities. In a practical sense the actual operations of such "undergrounds" as were possible may seem to us unheroic and limited; stealing blankets; "organizing" a few bandages, a little medicine, from the camp hospital; black market arrangements with a guard for a bit of extra food and protection for oneself and one's comrades; the circulation of news; and other such apparently trifling activities. But for the psychological balance of those involved, such activities were vital; they made possible a fundamentally different adjustment to the camp. To a prisoner so engaged, there were others who mattered, who gave real point to his existence—the SS was no longer the *only* one. Conversely, the role of the child was not the only one he played. He could take initiative; he could give as well as receive protection; he did things which had meaning in adult terms. He had, in short, alternative roles; this was a fact which made such a prisoner's transition from his old life to that of the camp less agonizing and destructive; those very prisoners, moreover, appear to have been the ones who could, upon liberation, resume normal lives most easily. It is, in fact, these people—not those of the ranks—who have described the camps to us.[32]

It was just such a difference—indeed, a much greater one—that separated the typical slave in Latin America from the typical slave in the United States. Though he too had experienced the Middle Passage, he was entering a society where alternatives were significantly more diverse than those awaiting his kinsman in North America. Concerned in some sense with his status were distinct and at certain points competing institutions. This involved multiple and often competing "significant others." His master was, of course, clearly the chief one—but not the only one. There could, in fact, be a considerable number: the friar who boarded his ship to examine his conscience, the confessor; the priest who made the rounds and who might report irregularities in treatment to the *procurador;* the zealous Jesuit quick to resent a master's intrusion upon such sacred matters as marriage and worship (a resentment of no small consequence to the master); the local magistrate, with his eye on the king's official protector of slaves, who would find himself in trouble were the laws too widely evaded; the king's informer who received one-third of the fines. For the slave the result was a certain latitude; the lines did not all converge on one man; the slave's personality, accordingly, did not have to focus on a single role. He was, true enough, primarily a slave. Yet he might in fact perform multiple roles. He could be a husband and a father (for the American slave these roles had virtually no meaning); open to him also were such activities as artisan, peddler, petty merchant, truck gardener (the law reserved to him the necessary time and a share of the proceeds, but such arrangements were against the law for Sambo); he could be a communicant in the church, a member of a religious fraternity[33] (roles guaranteed by the most powerful institution in Latin America— comparable privileges in the American South depended on a master's pleasure). These roles were all legitimized and protected *outside* the plantation; they offered a diversity of channels for the development of personality. Not only did the individual have multiple roles open to him as a slave, but the very nature of these roles made possible a certain range of aspirations should he some day become free. He could have a fantasy-life not limited to catfish and watermelons; it was within his conception to become a priest, an independent farmer, a successful merchant, a military officer.[34] The slave could actually—to an extent quite unthinkable in the United States—conceive of himself *as a rebel.* Bloody slave revolts, actual wars, took place in Latin America; nothing on this order occurred in the United States.[35] But even without a rebellion, society here had a network of customary arrangements, rooted in antiquity, which made possible at many points a smooth transition of status from slave to free and which provided much social space for the exfoliation of individual character.

To the typical slave on the ante-bellum plantation in the United States, society of course offered no such alternatives. But that is hardly to say that something of an "underground"—something rather more, indeed, than an underground—could not exist in Southern slave society. And there were those in it who hardly fitted the picture of "Sambo."

The American slave system, compared with that of Latin America, was closed and circumscribed, but, like all social systems, its arrangements were less perfect in practice than they appeared to be in theory. It was possible for significant numbers of slaves, in varying degrees, to escape the full impact of the system and its coercions upon personality. The house servant, the urban mechanic, the slave who arranged his own employment and paid his master a stipulated sum each week, were all figuratively members of the "underground." Even among those working on large plantations, the skilled craftsman or the responsible slave fore-man had a measure of independence not shared by his simpler brethren. Even the single slave family owned by a small farmer had a status much closer to that of house servants than to that of plantation labor gang. For all such people there was a margin of space denied to the majority; the system's authority-structure claimed their bodies but not quite their souls.

Out of such groups an individual as complex and as highly devel-oped as William Johnson, the Natchez barber, might emerge. Johnson's diary reveals a personality that one recognizes instantly as a type—but a type whose values came from a sector of society very different from that which formed Sambo. Johnson is the young man on the make, the ambitious free-enterpriser of American legend. He began life as a slave, was manumitted at the age of eleven, and rose from a poor apprentice barber to become one of the wealthiest and most influential Negroes in ante-bellum Mississippi. He was respected by white and black alike, and counted among his friends some of the leading public men of the state.[36]

It is of great interest to note that although the danger of slave revolts (like Communist conspiracies in our own day) was much overrated by touchy Southerners; the revolts that actually did occur were in no instance planned by plantation laborers but rather by Negroes whose qualities of leadership were developed well outside the full coercions of the plantation authority-system. Gabriel, who led the revolt of 1800, was a blacksmith who lived a few miles outside Richmond; Denmark Vesey, leading spirit of the 1822 plot at Charleston, was a freed Negro artisan who had been born in Africa and served several years aboard a slavetrading vessel; and Nat Turner, the Virginia slave who fomented the massacre of 1831, was a literate preacher of recognized intelligence. Of the plots that have been convincingly substantiated (whether they came to anything or not), the majority originated in urban centers.[37]

For a time during Reconstruction, Negro elite of sorts did emerge in the South. Many of its members were Northern Negroes, but the Southern ex-slaves who also comprised it seem in general to have emerged from the categories just indicated. Vernon Wharton, writing of Mississippi, says:

A large portion of the minor Negro leaders were preachers, lawyers, or teachers from the free states or from Canada. Their education and their independent attitude gained for them immediate favor and leadership. Of the natives who became their rivals, the majority had been urban slaves, blacksmiths, carpenters, clerks, or waiters in hotels and boarding houses; a few of them had been favored body-servants of affluent whites.[38]

The William Johnsons and Denmark Veseys have been accorded, though belatedly, their due honor. They are, indeed, all too easily identified, thanks to the system that enabled them as individuals to be so conspicuous and so exceptional and, as members of a group, so few.

Notes

1. The line between "accommodation" (as conscious hypocrisy) and behavior inextricable from basic personality, though the line certainly exists, is anything but a clear and simple matter of choice. There is a reason to think that the one grades into the other, and vice versa, with considerable subtlety. In this connection, the most satisfactory theoretical mediating term between deliberate role-playing and "natural" role-playing might be found in role-psychology.

2. Although the majority of Southern slaveholders were not planters, the majority of slaves were owned by a planter minority. "Considerably more than half of them lived on plantation units of more than twenty slaves, and one-fourth lived on units of more than fifty. That the majority of slaves belonged to members of the planter class, and not to those who operated small farms with a single slave family, in a fact of crucial importance concerning the nature of bondage in the ante-bellum south." Stampp, *Peculiar Institution*, p. 31.

3. See esp. below, n. 7.

4. "For just as the ego is a modified portion of the id as a result of contact with the outer world, the super-ego represents a modified portion of the ego, formed through experiences absorbed from the parents, especially from the father. The super-ego is the highest evolution attainable by man, and consists of a precipitate of all prohibitions and inhibitions, all the rules of conduct which are impressed on the child by his parents and by parental substitutes. The feeling of *conscience* depends altogether on the development of the super-ego." A. A. Brill, Introduction to *The Basic Writings of Sigmund Freud* (New York: Modern Library, 1938), pp. 12–13. "Its relation to the ego is not exhausted by the precept: 'You *ought to be* such and such (like your father)'; it also comprises the prohibition: 'You *must not be* such and such (like your father); that is, you may not do all that he does; many things are his prerogative.'" Sigmund Freud, *The Ego and the Id* (London: Hogarth Press, 1947), pp. 44–45. ". . . and here we have that higher nature, in this ego-ideal or super-ego, the representative of our relation to our parents. When we were little children we knew these higher natures, we admired them and feared them; and later we took them into ourselves." *Ibid.*, p. 47. "As a child grows up, the office of father is carried on by masters and by others in authority; the power of their injunctions and prohibitions remains vested in the ego-ideal and continues, in the form of conscience, to exercise the censorship or morals. The tension between the

demands of conscience and the actual attainments of the ego is experienced as a sense of guilt. Social feelings rest on the foundation of identification with others, on the basis of an ego-ideal in common with them." *Ibid.*, p. 49.

5.   Human *Behavior*, p. 136.

6.   Anna Freud, *The Ego and the Mechanisms of Defence* (London: Hogarth Press, 1948), p. 121. "In some illustrative case reports, Clara Thompson stresses the vicious circle put in motion by this defense-mechanism. The stronger the need for identification, the more a person loses himself in his omnipotent enemy—the more helpless he becomes. The more helpless he feels, the stronger the identification, and—we may add—the more likely it is that he tries even to surpass the aggressiveness of his aggressor. This may explain the almost unbelievable phenomenon that prisoner-superiors sometimes acted more brutally than did members of the SS. . . . Identification with the aggressor represented the final stage of passive adaptation. It was a means of defense of a rather paradoxical nature: survival through surrender; protection against the fear of the enemy— by becoming part of him; overcoming helplessness—by regressing to childish dependence." Bluhm, "How Did They Survive?" pp. 24–25.

7.   Leo Alexander, "War Crimes: Their Social-Psychological Aspects," *American Journal of Psychiatry*, CV (September, 1948), 173. "The super-ego structure is . . . in peril whenever these established guiding forces weaken or are in the process of being undermined, shifted, or perverted, and becomes itself open to undermining, shifting, or perversion even in adult life—a fact which is probably more important than we have been aware of heretofore." *Ibid.*, p. 175.

8.   My use of Sullivan here does not imply a willingness to regard his work as a "refutation" to that of Freud, or even as an adequate substitute for it in all other situations. It lacks the imaginative scope which in Freud makes possible so great a range of cultural connections; in it we miss Freud's effort to deal as scientifically as possible with an infinite array of psychological and cultural phenomena; the fragmentary nature of Sullivan's work, its limited scope, its cloudy presentation, all present us with obstacles not to be surmounted overnight. This might well change as his ideas are elaborated and refined. But meanwhile it would be too much to ask that all connections be broken with the staggering amount of work already done on Freudian models.

9.   Sullivan refined this concept from the earlier notion of the "generalized other" formulated by George Herbert Mead. "The organized community or social group [Mead wrote] which gives to the individual his unity of self may be called 'the generalized other.' The attitude of the generalized other is the attitude of the whole community. Thus, for example, in the case of such a social group as a ball team, the team is the generalized other in so far as it enters—as an organized process or social activity—into the experience of any one of the individual members of it." George H. Mead, *Mind, Self and Society: From the Standpoint of a Social Behaviorist* (Chicago: University of Chicago Press, 1934), p. 154.

10.   The technical term, in Sullivan's terminology, for the mechanism represented by these two elements functioning in combination, is the individual's "self- dynamism." David Riesman has refined this concept; he has, with his "inner-directed, other-directed" polarity, considered the possibility of different kinds of "self-dynamisms." The self-dynamism which functions with reference to specific aims and which is formed and set early in life is characterized as the "gyroscope." On the other hand the self-dynamism which must function in a cultural situation of constantly shifting significant others and which must constantly adjust to them is pictured as the "radar." See *The Lonely Crowd, passim.* The principles summarized in this and the preceding paragraphs are to be found most clearly set forth in Harry Stack Sullivan, *Conceptions of Modern Psychiatry* (Washington: William Alanson White

Psychiatric Foundation, 1945). Sullivan's relationship to the general development of theory is assessed in Patrick Mullahy, *Oedipus Myth and Complex: A Review of Psychoanalytic Theory* (New York: Hermitage House, 1948).

11. Actually, one of the chief functions of psychoanalysis as it has been practiced from the beginning is simply given more explicit recognition here. The psychiatrist who helps the patient exhibit to himself attitudes and feelings systematically repressed—or "selectively ignored"—becomes in the process a new and trusted significant other.

12. "Indeed . . . when the whole Sullivanian conception of the effect of significant others upon the origin and stability of self-conceptions is pushed farther, really revolutionary vistas of guided personality emerge. If the maintenance of certain characteristic patterns of interpersonal behavior depends upon their support by significant others, then to alter the composition of any person's community of significant others is the most direct and drastic way of altering his 'personality.' This can be done. Indeed, it is being done, with impressive results, by the many types of therapeutic groups, or quasi-families of significant new others, which have come up in the past few years." Patrick Mullahy (ed.), *The Contributions of Harry Stack Sullivan* (New York: Hermitage House, 1952), p. 193.

13. It should be noted that there were certain important exceptions. . . .

14. An outstanding instance of authorities who are exponents of both is of that of H. H. Gerth and C. Wright Mills, whose study *Character and Social Structure* ranges very widely in both interpersonal theory and role psychology and uses them interchangeably.

15. Conceptually, the purest illustration of this notion might be seen in such an analogy as the following. Sarah Bernhardt, playing in *Phèdre,* enacted a role which had not altered since it was set down by Racine two centuries before her time, and she was neither the first woman who spoke those lines, nor was she the last. Nor, indeed, was *Phèdre* her only triumph. Such was Bernhardt's genius, such was her infinite plasticity, that she moved from immutable role to immutable role in the classic drama, making of each, as critic and theatergoer alike agreed, a masterpiece. Now Bernhardt herself is gone, yet the lines remain, waiting to be transfigured by some new genius.

16. In the resources of dramatic literature a variety of insights may await the "social scientist" equipped with both the imagination and the conceptual tools for exploiting them, and the emergence of role-psychology may represent the most promising step yet taken in this direction. A previous area of contact has been in the realm of Freudian psychology, but this has never been a very natural or comfortable meeting ground for either the analyst or the literary critic. For example, in Shakespeare's *Hamlet* there is the problem, both psychological and dramatic, of Hamlet's inability to kill his uncle. Dr. Ernest Jones (in *Hamlet and Oedipus)* reduces all the play's tensions to a single Freudian complex. It should be at once more "scientific" and more "literary," however, to consider the problem in terms of role-conflict (Hamlet as prince, son, nephew, lover, etc., has multiple roles which keep getting in the way of one another). Francis Fergusson, though he uses other terminology, in effect does this in his *Ideal of a Theater.*

17. In this paragraph I duplicate and paraphrase material from Eugene and Ruth Hartley, *Fundamentals of Social Psychology* (New York: Knopf, 1952), chap. xvi. See also David C. McClelland, *Personality* (New York: Sloane, 1951), pp. 289–332. Both these books are, strictly speaking, "texts," but this point could be misleading, inasmuch as the whole subject is one not normally studied at an "elementary" level anywhere. At the same time a highly successful effort has been made in each of these works to formulate the role concept with clarity and simplicity, and this makes their formulations peculiarly relevant to the empirical

facts of the present problem. It may be that the very simplicity of the roles in both the plantation and concentration-camp settings accounts for this coincidence. Another reason why I am inclined to put a special premium on simplicity here is my conviction that the role concept has a range of "literary" overtones, potentially exploitable in realms other than psychology. For a recent general statement, see Theodore R. Sarbin, "Role Theory," *Handbook of Social Psychology*, I, 223-58.

18. Hartley, *Fundamentals of Social Psychology*, p. 485.

19. "Personality development is not exclusively a matter of socialization. Rather, it represents the organism's more or less integrated way of adapting to *all* the influences that come its way—both inner and outer influences, both social and nonsocial ones. Social influences, however, are essential to human personality, and socialization accounts for a very great deal of personality development.

From this point of view it would not be surprising to find that many personality disturbances represent some sort of breakdown or reversal of the socialization process." Theodore M. Newcomb, *Social Psychology* (New York: Dryden Press, 1950), p. 475.

20. Quoted in Leon Szalet, *Experiment "E"* (New York: Didier, 1945), p. 138.

21. Cohen, *Human Behavior*, pp. 173–74.

22. Theodore Newcomb is the only non-Freudian coming to my attention who has considered the concentration camp in the terms of social psychology. He draws analogies between the ex-inmates' problems of readjustment and those of returning prisoners of war. "With the return of large numbers of British prisoners of war . . . from German and Japanese camps, toward the end of World War II, it soon became apparent that thousands of them were having serious difficulties of readjustment. It was first assumed that they were victims of war neuroses. But this assumption had to be abandoned when it was discovered that their symptoms were in most cases not those of the commonly recognized neuroses. Most of the men having difficulty, moreover, did not have the kinds of personalities which would have predisposed them to neurotic disorders. Psychiatrists then began to wonder whether their disturbances represented only a temporary phase of the men's return to civilian life. But the difficulties were neither temporary nor 'self-correcting.' 'Even when men had been back for 18 months or even longer, serious and persistent difficulties were reported in something like one-third of the men.' . . . All in all . . . the authors were led to the conclusion that the returning war prisoner's troubles did not lie entirely within himself. They represented the strains and stresses of becoming *re*socialized in a culture which was not only different from what it had been but was radically different from that to which the men had become accustomed during their years of capture." "When a deliberate attempt is made to change the personality, as in psychotherapy, success brings with it changes in role patterns. When the role prescriptions are changed—as for . . . concentration-camp inmates—personality changes also occur. When forcible changes in role prescriptions are removed, the degree to which the previous personality is 'resumed' depends upon the degree to which the individual finds it possible to resume his earlier role patterns." Newcomb, *Social Psychology*, pp. 476–77, 482.

Social workers faced with the task of rehabilitating former concentration- camp prisoners rapidly discovered that sympathy and understanding were not enough. The normal superego values of many of the prisoners had been so thoroughly smashed that adult standards of behavior for them were quite out of the question. Their behavior, indeed, was often most childlike. They made extreme demands, based not on actual physical needs but rather on the fear that they might be left out, or that others might receive more than they. Those who regained their equilibrium most quickly were the ones who were able to begin new lives in social environments that provided clear limits, precise standards, steady goals, and specific roles to play. Adjustment was not easy, however, even for the most fortunate. On the collective farms of Israel, for example, it was understood that former concentration-camp inmates would be "unable to control their greed for food" for a number of months. During that time, concern for their neighbors' sensibilities was more than one could expect. Paul Friedman, "The Road Back for the DP's," *Commentary*, VI (December, 1948), 502–10; Eva Rosenfeld, "Institutional Change in Israeli Collectives" (Ph.D. dissertation, Columbia University, 1952), p. 278.

23.   The experience of American prisoners taken by the Chinese during the Korean War seems to indicate that profound changes in behavior and values, if not in basic personality itself, can be effected without the use of physical torture or extreme deprivation. The Chinese were able to get large numbers of Americans to act as informers and to cooperate in numerous ways in the effort to indoctrinate all the prisoners with Communist propaganda. The technique contained two key elements. One was that all formal and informal authority structures within the group were systematically destroyed; this was done by isolating officers, non-commissioned officers, and any enlisted men who gave indications of leadership capacities. The other element involved the continual emphasizing of the captors' power and influence by judicious manipulation of petty rewards and punishments and by subtle hints of the greater rewards and more severe punishments (repatriation or nonrepatriation) that rested with the pleasure of those in authority. See Edgar H. Schein, "Some Observations on Chinese Methods of Handling Prisoners of War," *Public Opinion Quarterly*, XX (Spring, 1956), 321–27.

24.   In a system as tightly closed as the plantation or the concentration camp, the slave's or prisoner's position of absolute dependency virtually compels him to see the authority-figure as somehow really "good." Indeed, all the evil in his life may flow from this man—but then so also must everything of any value. Here is the seat of the only "good" he knows, and to maintain his psychic balance he must persuade himself that the good is in some way dominant. A threat to this illusion is thus in a real sense a threat to his very existence. It is a common experience among social workers dealing with neglected and maltreated children to have a child desperately insist on his love for a cruel and brutal parent and beg that he be allowed to remain with that parent. The most dramatic feature of this situation is the cruelty which it involves, but the mechanism which inspires the devotion is not the cruelty of the parent but rather the abnormal dependency of the child. A classic example of this mechanism in operation may be seen in the case of Varvara Petrovna, mother of Ivan Turgenev. Mme Turgenev "ruled over her serfs with a rod of iron." She demanded utter obedience and total submission. The slightest infraction of her rules brought the most severe punishment: "A maid who did not offer her a cup of tea in the proper manner was sent off to some remote village and perhaps separated from her family forever; gardeners who failed to prevent the plucking of a tulip in one of the flower beds before the house were ordered to be flogged; a servant whom she suspected of a mutinous disposition was sent off to Siberia." Her family and her most devoted servants were treated in much the same manner. "Indeed," wrote Varvara Zhitova, the adopted daughter of Mme Turgenev, "those who loved her and were most devoted to her suffered most of all." Yet in spite of her brutality she was adored by the very people she tyrannized. David Magarshack describes how once when thrashing her eldest son she nearly fainted with sadistic excitement, whereupon "little Nicholas, forgetting his punishment, bawled at the top of his voice: 'Water! Water for mummy!' " Mme Zhitova, who knew Mme Turgenev's cruelty intimately and was herself the constant victim of her tyranny, wrote: "In spite of this, I loved her passionately, and when I was, though rarely, separated from her, I felt lonely and unhappy." Even Mme Turgenev's maid Agatha, whose children were sent to another village

when still infants so that Agatha might devote all her time to her mistress, could say years later, "Yes, she caused me much grief., I suffered much from her, but all the same I loved her! She was a real lady!" V. Zhitova, *The Turgenev Family*, trans. A. S. Mills (London: Havill Press, 1954), p. 25; David Magarshack, *Turgenev: A Life* (New York: Grove, 1954), pp. 14, 16, 22.

25. Bruno Bettelheim tells us of the fantastic efforts of the old prisoners to believe in the benevolence of the officers of the SS. "They insisted that these officers [hid] behind their rough surface a feeling of justice and propriety; he, or they, were supposed to be genuinely interested in the prisoners and even trying, in a small way, to help them. Since nothing of these supposed feelings and efforts ever became apparent, it was explained that he hid them so effectively because otherwise he would not be able to help the prisoners. The eagerness of these prisoners to find reasons for their claims was pitiful. A whole legend was woven around the fact that of two officers inspecting a barrack one had cleaned his shoes from mud before entering. He probably did it automatically, but it was interpreted as a rebuff of the other officer and a clear demonstration of how he felt about the concentration camp." Bettelheim, "Individual and Mass Behavior," p. 451.

26. Professor Stampp, in a chapter called "To Make Them Stand in Fear," describes the planter's resources for dealing with a recalcitrant slave. *Peculiar Institution*, pp. 141–91.

27. Edward A. Pollard, *Black Diamonds Gathered in the Darkey Homes of the South* (New York: Pudney & Russel, 1859), p. 58.

28. *Ibid.,* p. viii.

29. John Pendleton Kennedy, *Swallow Barn* (Philadelphia: Carey & Lea, 1832).

30. John Dollard, *Caste and Class in a Southern Town* (2nd ed.; New York: Harper, 1949), p. 255. The lore of "accommodation," taken just in itself, is very rich and is, needless to say, morally very complex. It suggests a delicate psychological balance. On the one hand, as the Dollard citation above implies, accommodation is fraught with dangers for the personalities of those who engage in it. On the other hand, as Bruno Bettelheim has reminded me, this involves a principle that goes well beyond American Negro society and is to be found deeply imbedded in European traditions: the principle of how the powerless can manipulate the powerful through aggressive stupidity, literal-mindedness, servile fawning, and irresponsibility. In this sense the immovably stupid "Good Soldier Schweik" and the fawning Negro in Richard Wright's *Black Boy* who allowed the white man to kick him for a quarter partake of the same tradition. Each has a technique whereby he can in a real sense exploit his powerful superiors, feel contempt for them, and suffer in the process no great damage to his own pride. Jewish lore, as is well known, teems with this sort of thing. There was much of it also in the traditional relationships between peasants and nobles in central Europe.

   Still, all this required the existence of some sort of alternative forces for moral and psychological orientation. The problem of the Negro in slavery times involved the virtual absence of such forces. It was with the end of slavery, presumably, that they would first begin to present themselves in generally usable form—a man's neighbors, the Loyal Leagues, white politicians, and so on. It would be in these circumstances that the essentially intermediate technique of accommodation could be used as a protective device beneath which a more independent personality might develop.

31. Even Negro officeholders during Reconstruction, according to Francis B. Simkins, "were known to observe carefully the etiquette of the Southern caste system." "New Viewpoints of Southern Reconstruction," *Journal of Southern History*, V (February, 1939), 52.

32. Virtually all the ex-prisoners whose writing I have made use of were men and women who had certain privileges (as clerks, physicians, and the like) in the

camps. Many of the same persons were also active in the "underground" and could offer some measure of leadership and support for others. That is to say, both the objectivity necessary for making useful observations and the latitude enabling one to exercise some leadership were made possible by a certain degree of protection not available to the rank and file.

I should add, however, that a notable exception was the case of Bruno Bettelheim, who throughout the period of his detention had no privileged position of any kind which could afford him what I am calling an "alternative role" to play. And yet I do not think that it would be stretching the point too far to insist that he did in fact have such a role, one which was literally self-created: that of the scientific observer. In him, the scientist's objectivity, his feeling for clinical detail and sense of personal detachment, amounted virtually to a passion. It would not be fair, however, to expect such a degree of personal autonomy as this in other cases, except for a very few. I am told, for instance, that the behavior of many members of this "underground" toward their fellow prisoners was itself by no means above moral reproach. The depths to which the system could corrupt a man, it must be remembered, were profound.

33. See Tannenbaum, *Slave and Citizen*, pp. 64–65.

34. *Ibid.,* pp. 4 ff., 56–57, 90–93; see also Johnston, *Negro in the New World*,p. 90.

35. Compared with the countless uprisings of the Brazilian Negroes, the slave revolts in our own country appear rather desperate and futile. Only three emerge as worthy of any note, and their seriousness—even when described by a sympathetic historian like Herbert Aptheker—depends largely on the supposed plans of the rebels rather than on the things they actually did. The best organized of such "revolts," those of Vesey and Gabriel, were easily suppressed, while the most dramatic of them—the Nat Turner Rebellion—was characterized by little more than aimless butchery. The Brazilian revolts, on the other hand, were marked by imagination and a sense of direction, and they often involved large-scale military operations. One is impressed both by their scope and their variety. They range from the legendary Palmares Republic of the seventeenth century (a Negro state organized by escaped slaves and successfully defended for over fifty years), to the bloody revolts of the Moslem Negroes of Bahia which, between 1807 and 1835, five times paralyzed a substantial portion of Brazil. Many such wars were launched from the *quilombos* (fortified villages built deep in the jungles by escaped slaves to defend themselves from recapture); there were also the popular rebellions in which the Negroes of an entire area would take part. One is immediately struck by the heroic stature of the Negro leaders: no allowances of any sort need be made for them; they are impressive from any point of view. Arthur Ramos has described a number of them, including Zambi, a fabulous figure of the Palmares Republic; Luiza Mahin, mother of the Negro poet Luiz Gama and "one of the most outstanding leaders of the 1835 insurrection"; and Manoel Francisco dos Anjos Fereira, whose followers in the *Balaiada* (a movement which drew its name from "Baliao," his own nickname) held the entire *province of* Maranhão for three years. Their brilliance, gallantry, and warlike accomplishments give to their histories an almost legendary quality. On the other hand, one could not begin to think of Nat Turner in such a connection. See Ramos, *The Negro in Brazil*, pp. 24–53; Herbert Aptheker, *American Negro Slave Revolts* (New York: Columbia University, 1943, *passim*).

36. See William R. Hogan and Edwin A. Davis (eds.). *William Johnson's Natchez; The Ante-Bellum Diary of a Free Negro* (Baton Rouge: Louisiana State University Press, 1951), esp. pp. 1–64.

37. Aptheker, *American Negro Slave Revolts*, pp. 220, 208–69, 295–96, and *passim.*

38. Vernon L. Wharton, *The Negro in Mississippi, 1865–1890* (Chapel Hill: University of North Carolina Press, 1942), p. 164.

The first of two critiques of Elkins' Slavery is presented here. The author, Earle E. Thorpe, criticizes Elkins' contention that Negro slaves in North America (in contrast to those in other parts of the New World) belonged to a "society of helpless dependents." He rejects the concentration camp analogy as well.

In Thorpe's view, Elkins exaggerates the differences between North and Latin American patterns and responses to them and minimizes the profound differences between the ongoing slavery system and the program of genocide that was the underlying raison d'être for the Nazi "slave labor" camps.

9

Chattel Slavery and Concentration Camps

Earle E. Thorpe

After criticizing the historical writings of Ulrich Bonnell Phillips as being strongly biased and based on faulty sources, Richard Hofstadter wrote in 1944:

> Let the study of the Old South be undertaken by other (unbiased) scholars who have absorbed the viewpoint of modern cultural anthropology, who have a feeling for social psychology . . . , who will concentrate upon the neglected rural elements that formed the great majority of the Southern population, who will not rule out the testimony of more critical observers, and who will realize that any history of slavery must be written in large part from the standpoint of the slave—and then the possibilities of the Old South as a field of research and historical experience will loom larger than ever.[1]

In 1959 the University of Chicago Press published a book entitled *Slavery: A Problem In American Institutional and Intellectual Life,*

From *Negro History Bulletin,* 25 (May 1962), 171–176, published by the Association for the Study of Negro Life and History, Inc.

which was written by a scholar who states that he accepted certain of the Hofstadter challenges as incentives for his study of the institution. This scholar, Stanley M. Elkins, in an opening chapter entitled. "Slavery as a Problem in Historiography," opines that studies of the Negro in American history made by Negroes themselves, as well as those by Ulrich Bonnell Phillips, James Ford Rhodes, Kenneth Stampp, Gunnar Myrdal, Herbert Aptheker, and just about everyone who has previously written on the subject have the serious defect of being biased, polemical, and overly dominated by moral considerations. Thus Professor Elkins clearly indicates that he is going to beware of the heavy hand of prejudice which he feels has done damage to previous writings about the Negro.

Elkins makes it clear that he does not believe the old charge that Negroes are biologically inferior. Although he shares the convictions that the slaves were indeed culturally inferior, this scholar goes to considerable length to disagree with U. B. Phillips and others who contended that plantation slaves in America were inferior because the African cultures from which they came were inferior. Unlike Phillips, Melville J. Herskovits, and others, Elkins agrees with those scholars who believe that very little of the African heritage survived in North America.[2] "No true picture . . . of African culture," he concludes, "seems to throw any light at all on the origins of what would emerge in American plantation society as the stereotyped 'Sambo' personality."[3]

On one aspect of his own thesis, Elkins writes:

> An examination of American slavery, checked at certain critical points against a very different slave system, that of Latin America, reveals that a major key to many of the contrasts between them was an institutional key: The presence or absence of other powerful institutions in society made an immense difference in the character of slavery itself. In Latin America, the very tension and balance among three kinds of organizational concerns—church, crown, and plantation agriculture—prevented slavery from being carried by the planting class to its ultimate logic. For the slave in terms of the space thus allowed for the development of men and women as moral beings, the result was an 'open system': a system of contact with free society through which ultimate absorption into society could and did occur with great frequency. The rights of personality implicit in the ancient traditions of slavery and in the chruch's most venerable assumptions on the nature of the human soul were thus in a vital sense conserved, whereas to a staggering extent the very opposite was true in North American slavery (which) operated as a 'closed system.'[4]

This scholar seeks to further buttress his conclusion with a contention that the impact of enslavement on the personality and character of Nazi concentration camp inmates was substantially identical with that which plantation slavery in North America had on the personality and character of Negroes. Utilizing the excellent and abundant literature which describes and analyzes the behavior of concentration camp inmates, Professor Elkins gives a concise but thorough picture of this behavior.[5] *Without any effort at all* to enumerate the *differences* between plantation slavery and the concentration camp, Elkins admits that there are differences but contends that this does not make comparison impossible.[6] He characterizes Negro slaves in North America as "a society of helpless dependents."[7] The dominant slave type, Elkins states, "corresponded in its major outlines to 'Sambo.'" This dominant type existed, he declares. because "there were elements in the very structure of the plantation system—its 'closed' character—that could sustain infantilism as a normal feature of behavior."[8] At the end of the volume, the author reminds us again, that in the analogy which he used, "the mechanism was the infantilizing tendencies of power."[9] Of what he feels was the dominant slave type, he writes:

> Sambo, the typical plantation slave, was docile but irresponsible, loyal but lazy, humble but chronically given to lying and stealing; his behavior was full of infantile silliness and his talk inflated with childish exaggeration. His relationship with his master was one of utter dependence and childish attachment.[10]

Of his acceptance of this stereotype, Professor Elkins writes:

> The picture has far too many circumstantial details, its hues have been stroked in by too many different brushes, for it to be denounced as counterfeit. Too much folk-knowledge, too much plantation literature, too much of the Negro's own lore, have gone into its making to entitle one in good conscience to condemn it as "conspiracy."[11]

"Why should it be, turning once more to Latin America," he continues, "that there one finds no Sambo, no social tradition, that is, in which slaves were defined by virtually complete consensus as children incapable of being treated with the full privileges of freedom and adulthood?" "There," he answers, "the system surely had its brutalities, (but) there . . . the system was not closed."[12]

The position taken in this article is that the Sambo stereotype was not the real Negro personality because, unlike the concentration camp, plantation slavery in North America had enough "elbow room" for the development of a more complex, better-rounded personality; that Sambo was often the side of his personality which the Negro chose to present to the white man; that although the child-posture is the one which whites generally sought to effect in their relationship with Negroes, because of the contradictions and "elbow room" in the system most bondsmen never internalized many of the planters' values. Elkins fails to recognize properly the complexity of slave personality. The bondsman wore many faces, of which Sambo usually was only his public and not his private one.[13]

With reference to the so-called Latin American contrast, it seems that there are at least three effective answers to the Elkins thesis. First, despite their differences, because of the high degree of similarity, it is erroneous to categorize Latin American slavery as an "open system" and the North American variety as the "closed system." A second point hinges on this scholar's often-repeated assertion that, "one searches in vain through the literature of the Latin-American slave systems for the 'Sambo' of our tradition—the perpetual child incapable of maturity."[14] This is so not because there were no slaves in Latin America who evidenced clear Sambo characteristics as one side of their personalities. Rather, the omission reflects Professor Elkins' own admission that in contrast to the situation in North America, Latin American culture *accepted the institution of slavery as a necessary evil.* Elkins fails to see that there was thus no need to create myths and stereotypes to justify the institution. In other words, the existence of the stereotype in North America is rooted not in a true estimate of slave personality but in the peculiar psychological needs of the slave owners. By their effort to convince themselves, and everyone else, that the institution was a positive good, the planters of North America were compelled to claim that Sambo was indeed the true slave personality.[15] Literature can be very misleading.

In addition to the objection that the personality differences are usually little more than mythical literary inventions created to satisfy the North American slave-owner's conscience, one reviewer of the Elkins volume shows that when the capitalist system matured in Latin America, there was practically no difference between treatment of slaves and freedmen there and the treatment meted out in North America. The reviewer concludes:

> The slave plantation . . . was a special, emergent capitalist form of industrial organization, which appeared earlier, and with more intensity, in the colonies of the north European powers than in the colonies of Spain. . . .
>
> The differentials in growth of slave plantations in different colonies are to be understood as resulting from different ecologies, differential maturation of metropolitan markets and industries, and different political relationships between creole governing bodies and the metropolitan authorities. The rate of growth of the slave plantation . . .

did not hinge on matters of race, civil liberties, protection of the rights of individuals slave and free, or the presence or absence of one or several religious codes.[16]

As dark as the picture of chattel slavery in North America was, because the theory, literature, law and actual practice were frequently at variance, the results on personality development were not as extreme as Professor Elkins would have us believe.[17]

It is wrong to study in an institution or culture, as he does "the infantilizing tendencies of power" without pointing out the countertendencies which were operative and which tended to minimize, negate, or eliminate many of the infantilizing tendencies. This omission makes his conclusions about the personalities of plantation slaves in North America erroneous in their simplicity. Among the significant omissions which would have to be included in a valid analogy are the following.

Differences

A major difference between the two systems is to be found in the extent of resistance to enslavement. Many observers have noted the almost complete lack of resistance among inmates of the concentration camps, pointing out that although guards were usually few the prisoners walked meekly into the gas chambers or quietly dug their graves and lined up beside them to be shot.[18] Bruno Bettelheim is severely critical of the prisoners for what he feels was their unrealistic lack of resistance.[19] Elkins agrees with this depiction of the behavior of camp inmates, but gives a similar characterization of the plantation slaves, whom he calls "a society of helpless dependents."[20] That he takes this statement literally can be seen in the disparaging remarks which he makes about Herbert Aptheker's study of slave revolts,[21] and in his own comparison of slave revolts in North and South America. Elkins does not perceive that, despite the absence of protracted large scale slave revolts in North America, the many forms of persistent resistance by the bondsmen to their enslavement is dramatic evidence of the very significant difference between the two systems.

Professor Elkins offers as one proof that Negro slaves were a docile mass the statement that, "the revolts that actually did occur were in no instance planned by plantation laborers but rather by Negroes whose qualities of leadership were developed well outside the full coercions of the plantation authority-system."[22] So anxious is he to prove his thesis that he apparently discounts the possibility that this may be so not because of the lack of leadership qualities among plantation slaves but because the opportunity to plan revolts was greater in or near towns or cities. Furthermore, although, as Elkins points out, Denmark Vesey was a freed artisan, Nat Turner, a literate preacher, and Gabriel a blacksmith who lived near Richmond, their hundreds and thousands of co-conspirators were not of this category, but were mostly the plantation slaves whom Elkins describes as humble, lazy, silly, immoral, docile, and loyal. In other words, to Elkins the leaders of the plots and revolts were the unusual or exceptional individuals. This and similar arguments leads the present writer to the conviction that Professor Elkins is here utilizing a version of the old argument which attributed the intelligence and achievements of some light-skinned Negroes to the amount of so-called white blood in their veins, thereby eliminating them from the race.[23]

Several observers have written of the manner in which the Nazis thought of and sought to operate the concentration camps with the same organizational and administrative emphases as are found in the most modern factory.[24] Absence of the mid-twentieth century level of organizational knowledge and efficiency was a major factor which kept plantation slavery from being as dehumanizing as was the case with concentration camps. It is not without justification that modern man uses the word "totalitarianism" to describe this century's mass state. "Every single moment of their lives was strictly regulated and supervised," one critic says of the camp inmates, "They had no privacy whatsoever."[25] Even after the work day was over, the camp inmate lived in barracks-style quarters which did not afford anything like the amount of freedom from the surveillance and oppressions of the ruling elite that slave quarters on the plantation usually offered. It is because he was so constantly under surveillance and oppression, together with the chronic possibility and fear of momentary extermination, that the camp inmate presents the classic picture of the ever-regressed personality and character which Elkins mistakenly attributes to plantation slaves.

Many camp inmates were made the subject of barbarous medical experiments.[26] Plantation slaves were not so used as human guinea pigs. A highly literate former camp inmate states that at the peak of its development, "the . . . slave labor and extermination policy (of the concentration camps) did away with all considerations for the value of a life, even in terms of a slave society. . . . In the Hitler state slaves (did not even have an) investment value. That was the *great difference* between exploitation by private capitalists and exploitation by a state answering only to itself."[27] Are we to suppose, as Elkins does, that this "great difference" between the two systems made no difference where the personalities which they bred or allowed is concerned? Whereas the concentration camp inmate, in order to keep from becoming an elected candidate for the incinerators or gas chambers, always had to act and work as if he were physically able to be of some service to the Third Reich, the plantation slave was usually free from this daily and hourly threat of a death sentence. Because he represented economic capital, usually the worst that the plantation slave could expect for dissatisfying the ruling class on such matters was a lashing or being sold, but of the camp inmates, we are told, "Everybody was convinced that his chances for survival were very slim; therefore to preserve himself as an individual seemed pointless."[28] "The prisoners' lives were in such extreme danger," continues this observer, "that little energy or interest was left over" for anything except concern with the problem of sheer survival.[29]

In his 1947 Presidential Address before the American Historical Association, Professor William L. Langer discusses the great psychological impact which the Black Death had on the personality and character of Europeans of the late medieval and early modern periods. A study might well be made of the consciousness of death in Negro thought, but, apart from the horrors of the Middle Passage, there is nothing in the history of plantation slavery to match the impact of the Black Death or the omnipresent hand of death in the concentration camps. This fact is doubtless one of several which kept plantation slavery from being as dehumanizing as was the Nazis' internment camps.

Elkins, Victor Frankl, Bettelheim, and others have commented on the weakness and almost disappearance at times of the emotional life of the camp inmates.[30] This is a marked contrast to the emotional life of the plantation slaves, an emotionality often so variegated and strong that it has added an indelible heritage of dance, song, laughter, and pathos to the American way of life. In the literature on concentration camps, many pages are filled with discussions of the *Muselmanner*, or Moslems, persons who had completely given up all interest in life. To this the literature on chattel slavery stands in marked contrast. A number of scholars state that throughout the slave era, among other attributes Negroes manifested "childlike qualities of happiness and good nature."[31] Where were these qualities to be found in the concentration camps? In great contrast to the plantation system, with concentration camp inmates, *the other side of child behavior*, a side which Elkins ignores entirely—that of the happy child—is missing.

Bettelheim tells us that concentration camp inmates were

deliberately kept on a starvation diet in order to make them easier to handle. "It is difficult," he writes, "to deeply terrorize a people that is well fed and well housed."[32] As inadequate as their diets usually were, plantation slaves were better fed than concentration camp inmates. Largely because of the poor quality and inadequate amounts of food given, after a few months of imprisonment, most of the latter were mere skin and bones suffering chronically from diarrhea and dysentery.[33]

The fact that most Ante-Bellum Negroes were *born into slavery*, while the concentration camp inmates were born and reared as free men and women must have considerable significance where the development of personality is concerned. Also, there were no state laws in Nazi Germany comparable to the "Black Codes" of the Old South. Although they were often honored more in the breach than in the observance, are we to suppose that the existence of laws setting limits to the cruelty which plantation slaves could be made the objects of, and actual court cases which resulted from the existence of these laws, had no effect on the personality and character development of the slave?

We are informed that "No prisoner was told why he was imprisoned, and never for how long."[34] In contrast to this, are we to suppose that the elaborate biblical, historical, and other justifications for his race's enslavement which were constantly presented to the plantation bondsman had no effect on the development of his personality and character? As ridiculous as these justifications now appear, may it not be that such rationalizations given to an enslaved race may affect their personality development in a more positive way than is the case with enslavement of selected members of a free populace, with no justification at all given?

Professor Elkins calls both the concentration camps and antebellum plantations highly similar "closed systems." Yet where in the concentration camps was there anything comparable to the ebonyhued slave women suckling white infants at their breasts, or free white children and slave children playing together, or planters paying high cash prices for colored mistresses and concubines? Where in Nazi Germany was there an Underground Railroad, or a geographically contiguous region rife with abolitionism, or anything even comparable to the colonization society? How many SS officers or Capos encouraged the camp inmates to sing while they worked as was the case with the Negro slaves? While the plantations produced the enchanting slave songs and tales, and eternally beautiful spirituals, what of comparable beauty has come out of the concentration camps?[35] And can we imagine inmates being in such physical and psychical condition so as to be considered for last-ditch military service in the manner of the Confederate Congress voting to enlist and arm Negro slaves? Because their fruits were so different, we must conclude that the personalities of slaves and camp inmates were different.

So absolute and unmitigated was the cruelty of the concentration camps that they were indeed the closed systems to which Elkins refers. In them it is true that prisoners had to make a total adjustment to enslavement, and for most dehumanization was well nigh complete. But in the United States even the slaves knew that the basic national creed as encouched in such documents as the Declaration of Independence and the Federal Constitution ran counter to the prospect of their remaining eternally in bondage. Where in Nazi Germany did a similar conflict exist between ideal and reality?

Professor Elkins' failure adequately to consider these differences means that his conclusion that the effect which the concentration camp had on its inmates is the same effect that plantation slavery in North America had on Negroes is in need of drastic revision. While he seems to understand fairly well the mind and personality of the camp inmate, his understanding of the mind of the Negro slaves leaves much to be desired.

Despite their similarities, the differences between the two systems are so significant that, for the development of a more healthy or adult personality, when compared to the concentration camps the plantation system in North America had considerably more "elbow room." It was not on the plantations of North America as Elkins claims, but in such products of Occidental efficiency and technology as Belsen, Sachsenhausen, Dachau, and Buchenwald that our Christian civilization first saw the institution of slavery "carried to its ultimate logic."[36]

It is not without significance that plantation slavery existed in a culture which was peace oriented, while the concentration camps were vital parts of a war-oriented culture. Just as the twentieth century has produced total war, in these camps it also has produced total enslavement. However, although the Nazis may be said to have perfected the institution of slavery, from the long record of North America's treatment of Africans and their descendants the Nazis could have and probably did learn much.

Because his own biases blurred his vision,[37] and because of the too-loose fashion in which Elkins handles his analogy, we must conclude that the challenge laid down for historical scholars in 1944 by Professor Hofstadter has not yet been met. Professor Elkins should have been more impressed with the words of Herbert J. Aptheker, written in 1943, which state—"The dominant historiography in the

United States either omits the Negro people or presents them as a people without a past, as a people who have been docile, passive, parasitic, imitative."[38] "This picture," Aptheker declares, "is a lie." Elkins should have been more impressed with the words of a planter who wrote in 1837—

> The most general defect in the character of the Negro is hypocrisy: and this hypocrisy frequently makes him pretend to more ignorance than he possesses; and if his master treats him as a fool, he will be sure to act the fools part.[39]

Finally, Professor Elkins should have been more impressed with the work of the Association for the Study of Negro Life and History, which has devoted almost a half century of labor directed toward disproving the Sambo and similar stereotypes.

Notes

1. Richard Hofstadter, "U. B. Phillips and the Plantation Legend," *Journal of Negro History*, XXIX (April, 1944) pp. 109–124.
2. See Melville J. Herskovits, *The Myth of the Negro Past* (New York: Harpers, 1941), and E. Franklin Frazier, *The Negro in the United States* (New York: Macmillan, 1949).
3. Elkins, *Slavery*, p. 97.
4. *Ibid.*, p. 82.
5. *Ibid.*, pp. 103 ff.
6. *Ibid.*, p. 104.
7. *Ibid.*, p. 89.
8. When he holds that the Sambo stereotype is a factual representation of the plantation slave's personality, Elkins apparently fails to perceive that he may at the same time be ascribing this same personality to the masses of antebellum Southern whites. Bruno Bettelheim (See Chapter 7 of his *The Informed Heart: Autonomy in a Mass Age*, (Glencoe, Illinois: The Free Press, I960), and other observers state that the same psychological forces operative within the concentration camps were the dominant ones operative on the German populace outside the camps, and the effect was the same, with the difference being largely one of degree. Wilbur Cash and other critics of southern culture have pointed out that the masses of southern whites were subjected to the same frontier forces, similar patterns of control, paternalism, general illiteracy, and exclusion from the political, social, and cultural mainstream as was the Negro slave, with the difference being one of degree. These same critics often have ascribed to southern whites, ante- and post-bellum, virtually the same negative personality traits and characteristics as those often attributed to the Negro.

    It is doubtless true, as Professor Elkins writes, that certain situations or settings put premiums on certain types of behavior, while severely penalizing certain other types of behavior (*Slavery*, p. 228). In order for the rigid Sambo stereotype to emerge as the true slave personality, however, a high degree of constancy or consistency in behavior would have to be maintained. Such has never been the case where race relations in the South is concerned. The strange career of Jim Crow did not begin with Appomattox, as Elkins thinks (p. 133), but was a prominent feature of Old South culture.

Also, the rather common belief which Elkins appears to accept completely (pp. 82 ff) to the effect that the old South accepted the Negro only in the posture of a child is an erroneous oversimplification. Here again consistency was too lacking for the image to be true, for it is largely in the social relations or amenities that the child-posture was insisted on. At working time, which existed far more frequently and lasted much longer than the brief periods of what may be termed points of social contact, the white South sought to get the bondsman to give a very efficient and adult-like performance. The same is true where the matter of obeying the laws was concerned, for here the white South wanted not child-like irresponsibility, but adult-like respect for the law. The notion that the Old South always encouraged and wanted the child-posture from Negroes needs considerable revision.

9. Elkins, *Slavery*, p. 225.
10. *Ibid.*, p. 82.
11. *Ibid.*, p. 84.
12. *Ibid.*, p. 134.
13. On the more positive side, it may be pointed out that Elkins' discussion of the role of guilt in liberal and reform movements is highly provocative. Too, unfortunately for the scholar who is interested in plantation slavery in America, there were no professional psychologists and psychiatrists among the Negro bondsmen. Therefore, if the student of this institution will avoid the pit-falls into which Elkins stumbled, from a careful study and comparison of the behavior of concentration camp inmates he may gain great insights into many aspects of this "problem in American institutional and intellectual life."

The growth of anthropology, psychoanalysis, social psychology and related disciplines, and the significance of the new insights into human behavior which they offer, means that the historian of the second half of the twentieth century will probably not be counted adequately literate who does not have an acquaintance with these disciplines. In calling for this broader approach to the study of the Negro in American history, Professors Hofstadter and Elkins are correct. In his December, 1957 address before the American Historical Association entitled, "The Next Assignment," William L. Langer had as his central concern "the directions which historical study might profitably take in the years to come," (in *American Historical Review*, LXIII, No. 2, January, 1958, p. 284). Here he urged historians to cease to be "buried in their own conservatism" and to recognize "the urgently needed deepening of our historical understanding through exploitation of the concepts and findings of modern . . . psychoanalysis and its later developments and variations as included in the terms 'dynamic' or 'depth psychology.'" The whole of Professor Langer's Presidential address was an attack on what he called the "almost completely negative attitude toward the teachings of psychoanalysis" which historians have traditionally held together with some illustrations and suggestions as to specific applications of this knowledge which historians may make. The present writer believes that scholars who are interested in Afro-American studies would do well to take Professor Langer's suggestions seriously.

14. Elkins, *Slavery*, p. 84.
15. Any historian who denies that Sambo, *often feigned* but sometimes genuine, was *one side* of the bondsman's personality is probably guilty of being unrealistic. What is now known about both human behavior and totalitarian systems calls

for a change in some aspects of the slave image which some Negro Historians have favored. Since these were their immediate blood and cultural forebearers, and in view of the overly-narrow image of them which the Slavocracy projected, it is understandable that they sometimes have given great stress to the neater side of the bondsman's personality and character. Thus in reacting against one stereotype, they have been in danger of creating another one, equally false.

Contemporary knowledge ought to have put beyond the bounds of controversy that slavery is generally debasing and degrading to human personality. Rather than fly in the face of this fact and deny the whole of the Slavocracy's propaganda, the truths that should be insisted upon are: (1) These negative behavior characteristics are not innate racial traits. (2) They indict the slave system and not the enslaved, and (3) They do not constitute the whole picture.

16. S. W. Mintz, in *American Anthropologist*, Vol. 63, No. 3 (June, 1961), p. 586. Professor Elkins appears to be essentially correct in his contention that in the case of plantation slavery and the concentration camps each became "a kind of grotesque patriarchy." (*Slavery*, pp. 104, 113). The present observer does not find this the startling discovery which Professor Elkins seems to think it is. There is a sense in which practically every highly authoritarian system is a grotesque patriarchy, and Elkins seems to miss Wilbur Cash's often repeated assertions in his volume, *The Mind of the South* (New York: A. Knopf, 1941), that the total southern culture, both ante- and post-bellum, has been essentially such a grotesque patriarchy. The present observer has even noticed that in several small colleges and universities the college president represents for a number of students and faculty members a father image and paternalism is the dominant basis of their relationships. This paternalistic factor is the major argument against highly authoritarian systems and, therefore, the major argument in favor of democracy as a way of life which does not treat adults as if they are children.

17. Apparently the only subject on which Professor Elkins is willing to accept the judgment of the slave-owners is their conclusion that Negroes constitute an inferior human type. As indicated, to be sure he does not accept the reasoning on which his conclusion rests, but he devotes one-half of his book in an effort to prove that the slave owners' conclusion was a correct one. Yet, near the end of his volume, when discussing, "Slavery, Consensus, and the Southern Intellect," he is well-nigh completely denunciatory of the southern intellect which he says, mainly because of its rigidity, single-mindedness, and hysterical fears (p. 207) was not able to think objectively about slavery. "At most," he writes, the southern intellect "thought in the vicinity of slavery." (*Ibid.*) On this point, Elkins further states:

"The existence of thoroughgoing consensus in a democratic community appears to create two sorts of conditions for the functioning of intellect. One is sternly coercive, the other, wildly permissive. On the one hand, consensus narrows the alternatives with which thought may deal; on the other, it removes all manner of limits—limits of discrimination, circumspection, and discipline—on the alternatives that remain. The former function is probably better understood than the latter; both, however, were fully at work in the intellectual life of the ante-bellum South. (pp. 212–213)."

Elkins declares that the Southern intellect made "a general agreement" to stop "[objective] thinking about slavery altogether," and points up the ineffectiveness of pro-slavery propaganda by reminding us that though the slave's way of life was declared to be a better one than that of northern industrial workers, there was an absolute failure of "any free workers to present themselves for enslavement." (216) "In reality," he concludes, "the contour of this body of thought was governed by the fact that the South was talking no longer to the world, or even to the North, but to itself. It is this fact—the fact of internal consensus and the peculiar lack of true challenge-points at any level of Southern society—that gives the pro-slavery polemic its special distinction." (p. 217). In this chapter Elkins is clearly describing the southern mind as a diseased one and he rejects its conclusions on practically all points except one, this being the concept of Negro inferiority.

18. See Otto Kurst, *Auschwitz*, Hillman Books (New York: Hillman Periodicals, 1960); Eugen Kogon, *The Theory and Practice of Hell*, tr. by Heinz Norden, Berkley Medallion Book (New York: Berkley Publishing Corp., 1960 ed.); Rudolf Hoess, *Commandant of Auschwitz*, tr. by Constantine FitzGibbon, Popular Library Book (New York: 1961); Victor Frankl, *From Death Camp to Existentialism*, tr. Ilse Lasch (Boston: Beacon Press, 1959).

19. B. Bettelheim. *The Informed Heart*, see especially the last three chapters.

20. Elkins, *Slavery*, p. 98.

21. Aptheker's sources he calls "unsubstantiated rumors gleaned from rural Southern newspaper."

22. Elkins, *Slavery*, p. 139.

23. For other examples of the evidence of slave resistance which Elkins treats as of little significance see Harvey Wish, "American Slave Insurrections before 1861," *Journal of Negro History*, XXII (July, 1937), pp. 299–320; R. A. and A. H. Bauer, "Day to Day Resistance to Slavery," *Ibid.*, XXVII (October, 1942), pp. 388–419; Kenneth W. Porter, "Florida Slaves and Free Negroes in the Seminole War, 1825–1842," *Ibid.*, XXVIII (October, 1943), pp. 390–421; John Hope Franklin, *From Slavery to Freedom* (New York: A. Knopf, 1947); and Earle E. Thorpe, *The Mind of the Negro* (Baton Rouge, Louisiana: Harrington Publications, 1961), Chapters III, IV, and V.

Not only is Elkins' picture of what oppression did to the personality and character of plantation slaves overdrawn, the same is true of the picture which he paints of the results of oppression in the concentration camp. On this Victor Frankl has written:

"The sort of person the prisoner became was the result of an inner decision, and not the result of camp influences alone. Fundamentally, therefore, any man can, even under such circumstances, decide what shall become of him—mentally and spiritually. He may retain his human dignity even in a concentration camp" (in his *From Death Camp to Existentialism*, p. 66).

Of the changes in personality and character which took place, Bettelheim states— "Given the conditions of the camp, these changes were more often for the worse, but sometimes definitely for the better. So one and the same environment could bring about radical changes both for better and worse" (in his *The Informed Heart*, p. 14).

24. See, for example, works already cited by Bruno Bettelheim, Otto Kurst, Eugen Kogon, Rudolf Hoess, and V. Frankl.

25. B. Bettelheim, *op. cit.*, p. 108.

26. See A. Mitscherlich and F. Mielke, *Doctors of Infamy* (New York: Henry Schuman, 1949).

27. B. Bettelheim, *op. cit.*, p. 243. Italics supplied.

28. *Ibid.*, p. 138.

29. *Ibid.*, p. 203.

30. *Ibid., passim*; S. M. Elkins, *op. cit.*, p. 115.

31. Otto Klineberg, ed., *Characteristics of the American Negro* (New York: Harpers, 1944).

32. B. Bettelheim, *op. cit.*, p. 297.

33. Elkins states that in the concentration camps, because of chronic hunger due to the scanty meals, "even the sexual instincts no longer functioned." (*Slavery*, p. 107). Bettelheim denies this and states that both homosexuality and masturbation were practiced in the camps, though often more because of anxiety as to whether one had lost his sexuality than for any other reason.

34. Bettelheim, *op. cit.*, p. 108.

35. There were, of course, similarities in the reactions of inmates of the concentration camps and the plantation slaves. Among those similarities, both groups tended to be highly interested in food and other bodily needs, to day-dream a lot as an escape from the harsh realities of their lives, and to internalize the values of the ruling class. Because of fear of the ruling elite, both tended to direct many of their aggressions against one another, and, as was the case with the camp prisoner-leaders known as Capos, sometimes Negroes put in positions of leadership outdid the Slavocracy in manifestations of anti-Negroism. Among both, stealing from or cheating the ruling elite was often considered as honorable as stealing from fellow slaves was thought despicable.

36. A number of psychologists and psychiatrists have pointed out that the radical alterations in personality and character which occurred in concentration camps prove that some long-accepted Freudian concepts, valid under normal life-circumstances, are invalid where the behavior of man under extreme stress is concerned. Here is a situation roughly analogous to that of Newtonian physics, which twentieth-century scientists have shown to break down at both of the extreme ends of the matter and space continuities. It has been pointed out that much in Freudian psychology was peculiarly applicable to the nineteenth-century society in which Freud lived, "the stability of whose institutional and status relationships could always to a large extent be taken for granted," but less appropriate for a dynamic culture such as that long characteristic of the United States (Elkins, *Slavery*, p. 119). That Freud failed to perceive these particular limitations of his psychology, Elkins attributes in part to the fact that in modern occidental civilization, before the Nazi concentration camps chattel slavery in America was the only large-scale social laboratory which might have given Freud the evidence that he needed for a more inclusive psychology. Thus it seems that Freud might have benefited greatly from a close study of slavery in America. (For other comments on the changes in Freudian psychology wrought by the concentration camp experiences see Eli Cohen, *Human Behavior in the Concentration Camp*, New York: Norton, 1953; Bruno Bettelheim, *The Informed Heart: Autonomy in A Mass Age*, p. 14, *passim*; Leo Alexander, "War Crimes: Their Social-Psychological Aspects," *American Journal of Psychiatry*, CV (September, 1948) p. 173; and Victor Frankl, *From Death Camp to Existentialism*, *passim*.

 On the subject of this paper, see also Kenneth Stampp. "The Historian and Southern Negro Slavery," *American Historical Review*, LXII (April, 1952).

37. Although Professor Elkins usually has rejected the mood and methodology of the Slavocracy, he makes the mistake of accepting its conclusions about the nature of the bondsman's personality and character. Throughout the volume Professor Elkins reveals himself as a staunch elitist and conservative, in whose philosophy, like that of most conservatives, the word "gradualism" is sacrosanct. Further evidence of his biases in favor of the Slavocracy are evident

in the strongly denunciatory tone which he takes where the American abolitionists are concerned. Calling them "Intellectuals without Responsibility," he writes as if they were all hate and guilt- ridden neurotics who should have been incarcerated for their own sake and for that of society (see pp. 140–192 of his *Slavery*). Elkins erroneously states that the "loftiest manifestation" of slave religion was "at about the level of Green Pastures," (p. 195), and he feels that had not irresponsible extremists, such as the Abolitionists, had their way slavery would have been eliminated by a gradual, hence to him more adult, approach. This adult approach would have had as one step the insistence that each slave "be offered a spiritual life marked by dignity and be given instruction in Christian morality," (p. 195). That this would have involved a denial of the "positive good" argument of the South, or how a slave society can effectively teach Christian morality are points on which Elkins is silent.

Professor Elkins has great admiration for the English abolitionists and thinks that they were realistic, objective and dispassionate about their cause because they were men of wealth who operated through parliament and other well-established institutions, in contrast with the American abolitionists who were a displaced elite, anti-institutional, and each speaking for no one but himself. He ignores the fact that declining profits from slave produced products was a key factor in the success which English abolitionists had, while abolitionism in the United States was fighting a system which could boast of almost steadily rising prices from about 1810 to 1860. Too, he omits the fact that when England abolished slavery she had a diversity of economic interests while the Old South's economy rested almost exclusively on cotton culture. Finally, Elkins fails to consider another significant difference between the two abolitionist movements. "The United States alone, of all the great powers," comments one observer, "had to fight for the abolition of slavery within its own national territory. . . . The irreducible conflict, in the case of other nations, was fought by under-mining mercantilism, pushing free trade, and shifting power to the industrial capitalists . . . this was accomplished within the metropolis, far from the colonies themselves. The American South, however, was integrated with United States institutions in a way that the British West Indies never were, and never could be, with the institutions of Great Britain." (S. W. Mintz, *op. cit.*, p. 587.)

Professor Elkins repeatedly makes it clear that he detests uncompromising idealists, and has great admiration for "men with specific stakes in society, men attached to institutions and with a vested interest in one another's presence, men aware of being engaged with concrete problems of power." (pp. 146–47.) By his standards not only do Margaret Fuller, Ralph Waldo Emerson, William Ellery Channing, Orestes Browning, Theodore Parker, James Freeman Clark, Bronson Alcott, Henry David Thoreau and other persons mentioned flunk the course, but Socrates, Jesus Christ and similar non-propertied idealists and reformers who worked largely outside of institutional frameworks also fail to pass. Elkins apparently fails to appreciate the fact that a dynamic society probably needs critics operating without as well as within the institutional framework, for if the man outside of institutions is liable to exaggerate the role of the individual, those who operate within institutions are liable to become organization and institution-bound and lose sight of human beings.

38.   Herbert J. Aptheker, *American Negro Slave Revolts* (New York: Columbia University Press), 1943.

39.   In Kenneth Stampp, *The Peculiar Institution* (New York: A. Knopf, 1956), p. 99, quoting *The Farmer's Register*, V (1837), p. 32.

Mina Davis Caulfield argues that Elkins' thesis is based on the fallacious assumption that the slave had no sense of his own identity, no community, and no culture.

According to this critic, parallel institutions developed from (and were insured by) the social structure of the plantation system. And, as in all societies, various roles were learned—and played. Undoubtedly, "Sambo" was one such role, a role played for the benefit of white masters (and, some might facetiously say, for white historians as well).

This last essay in the first part of Americans from Africa *touches on all that has gone before and raises many questions that will be discussed throughout the remainder of this volume and in Volume II,* Old Memories, New Moods.

10

Slavery and the Origins of Black Culture: Elkins Revisited

Mina Davis Caulfield

As white Americans are increasingly becoming aware, often to their distress and puzzlement, the more prominent leaders of black communities in this country are currently overwhelmingly concerned not with integration or assimilation into our white culture but with defining and promoting a growing sense of a separate and distinct black identity, a black culture. As Robert Blauner has pointed out in his essay "Black Culture: Myth or Reality?" the conventional wisdom of white social science in the United States has long obscured the fact of a separate Negro culture, largely by applying to this group the same model for subcultural "ethnicity" which they have used in studying immigrant national minorities, a model that simply does not fit the Negro experience here. As Blauner puts it:

> The black man did not enter this country with a group identity as a
> Negro. This group category could only be formed by the slave-making

Original for this volume.

operation which vitiated the meaning and relevance of the traditional, specific African identities. Therefore the cultural process could not be one of movement from ethnic group to assimilation, since Negroes were not an ethnic group. What took place first was a kind of too quick and too total "assimilation" without the group autonomy, social and economic equality that was the concomitant of assimilation for other minorities. Hut at the same time, beginning with the dark era of slavery, the group and culture-building process began among the black population, and the development of an ethnic group identity and distinctive culture has been going on ever since. [1]

If Blauner and the Black Culture advocates in the Negro liberation movement are right, and it is my contention that they are, then the first place to look for evidences of the culture-building process is in the slavery experience, and here we come up against a seemingly solid phalanx of white and Negro sociologists and historians who have developed and maintain what amounts to an "official liberal ideology" on slavery. The first main tenet of this position is that African cultures and traditions were completely smashed in the process of enslavement. It has apparently been easier to write off Melville Herskovits' *Myth of the Negro Past* in toto rather than to examine his evidence and evaluate each item for what it is worth; there is a great deal to examine, and in my opinion a great deal of it is valid, although he certainly overstates his case on the whole. Writing off the evidence of Africanisms in American Negro cultures was made particularly simple for white liberal social scientists, largely I think because it was a Negro sociologist, E. Franklin Frazier, who played the major role, initially, in refuting the African-survival argument. The blanket denial of African elements in North American Negro life has obviated the need to study the whole process of early culture-building in this group—the process of adaptation and transformation of "Africanisms" to fit the new environment.

Furthermore, in refuting Herskovits, Frazier went much farther, and firmly allied himself with the second item in the official liberal position on black culture: that there is none, African or otherwise. Thus the argument goes, that just as the brutality of the slave system robbed Negroes of their cultural traditions, it likewise forced them to adopt the dominant white culture and prevented them from forming a new culture which could be called their own. Frazier says:

> Although the Negro is distinguished from other minorities by his physical characteristics, unlike other racial or cultural minorities the Negro is not distinguished by culture from the dominant group. Having completely lost his ancestral culture, he speaks the same language, practices the same religion, and accepts the same values and political ideals as the dominant group.[2]

Substantially the same position has been voiced, and widely accepted, by Gunnar Myrdal, Kenneth Stampp, Kardiner and Ovesey, and more recently by Glazer and Moynihan, Charles Silberman, and many others.

The third point in the official liberal position on the Negro in America is that whatever *has* been distinctively Negro in culture or personality is socially and psychologically pathological. Myrdal set the tone for this interpretation when he described the Negro as "an exaggerated American" with pathological variations on American values, and Kardiner and Ovesey have elaborated the theme extensively in *The Mark of Oppression*, a mark which they see as productive *only* of negative personality anomalies in Negro Americans. Here again, the slavery experience is the crucial starting-point for the argument, and historian Stanley Elkins has provided what is undoubtedly the most influential and probably the most ingenious interpretation of what slavery has done to Negro personality. Elkins' analogy between the psychological infantilization process observed in Nazi concentration camp inmates and the experience of slaves in the United States has been almost universally accepted in white social scientific circles, in spite of what seem to me to be glaring inconsistencies, faulty logic, and almost total lack of historical substantiation. I can only assume that the amazing popularity of this rather far-fetched idea is due primarily to the truly beautiful "fit" it accomplishes with the other elements of the official liberal position on the Negro. As a step toward the re-thinking of this position, I would like to re-examine Elkins' interpretation of the slavery experience and point to some evidence indicating that the period of American slavery was indeed, as Blauner suggests, a culture-*building* era, and a crucial one.

I will not attempt to deal in any detail with the African-survivals debate, not because it is uninteresting or unimportant, but because the question is largely peripheral to the main point I wish to make. I think it should be clear to even a casual observer of American Negro music, dance, and religion, particularly, that some African origins are evident even today; the point is not to look for "pure" African elements but to recognize that, as with all culture growth and change, black culture has developed from diverse sources into a distinctive and unique way of life. The fact that slaves, unlike other immigrant groups, were unable to bring into their new land a functioning, "whole" culture has meant that they and their descendants have brought together cultural elements from many sources, changed them, restructured them, and combined them with original innovations; it has not meant that no distinctive culture exists. As with so many other attempts to legislate or coerce cultural process, we find that although white racism has profoundly affected black cultural development, the results have been dramatically different from those intended.

This is precisely where Elkins, in his attempt to delineate typical slave psychological functioning, has started off on the wrong foot. He has taken the *wish* (of the white planter class) for the *deed*, and swallowed whole the stereotyped characterization of the happy, childlike slave:

> Sambo, the typical plantation slave, was docile but irresponsible, loyal but lazy, humble but chronically given to lying and stealing; his behavior was full of infantile silliness and his talk inflated with childish exaggeration. His relationship with his master was one of utter dependence and childlike attachment: it was indeed this childlike quality that was the very key to his being.[3]

Elkins, of course, recognizes this picture as a white racist stereotype, but argues, quite correctly, that one cannot therefore assume its necessary untruth. What he does instead is an interesting inversion of the scientific process: he assumes its *truth*, rather on the principle that where there's smoke there's fire, without examining the relevant historical evidence, and proceeds to construct on theoretical grounds "the mechanisms whereby this adjustment to absolute power—an adjustment whose end product included infantile features of behavior —may have been effected."[4]

When I say that he fails to examine the relevant historical data, I do not mean that Elkins fails to examine any historical data at all. His opening chapter on the historiography of slavery indicates his command of the material, and his comparison between North American and Latin American slave systems, though it is essentially the same as that developed in 1946 by Frank Tannenbaum,[5] has contributed valuable dimensions to that comparison. However, when he comes to discuss the psychological functioning of slaves, he operates almost entirely by speculation, assumption, and analogy. Because he persistently refuses to entertain the possibility of cultural values and traditions peculiar to slaves, he fails to consider the most useful kinds of evidence for assessing a slave "modal personality"—cultural evidence. Thus, I would argue, his psychologizing is hampered by being largely culture-bound, and he fails in precisely that task which he says he set out to accomplish: to write a history of slavery "largely from the standpoint of the slave."[6]

Elkins sets the stage for his argument on slave personality by comparing the North American variety of the system with its relatively more "open" counterpart in Latin America. Basing himself on the legal codes governing the systems, he contends that in Latin America both the Church and the Crown maintained an active interest in slaves, frequently acting in opposition to the interests of the owners and thus providing a range of "significant others" for the slave that included agents of powerful institutions. The friar and the magistrate were empowered to protect him from illegally harsh punishment and to assure him proper instruction for the good of his immortal soul. The openness of the system was evident also in the variety of potentially available roles for the slaves. Not only were his rights to familial, occupational, and religious roles guaranteed by institutions outside the plantation, but freedom itself was a far more distinct possibility than in North America, through a "network of customary arrangements, rooted in antiquity."[7] Furthermore, there were important differences in the status of free Negroes in the two areas, such that the slave in Latin America was seen as a man, and a potential citizen, rather than a being inherently unfit for anything but servitude, who if freed was customarily assigned a position in society very little different from that of slave. Following Elkins' argument, then, the North American slave was comparatively limited in the range of significant others and in the social roles actually or potentially open to him—outside the plantation. I think we can grant that these facts had important psychological and cultural consequences for slaves, in the Southern United States, but I do not believe it is necessary to conclude with Elkins that "infantilization" was the inevitable result.

Elkins maintains that the conditions of servitude produced a childlike dependence and identification with the master, because "virtually all avenues of recourse, all lines of communication with society at large, originated and ended with [him]," [8] and therefore he was the only really "significant other" for the slave.

> Cruelty per se cannot be considered the primary key to this; of far greater importance was the simple "closedness" of the system, in which all lines of authority descended from the master and in which alternative social bases that might have supported alternative standards were systematically suppressed. The individual, consequently, for his very psychic security, had to picture his master in some way as the "good father."[9]

Can one really assume that because society at large could offer no significant others there were none in slave society itself? Is naked power the only, or even the major, incentive to the internalization of cultural values? Can it really be true that because of the "absolute dependency" on his master, the slave was compelled to see the authority figure as somehow "good"?

I think not. North American slaves may have been effectively cut off from society at large, they may have been lacking in ultimate power over some important aspects of their lives, or even over the lives themselves, but in spite of all attempts in that direction, "alternative social bases" that could support alternative standards were not, in most cases, *successfully* suppressed. Being cut off from society at large did not mean that slaves existed with *no society at all;* inability to merge with Southern white culture did not preclude the possibility of having cultural identity of their own. Slave communities on large plantations, I would argue, constituted functioning cultural units, and as such they embodied alternative standards of behavior to the Sambo stereotype.

It is in this context that Elkins' analogy between plantation and concentration camp overlooks a crucial distinction. Taking an extreme case of the "closed system," Elkins has tried to extend to the slavery situation the psychological dynamics leading to infantilism among inmates in Nazi death camps. The analogy, as he poses it, is far-reaching: he makes it clear that he is speaking not only of the "shock and detachment" phase of the Middle Passage but also of the "stability" of life adjustment to a paternal system. What Elkins' analogy overlooks is the fact that concentration camps were instruments of death and terror, while slave quarters were functioning communities involved in subsistence, procreation, and the socialization of the young. Death and terror unquestionably were essential to North American slavery as it existed, but they were not its *raison d'être*, and consequently their effects on the personality of the slave were quite different. In Elkins' own terms, those of interpersonal theory and role theory of personality, his analogy is unworkable, as I will try to demonstrate.

Looking, then, for the life situation of the "typical" plantation slave in the United States, we find the majority living in units of more than twenty, with one fourth in units of more than fifty.[10] Occupationally quite diverse, ranging from blacksmith to mill hand to wet nurse, they were still in the main field hands, working in gangs under supervision, living in separate quarters, and having little contact with the master class.[11] According to Elkins' theory, the psychological forces making for infantilization would have been most powerful in these situations of greatest oppression, where slaves were most closely governed by naked terror, where conditions most closely approached those of the concentration camp.

Viewing this type of cultural community as an anthropologist, the most immediately salient feature is admittedly the slaves' lack of power in the control of their own lives. Kenneth Stampp, the most noted authority on the "peculiar institution" in the United States, sees this lack of power as the crucial factor in the no-slave-culture argument. He maintains that "in bondage, the Negroes lacked cultural autonomy—the authority to apply rigorous sanctions against those who violated or repudiated their own traditions."[12] There can be no doubt that the sanctions of the white rulers were rigorous, including the power of life and death, extreme physical punishment, and banishment from the community itself (sale to another owner). To conclude, however, that slaves were unable therefore to apply their own rigorous sanctions in support of independent values and traditions, would be to overlook crucial factors in the cultural ethos and psychological dynamics of slave life.

Stampp himself, in another passage, describes what is clearly an example of cultural autonomy, when he speaks of the difference between the "master's code" and the "slave's code" in regard to stealing:

> The slaves, however, had a somewhat different definition of dishonesty in their own code, to which they were reasonably faithful. For appropriating their master's goods they might be punished or denounced by him, but they were not likely to be disgraced among their associates in the slave quarters, who made a distinction between "stealing" and "taking." Appropriating things from the master mean simply taking part of his property for the benefit of another part, or, as Frederick Douglass phrased it, "taking his meat out of one tub, and putting it in another." . . . Stealing, on the other hand, meant appropriating something that belonged to another slave, and this was an offense which slaves did not condone.[13]

Likewise, Stampp says, "No slave would betray another, for an informer was held 'in greater detestation than the most notorious thief.'"[14] The sanction of social disapproval may not be "rigorous" in the same sense that a flogging is rigorous, but I can't imagine any social psychologist would argue that it was ineffectual.

Furthermore, the social *approval* accorded the successful pilferer of the master's goods was founded on a more basic feeling than "loose morals" or even simple rebelliousness. The frequency of petty thievery, especially of food, has been remarked again and again. Far from being the occasional aberration of a few social deviants, petty theft was, as Stampp tells us, "an almost universal vice; slaves would take anything not under lock and key."[15] Now, if one takes the Sambo stereotype seriously, the process of "taking care of themselves" was widely assumed to be the one thing beyond the capacity of the childlike plantation slave.[16] Indeed, Elkins' argument on infantilism is based largely on the idea that lack of opportunity, and thus incentive, for independent providing or ambition bred personalities incapable of any psychological adaptation but complete dependency. However, in the life situation which obtained on most of the larger plantations, where slaves were systematically issued rations at or near the starvation level, "taking care of themselves" involved, probably in all cases, supplementing the rations by various "illegal" means, regardless of harsh punishments on discovery. Thus petty thievery, secret hunting and fishing late at night, and so forth, were not only necessary and accepted (by the slaves) means of subsistence but also acts of highly courageous independence in the important social role of family or personal provider.

Many accounts in the words of the slaves themselves attest not only to the frequency of theft and "illegal" hunting but also to the dedication of the fruits to family or even communal subsistence. The pride and social value attached to such provisioning is obvious when we read such slave accounts as the following:

> I had, by this time, become . . . acquainted with the country, and began to lay and execute plans to procure supplies of such things as were not allowed me by my master. I understood various methods of entrapping raccoons, and other wild animals that abounded in the large swamps of this country; and besides the skins, which were worth something for their furs, I generally procured as many rackoons, opossums, and rabits, as afforded us two or three meals in a week. The woman with whom I lived, understood the way of dressing an opossum, and I was careful to provide one for Sunday dinner every week, so long as these animals continued fat and in good condition. . . . My principal trapping ground was three miles from home, and I went three times a week, always after night, to bring home my game, and keep my traps in good order. Many of the families in the quarter caught no game, and had no meat, except that which we received from the overseer, which averaged about six or seven meals in the year. [17]

A recurrent theme in the slave narratives is the problem of feeding the children, for whom a very small allowance was usually made by the master. Not only are there numerous tales of suffering, sacrifice, and danger in providing for the children, but ex-slaves often recall how they learned the gentle art of "taking care of themselves" at an early age:

> The children never did get no meat. The grown folks got a little meat, 'cause they had to work; but we didn't. . . . My aunt, she'd slip meat skins through the crack to us chillen till that hole would get right greasy. She had a little hole in the floor that she could use; and we would go down to the orchard and broil them or cook 'em some way. We'd put the little ones in the henhouse, through the hole they left

for the hens; and they'd come out with an apron full of eggs, and we'd take them out to the woods and cook 'em someway; and we would steal chickens too.[18]

The numerous accounts of stealing food in the "slave narratives," published in the North by abolitionists, characteristically give moral justifications in terms of the necessity to supplement meager rations, and to the effect that it was not really theft, since both the slave and the food were the master's property. These narratives are clearly addressed to the sympathies of the white population, and it is difficult to tell, frequently, how much of the wording has been supplied by the abolitionist editors; the stories themselves, however, can hardly be discounted. The much simpler accounts of these activities found in the collections of interviews with ex-slaves (Botkin, *Lay My Burden Down*, and the Fisk University *Unwritten History of Slavery*) are characterized by pride, pleasure, and most especially by humor at fooling the master, as in the following:

> One night they come down and there was three dozen eggs in the fire where they done stole. Mother give me a look, and looked over to the bed, and that meant for me to get up and go to bed; I better had went too. The fire was hot and one of them eggs popped. Old master looked around trying to see what it was. My mother looked at me for she was scared I was gonna tell. But master didn't stay long, but if he had he would have heard all them eggs. Soon as he left they began pulling eggs out and such a feast they did have.[19]

Frequent mention is also made, in the accounts of the slaves themselves, of sharing stolen food with slaves from neighboring plantations or with runaways.

> I would always have something hid in the spring house, and I would prize the log on the spring house open, and when the white folks would come down to the spring house to get butter and stuff they would be taken out and we would have gotten it and given it to the runaway Negroes.[20]

Insignificant as such activities may appear in larger economic terms or in our own view of personal autonomy and responsibility, it seems logical from the circumstances of slave life that they would have been crucial both for subsistence itself (no small matter!) and for feelings of personal worth in the slaves. If one can free oneself of the cultural presuppositions that pose complete autonomy in a free society as the only condition for adult personality structures, and see responsibility for subsistence as the slave must have seen it, the cultural and psychic value of such "petty" behavior should appear in a different light. Stampp comments:

The generality of slaves believed that he who knew how to trick or deceive the master had an enviable talent, and they regarded the committing of petit larceny as both thrilling and praiseworthy. One former slave recalled with great satisfaction the times when he had caught a pig or chicken and shared it with some "black fair one." These adventures made him feel "good, moral, [and] heroic"; they were "all the chivalry of which my circumstances of life admitted."[21]

Interestingly enough, Elkins, in discussing concentration camp adjustment, makes a point of the significance of just such petty means of securing illegal food and supplies, for the psychological life of some inmates:

In a practical sense the actual operations of such "undergrounds" as were possible may seem to us unheroic and limited: stealing blankets; "organizing" a few bandages, a little medicine, from the camp hospital; black market arrangements with a guard for a bit of extra food and protection for oneself and one's comrades; the circulation of news; and other such apparently trifling activities. But for the psychological balance of those involved, such activities were vital; they made possible a fundamentally different adjustment to the camp. To a prisoner so engaged, there were others who mattered, who gave real point to his existence—the SS was no longer the *only* one. Conversely, the role of the child was not the only one he played. He could take the initiative; he could give as well as receive protection; he did things which had meaning in adult terms. He had, in short, alternative roles.[22]

Curiously, Elkins fails to make the obvious extension of this cogent argument to the similar activities of North American slaves, but rather goes on to make an opposing point. Because alternative roles were not "legitimized and protected *outside* the plantation," but were dependent on the master's pleasure, he argues, infantilism was effectively guaranteed.[23]

The only "underground" which Elkins perceived in the American South was, surprisingly, of a completely different sort from that he describes in the concentration camp. He casts in the underground role those slaves who were privileged to partake in some measure of "society at large":

The house servant, the urban mechanic, the slave who arranged his own employment and paid his master a stipulated sum each week, were all figuratively members of the "underground."[24]

Once again, Elkins' culture-bound approach has led him into a clear inconsistency. With his eye always on the society at large and the social/psychological distance between the slave and the dominant culture, he fails to see that what was significant for the psychology of the concentration camp inmate must have been far more significant for the plantation slave, who carried on his illegal, autonomous acts in the context of a functioning slave culture which had independent values, traditions, and a considerable degree of solidarity, over a number of generations.

That these functioning cultures were narrow, limited, and warped by the absence of final authority is clear. I would agree with Stampp that "before the Civil War, American Negroes developed no cultural nationalism [based on African heritage],"[25] and further, that conditions of life varied considerably between plantations made the character of individual cultural settings quite distinct. But I cannot agree when he says that "in slavery the Negro existed in a kind of cultural void. He lived in a twilight zone between two ways of life [African culture and white Southern culture] and was unable to obtain from either many of the attributes which distinguish man from beast."[26] *Homo sapiens* has been defined as the animal with culture, and while there are certainly some cultures more complex, extensive, and "open" than others, it seems to me that even a culture operating under such constricted conditions as those of a slave quarter can be viewed in the same basic terms as the generality of human cultures. Stampp, in outlining the "cultural void" of slave life, paints a seemingly desolate picture:

> The average bondsman, it would appear, lived more or less aimlessly in a bleak and narrow world. He lived in a world without schools, without books, without learned men; he knew less of the fine arts and of aesthetic values than he had known in Africa; and he found few ways to break the monotonous sameness of all his days. His world was the few square miles of earth surrounding his cabin—a familiar island beyond which were strange places (up North where people like him were not slaves), frightening places ("down the river" where overseers were devils), and dead places (across the ocean where his ancestors had lived and where he had no desire to go). His world was full of mysteries which he could not solve, full of forces which he could not control. And so he tended to be a fatalist and futilitarian, for nothing else could reconcile him to his life.[27]

Mr. Stampp has chosen to leave out of his picture all those positive aspects of the slave world view—humor, courage, resistance to oppression, solidarity, "soul"—but even so, is this long string of negatives (if true) really a "cultural void"? Is it qualitatively different from the world views of some very small, isolated, and "poor" cultural groups elsewhere in the world? The African Bushmen live in a closely circumscribed world, likewise without the "advantages" of schools, books, or what Mr. Stampp would consider "learned men." They have lost the complex structure, rich lands, and aesthetic attainments which characterized their culture in past centuries. For them, too, the world is frightening, subsistence on the border of starvation, and they are subject to sudden, arbitrary disruption, death and capture by the Bantu, against whom they are virtually powerless. Their modal personality is distinct from that of neighboring peoples (and also, I would think, quite different from that of North American slaves): they are unaggressive, affectionate, full of humor, and they call themselves "the harmless people." But they do not live in a cultural void, and they think and act as adults, not as children.

The infantilism which Elkins describes as typical for surviving inmates of concentration camps was produced by a life situation which had virtually none of the characteristics of a functioning culture. A concentration camp was bounded by death, without procreation, without the transmission of learned behavior from one generation to the next—indeed, impotence and the irrelevance of sex and child bearing were among the first psychological effects of the induction experience. Only the rare incidence of underground activities maintained some prisoners above the childlike state of their fellows, and I would argue that these constituted the faint glimmerings of the urge to form a new cultural adaptation in virtually impossible conditions. This was a true cultural void.

For the American slave, however, generation followed generation, and the formation of recognizable social structure was apparent in most slave communities.[28] Here it is important to distinguish between social structure based on the authority of the master, which was little more than an extension of oppression through agents from among the slaves themselves (black drivers), and that based on the esteem accorded by virtue of cultural attributes respected independently of white patronage. The line is of course hard to draw, since many of the values in slave society were necessarily drawn directly from white society. The relative independence of those slaves granted the privilege to hire out, and the easier physical life of house servants tended to make such slaves objects of envy, if not of respect, to less fortunate field hands. These individuals were not always in a position of leadership, however, and this says much for the importance of independent value systems. The adoption of white standards and manners, indeed, frequently alienated house servants from the rest of their community: "Former slaves described the envy and hatred of the 'helots' for the 'fuglemen' who 'put on airs' in imitation of the whites."[29] On the other hand, the real leaders in the quarters were not looked upon with favor by the masters, and their qualities of leadership were most often exactly those which put them in opposition to the white oppressor.

> Each community of slaves contained one or two members whom the others looked to for leadership because of their physical strength, practical wisdom, or mystical powers. It was a "notorious" fact, according to one master, "that on almost every large plantation of Negroes, there is one among them who holds a kind of magical sway over the minds and opinions of the rest; to him they look as their oracle. . . . The influence of such a Negro, often a preacher, on a quarter is incalculable."[30]

Of these social leaders, probably the most important was the preacher. The official liberal position on the Negro would maintain that this is another indication of the lack of cultural autonomy. Kardiner and Ovesey, for example, argued that since African culture could not survive under the repressive conditions of slavery, the *"new* culture in which the slave found himself . . . was forced upon him. . . . He was thus obliged to learn the new language and adopt a new religion, which was not evolved out of his old cultural conditions, but was foisted on him as a new credo, with no bearing . . . on his current problem of adaptation."[31] Not only does this statement contradict what is known about acculturative process, i.e., that cultural elements are capable of adoption only in a form which has bearing on the adaptation of the group, but it ignores the evidence of history on the actual process by which the slaves acquired Christianity.

The attempt to convert slaves to Christianity was actively opposed by a large segment of the master class throughout the eighteenth century and in many cases beyond; and those missionizing attempts made were notably without success until the campaigns mounted by the Baptists and Methodists. On the other hand, there is considerable evidence that in many if not most localities slaves held *secret* meetings for the dissemination of what knowledge they had of the Scriptures (and other things, such as voodoo, insurrection, and the Underground Railway): meetings held at night in the woods, the swamps, in some cases in "praise houses." These meetings were regarded with fear by the masters, and with reason, for they were foci of feelings, and in some cases actions, of revolt and escape.[32] The fact that such secret meetings were repeatedly prohibited in most areas of the South, with severe penalties attached to discovery, far from proving that the Negro was prevented from developing his own cultural forms, proves in my opinion just the opposite—that he developed them in spite of massive opposition. One does not repeatedly outlaw an activity and send out armed patrols to prevent its occurrence, unless that activity is being carried on, and on a scale large enough to cause concern.

There is scarcely a single slave account in the Fisk collection or in Botkins' which does not mention the secret praise meetings, and the practice of "turning the pot down" appears so often that it seems almost to achieve the status of a ritual. Here is a typical account from the Fisk collection:

> When they had meetings that way they came from other men's farms, and they would slip over and keep the padderollers from getting you, and they would turn the kettle down outside the door, raised so that the sound can get under there and you couldn't hear them. If they heard women pray, the next morning they would hit them fifty lashes for praying. . . . Oh, yes'm, prayed for the children that the time would come when they would be free, and they could serve God under their own vine and fig tree.[33]

This same informant, in speaking of the slaves' attendance at *church*, as distinct from praise meetings, makes clear the enormous difference between the two. The same slaves that received fifty lashes when discovered at a praise meeting, were perfectly free, even encouraged to attend church:

> No, they allowed them to go to church. White folks have a morning service, and in the afternoon colored folks would go to the same church. The biggest thing I heard them preach about was, "Servants, obey your mistress and master." They would tell them not to steal. Very few of them told you about religion. They didn't have any time.[34]

This informant, at least, was in no confusion such as Kardiner and Ovesey suffer—the *real* religion was the slaves' own, and what was foisted on them wasn't religion at all.

When the Baptists had such notable success in converting slaves, one decisive factor was, according to both Herskovits[35] and Frazier,[36] the large degree of local autonomy granted to slave congregations, and the willingness to make use of slave preachers. One does not need the evidence that such missionaries as Bishop Asbury actually visited pre-existing praise meetings,[37] to recognize that the slaves had, in many places at least, created their own religious forms, which were extended and standardized throughout the South following the formation of institutionalized Negro churches. Frazier, curiously, doesn't even mention the secret meetings in his history of the Negro church, but he retells one account by a slave indicative of my point:

> The coloured folks had their code of religion, not nearly so complicated as the white man's religion, but more closely observed. . . .

> When we had our meetings of this kind, we held them in our own
> way and were not interfered with by the white folks.[38]

Frazier also, unlike Kardiner and Ovesey, stresses that the Negro slave
"adapted the Christian religion to his psychological and social needs."[39]

It is impossible to discuss the religious adaptation of the black man in
America without discussing the role of music in his religion, and here it
is more difficult to ignore the dispute as to the survival of Africanisms.
The central importance of song and song-like exhortation in the form
of worship peculiar to the American Negro has been discussed with
great force and insight by LeRoi Jones, who quotes another student of
Negro music, Ernest Borneman, as follows:

> The Methodist revival movement began to address itself directly to
> the slaves, but ended up not by converting the Africans to a Christian
> ritual, but by converting itself to an African ritual.[40]

Whether or not one accepts this extreme formulation, Negro "spirituals" are recognized by virtually all commentators on slave life as original
productions, and all recognize in them some African origins, with the
exception of Kardiner and Ovesey, whose discussion is in all respects
the least satisfactory. These authors approach the spirituals as projective
expressions of slave personality, and find in them an "accommodative
trend toward slavery," containing no protest or hatred, but a "resignation
to the slave status and a wish for liberation by a higher power," having
a high "release value" for repressed emotions.[41] This interpretation is
highly compatible with Elkins' thesis, but a singularly shallow view of
the significance of this body of folklore.

Consider the context in which these songs were performed: a
secret meeting late at night in a clearing in the woods, or a tiny cabin
with a pot turned down and the shutters drawn, patrols on all the
roads outside. It hardly seems plausible that the feelings associated
with such lyrics as those of "Jine Jerusalem's Band," for example,
were resignation and accommodation. Because of the nature of the
evidence, it is difficult to assign historical certainty to any interpretation, but the approach of Miles Mark Fischer in his study of
Negro slave songs appears far more convincing. He maintains that
the "Jerusalem Band" was Nat Turner's band of insurgents, and that
the song was used both for recruiting purposes and for spreading
news of the rebellion, celebrating it, for many years after. According
to Fischer, the word "Jerusalem" thus became a kind of code word,
and "Negroes in Georgia thrilled at its mention even in the 1850's."[42]

Thus he sees spirituals *not* simply as "fantasy productions" of slave personality, but in most cases as a form of *code* operating on a conscious level within a group severely restricted in the free interchange of illicit information and plans. Fischer details the use of whole bodies of songs to convey information and propaganda for the Liberian colonization movement, slave revolts, in particular the Nat Turner rebellion, and escape, in addition to the ubiquitous calls to the secret meetings in the "wilderness."[43] It is easy to imagine (as has been reported by many ex-slaves) the amusement of the slaves at fooling their masters with their humble-sounding songs with not-so-latent hostile intent. What emerges is the psychology, not of a passive, infantile Sambo, but of a plotting, planning adult under severe oppression, who has evolved an intricate cultural adaptation to meet a pressing cultural need.

This is not to deny that there was also expressed in these songs a deeply felt, beautifully rendered lament—an emotional release, if you will, of repressed feelings. W. E. B. Du Bois called them the "Sorrow Songs," the "siftings of centuries":

> They are the music of an unhappy people, of the children of disappointment; they tell of death and suffering and unvoiced longing toward a truer world, of misty wanderings and hidden ways.[44]

But it is hard to imagine how one can argue that the generality of the spirituals were the fantasy productions of a happy, childlike personality which idealized the master and saw him as "good."

That slave personality is still seriously seen in these terms by some whites indicates, perhaps, more about the unconscious needs of the white population than those of the Negro. There is considerable evidence that Sambo, far from being a stereotype based ultimately on the facts of objectively perceived slave personalities, was rather a creation of the guilt-ridden, fearful psyche of the Southern white. Winthrop Jordan, after an extensive study of journals, travelers' accounts, and other sources in the eighteenth and nineteenth centuries, has concluded that the Sambo image of the slave simply was not reported (with one or two exceptions, in the observations of British travelers) prior to the 1830's; the prevailing characterization before that time was of the "recalcitrant" slave, constantly running off to the woods for days or months, stealing, lying, deceiving, loafing or deliberately doing the job wrong—in short, causing endless trouble.[45]

Why did the 1830's mark a turning point in the white man's perception of the slave? The thirties were highly significant in the history of master-slave relations, being marked by the Nat Turner Rebellion and the severe reprisals following it, the great debates on the whole subject of slavery in the Virginia legislature, a marked increase in Northern abolitionist agitation, and, as Fischer notes, a marked change in the tenor of the spirituals, which began to reflect fear of the widespread reprisals and to exhort the slaves, "You better min."[46] It could be argued, from this latter change, that the "reality" of the Sambo type was more prevalent in the years following 1831, and that this accounted for the creation of the stereotype. If true, of course, this would not conform to Elkins' theory cither, since by this time more slaves were farther removed from the shock and detachment of the Middle Passage, and more had mastered crafts, learned to read, and in general come in closer contact with the dominant culture. I would argue quite differently, that the Sambo stereotype, in addition to serving as a ready argument against abolitionists, arose from the psychological shock to the planters at the realization that behind simple recalcitrance lay bitter hostility and danger; their own guilt for provoking this hostility evoked a denial: slaves were "really" simple, child-like, happy, and their owners loved them and wanted to treat them well.

To return to the analysis of folklore as expressive data, there is a considerable body of slave tales, rhymes, and secular songs celebrating the trickster hero, which have been interpreted in various ways. The well-known Uncle Remus stories, starring the great trickster Brer Rabbit, who outwits the larger and more powerful fox, are paralleled by the "Old John" stories, in which the clever slave outwits his master. Botkin has suggested that the former are simply a politer form of the latter, reserved for telling when whites were present.[47]

Roger Abrahams, in his discussion of the trickster as hero, relies largely on a Jungian analysis, and concludes:

> Indeed, in almost every sense the trickster *is* a child. He has no perceptible set of values except those dictated by the demands of his id. One could not say that he is immoral; he is, rather, amoral because he exists in the stage before morality has had a chance to inculcate itself upon his being.[48]

Although Abrahams' collection of contemporary folklore appears clearly to attest to a separate black cultural tradition,[49] his interpretation here fits right in with the "official" no-Negro-culture position by suggesting amorality or pre-morality rather than an autonomous moral code.

> The trickster provides a full escape for those Negroes who have been offered no opportunity to feel a control over their own lives, no method

> for developing their egos through a specific action. As such, the trickster may reflect a real childlike state of a severely stunted ego, or a veiled revolt against authority in the only terms available. At the same time the performer and audience are enabled to express some of their aggressive impulses in this acceptable form.[50]

I would certainly agree with the second part of this comment, that the trickster stories express aggressive feelings in author and in audience, but the predication of a stunted, childlike, pre-moral ego seems somewhat unfounded. Was Old John pre-moral when he tricked his master into turning over the season's pork supply to the slave quarters?[51] Or was he operating with a code of morals in *opposition* to those of the master? The type of actions celebrated in these tales are precisely the sort actually reported with pride in the slave narratives as performed by slaves in the process of getting enough to eat, and in getting around the severe limitations on their personal freedom, as discussed above. As a capsule statement on the real meaning of the trickster tales for the black culture which created them, I can hardly do better than to quote Charles Keil, in my opinion the most perceptive commentator on modern black culture, who remarks in another connection that "the art of the 'put on' has of necessity been developed to an exceptionally high level in Negro culture."[52]

The socialization of children in a culture is one of the most crucial areas in which to look for evidence of cultural autonomy and continuity, and here the available data is not only scarce but variable. In this variation, I think, is the key to the actuality of the Sambo personality as it did in some cases exist.

The typical manager of a large-scale plantation, run on businesslike lines, seems to have been concerned with educating only the *working* slave to absolute submission. Stampp's summary of the rules most commonly employed "to make them stand in fear" do not deal with slaves below the age of useful labor, usually six to ten years.[53] Infants and very young children, in cases where the mother was working in the fields all day, were generally under the supervision of an older child, a superannuated slave woman, or the cook.[54] In the critical years for the internalization of values, then, slave children appear to have been for the most part neglected by the white system, regarded as only potentially valuable property, and left to absorb the prevailing standards and values of the slave quarters.

Exceptions to this rule were some small plantations or farms, such as those described by three ex-slaves in Botkin's collection, where the white mistress took a motherly interest in the black children, caring for them herself while their mothers worked. Millie Evans describes a plantation situation of this sort, which has many features of a truly paternal system:

> I stayed with my ma every night, but my mistress raised me. My ma had to work hard, so every time Old Mistress thought we little black children was hungry 'tween meals she would call us up to the house to eat.... And we had plenty to eat. Whooo-eee! Just plenty to eat.[55]

On this plantation the master led teaching sessions on the Bible, and the self-identification of the slaves as in a sense his children appears to have been, at least in the case of Millie Evans, much deeper than mere accommodation. The adults saw their economic efforts as communal tasks, and there was a fierce pride in the self-sufficiency of the plantation, as evidenced by the memories of this ex-slave.[56]

This pattern of "plenty to eat," maternal and paternal interest by the mistress and master in the very young slaves, and the assumption of religious teaching by the master appears to be correlated with the only instances of what I would call infantile personality. Millie Evans says:

> Now, child, I can't 'member everything I done in them days, but we didn't have to worry 'bout nothing. Old Mistress was the one to worry.... We had such a good time, and everyone cried when the Yankees cried out: "Free."[57]

In another instance, Nicey Kinney, remembering her old master and mistress, says:

> I sure does thank 'em to this day for the pains they took with the little nigger gal that growed up to be me, trying to show her the right road to travel. Oh! if I could just see 'em one more time![58]

In this case, too, there was plenty to eat, and pride in the ability of the community to produce everything needed, an identification of interest with the master. Again, Charley Williams recalls a life with plenty to eat, where everything was made on the plantation, and he can even recount with pride the methods of manufacture of various articles from hats to bedsteads to shoes. His master took a personal interest in him from boyhood, and he still thinks of himself as a child, looking forward to meeting Old Master in heaven:

> I reckon maybe I'll just go up and ask him what he want me to do, and he'll tell me, and iffen I don't know how he'll show me how, and I'll try to do it to please him. And when I git it done, I wants to hear him grumble like he used to and say, "Charley, you ain't got no sense but you is a good boy. This here ain't very good but it'll do, I reckon.

Git yourself a little piece of that brown sugar, but don't let no niggers see you eating it—if you do I'll whup your black behind!"[59]

I have quoted at length from these three accounts not because they are typical (they are not), but because they seem to me to demonstrate that the childlike personality structure that Elkins tried to correlate with North American slavery in general was in fact associated with exceptional cases in which conditions were least favorable for the development of a separate cultural identity—where transmission of cultural values to the young was in the hands of the master; where adult economic self-interest was perceived as communal and associated with the master's interest (not only were the slaves well fed, but the masters were not very well-to-do); and where religious teaching was conducted by the master. These childlike slaves were thus *closer* to white Southern culture (rather than farther, as Elkins' theory would predict) than the field hands on larger, more capitalistically run establishments, close enough to take their cultural identity almost completely from their masters and to interact on intimate terms with them. Significant others were indeed limited, and the available social roles of transmitter of tradition, independent provider, and social leader were pre-empted more or less effectively by the master and mistress.

Elkins' personality theory approach seems relevant, therefore, in the quite special cases noted, but his failure to recognize the decisive importance of cultural frame of reference has, I think, led him to give the Sambo personality a reality for a much broader range of life situations than is warranted. He assumes that all cultural meaning and value must flow *from the dominant culture*, and concludes that since all plantation slaves were limited in choice of significant others *from that culture*, and effectively cut off from available social roles *in that culture*, that infantile behavior analogous to that in concentration camps must have resulted. The widespread myth of the Sambo personality lends credence to his theory, on the surface, but I think there can be little doubt that the major part of the basis in perceived behavior for this myth can be attributed to conscious role playing on the part of slaves who were well aware of the role expectations of their masters. What I have tried to demonstrate is that the predominant pattern of slavery, that of large plantations, very little contact with the master, and severe restrictions in food and leisure, was correlated with the development of distinct cultural identity. The slave not only could but was also forced to find his significant figures within his own society, to himself adopt the important social roles of provider, transmitter of tradition, and leader among his own people. The personality configurations produced within this culture could not have been, of course, the same as those in the dominant society. But to conclude, as Elkins does, that "Sambo" was the actual modal personality type, simply does not stand up to the available evidence.

The fact that Elkins' theory has been so widely accepted by white liberals is an interesting social-psychological phenomenon in itself. It seems to be peculiarly gratifying to the white liberal burdened with a pervasive sense of guilt in relation to the black man, to be able to say, "Yes, it is sad but true that Negro life is socially and psychologically pathological (I don't have to feel guilty about not wanting to associate with them). Of *course*, this is not biologically determined (I'm not a racist!), and the poor Negro is not himself at fault; it's those Southern white racists that made him what he is. I, on the other hand, am a guiltless man of good will who is possessed of a true scientific understanding of how it all happened."—To my mind, there is an urgent need for the replacement of the Elkins brand of "scientific understanding" with a humanist understanding of, and respect for today's Black Culture. Furthermore, as I have tried to show, a cultural approach to the slavery experience can provide insight into an important source of the modern patterns.

Notes

1. Robert Blauner, "Black Culture: Myth or Reality?" in Volume II of this book, p. 417.
2. *The Negro in the United States*, rev. ed. (New York: Macmillan, 1957), p. 680.
3. Stanley M. Elkins, *Slavery: A Problem in American Institutional and Intellectual Life* (Chicago: University of Chicago Press, 1959), p. 82.
4. *Ibid.*, pp. 86–87.
5. *Slave and Citizen: The Negro in the Americas* (New York: Alfred A. Knopf, 1946).
6. Elkins, pp. 18–19.
7. Elkins, p. 137. This interpretation has been challenged by Marvin Harris, whose *Patterns of Race in the Americas* (New York: Walker and Co., 1964) presents a more meaningful comparison between the two systems, based not just on the legal definitions of slavery but on the differing economic and class structures of the total societies. Harris makes clear that one cannot make broad-gauge assumptions on the basis of legal codes alone, as both Tannenbaum and Elkins tend to do. Harris says: "What the laws of the Spanish and Portuguese kings had to do with the attitudes and values of the Spanish and Portuguese planters . . . baffles one's imagination. The Crown could publish all the laws it wanted, but in the lowlands, sugar was king. If there were any Portuguese or Spanish planters who were aware of their legal obligations toward the slaves, it would require systematic misreading of colonialism, past and present, to suppose that these laws psychologically

represented anything more than the flatus of a pack of ill-informed Colonel Blimps who didn't even know what a proper cane field looked like" (p. 76).

8. Elkins, p. 63.

9. *Ibid.*, pp. 128–129.

10. Kenneth Stampp. *The Peculiar Institution; Slavery in the Ante-Bellum South* (New York: Alfred A. Knopf, 1956), p. 31.

11. *Ibid.*, p. 325.

12. *Ibid.*, p. 362.

13. Stampp, pp. 126–127.

14. *Ibid.*, p. 125.

15. Stampp, p. 125. See also Frederick L. Olmsted, A *Journey in the Seaboard Slave States* (New York: Mason Bros., 1856), p. 117; B. A. Botkin (ed.), *Lay My Burden Down: A Folk History of Slavery* (Chicago: University of Chicago Press. 1945), *passim;* Social Science Institute, *Unwritten History of Slavery* (Nashville; Fisk University, 1945), pp. 9, 11–12, 76, 97, 137, 279.

16. U. B. Phillips, *Life and Labor in the Old South* (Boston: Little, Brown, 1930), p. 196; Olmsted, p. 131.

17. Charles Ball, *Slavery in the United States: A Narrative of the Life and Adventures of Charles Ball, A Black Man* (Pittsburgh, 1853). Similar accounts of hunting and trapping can be found in many other slave narratives, and in Botkin, p. 90, and the Fisk collection, p. 36.

18. *Unwritten History of Slavery*, p. 279.

19. *Ibid.*, p. 137.

20. *Unwritten History of Slavery*, p. 97.

21. Stampp, pp, 334–335.

22. Elkins, pp. 134–135.

23. *Ibid.*, p. 136.

24. *Ibid.*, p. 137.

25. Stampp, p. 362.

26. *Ibid.*, p. 364.

27. Stampp, p. 361.

28. Phillips, p. 206; Stampp, pp. 335–338.

29. Stampp, p. 338.

30. *Ibid.*, pp. 335–336.

31. Abram Kardiner and Lionel Ovesey, *The Mark of Oppression: Explorations in the Personality of the American Negro* (Cleveland: Meridian Books, 1951), p. 44.

32. Miles Mark Fischer, *Negro Slave Songs in the United States* (New York: Citadel Press, 1953), *passim.* See especially p. 186.

33. *Unwritten History of Slavery*, pp. 98–99.

34. *Unwritten History of Slavery*, p. 98.

35. P. 209.

36. E. Franklin Frazier, *The Negro Church in America* (New York: Schocken Books, 1963), p. 18.

37. Fischer, pp. 75–76.

38. Frazier, *The Negro Church*, p. 16.

39. *Ibid.*, p. 12.

40. Ernest Borneman, quoted in LeRoi Jones, *Blues People: The Negro Experience in America and the Music that Developed from It* (New York: Morrow, 1963), p. 42.

41. Kardiner and Ovesey, p. 340.
42. Fischer, pp. 85–86.
43. Fischer, pp. 41–65, 111–132, 66–87, 108–110.
44. *The Souls of Black Folk* (Greenwich, Conn.: Fawcett, 1953), p. 183.
45. Winthrop Jordan, personal communication. These findings were presented in a paper given at the American Historical Association meetings in December 1964.
46. Fischer, pp. 88–110.
47. Botkin, p. 2.
48. Roger Abrahams, *Deep Down in the Jungle: Negro Narrative Folklore from the Streets of Philadelphia* (Hatboro, Pa.: Folklore Associates, 1964), p. 67.
49. See the excellent discussion of Abrahams in Charles Keil, *Urban Blues* (Chicago; University of Chicago Press, 1966), pp. 20–28.
50. Abrahams, p. 69.
51. Botkin, p. 4.
52. Keil, p. 12
53. Stampp, pp. 149–150.
54. Botkin, pp. 89, 99, 126, 139, 147.
55. *Ibid.*, p. 61.
56. Botkin, pp. 63–64.
57. *Ibid.*, p. 64.
58. *Ibid.*, p. 80.
59. Botkin, p. 110.

Suggested Readings

Elkins, Stanley M. *Slavery: A Problem in American Institutional and Intellectual Life.* Chicago: University of Chicago Press, revised 1968.
A reassessment of the relationship between the master and slave and a discussion of the "Sambo" personality.

Davis, David Brion. *The Problem of Slavery in Western Culture.* Ithaca: Cornell University Press, 1966.
A Pulitzer-Prize-winning study dealing with slavery in the Americas.

Drimmer, Melvin, editor. *Black History: A Reappraisal.* New York: Double-day, 1968.
A very recent, very fine collection of excerpts from major historical works, with interpretations by the editor.

Franklin, John Hope. *From Slavery to Freedom.* New York: Alfred A. Knopf, revised 1956.
This historical account has become a classic. Of special interest are Chapters IV, V and VI which deal with the slave trade, "seasoning" in the West Indies, and servitude in the Old South.

Genovese, Eugene D. *The Political Economy of Slavery.* New York: Pantheon, 1965.
A series of penetrating studies on the economic bases of slavery and the nature of life in the slave south.

Phillips, Ulrich B. *Life and Labor in the Old South.* Boston: Little, Brown, 1929.
An excellent introduction despite its "benign view of slavery."

Weinstein, Allen, and Frank Otto Gattell, editors. *American Negro Slavery.* New York: Oxford University Press, 1968.
A useful modern reader which includes articles on slaves, masters, and "the system."

II

This Side of Jordan

Down Home and Up North

In relation to their Southern background, the cultural history of Negroes in the North reads like the legend of some tragic people out of mythology, a people which aspired to escape from its own unhappy homeland to the apparent peace of a distant mountain; but which, in migrating, made some fatal error of judgment and fell into a great chasm of maze-like passages that promise ever to lead to the mountain but end ever against the wall.

Ralph Ellison

Many of those whose essays appear in both the preceding and following sections mention folk tales told by slaves and passed on to their descendants. None are more important than the "Uncle Remus" stories, although, as Bernard Wolfe points out, these have often been misunderstood.

A principal character in the stories is Brer Rabbit. Weak and supposedly stupid, he triumphs in one struggle after another, often by employing the most diabolical techniques and inflicting pain and torture at every turn. To Wolfe, Brer Rabbit is really the embittered Negro in the habit of the hare. The un-Aesopian Remus tales tell much about what goes on behind the mask. As the reader will note, the stories tell much about life in the Old South as well.

11

Uncle Remus and the Malevolent Rabbit

Bernard Wolfe

"Takes a Limber-Toe Gemmun fer ter Jump Jim Crow"

Aunt Jemima, Beulah, the Gold Dust Twins, "George" the Pullmanad porter, Uncle Remus. . . . We like to picture the Negro as grinning at us. In Jack de Capitator, the bottle opener that looks like a gaping minstrel face, the grin is a kitchen utensil. At Mammy's Shack, the Seattle roadside inn built in the shape of a minstrel's head, you walk into the neon grin to get your hamburger. . . . And always the image of the Negro—as we create it—signifies some bounty—for us. Eternally the Negro gives—but (as they say in the theater) *really gives*—grinning from ear to ear.

Gifts without end, according to the billboards, movie screens, food labels, soap operas, magazine ads, singing commercials. Our daily bread: Cream O' Wheat, Uncle Ben's Rice, Wilson Ham ("The

---

From *Commentary* (July 1949), 31–41. Copyright © 1949 by *Commentary*. Re-printed by permission of Harold Matson Co., Inc.

Ham What Am!"), those "happifyin'" Aunt Jemima pancakes for our "temptilatin'" breakfasts. Our daily drink, too: Carioca Puerto Rican Rum, Hiram Walker whiskey, Ballantine's Ale. Through McCallum and Propper, the Negro gives milady the new "dark Creole shades" in her sheer nylons; through the House of Vigny, her "grotesque," "fuzzy-wuzzy" bottles of Golliwogg colognes and perfumes. Shoe-shines, snow-white laundry, comfortable lower berths, efficient handling of luggage; jazz, jive, jitterbugging, zoot, comedy, and the wonderful tales of Brer Rabbit to entrance the kiddies. Service with a smile. . . .

"The Negroes," writes Geoffrey Gorer, "are kept in their subservient position by the ultimate sanctions of fear and force, and this is well known to whites and Negroes alike. Nevertheless, the whites demand that the Negroes shall appear smiling, eager, and friendly in all their dealings with them."

But if the grin is extracted by force, may not the smiling face be a falseface—and just underneath is there not something else, often only half-hidden?

Uncle Remus—a kind of blackface Will Rogers, complete with standard minstrel dialect and plantation shuffle—has had remarkable staying power in our popular culture, much more than Daddy Long Legs, say, or even Uncle Tom. . . . [He] has inspired a full-length Disney feature, three Hit Parade songs, a widely circulated album of recorded dialect stories, a best-selling juvenile picture book, a syndicated comic strip. And the wily hero of his animal fables. Brer Rabbit—to whom Bugs Bunny and perhaps even Harvey owe more than a little—is today a much bigger headliner than Bambi or Black Beauty, outclassing even Donald Duck.

For almost seventy years, Uncle Remus has been the prototype of the Negro grinner-giver. Nothing ever clouds the "beaming countenance" of the "venerable old darky"; nothing ever interrupts the flow of his "hearty," "mellow," "cheerful and good-humored" voice as, decade after decade, he presents his Brer Rabbit stories to the nation.

But Remus, too, is a white man's brainchild: he was created in the columns of the Atlanta *Constitution*, back in the early 1880's, by a neurotic young Southern journalist named Joel Chandler Harris (1848–1908).

When Remus grins, Harris is pulling the strings; when he "gives" his folk stories, he is the ventriloquist's dummy on Harris's knee.

The setting for these stories never varies: the little white boy, son of "Miss Silly" and "Mars John," the plantation owners, comes "hopping and skipping" into the old Negro's cabin down in back of the "big house" and the story telling session gets under way. Remus's face "breaks up into little eddies of smiles"; he takes his admirer on his knee, "strokes the child's hair thoughtfully and caressingly," calls him "honey." The little boy "nestles closer" to his "sable patron" and listens with "open-eyed wonder."

No "sanctions of fear and force" here, Harris insists—the relationship between narrator and auditor is one of unmitigated tenderness. Remus "gives," with a "kindly beam" and a "most infectious chuckle"; the little boy receives with mingled "awe," "admiration," and "delight." But, if one looks more closely, within the magnanimous caress is an incredibly malevolent blow.

Of the several Remus collections published by Harris, the first and most famous is *Uncle Remus: His Songs and His Sayings*. Brer Rabbit appears twenty-six times in this book, encounters the Fox twenty times, soundly trounces him nineteen times. The Fox, on the other hand, achieves only two very minor triumphs—one over the Rabbit, another over the Sparrow. On only two other occasions is the Rabbit victimized even slightly, both times by animals as puny as himself (the Tarrypin, the Buzzard); but when he is pitted against adversaries as strong as the Fox (the Wolf, the Bear, once the whole Animal Kingdom) he emerges the unruffled winner. The Rabbit finally kills off all three of his powerful enemies. The Fox is made a thorough fool of by all the weakest animals—the Buzzard, the Tarrypin, the Bull-Frog.

All told, there are twenty-eight victories of the Weak over the Strong; ultimately all the Strong die violent deaths at the hands of the Weak; and there are, at most, two very insignificant victories of the Strong over the Weak. . . . Admittedly, folk symbols are seldom systematic, clean-cut, or specific; they are cultural shadows thrown by the unconscious, and the unconscious is not governed by the sharp-edged neatness of the filing cabinet. But still, on the basis of the tally-sheet alone, is it too far-fetched to take Brer Rabbit as a symbol—about as sharp as Southern sanctions would allow—of the Negro slave's festering hatred of the white man?

It depends, of course, on whether these are animals who maul and murder each other, or human beings disguised as animals. Here Harris and Remus seem to differ. "In dem days," Remus often starts, "de creeturs wuz santer'n 'roun' same like fokes." But for Harris—so he insists—this anthropomorphism is only incidental. What the stories depict, he tells us, is only the "roaring comedy of animal life."

Is it? These are very un-Aesopian creatures who speak a vaudeville dialect, hold candy-pulls, run for the legislature, fight and scheme over gold mines, compete for women in elaborate rituals of courtship and self-aggrandizement, sing plantation ditties about "Jim Crow," read the newspapers after supper, and kill and maim each other—not in gusts of endocrine Pavlov passion but coldbloodedly, for prestige, plotting their crafty moves in advance and often using accomplices. . . . Harris sees no malice in all this, even when heads roll. Brer Rabbit, he explains, is moved not by "malice, but mischievousness." But Brer Rabbit "mischievously" scalds the Wolf to death, makes the innocent Possum die in a fire to cover his own crimes, tortures and probably murders the Bear by setting a swarm of bees on him—and, after causing the fatal beating of the Fox, carries his victim's head to Mrs. Fox and her children, hoping to trick them into eating it in their soup. . . .

One dramatic tension in these stories seems to be a gastronomic one: *Will the communal meal ever take place in the "Animal" Kingdom?*

The food-sharing issue is posed in the very first story. "I seed Brer B'ar yistiddy," the Fox tells the Rabbit as the story opens, "en he sorter rake me over de coals kaze you en me ain't make frens en live naborly." He then invites the Rabbit to supper—intending that his guest will be the main course in this "joint" feast. Brer Rabbit solemnly accepts the invitation, shows up, makes the Fox look ridiculous, and blithely scampers off: "En Brer Fox ain't kotch 'im yit, en w'at's mo', honey, he ain't gwine ter." The Rabbit can get along very well without the communal meal; but, it soon develops, Brer Fox and his associates can't live without it.

Without food-sharing, no community. Open warfare breaks out immediately after the Fox's hypocritical invitation; and the Rabbit is invariably the victor in the gory skirmishes. And after he kills and skins the Wolf, his other enemies are so cowed that now the communal meal finally seems about to take place: "de animals en de creeturs, dey kep' on gittin' mo' en mo' familious wid wunner nudder—bunchin' der perwishuns tergidder in de same shanty" and "takin' a snack" together too.

But Brer Rabbit isn't taken in. Knowing that the others are sharing their food with him out of fear, not genuine communality, he remains the complete cynic and continues to raid the Fox's goober patch and the Bear's persimmon orchard. Not until the closing episode does the Fox make a genuine food-sharing gesture—he crawls inside Bookay the Cow with Brer Rabbit and gratuitously shows him how to hack out all the beef he can carry. But the communal overture comes too late. In an act of the most supreme malevolence, the Rabbit betrays his benefactor to the farmer and stands by, "makin' like he mighty sorry," while the Fox is beaten to death. . . . And now the meal which aborted in the beginning, because the Fox's friendliness was only a ruse, almost does take place—with the Fox as the main course. Having brutally destroyed his arch enemy, Brer Rabbit tries to make Mrs. Fox cook a soup with her husband's head, and almost succeeds.

Remus is not an anthropomorphist by accident. His theme is a *human* one—neighborliness—and the communal meal is a symbol for it. His moral? There are no good neighbors in the world, neither equality nor fraternity. But the moral has an underside: the Rabbit can never be trapped.

Another tension runs through the stories: *Who gets the women?* In sex, Brer Rabbit is at his most aggressive—and his most invincible. Throughout he is engaged in murderous competition with the Fox and the other animals for the favors of "Miss Meadows en de gals."

In their sexual competition the Rabbit never fails to humiliate the Fox viciously. "I'll show Miss Meadows en de gals dat I'm de boss er Brer Fox," he decides. And he does: through the most elaborate trickery he persuades the Fox to put on a saddle, then rides him past Miss Meadows' house, digging his spurs in vigorously. . . . And in sex, it would seem, there are no false distinctions between creatures—all differences in status are irrelevant. At Miss Meadows' the feuds of the work-a-day world must be suspended, "kaze Miss Meadows, she done put her foot down, she did, en say dat w'en dey come ter her place dey hatter hang up a flag er truce at de front gate en 'bide by it."

The truce is all to the Rabbit's advantage, because if the competitors start from scratch in the sexual battle the best man must win—and the best man is invariably Brer Rabbit. The women themselves want the best man to win. Miss Meadows decides to get some peace by holding a contest and letting the winner have his pick of the girls. The Rabbit mulls the problem over. He sings ironically,

> Make a bow ter de Buzzard en den ter de Crow
> Takes a limber-toe gemmun fer ter jump Jim Crow.

Then, through a tricky scheme, he proceeds to outshine all the stronger contestants.

Food-sharing, sex-sharing—the Remus stories read like a catalogue of Southern racial taboos, all standing on their heads. The South, wearing the blinders of stereotype, has always tried to see the Negro as a "roaringly comic" domestic animal. Understandably; for animals of the tame or domestic variety are not menacing—they are capable only of mischief, never of malice. But the Negro slave, through his anthropomorphic Rabbit stories, seems to be hinting that even the frailest and most humble of "animals" can let fly with the most bloodthirsty aggressions. And these aggressions take place in the two most sacrosanct areas of Southern racial etiquette: the gastronomic and the erotic.

The South, with its "sanctions of fear and force," forbids Negroes to eat at the same table with whites. But Brer Rabbit, through an act of murder, *forces* Brer Fox and all his associates to share their food with him. The South enjoins the Negro, under penalty of death, from coming near the white man's women—although the white man has free access to the Negro's women. But Brer Rabbit flauntingly demonstrates his sexual superiority over all the other animals and, as the undisputed victor in the sexual competition, gets his choice of all the women.

And yet, despite these food and sex taboos, for two solid centuries—for the Rabbit stories existed long before Harris put them on paper—Southerners chuckled at the way the Rabbit terrorized all the other animals into the communal meal, roared at the Rabbit's guile in winning the girls away from the Fox *by jumping Jim Crow*. And they were endlessly intrigued by the O. Henry spasm of the miraculous in the very last story, right after the Fox's death: "Some say dat . . . Brer Rabbit married ole Miss Fox. . . ."

An interesting denouement, considering the sexual fears which saturate the South's racial attitudes. Still more interesting that Southern whites should even have countenanced it, let alone revelled in it. . . .

Significantly, the goal of eating and sex, as depicted in Uncle Remus, is not instinct-gratification. The overriding drive is for *prestige*—the South is a prestige-haunted land. And it is in that potent intangible that the Rabbit is always paid off most handsomely for his exploits. Throughout, as he terrorizes the Strong, the "sassy" Rabbit remains bland, unperturbed, sure of his invincibility. When he humiliates the Fox by turning him into a saddle-horse, he mounts him "same's ef he wuz king er de patter-rollers." ("Patter-rollers," Harris cheerfully points out, were the white patrols that terrorized Negro slaves so they wouldn't wander off the plantations.)

Brer Rabbit, in short, has all the jaunty topdog airs and attitudes which a slave can only dream of having. And, like the slave, he has a supremely cynical view of the social world, since he sees it from below. The South is the most etiquette-ridden region of the country; and the Rabbit sees all forms of etiquette as hypocritical and absurd. Creatures meet, address each other with unctuous politeness, inquire after each other's families, pass the time of day with oily clichés— and all the while they are plotting to humiliate, rob, and assassinate each other. The Rabbit sees through it all; if he is serene it is only because he can plot more rapidly and with more deadly efficiency than any of the others.

The world, in Brer Rabbit's wary eyes, is a jungle. Life is a battle-unto-the-death for food, sex, power, prestige, a battle without rules. There is only one reality in this life: who is on top? But Brer Rabbit wastes no time lamenting the mad unneighborly scramble for the top position. Because it is by no means ordained that the Weak can never take over. In his topsy-turvy world, to all practical purposes, the Weak *have* taken over. In one episode, the Rabbit falls down a well in a bucket. He can get back up only by enticing the Fox to climb into the other bucket. The Fox is duped: he drops down and the Rabbit rises, singing as he passes his enemy:

> *Good-by, Brer Fox, take keer yo' cloze*
> *Fer dis is de way de worril goes*
> *Some goes up en some goes down*
> *You'll git ter de bottom all safe en soun'.*

This is the theme song of the stories. The question remains, who sings it? The Rabbit is a creation of Uncle Remus's people; is it, then, Uncle Remus singing? But Uncle Remus is a creation of Joel Chandler Harris. . . .

There is a significant difference in ages—some hundreds of years—between Uncle Remus and Brer Rabbit. The Rabbit had been the hero of animal stories popular among Negroes from the early days of slavery; these were genuine folk tales told by Negroes to Negroes and handed down in oral form. Uncle Remus was added only when Harris, in packaging the stories—using the Negro grin for gift-wrapping—invented the Negro narrator to sustain the dialect.

Harris, then, fitted the hate-imbued folk materials into a framework, a white man's framework, of "love." He took over the animal characters and situations of the original stories and gave them a human setting: the loving and lovable Negro narrator, the adoring white auditor. Within this framework of love, the blow was heavily padded with caresses and the genuine folk was almost emasculated into the cute folksy.

Almost, but not quite. Harris all his life was torn between his furtive penchant for fiction and his profession of journalism. It was the would-be novelist in him who created Remus, the "giver" of interracial caresses; but the trained journalist in him, having too good an eye and ear, reported the energetic folk blow in the caress. Thus the curious tension in his versions between "human" form and "animal" content.

Before Harris, few Southerners had ever faced squarely the

aggressive symbolism of Brer Rabbit, or the paradox of their delight in it. Of course: it was part of the Southerner's undissected myth—often shared by the Negroes—that his cherished childhood sessions in the slave quarters were bathed in two-way benevolence. But Harris, by writing the white South and its Negro tale-spinners into the stories, also wrote in its unfaced paradoxes. Thus his versions helped to rip open the racial myth—and, with it, the interracial grin.

What was the slippery rabbit-hero doing in these stories to begin with? Where did he come from? As soon as Harris wrote down the oral stories for mass consumption, these questions began to agitate many whites. The result was a whole literature devoted to proving the "un-American" genealogy of Brer Rabbit.

Why, one Southern writer asks, did the Negro pick the Rabbit for a hero? Could it be because the Rabbit was "symbolic of his own humble and helpless condition in comparison with his master the owner of the plantation"? Perhaps the Rabbit represents the Negro "in revolt at . . . his own subordinate and insignificant place in society"?

But no: if the Negro is capable of rebelling against society—American society—even symbolically, he is a menace. The Negro must be in revolt against *Nature*, against the "subordinate and insignificant place" assigned to him by biological fate, not America. The writer reassures himself: the Negro makes animals act "like a low order of human intelligence, such as the Negro himself [can] comprehend." The Negro naturally feels "more closely in touch with [the lower animals] than with the white man who [is] so superior to him in every respect." No threat in Brer Rabbit; his genealogy, having no *American* roots, is a technical matter for "the psychologist or the student of folklore."

However, uneasy questions were raised; and as they were raised they were directed at Harris. Readers sensed the symbolic taunts and threats in the Rabbit and insisted on knowing whether they were directed against white America—or against "Nature." Harris took refuge from this barrage of questions in two mutually contradictory formulas: (1) he was merely the "compiler" of these stories, a non-intellectual, a lowly humorist, ignorant of "folkloristic" matters; and (2) Brer Rabbit was most certainly, as Southerners intuited, an undiluted African.

"All that I know—all that we Southerners know—about it," Harris protested, "is that every old plantation mammy in the South is full of these stories." But, a sentence later, Harris decided there *was* one other thing he knew: "One thing is certain—the Negro did not get them from the whites; *probably they are of remote African origin.*"

And if they come from the Congo, they offer no symbolic blows to Americans; they are simply funny. So Harris warns the folklorists: "First let us have the folktales told as they were intended to be told, for the sake of amusement. . . ."

But if the folklorists *should* find in them something "of value to their pretensions"? Then "let it be picked out and preserved with as little cackling as possible."

The South wavered; it could not shake off the feeling that Brer Rabbit's overtones were more than just funny. And Harris, too, wavered. To a British folklorist editor he wrote, suddenly reversing himself, that the stories were "more important than humorous." And in the introduction to his book he explains that "however humorous it may be in effect, its intention is perfectly serious. . . . It seems to me that a volume written wholly in dialect must have its solemn, not to say melancholy features."

What was it that Harris sporadically found "important," "solemn," even "melancholy" here? It turns out to be the *Americanism* of Brer Rabbit: "it needs no scientific investigation," Harris continues in his introduction, "to show why he [the Negro] selects as his hero the weakest and most harmless of all animals. . . . It is not virtue that triumphs, but helplessness. . . . Indeed, the parallel between the case of the 'weakest' of all animals, who must, perforce, triumph through his shrewdness, and the humble condition of the slave raconteur, is not without its pathos."

A suggestive idea. But such a "parallel" could not have been worked out in the African jungle, before slavery; it implies that Brer Rabbit, after all, was born much closer to the Mississippi than to the Congo. . . . This crucial sentence does not occur in later editions. Instead we read: "It would be presumptious [*sic*] in me to offer an opinion as to the origins of these curious myth-stories; but, *if ethnologists should discover that they did not originate with the African, the proof to that effect should be accompanied with a good deal of persuasive eloquence.*"

In this pressing sentence we can see Harris's whole fragmented psyche mirrored. Like all the South, he was caught in a subjective tug-of-war: his intelligence groped for the venomous American slave crouching behind the Rabbit, but his beleaguered racial emotions, in self-defense, had to insist on the "Africanism" of Brer Rabbit— and of the Negro. Then Miss Sally and Mars John could relish his "quaint antics" without recognizing themselves as his targets.

Against the African origin of Brer Rabbit one may argue that he is an eloquent white folk-symbol too, closely related to the lamb as the epitome of Christian meekness (the Easter bunny). May not the Negro, in his conversion to Christianity, have learned the standard Christian animal symbols from the whites? Could not his constant tale-spinning about the Rabbit's malevolent triumphs somehow, in some devious way, suggest the ascent of Christ, the meekness that shall inherit the earth; suggest, even, that the meek may stop being meek and set about inheriting the earth without waiting on the Biblical timetable?

But, there *is* more definite evidence as to Brer Rabbit's non-African origins—skimpy, not conclusive, but highly suggestive. Folklore study indicates that if the Negro did have stories about a rabbit back in Africa, they were not these stories, and the rabbit was most decidedly not this rabbit. Brer Rabbit's truer ancestor, research suggests, hails from elsewhere.

"Most of these Negro stories," reported a Johns Hopkins ethnologist—one of the "cackling" folklorists—". . . bear a striking resemblance to the large body of animal stories made on European soil, of which the most extensive is that known as the *Roman de Renard.* The episodes which form the substance of this French version circulated in the Middle Ages on the Flemish border. . . . The principal actors . . . are the fox, who plays the jokes, and the wolf, most frequently the victim of the fox."

In incident after incident, the Brer Rabbit situations parallel the Reynard the Fox situations: the same props appear, the same set-to's, the same ruses, the same supporting characters, often the same dialogue. But there is one big difference: "In *Uncle Remus* the parts are somewhat changed. Here the rabbit, who scarcely appears (under the name Couard) in the *Renard*, is the chief trickster. His usual butt is the fox. . . ."

In Christian symbolism, then, the rabbit is the essence of meekness and innocence. And in an important part of white folk culture he stands for the impotent, the cowardly, as against the cunning fox. Suddenly, with the beginning of slavery, the Negro beings to tell stories in which the rabbit, now the epitome of belligerence and guile, crops up as the *hero*, mercilessly badgering the fox.

Could the Negroes have got the Reynard fables from the whites? Not impossible. The stories originated among the Flemish peasants. During the 12th century they were written down in French, Latin, and German, in a variety of rhymed forms. The many written versions were then widely circulated throughout Western Europe. And more than a few of the first Negro slaves were brought to France, Spain, and Portugal; and some of their descendants were transplanted to America. Also, many early slaves were brought to plantations owned by Frenchmen—whether in the Louisiana Territory, the Acadian-French sections of North Carolina, or the West Indies.

And many white masters, of French and other backgrounds, told these delightful fox tales to their children. And, from the beginning of the slave trade, many Negroes—who may or may not have had pre-Christian rabbit fables of their own back in Africa—could have listened, smiling amiably, slowly absorbing the raw materials for the grinning folk "gift" that would one day be immortalized by Joel Chandler Harris, Walt Disney, Tin Pan Alley, and the comics. . . .

The Harris research technique, we learn, was first-hand and direct. Seeing a group of Negroes, he approaches and asks if they know any Brer Rabbit stories. The Negroes seem not to understand. Offhandedly, and in rich dialect, Harris tells one himself—as often as not, the famous "Tar-Baby" story. The Negroes are transfixed; then, suddenly, they break out in peals of laughter, kick their heels together, slap their thighs. Before long they are swapping Rabbit yarns with the white man as though he were their lifelong "hail-feller." "Curiously enough," Harris notes, "I have found few Negroes who will acknowledge to a stranger that they know anything of these legends; and yet to relate one of the stories is the surest road to their confidence and esteem."

Why the sudden hilarity? What magic folk-key causes these wary, taciturn Negroes to open up? Harris claims to have won their "esteem"; but perhaps he only guaranteed them immunity. He thinks he disarmed the Negroes—he may only have demonstrated that he, the white boss-man, was disarmed.

And how much did the Negroes tell him when they "opened up"? Just how far did they really open up? Harris observes that "there are different versions of all the stories—the shrewd narrators of the mythology of the old plantation adapting themselves with ready tact to the years, tastes, and expectations of their juvenile audiences." But there seem to be gaps in Harris's own versions. At tantalizingly crucial points Uncle Remus will break off abruptly—"Some tells one tale en some tells nudder"—leaving the story dangling like a radio cliff-hanger. Did these gaps appear when the stories were told to Harris? When the slave is obliged to play the clown-entertainer and "give" his folk tales to his masters, young or old, his keen sense of the fitting might well delete the impermissible and blur the dubious—and more out of self-preservation than tact.

Of course, the original oral stories would not express the slave's aggressions straightforwardly either. A Negro slave who yielded his mind fully to his race hatreds in an absolutely white-dominated situation must go mad; and the function of such folk symbols as Brer Rabbit is precisely to prevent inner explosions by siphoning off these hatreds before they can completely possess consciousness. Folk tales, like so much of folk culture, are part of an elaborate psychic drainage system— they make it possible for Uncle Tom to retain his facade of grinning Tomism and even, to some degree, to believe in it himself. But the slave's venom, while subterranean, must nonetheless have been *thrillingly* close to the surface and its symbolic disguises flimsier, its attacks less roundabout. Accordingly his protective instincts, sensing the danger in too shallow symbolism, would have necessarily wielded a meticulous, if unconscious, blue pencil in the stories told to white audiences.

Harris tried hard to convince himself that Uncle Remus was a full-fledged, dyed-in-the-denim Uncle Tom—he describes the "venerable sable patron" as an ex-slave "who has nothing but pleasant memories of the discipline of slavery." But Harris could not completely exorcise the menace in the Meek. How often Remus steps out of his clown role to deliver unmistakable judgments on class, caste, and race! In those judgments the aggressions of this "white man's nigger" are astonishingly naked.

"Why the Negro Is Black" tells how the little boy makes the "curious" discovery that Remus's palms are white. The old man explains: "Dey wuz a time w'en all de w'ite folks us black—blacker dan me. . . . Niggers is niggers now, but de time wuz w'en we 'uz all niggers tergedder. . . ." How did some "niggers" get white? Simply by bathing in a pond which washed their pigmentation off and using up most of the waters, so that the latecomers could only dabble their hands and feet in it.

But the stragglers who were left with their dark skin tone are not trapped—they may be able to wriggle out of it. In "A Plantation Witch," Remus, explaining that there are witches everywhere in the world that "comes en conjus fokes," hints that these witches may be Negroes who have slipped out of their skins. And these witches conjure white folks from all sides, taking on the forms of owls, bats, dogs, cats—and rabbits.

And in "The Wonderful Tar-Baby Story"—advertised on the dust-jacket as the most famous of all the Remus stories—Remus reverts to the question of pigmentation. ("There are few negroes that will fail to respond" to this one, Harris advises one of his folklore "legmen.") The Fox fashions a "baby" out of tar and places it on the side of the road; the Rabbit comes along and addresses the figure. Not getting any answer, he threatens: "Ef you don't take off dat hat en tell me howdy, I'm gwineter bus' you wide open." (Here the

Rabbit's bluster reads like a parody of the white man's demand for the proper bowing-and-scraping etiquette from the Negro; it is a reflection of the satiric mimicry of the whites which the slaves often indulged in among themselves.) He hits the Tar-Baby—his fist sticks in the gooey tar. He hits it with the other hand, then kicks it—all four extremities are stuck.

This is "giving" in a new sense; tar, blackness, by its very yielding, traps. Interesting symbol, in a land where the mere possession of a black skin requires you, under penalty of death, to yield, to *give*, everywhere. The mark of supreme impotence suddenly acquires the power to render impotent, merely by its flaccidity, its inertness; it is almost a Gandhi-like symbol. There is a puzzle here: it is the Rabbit who is trapped. But in a later story, "How Mr. Rabbit Was Too Sharp for Mr. Fox," it turns out that the Rabbit, through another cagey maneuver, gets the Fox to set him free from the tar-trap and thus avoids being eaten by his enemy. The Negro, in other words, is wily enough to escape from the engulfing pit of blackness, although his opponents, who set the trap, do their level best to keep him imprisoned in it. But it is not at all sure that anyone else who fell victim to this treacherous black yieldingness—the Fox, say—would be able to wriggle out so easily.

The story about "A Plantation Witch" frightens his young admirer so much that Remus has to take him by the hand and lead him home to the "big house." And for a long time the boy lies awake "expecting an unseemly visitation from some mysterious source." Many of the other stories, too, must have given him uneasy nights. For within the "gift" that Uncle Remus gives to Miss Sally's little boy is a nightmare, a nightmare in which whites are Negroes, the Weak torture and drown the Strong, mere blackness becomes black magic—and Negroes cavort with cosmic forces and the supernatural, zipping their skins off at will to prowl around the countryside terrorizing the whites, often in the guise of rabbits. . . .

Harris's career is one of the fabulous success stories of American literary history. Thanks to Uncle Remus, the obscure newspaperman was catapulted into the company of Mark Twain, Bret Harte, James Whitcomb Riley, and Petroleum V. Nasby; Andrew Carnegie and Theodore Roosevelt traveled to Atlanta to seek him out; he was quoted in Congress. And all the while he maintained—as in a letter to Twain—that "my book has no basis in literary merit to stand upon; I know it is the matter and not the manner that has attracted public attention . . . my relations towards Uncle Remus are similar to those that exist between an almanac-maker and the calendar. . . ."

But how was it that Harris could apply his saccharine manner to such matter, dress this malevolent material, these nightmares, in such sweetness and light? For one thing, of course, he was only recording the tottering racial myth of the post-bellum South, doing a paste-job on its fissioning falseface. As it happened, he was peculiarly suited for the job; for he was crammed full of pathological racial obsessions, over and above those that wrack the South and, to a lesser degree, all of white America.

Even Harris's worshipful biographer, his daughter-in-law, can't prevent his story from reading like a psychiatric recital of symptoms. The blush and the stammer were his whole way of life. From early childhood on, we are told, he was "painfully conscious of his social deficiencies" and his "lack of size"; he felt "handicapped by his tendency to stutter" and to "blush furiously," believed himself "much uglier than he really was"; in his own words, he had "an absolute horror of strangers."

During his induction into the typographical union, Harris stutters so badly that he has to be excused from the initiation ceremony; trapped in a room full of congenial strangers, he escapes by jumping out of the window. "What a coarse ungainly boor I am," he laments, "how poor, small and insignificant. . . ." He wonders if he is mad: "I am morbidly sensitive . . . it is an affliction—a disease . . . the slightest rebuff tortures me beyond expression. . . . It is worse than death itself. It is *horrible*." Again, he speculates about his "abnormal quality of mind . . . that lacks only vehemence to become downright insanity. . . ." Harris's life, it appears, was one long ballet of embarrassment.

"I am nursing a novel in my brain," Harris announced archly more than once. All along he was consumed with the desire to turn out some "long work" of fiction, but, except for two inept and badly received efforts (published after his forty-eighth year), he never succeeded. Over and over he complained bitterly of his grinding life in the journalistic salt mines—but when the Century Company offered him a handsome income if he would devote all his time to creative work, he refused. This refusal, according to his daughter-in-law, "can be explained only by his abnormal lack of confidence in himself as a 'literary man.'"

The urge to create was strong in Harris, so strong that it gave him no peace; and he could not create. That is the central fact in his biography: his creative impulses were trapped behind a block of congealed guilts, granite-strong; the works he produced were not real gushings of the subjective but only those driblets that were able to seep around the edges of the block.

Harris's stammer—his literal choking on words—was like a

charade of the novelist *manqué* in him; his blush was the fitful glow of his smothered self, a tic of the guilty blood. And that smothered self had a name: Uncle Remus.

Accused of plagiarizing folk materials, Harris replies indignantly: "I shall not hesitate to draw on the oral stories I know for incidents. . . . The greatest literary men, if you will remember, were very poor inventors." Harris all his life was a very poor inventor; his career was built on a merciless, systematic plagiarizing of the folk-Negro. Small wonder, then, that the "plantation darky" was such a provocative symbol for him. For, ironically, this lowly Negro was, when viewed through the blinders of stereotype, almost the walking image of Harris's ego-ideal— the un-selfconscious, "natural," free-flowing, richly giving creator that Harris could never become. Indeed, for Harris, as for many another white American, the Negro *seemed* in every respect to be a negative print of his own uneasy self: "happy-go-lucky," socializing, orally expressive, muscularly relaxed, never bored or passive, unashamedly exhibitionistic, free from self-pity even in his situation of concentrated pain, emotionally fluid. And every time a Remus opened his mouth, every time he flashed a grin, he wrote effortlessly another novel that was strangled a-borning in Harris.

"I despise and detest those false forms of society that compel people to suppress their thoughts," Harris wrote. But he was himself the most inhibited and abashed of men. What fascinates him in the Rabbit stories, he confesses, is "the humor that lies between *what is perfectly decorous in appearance* and *what is wildly extravagant in suggestion*." But, a thorough slave to decorum, he was incapable of the "wildly extravagant," whether in his love-making ("My love for you," he informs his future wife, "is . . . far removed from that wild passion that develops itself in young men in their teens . . . it is not at all wild or unreasoning.") or in his writing.

Harris, then, was *awed* by Uncle Remus. It was the awe of the sophisticate before the spontaneous, the straitjacketed before the nimble. But was the Negro what Harris thought him to be? It is certainly open to question, for another irony of the South is that the white man, under his pretense of racial omniscience, actually knows the Negro not at all—he knows only the false-face which he has forced on the Negro. It is the white man who manufactures the Negro grin. The stereotype reflects the looker, his thwartings and yearnings, not the person looked at; it is born out of intense subjective need.

Harris's racial awe was only an offshoot of the problem that tormented him all his life: the problem of identifying himself. He was caught in the American who-am-I dilemma, one horn of which is white, the other often black. And there is abundant proof that, at least in one compartment of his being, Harris defined himself by identifying with the Negro.

As a child, Harris started the game of "Gully Minstrels" with his white playmates; and later in life, whenever he felt "blue" and wanted to relax, he would jump up and exclaim, "Let's have some fun—let's play minstrels!" Often, in letters and newspaper articles, and even in personal relations, he would *jokingly* refer to himself as "Uncle Remus," and when he started a one-man magazine, he decided to name it *Uncle Remus's Magazine* instead of *The Optimist*! Frequently he would lapse into a rich Negro dialect, to the delight of his admirers, from Andrew Carnegie down to the local trolley conductor. And, like Uncle Remus, he even toys with the idea that whites are only blanched Negroes: "Study a nigger right close," he has one of his characters say, "and you'll ketch a glimpse of how white folks would look and do without their trimmin's."

Harris seems to have been a man in permanent rebellion against his own skin. No wonder: for he was driven to "give," and it was impossible for him to give without first zipping out of his own decorous skin and slipping into Uncle Remus's. To him the artist and the Negro were synonymous.

And Harris virulently *hated* the Negro, too. "The colored people of Macon," he writes in his paper, "celebrated the birthday of Lincoln again on Wednesday. This is the third time since last October. . . ." And: "A negro pursued by an agile Macon policeman fell in a well the other day. He says he knocked the bottom out of the concern." Again: "There will have to be another amendment to the civil rights bill. A negro boy in Covington was attacked by a sow lately and narrowly escaped with his life. We will hear next that the sheep have banded together to mangle the downtrodden race."

The malice here is understandable. Can the frustrate—the "alma-nac-maker"—ever love unequivocally the incarnation of his own taboo self—the "calendar"? What stillborn novelist can be undilutedly tender towards the objectivization of his squelched alter-ego, whose oral stories he feels impelled to "draw on" all his life?

Most likely, at least in Harris, the love went deeper than the hate—the hate was, in some measure, a *defense* against the love. "*Some goes up en some goes down.*" Who sings this theme song? A trio: the Rabbit, Remus, *and* Harris. Literally, it is only a rabbit and a fox who change places. Racially, the song symbolizes the ascent of the Negro "Weak" and the descent of the white "Strong."

But to Harris, on the deepest personal level, it must have meant:

the collapse of the "perfectly decorous" (inhibition, etiquette, embarrassment, the love that is never wild, the uncreative journalist-compiler, the blush and the stammer) and the triumph of the "wildly extravagant" (spontaneity, "naturalness," the unleashed subjective, creativity, "Miss Meadows en de gals," exhibitionism, the folk-novelist). The song must have been *deliciously* funny to him. . . .

The Remus stories are a monument to the South's ambivalence. Harris, the archetypical Southerner, sought the Negro's love, and pretended ho had received it (Remus's grin). But he sought the Negro's hate too (Brer Rabbit), and revelled in it in an unconscious orgy of masochism—punishing himself, possibly, for not being the Negro, the stereotypical Negro, the unstinting giver.

Harris's inner split—and the South's, and white America's—is mirrored in the fantastic disparity between Remus's beaming face and Brer Rabbit's acts. And such aggressive acts increasingly emanate from the grin, along with the hamburgers, the shoeshines, the "happifyin'" pancakes.

The first of several descriptions of life "Down Home and Up North" is Hylan Lewis' discussion of the social structure and cultural norms of the black citizens of Kent, a southern community he studied in the late 1940s.

The underlying theme of this and all studies of the social life of black Americans, past and present, is their "race-ridden character." As Lewis says, "The Kent Negro has two public personailities—one for the white community and one for the Negro. . . " The same could be said for blacks living in every other American town in the days before the current Black Revolution began (and it is still true in many places).

12

The Blackways of Kent

Hylan Lewis

In observing and living in the Negro culture of [the Southern community of] Kent, one notes characteristic group "leanings" and emphases. Organized customs tend to be "pointed"—consciously or unconsciously—in a desirable direction or directions. The desired ends of behavior and the activities and qualities that seem to occupy people most are elements that help to characterize a culture in social psychological terms.

This is no attempt to idealize, or to oversimplify, complex and ever-changing behavior; nor is this a search for a "folk soul" or "folk spirit." Our interest is in the demonstrable value-emphases of this subculture. The clues taken from the examination of customs and institutions indicate that there is no single orientation or value which will adequately explain everything, nor is there necessarily any logical consistency among the many that are to be found.

From Hylan Lewis, "Orientations and Values," in *The Blackways of Kent*, Chapel Hill: The University of North Carolina Press, 1955, pp. 194–222.

The significant things that concern and occupy people most in the Kent Negro subculture involve considerations of race; religion; self-expression and release as measured in whisky, sex, and leisure-time activity; touchiness of the ego as measured in querulousness and ingroup aggression and violence; and a desire for appreciation of the person and for respect. Many of these emphases are functionally linked, and they conceivably are colored significantly by the same situational factors, the most important of which is, of course, the color line.

The Race-Ridden Character of Life

In general, life for the Negro in Kent tends to be race-ridden: considerations of ethnic role and status pervade every aspect of the life-death cycle and color a great deal of the minutiae of everyday life; much of life consists of adjusting to, rationalizing, making consistent, or combatting the force and implications of ethnic role and status. Group consciousness, and a not-always-too-comfortable identification with one's own, derive from the facts of minority status. Invidious inter-group comparisons are frequent, and there are elements of defensiveness, pride, defiance, individuation, and sharp criticism, condemnation, and rejection of one's own.

An implicit and explicit dominating theme is "white folks is white folks."* It can he said in different ways, in different contexts, or in tones ranging from awe and respect through sardonic humor to disgust and bitterness. As indicated earlier, it bespeaks a feeling that there is a gulf or wall between the groups; that there are certain things that are categorically true of the white group: in a crucial situation, loyalty to one's own will over-ride considerations of fair play, sentiment, and personal relationships. It means that a white man can never be thoroughly trusted or incorporated into the intimate ongoing life of the Negro community. It means that there tends to be an item of reservation in any relationship, no matter how cordial or benevolent.

A corollary of the above is the map that every Negro carries around in his head of "how far to go with white folks." It is marked by a sensitivity that every Negro has in his relations with whites, along with a set of reservations and restrictions on free expression and

---

* This does not mean the qualitative difference are not recognized among Negroes; for instance, there is a general disposition to "look down upon" the poor white mill villagers as a different bread of whites who do not get—and often cannot demand—the same deference and respect accorded upper class "town whites." The taken-for-granted "low-class" behavior of "Mill Hill" folks is a matter of amusement and give some sense of superiority. Still there is recognition of the stubborn fact that they too are white.

behavior with whites. "I ain't going to do that"; "I know better than to go too far," typify expressions of restraint. The line separating that which is permitted and that which is "too far" is not a straight and consistent line, nor is it absolute, as it is broken on occasions and by special persons. Part of this sensitivity flows from a knowledge of the stereotypes that whites have about Negroes. In this way, the stereotype serves a social-control function. A case in point is cited by a colleague;

> We had told the Negro grocery delivery boy to pick up and take back to the store any empty Coca-Cola bottles that might be in the kitchen when he delivered groceries. He never took them however. The owner of the grocery store said that he does not like to take anything from a kitchen, even though he has been told to do so, for fear he will be accused of stealing. This Negro man enters the kitchens of white people whether or not they are at home and delivers groceries. Due to the prevalence of the belief that "all Negroes steal," he probably has to avoid anything that would give the slightest grounds for suspicion. His job no doubt hangs on his avoidance of any such suspicions.

In another category was the wry but facetious comment of a young man who works in the business section:

> Man, the cops is after me because I don't get drunk. They think that because I don't get drunk like these other cats that I'm a smart nigger. They talk around sometime and try to trick me into a smart answer; but I'm too wise for them.

Another illustration of the mental restraints on normal behavior that race imposes is the case of an elderly man who told of losing a wallet. In retracing his steps immediately he met a white woman and saw what appeared to be his wallet in her hand; he asked her if she had found a wallet; after some hesitation she said she had not. The man said that he started to go back and approach the woman but "something told me not to, for you see, that woman was a white woman, and I figured I would get in some kind of trouble that would cost me more than was in the wallet. . . . But I am as sure as anything that she found it."

A Negro man reports that in his early manhood he made enough from a cotton crop and odd jobs to purchase a particular brand of car that he wanted; he asked his father about it. His father consulted with a white friend to see "if it would be all right." The white friend advised: "Moe, go on and get the car; if anybody says anything to you, come and see me." This incident illustrates also the white patron- intermediary-friend pattern that is almost a necessary adjunct to successful adjustment on the local scene.

The role of the race factor in establishing status is shown in the following; there are also indications of ingroup criticism:

I know practically everybody in town—white and colored—and they all know me. When I walk down the street, they all call me by name, and I don't mean no nickname. I can get favors out of any of them—and I don't "Charlie" to them either. These white people are generally decent; they treat you much more decent than some of those whites up North. . . . Some Negroes don't know that you don't have to "Charlie" white folks; they really don't like it, and they respect you when you talk straight to them. They know them; white folks can tell you every respected Negro in this town. I kept my uniform on ninety days after I returned. One old peckerwood down there in front of the ten cent store told the Chief that I was impersonating. The Chief told him, "You're a damn liar. Don't start that stuff. I've known that boy all his life. He ain't never got in trouble; what he's got, that's what he is."

Condemnation of one's own and rationalization of the implications of ethnic status are indicated in the following comments which are not necessarily typical in content but tend to be in tone. A middle-aged Negro businessman said:

Negro been petted in the North. They brought on themselves a lot of trouble and discrimination. That Chicago riot was their fault, or at least a good part of it. They don't keep and know their place. I like to know my place.

A middle-aged Negro mill worker:

I thinks the Negroes knows they's free but they's got so much cowardism in them, they don't act like it. . . . These white folks is funny; if you acts like a man, you can talk up to them like a man. They appreciates it and don't do nothing about it. I believes a man's a man.

An elderly Negro widow of the "old school":

Hoover had the nigger down to fifty cents a day. I reckon if he had kept on he'd had 'em all in county home. Roosevelt straightened all that out. . . . This man Truman's trying to carry all that out that Roosevelt started. I'd like to see him continue but I fear he gonna lose out. But he didn't have to do all he did. . . . We's got so many bad niggers don't need no rights. If they could just give the rights to the good niggers would be all right. Leastwise till you could bring the bad niggers up. I tell you, we's got a heap of bad niggers; they'd get in there and ruin everything. . . . Whites don't want to change. . . . Niggers ain't had enough experience. Niggers ain't got equipment and stuff; they can't run the courthouse. Whites feared they'd git up with them and be looking at their women. . . . Better not do that; you gits kilt.

More nearly typical of the younger group is this Navy veteran's statement on civil rights:

> They don't know what they're talking about. All I want for them to do is just give me room on the streets—and don't try to brush me out of the way. I don't want to socialize with them.

As indicated, invidious ethnic comparisons are frequent; all indicate group consciousness although all are not self-critical. The disposition to compare Negro and white ways is a constant one. Comments may be streaked with bitterness, disgust, or shame; or they may show a tolerant sardonic humor. Some miscellaneous examples: "That's a spook [Negro] for you!" "Negroes don't stick together." "You can never trust a Negro with your business; he'll put it in the street every time." "Negroes haven't learned to respect their own women." "Anything happens the first thing the Negro will do is run to the white man." "My Negro (or nigger) came out." However, all comparisons are not unfavorable, and there is a legitimate question as to whether these verbalizations are indications of true feelings: some of them have a catchword quality and others are family-like outbursts indicating annoyance and frustration as much as anger and hatred.

Actually, in many generalizations and categorical statements there is significant pride and a feeling that Negro ways are superior. Here are four generalizations expressing criticism or disdain of the ways of whites; these were all made at the same poolroom "bull-session" devoted to comparisons and reminiscences.

> When a Negro can really do something, he can do it better than a white man.
> The white man knows when you're right; he sees but acts like he don't.
> A white man will recognize a smart Negro but he won't tell the Negro; he'll tell some other white man.
> A white man never says he let a Negro go, or fired him; he'll always say "I had to run that nigger off the place."

One of the most constant generalizations critical of whites is that the Negro in many ways is morally superior to the white; it is usually stated in the form, "The Negro ain't as 'dirty' as the white man." For example, a trusted Negro employee of a fairly large business just outside of Kent explained why his boss preferred Negro employees:

> White man'll take it all. A Negro'll take a little bit for himself and leave you a little bit. A Negro ain't like a peckerwood.

These feelings are often linked up with a comparison of opportunities; for example, the feeling that whites are "dirtier" in terms of sex morals, taking advantage of the weaker, large-scale larceny, and lack of loyalty to country, is sometimes related to the notion that whites have more opportunity to commit such acts.

> Ain't white folks dirty? A Negro ain't as dirty as a white man. . . . One thing, they don't give the Negro the opportunity to get up in them big places and positions.

A veteran commented on one of the federal spy trials:

> Ain't it a damn shame that white woman doing like that—betraying her country. There ain't never been a Negro was a traitor to his country. And yet a foreigner can come here and be anything he want and a poor Negro can't get nothing.

These expressions indicate, among other things, the Negro's observation of the white from his vantage point as servant, his one-sided relationships with whites, and an acute interest in newspaper accounts of tragedies and crises, successes and failures. They are a part of an attitude of detachment—a process of dissociation—that comes from observing rather than participating and feeling fully a part of the local and larger world. "The white folks are doing" or "the white folks have done" become almost standard ways of introducing accounts of happenings that are remote because of a lack of participation and identification. To say this is not to deny that there are some employee-employer relationships where the Negro for a variety of reasons may speak of "we" or "our place"; but the few such Negroes are likely to be laughed at or looked down upon. Locally, there is one Negro of mixed background who is a sort of man-of-all-duties for "Rocky" Rhodes, a prominent white; the Negro is looked upon for this and other reasons as something of a renegade—a traitor to his group; this Negro speaks of "me and 'Rocky'" doing many things—to the amusement and disgust of other Negroes. An older woman refers to them as "two bad niggers together."

Reports from Negro servants and workers as to the sex and drinking behavior of whites are common. They are usually told with an air of amused superiority, with emphasis upon the low-down or dirty aspects of the behavior. There is one young woman who has a minor obsession about Caldwell's *Tobacco Road*. She reports having read it several times and seeing the picture six times. When asked if the reason were the off-color language she replied:

> No, I just likes to have those white folks see how bad some white folks lives. I used to have me a job and I would carry the book to work and talk about it every chance I would get. Once the lady sent me up the street and she said, "Mary, leave *Tobacco Road* here; you'll stop on every street corner and sit down and read it." I just likes that book

The race orientation as seen in the race-ridden character of all phases of life is probably the closest approach to a universal emphasis; race is something that colors a considerable portion of the behavior of everyone. It is at once a factor making for group consciousness and a factor making for ingroup tensions and divisiveness.

The value correlate of this pervasive orientation is related to survival and getting along—adaptability—in a society where "white folks is white folks" and "colored folks is colored folks." This is the closest approach to an over-all unifying value; it reflects a kind of folk realism and opportunism. This doesn't mean that there is absolute resignation to *status quo*, because there are other values that operate also. For instance, the democratic value involving opportunity and equality before the law has some force; there is also considerable belief in all areas that things will get better—a belief spurred by recent happenings on the national and world scene. Patience comes to be an important subsidiary value.

The Salvation Myth

. . . Religion in this society is a sort of talisman, a magical guarantee giving assurance about salvation. Salvation is the meaningful goal; religious behavior to some extent gives reassurance and a sense of security. The projected goal of salvation ties in with the immediate value of survival and getting along. Salvation is one of the chief myths of this society: "Sometimes you get gypped here—but Jesus will make it up to you"; "Everything is going to be all right." A local minister sketched the recurrent theme in this fashion:

> Man's earthly treasure is liable to be destroyed at any time; worldly riches have in themselves a principle of corruption and decay. They will wither away themselves. Jesus points out to us the different forces that will destroy the earthly treasures. There are some whose treasure is fine clothes, but it is not to put your highest joy in them. For they breed moths and moths will eat holes in your clothes. . . . There are others who cherish their food, but it is not wise to put your trust solely in food for the mice will eat your wheat, and you will be left hungry. And there are others whose treasure is their bank account; don't treasure that too highly. Because gold and silver canker and will become less even if we don't use them. . . . During World War I, the people of this country laid up treasures upon the earth for themselves. Most everybody had a large bank account and they glorified it. But it was not long before the moths and rust corrupted it; and thieves broke through and stole all they had.
>
> But lay up for yourselves treasures in Heaven, there where moths cannot eat it, the rust cannot canker it, and thieves cannot break through the Pearly gates and steal them. If you want treasures in Heaven, you must send something up there. Send up good counseling, good will for all mankind, and send up prayer. Send up truth and

righteousness and not anything will be lost or forgotten. In Heaven there is a book of remembrance and we will be paid according to the book. Down here in this world, unfortunately some of us cannot read books, but that book that is called the Book of Life—every child of God can read it for himself. Yes, lay not up for yourselves treasures upon earth. . . .

Self-Indulgence and Self-Expression

Whisky drinking is a central pattern among men of all strata, and concern over male drinking is a common anxiety among wives and mothers. It is an admitted type of self-indulgence, and, as such, it ties in with a general design for self-indulgence and release that would include much of the nonmarital sex activity, much of the idling, and much of the tavern behavior of the nonrespectable. Whisky is also an essential ingredient in a pattern of behavior that is marked by individual touchiness and ingroup aggression. The people tend to think of themselves as drinkers of large quantities of whisky. That much of the drinking is sectional or situational—and not unique to the Negro community—is shown by the fact that comments and behavior in both the white and Negro communities parallel each other. Here are two statements typifying the local person's assessment of the community; the first is from the Negro community and the second from the white community:

> There's more whisky drunk here than any other little town in the country.
> You'll find more old drunks in Kent than any town of its size around here. . . . Kent is a town of drunks and old maids.

It is theoretically possible that the behavior here might be the same in both communities but that the basic motivations might differ. The chances are, however, that drinking is a pattern available to all that has become widely diffused here; any different meaning that it may have in the Negro community would come from the fact that it fits into a slightly different social and value situation. . . .

. . . The etiquette of drinking is roughly this: the bottle is usually shared among persons who are close acquaintances and have some kind of informal reciprocity pattern, or persons who have contributed to the price of the whisky. Under conditions other than these, the offer of a drink is a gesture of hospitality or good will and a sign of acceptance. When drinking among casual acquaintances, rather than thoroughly trusted intimates, the person who owns or offers the whisky must always take the first drink to allay suspicion. The great bulk of drinking is group drinking, i.e., two or more persons. "Let's get one!" or "I don't enjoy drinking by myself" are recurrent statements. An older man who has stopped drinking because of the doctor's orders said:

> I tell you I used to drink. I used to be one of the biggest drinkers in this here town. And when I used to drink, I had plenty of friends. I ain't got no friends now since I stopped drinking.

In a similar vein, a younger man said:

> A man has almost got to drink. If a man don't drink, he ain't got no friends.

Except for the few emancipated, the respectable woman doesn't drink or at least doesn't admit it except to intimates.

Drinking, as indicated, is in some respects a social or group phenomenon; it is an available accepted pattern of sociability and sharing. The rhythm of economic life, with its stretches of leisure and uncertainty, provides opportunity and reinforcement. Questioning of drinkers indicates that, for most of them, custom, curiosity, and social pressure were factors in the initiation into drinking. It becomes apparent then that the purely personal satisfactions that reinforce the drinking habit among many—relief from boredom or monotony, frustration, fear, and inferiority feelings—are at first secondary, although they eventually become primary motivations.

The fact that rarely is there an attempt made to rationalize or justify heavy and regular whisky drinking beyond "I just likes my whisky" or "I've just got to have me a little drink," indicates a feeling that drinking is something of a personal privilege or right, and underscores its nature as a type of self-indulgence and a means of self- expression. An old ritualistic drinker explained:

> When I was a younger man I was just crazy after the women, but now that I done got old and can't do nothing, I done took up a worser habit—whisky.

A middle-aged week-end drunk and brawler who lacks status, even among chronic drinkers, because of his extreme "low class" behavior said:

> Everbody knows I drinks. I tell anybody I can drink plenty of liquor and if there's any to be got I'm going to have me some. But I don't harm nobody. I tries to treat everybody right. The biggest harm is what I does to myself.

The desire to get money for whisky underlies the great bulk of small loan and pawning transactions among friends and acquaintances; there is rarely any attempt to conceal the purpose for which the money is wanted.

The pervasiveness of whisky drinking among the adult males and lower status women; the indulgent and tolerant attitudes toward it in all quarters except among the females who perhaps feel strongest about its effects upon family income and expenditures, status, and personal relations; the frequency with which whisky appears as a factor in nonmarital sex play, "touchy" behavior, and "having a good time," whether attending baseball games, hunting, or idling; and the lack of elaborate rationalizations or justifications for its use or abuse—all these indicate a near-successful integration with other aspects of the culture. Here, whisky tends to be an individual or family problem rather than a social problem. It is an essential aspect of normal social ritual and leisure-time activity; it eases personal tensions (while at the same time creating new ones) in a culture that has many "tough" features—status and respect hunger, limited access to rewards, a measure of economic uncertainty. It is also, for many, a temporary ego-booster and a gesture of defiance to family and community. The emphasis upon alcohol as a sort of personal and social "lubricant" suggests the importance of individual release and selfexpression as values. It is significant that these same two values are important ingredients of the more active and emotional religious behavior.

Dionysian Tendencies in the Culture

The evidence shows that among the Negroes of Kent there is a significant disposition to escape the humdrum and monotonous. This, plus the seasonal character of economic activity, gives emphasis to leisure-time and idling behavior. Whisky drinking, tavern frequenting, and nonmarital sex experiences are patterns involving a certain amount of release and self-indulgence. Public release and indulgence in any area are frowned upon by the respectables, although it is probable that the design for release is no less strong among them even if channeled in other directions or levels. When we add a marked disposition to querulousness or "touchiness" and ingroup violence, we get intimations at least of a Dionysiac way of life, particularly among the lower status groups.

This lack of restraint applies primarily to ingroup behavior and is in marked contrast to the necessity for restraint in intergroup relations. The Kent Negro has two public personalities—one for the white community and one for the Negro community; they need not coincide. In fact, the incompatibility of the role demands of each may account for the high content of random and disorganized behavior in the Negro community. The concept, Dionysian, is not used here in an attempt to characterize a whole culture; rather it is used to "bring clearly to the fore the major qualities that differentiate"[1] this segment of culture from others. Ruth Benedict used the concept to contrast American Indian cultures:

> The basic contrast between the Pueblos and the other cultures of North America is the contrast that is named and described by Nietzsche in his studies of Greek tragedy. He discusses two diametrically opposed ways of arriving at the values of existence. The Dionysian pursues them through the annihilation of the ordinary bounds and limits of existence; he seeks to attain in his most valued moments escape from the boundaries imposed upon him by his five senses. The desire of the Dionysian, in personal experience or in ritual, is to press through it toward a certain psychological state, to achieve excess. The closest analogy to the emotions he seeks is drunkenness, and he values the illuminations of frenzy. With Blake, he believes the path of excess leads to the palace of wisdom. The Appolonian distrusts all this. . . .[2]

Gertrude D. Stevens, after an independent content analysis of field notes collected for this study, concluded that frustration-aggression and religion were two of the basic controlling patterns in the Kent Negro subculture. She pointed out:

> It seemed clear . . . that the greater amount of events measurable as the immediate cause of aggression are those arising within the Negro section of Kent, verbal and circumstantial, rather than violent. The fact that they result in so much aggression indicates a "touchiness" of personality. . . . Drinking. . . seems to be antecedent to and coincidental with much of the aggression.[3]

The ranking of the types of initial acts in the aggression sequence based on the data Miss Stevens analyzed were: verbalization, sex patterns, attitudes, violence, law breaking, economic and competitive. The conditions of aggression ranked as follows: drunk (or liquor), suspicion, sex, caste, insanity, fighting, irresponsibility.[4]

"Touchiness" and the disposition to violence are more prevalent among lower status groups; in fact, this is conceded to be an ingredient of "low class" behavior and an inevitable accompaniment of public drinking and tavern behavior. However, such characteristics are not exclusive with nonrespectables.

A constant and highly significant element in the pattern of querulousness and aggression is the use of the profane and obscene phrase. Intent and tone are important factors defining response to cursing; the same expressions can be used jocularly, or impersonally for conversational emphasis and as extremely aggressive vocal gestures and deprecations. In any event, the very frequent use of profanity and obscenity—and the fact that such expressions are conventional for the nonrespectable, low-status male, in particular[5]—suggest the "outlet" function; satisfaction is undoubtedly received from using freely words that are normally taboo. The words used are common elements in the substandard language of America; there is nothing unique about them, except probably the incidence of their use in certain settings and the psychological content for that group. In cultural terms, the pattern of profanity and obscenity among certain categories of the Kent Negro population, with its spontaneous use in certain situations marked by balking or frustration, has an adaptive function; it is "natural." The mechanisms involved are suggested in the following explanation of soldiers' responses to the frustrations, conflicts, and deprivations of army life:

> Soldiers have the reputation of assuming less responsibility toward society's ideals and values. In the American Army the soldier often comes not only to realize this reputation but to accept it as a prerogative. . . . The expression of this self-image manifests itself in his thoughts, his behavior, his language.
>
> In his image of himself, then, the soldier tends to feel a freedom from civilian society's taboos and controls. This image would, in most cases, never exist in an isolated individual; it is a feature of the crowd. In a group of similarly minded men these expressions are no longer taboo; on the contrary, they are often the conventional way of speaking. In his own mind, however, the soldier is aware that he is expressing what was formerly a taboo and is thus freer from social restraint. The expression of this soldier self-image is primarily in profanity.
>
> The expression of obscenity obviously gives the soldier certain indulgences. Violating the taboos of language gives feelings of courage and freedom; it is in itself satisfying. It seems, however, that more can be derived from the given expressions than the mere fact that the soldier obtains indulgences, for each expression manifests something of a repressed sphere. In most respects, however, this is a field of study for the psychoanalyst.
>
> As obscene words come into such universal usage and as seemingly indiscriminate usage, they tend to lose their original sexual significance. As casually spoken by soldiers, obscene expressions do not mean that the users actually are thinking on the sexual level; they are merely speaking the language of their social group.[6]

There are many analogous features. Profanity and obscenity in the Kent subculture are in part an expression of freedom from the restraints of the larger society; they give a sense of courage and freedom to the Negro who indulges. Obscenity does not always have its ordinary denotative meaning; it is the language of a special category of the population with complex psychological implications.

Hair-trigger sensitivity to word and gesture is accentuated by whisky drinking, but whisky is not a necessary condition. This sensitivity has compulsive features and involves the ego and "face." It is most commonly expressed as "I don't bother nobody and I don't allow nobody to do nothing to me." It is also marked by a significant element of fatalism: "If I gets killed, I just gets killed"—"I couldn't see nothing but for me to die." In looking at the disposition to violence and "touchiness" as a research problem, we must keep in mind that personal violence is something of a southern regional pattern and therefore there is a question as to how much is related primarily to—or aggravated by—the Negro's status. The nearby Stone Valley Bugle editorialized:

Shoot 'N' Cut

> You know, in a year's time, quite a few people in this section got shot or cut up.
> Oh, no, not YOUR family.
> Oh, no, not YOUR kind of folks.
> But you know what we're writing about: you know that in a year's time quite a few people in this section get shot or cut up.
> Some white. Some Negro.
> It doesn't do anybody any good.
> Sometimes "the law" doesn't even get to arrest anybody. Other times, somebody gets into court, maybe is sentenced. But that doesn't undo what has been done. . . .
> What can we do about it?
> There's just no sense in the cuttings and shootings.
> Sometimes there's liquor mixed up in it. But usually it isn't the liquor that makes the trouble; it was just that somebody who is liquored lets loose. It would be hard to say whether the same person, cold sober, might not have done the same thing sooner or later.
> No, it's something inside folks that causes them to do such things, that lets them do such things.
> What can be done to change that "something inside folks" which ends up in shootings and cuttings?
> Church going helps. Being self-respecting helps. Going to school enough when a child helps. Friends help. More attention by YOUR kind of people (who don't get mixed up in such things) to the lives led by the kind of people who do get mixed up in cuttings and shootings could help some.

In the same way that hardly a person or a family has escaped some contact with "the law," scarcely a person or a family has not been touched by violence and querulousness. Identifying references such as "he's a bad man to fool with," "he killed a man," "he'll cut you in a minute," "he slapped hell out of a woman," are frequent among lower status groups. A large number of persons, mainly men, are marked with knife scars on the neck and face, some of them having been cut or wounded several times. A young veteran who had just been cut in a Saturday tavern scrape remarked:

> That's the fourth time I been cut. But there ain't nobody I know around here ain't got some kind of mark or something where they been in a

ramble. I told my dad, I got a bad record behind me—four members of my family, aunts and uncles—is murderers. I tries to hold myself in because I done shot a "cat" once. I tries to avoid getting in a corner where you's got to do something.

There is significant conversational interest in disputes, scrapes, and violence. The majority of the adult males own and carry pocket knives; many nonrespectables feel uncomfortable and unprepared without them. Illustrative is the case of the young man on his way to church who retraced his steps home, and when he returned said: "I had to go back and get my knife; I just don't feel right without it." The gestures of drawing the knife or references to using it are frequent in jest and play behavior. The knives used are pocket knives with folding blades from three and a half to six inches long. In many cases when trouble is anticipated, the knife is carried "at the ready" that is, in an outer pocket open and ready for action. The most frequent technique used is the quick slash at the face or body; this is often a surprise attack. Stabbings or multiple slashings on the other hand usually involve some degree of premeditation or brooding and tend to exhibit significant sadism. In cases of knife play, the only elements of skill involved that suggest some training or aptitude are in the speed with which the knife is opened and made ready and the ability to ward off counter thrusts and strike quickly. For the most part, altercations involving knife play are not exhibitions of skill and finesse, rather they are one or more passionate and often wild thrusts that usually come at the end of an exchange of threats and/or blows. Persons are ranked in terms of their dispositions to use knives rather than in terms of skill.

A smaller number of persons carry pistols; a few carry them, especially when "going out" or anticipating attack or trouble. "Touchiness" of personality and hostility to intimates is indicated in the fact that a large number of altercations—both verbal and physical—involve relatives or close acquaintances.

That a great deal of this behavior is unpremeditated and rationally disapproved is indicated by the fact that persons who themselves have a record of violence or contentiousness will decry both. They will even advise others that such situations are not worth getting in trouble about. The point to be emphasized is that the typical person, given a situation and the proper cues, will act immediately: there is little disposition to "take things" from other Negroes. In many cases observed, the causes of violence have been objectively trivial or vague, and the incident is the inevitable culmination of an exchange of aggressive gestures.

Illustrative is the account by a well-known and active person in the community of his "reformation."

Dub pointed out that since he had stopped carrying a gun he had gotten along much better. If he were carrying a gun, he would, in fact, be looking for trouble—"and that is the easiest thing in the world to find." At one time he used to feel and tell himself that he wouldn't take anything off of anybody—"but I've got more sense now." The incident that "cured" him occurred on Christmas Gift Night at his home church just outside Kent. Fortunately, he had taken his gun from his pocket and put it in the house before leaving for the church with his family. While on the church ground, his children were shooting firecrackers. One of his fellow church members objected and told him that children who did such showed that they had no raising. Dub immediately attacked him; after a scuffle, he ran to a nearby house, broke the door in and grabbed a shotgun and returned. Luckily, other persons intervened. Dub says that he would have surely shot the man if he had had his pistol; that "learned" him. The police came but the participants would not prosecute each other. Dub told his opponent: "If I didn't do nothing to you while I was mad, I don't see the point in trying to harm you further when I'm in my good senses."

In this setting, it is well to note, a "bad guy" or a "tough guy" is not necessarily a braggart who parades his toughness—although there are a few; he may in fact be a mild-mannered person ordinarily. Usually he is a person who is known to have few qualms about fighting or hurting another person with little provocation. It is the code rather than mannerisms that makes one tough; each individual in self-protection is "tough" to some degree. This is hair-trigger sensitivity rather than chip-on-the-shoulder behavior. . . .

Symptomatic of the sensitivity over status and respect is the often aggressive reaction to the use of the term "nigger" by a Negro to another Negro. Illustrative are these two instances:

"BB" is a mild-mannered fellow who is given to considerable beer-animation on Saturdays. He was dancing in one of the taverns with Mae Lee, As they finished one very passionate dance, Mae casually said something to him and used the word "nigger." "BB" asked her firmly not to use that word, saying that was not what he is. Mae stood her ground, repeated the term and told him that was all he was and that was what the white man called him. The audience laughed. The exchange continued and got more heated. "BB" invited Mae outside to settle the matter physically. Mae was on the verge of going outside to accept the challenge when the proprietor stepped in. Mae said that she would have gone out there and beaten the hell out of him; furthermore, no man had ever messed up her face or body like some girls had let them do.

Oscar and Albert were at a dance following a basketball game. Oscar saw a boy from a nearby community open his knife and mumble, "He called me a nigger," as he prepared to plunge it in Albert's back. Oscar pulled his knife and told the boy that if he tried that the two of them would have to cut it out. The boy desisted but later told his friends about it and "spotted" Oscar for them. Oscar was afraid that if he went to the taverns on a Friday or Saturday night that he might "get it." He later talked it out with the boy and explained that the both of them were drunk and meant no harm; they "got straight" but he continued to be concerned about the boy's buddies.

... Ingroup querulousness and the possibility of violence and physical hurt are constant and expected risks characteristic of the way of life of the tavern habitues, the chronic public drinkers, and the males and females who indulge significantly in nonmarital sex exploits. Indeed, to a significant degree it is anticipated in all areas of contact and group behavior. The small size and relative homogeneity of the community mean that in some way all people tend to have access to each other; this in turn means that everyone is influenced or is aware of this feature of Negro ways, whether he takes it for granted or has strong negative feelings. Those who have strong negative feelings are in some degree isolated and characteristically avoid active participation in many areas of group activity. In any event, the disposition outlined above indicates the importance of respect for the person as a pervasive value. Practically every Negro in this bi-racial situation tends to be respect-starved. When the opportunity affords, he will demand it, or satisfy his need for it indirectly or subtly, when whites are involved; the use of direct aggression varies with the person and the situation. Consistent with this "having to take it" is the Negro's behavior within his own group: it is the one place where he doesn't have to "take it." Aggressiveness and querulousness are symptomatic of a respect-starved group; they have a cumulative and persistent quality insofar as "touchiness begets touchiness."

The Premium on "Treating People Right"

The Kent Negro's implicit and explicit emphasis upon appreciation for the person is clear when he exhibits his basic warmth, generosity, and hospitality to those who appreciate and recognize him as a person regardless of status. Friendliness, courtesy and kindness are important values that are graciously reciprocated; they are the chief weapons that can be used to break through sensitivity and suspiciousness. To some extent they become "values by contrast" in a society that is marked by a great deal of touchiness and latent resentment. The burden of proof tends to be on the newcomer to the community and also upon those who, for any reason, are differentiated from the mass

—the educated, the leaders, the conspicuously successful. The words "appreciated everybody," "treat people" are recurrent. Illustrative were the remarks to the writer of a woman who herself was of low status:

> You sure is like around here. . . . You appreciates everybody. Of course, you's got sense; you ain't like these ignorant niggers around here. Just because a person's done something bad, you ain't got to treat him bad.

There is great respect for the person who "can get out among the people." Where class lines are virtually nonexistent and the range of statuses is small, personal characteristics loom large. There is a tendency for every person to think "I'm as good as anyone else"; at least, that is a frequent bristling response to the slight, or intimation of a slight. Yet, paradoxically, each person tends to have a personal definition of the limits of association; there is no person who would not define some others as unfit for association. Hence the paradox for the newcomer who seeks mobility: he can't afford to associate with just certain people, yet he is not supposed to associate with every "Tom, Dick, and Harry." But "Tom, Dick, and Harry" are as appreciative of recognition as anyone else.

In a society where so many persons have meager means, low status, and limited contact, the essential dignity of the "common people" is an important implicit value. The worth of ordinary people is implicit in a statement by the previously mentioned Billy: "It ain't your fault how much education you got. It ain't your fault if you didn't go to school. The only thing your fault is how you treats people."

Notes

1. Ruth Benedict, *Patterns of Culture* (New York: First Pelican Books Edition, 1946), p. 72.
2. *Ibid.*
3. Gertrude D. Stevens, Application of Content Analysis to Anthropological Field Notes (unpublished M.A. thesis, Department of Sociology and Anthropology, University of North Carolina, 1949), p. 66.
4. *Ibid.*, pp. 65–66.
5. Knowledge of profane words and use of them is not confined to the lower-status groups, although there is undoubtedly a significant difference in incidence of both; and there is certainly more discrimination in their use among respectables. One certain way of identifying a nonrespectable woman is in terms of whether males curse freely around or at her, or whether she curses rather indiscriminately herself.
6. Frederick Elkin, "The Soldier's Language," *American Journal of Sociology*, LI (March 1946), 418–19.

Too often those writing about southern Negroes have given the impression that all respond similarly to what Hylan Lewis has called the "race-ridden character" of southern life. While certain modal personality types ("Sambo" for instance) have come to be discredited, others have been suggested as substitutes (including "Brer Rabbit").

In the following essay ten profiles of very different black youths are presented Charles Johnson's case studies were drawn from his research conducted in the late 1930s. They should he compared and contrasted to those presented by such contemporary writers as William H. Grier and Price Cobbs (authors of Black Rage*), who may well be portraying the children of "Hesekie Parker," "Sadie Randolph," "Essie Mae Jones," and the others*

13

Growing Up in the Black Belt: Ten Profiles

Charles S. Johnson

Descriptions of ten Negro youth are given by way of introduction to the study of the personality development of southern rural Negro youth. The common everyday experiences of these young people on the plantations and in the other rural areas of the South are described in these profiles, frequently in the words of the young people themselves. These particular young people were not selected because they are striking or unique but because they are typical and have problems common to the section. The profiles include boys and girls from all types of areas and from all classes of the Negro population in approximately their true proportions in the area. . . .

Hesekie Parker: Plantation Youth

Coahoma County in Mississippi has a teeming Negro population, vast plantations, and a complete and traditional devotion to the

From Charles S. Johnson, "Personality Profiles," in *Growing Up in the Black Belt*, Washington D.C.: American Council on Education, 1941, pp. 1–37.

cultivation of the commercial crop of cotton. Three-fourths of the rural population of the county are Negroes and practically all of them are tenants and sharecroppers. Hesekie Parker is a youth of 18 who lives with his grandparents in the Yazoo-Mississippi delta section of Coahoma County, which has rich and well-nigh inexhaustibly fertile soil.

He is well built physically and is still boyish and lively. He talks with a thick accent and a careless drawl, and his complexion is so dark his associates have affectionately labeled him "Crow." He does not object to this label. Hesekie grew up in a little community of sharecroppers called New Africa. By the time he was 6 years old his mother had taught him how to milk a cow. At 10 his father had started him chopping cotton.

> First, I wanted it, but after a week I was ready to quit. I had to go to the fields though, 'cause they made me. The same year I commenced a-pickin'. Mama was fixin' sacks and she just made me one. I was glad to get it then. I reckon I was pickin' 'bout fifty when I started.

When he was 12 he began plowing.

> I used to watch 'em and figured I could do it. When I asked Dad to let me have it he was breaking with four mules, but I knew I could handle them. He gave it over and I been plowing since. Every evening when I come home from school I'd plow till dark. I still like to do it better than anything else around the place.

Family Trouble and Separation

When Hesekie was 13 years old his mother and father separated. He does not know why. They never told him and he did not inquire. One day his mother just went off and did not come back. His father found her in a nearby town, but she refused to return. Later his father left for Illinois. His mother went back to him once, but she did not stay because by that time he had two children by another woman. Now both have remarried and Hesekie is living with his grandparents who, as tenants go in this section, are fairly well off.

Routine of Work on the Farm

Hesekie's working schedule is typical. In the spring and summer he rises at four o'clock and feeds the chickens, hogs, mules, and cows. Then he milks the cows, eats his breakfast of molasses and bread and milk, and goes to the fields. In the spring he starts "breaking."

When chopping time comes it is his job to plow up the center of the rows and "dirt" behind the choppers. ("Dirting" is done with a double-shovel or a Gary plow. The chopping hands loosen and pull the dirt away from the cotton and "dirting" is simply throwing it back again.) At twelve o'clock he stops for dinner, the heaviest meal of the day—greens, beans, corn bread, middle-pork, molasses—and returns to the field at one o'clock, to remain until sundown. This is his schedule until cotton picking begins.

In the middle of August picking begins. In the early morning and late evening working conditions in the cotton fields are tolerable, but in the late morning and early afternoon the sun beats down mercilessly, and there are few hands, young or old, who can be indifferent to it. They stop work and rest under the shade of a convenient tree, or trudge back to the cabin for a nap and dinner. Where several children are picking cotton they can sometimes make a contest of picking—a nickel or a dime for the winner. This is their pay and they are lucky if they can get that.

During the "laying-by" season, when work is slack, Hesekie has a lighter schedule and he may go to the nearest town to visit friends or just for a lark.

Acquiring New Skills

At 18 Hesekie is tired of farming, but just keeps on. "I reckon that's because I been doing it all my days," he says. He likes carpentry and has been "trying a hand to it for seven or eight years." He began by making log play wagons at home. Now he can shingle a house, build a chicken coop or hog pen, and do various kinds of ordinary "fixing." He learned to shoe a mule, but does not like it. His grandfather taught him to drive a well. He says the rope and rigging and pulleys "wore him down."

Once he and his brother Bennie tried to escape from the farm by selling fish. They would go along the Mississippi and buy the fish caught by men who liked to fish for fun. It was a good idea but the capital of larger traders put them out of business.

With his cousin he worked a cane mill for a while. His job was feeding the cane to the mill. The improvised mill which they operated consisted of a couple of spools with a long pole attached which was turned by a mule. He can cut and strip cane.

At home with his grandparents he is comfortable but not happy. His total personal possessions consist of one suit, two extra pairs of trousers, two pairs of shoes, four shirts, and an old twelve-gauge shotgun left by his father.

> My grandpa don't have much to say 'bout things, 'ceptin' his own business. He runs that and nobody tells him nothing. He could do better, but I dassen't tell him. That's one reason I don't want to stay on the farm with him. Long as he's boss I can't make nothing, and he ain't doing much. He's nice enough to all of us, but he can't give us much and we sure have plenty of work to do.

Hesekie's teachers call him ambitious and energetic, and say that he does a pretty fair job of anything he tries.

Religion and Play

When Hesekie was 11 years old he followed the pattern of the community and "got religion" and joined the church.

> I just went to the mourners' bench because my brother was there. 'Course I got 'ligion. I don't know how it happened or what it was, but I just felt somepin in me and I wanted to jine. Grandma was glad and kinda cried when I got 'ligion.

In the fall of the year he and his gang pick hickory nuts and pecans for fun. They sit on the river bank and eat them and then go swimming. The also hunt rabbits, birds, coons, and possums, and steal cane from the fields and carry it into the woods to eat.

Thoughts of Escape

He thinks he would rather be up North "where you don't have to say 'Yes, suh' and 'No, suh' to every white man." "If you don't do it here," he says, "they are going to try to see what's ailin' you." These observations, thoughtfully made if crudely expressed, suggest the influence of his racial past upon his present behavior and outlook.

> Now, the white folks that lived in front of us was good. There was fifteen of them in the family and we never had any trouble. Lots of white boys around would pick fights with colored boys because they wouldn't do too much fighting back. I fought plenty of white boys and whipped 'em too. Some mean, poor white folks around would ketch niggers' cows and sell 'em, or do other mean things.
>
> Niggers and white folks often get into it and kill each other. Well, one day a white man came to see a colored woman and a nigger was there; so he got mad and went home for his gun. Time he got back the nigger was out in the field working. The white man shot the nigger, then another old nigger got on the white man's side and said that the white man was going to hunt ducks and the nigger told him he couldn't

hunt around his place. He said the nigger drawed for his gun and the white man had to kill him to save his life. That wasn't so 'cause that colored man never even had a gun. A little later the white man's own son killed him for beating his mother.

Some white men fool around with Negro women and nigger men are too scared to do anything. 'Course once in a while niggers kill 'em up. Then they got to take to the bushes and go ahead. If they ketch him, they just hang him to a bridge. Lynchings often happen. They are different to what they used to be, though. They used to be big mobs hunting for a nigger, but now you just hear about some nigger found hanging off a bridge.

They came right through by home one evening. I reckon there was 'tween thirty and forty men riding on horses, with guns and pistols. They was men from 'round that go for bad. They didn't make any fuss, just rode quiet like. I didn't do nothin'—just set on the porch and looked. Them mobs don't hardly bother nobody 'ceptin' the one they're after, 'lessen they figger you know somethin' 'bout who they want. Now if you happen to run up on 'em at night they are more than apt to kill you, 'cause when they holler for you to stop, you gets scared of the mob and cuts out runnin'. Then they shoot you down. If you do stop some bad white man is likely to kill you for sport.

Sometimes the agents ride at the head of a mob, but round here there is a bad scoundrel called Dan Ashby who usually gets mobs together. They only get them after niggers—I never seen or heard tell of one after any white man.

Some white folks are just natcherly low-down and no good. A white man next to our place did something that wasn't right to his own daughter and his son killed him for it. There was a little white girl 4 years old down in Duncan what asked a little nigger boy about 3 to pull her bloomers up for her. They was just little kids playing along together. Some old white man saw it and grabbed up the little boy and castrated him. Then he took the boy and threw him in the lake. Nobody ever did anything about that.

I never had much to do or say with white people, and I don't either like or dislike them. I ain't scared of them, though, like some niggers. I fight white boys quick as they meddle with me.

Thousands of youth are "dammed up" on the farms of the South. They are unable to make a satisfactory living there and are unwanted in the cities and industrial centers. Hesekie represents a class of rural Negro youth in the plantation area capable of growth and confident in his rural skills but bound in by a complex of barriers, small in their separate details but fairly paralyzing in their totality. He is, however, a part of the raw material from which the cities recruit their surplus populations and which the rural South all too casually loses to the city.

Sadie Randolph: Girl in a Sharecropper Family

Sadie Randolph's family is one of the thousands of Negro sharecropper families living along the Yazoo in Bolivar County, Mississippi. She is a placid girl of 18. Her complexion is dark-brown and she has short, straightened hair. In her new gingham dress, which she herself made, she is neat and clean.

The house in which she lives is a four-room frame dwelling in fairly good condition, although about twenty-five years old. Its chief defects are a leaky roof and a broken back door. Beside the house is a small well-kept vegetable and flower garden. In the back yard is a motor truck, worth about $300. There are many chickens, nine hogs, and two cows—a conspicuous affluence by the standards of the Negro community. The family cleared $160 from the cotton crop last year.

Sadie Randolph is interesting because she belongs to one of the numerous sharecropper families that find it necessary to compromise with the conventions in order to achieve a practical economic unit for sharecropping. The fact of irregular family organization is often noted statistically. The effects of such organization on the personality of youth is not so often indicated.

The head of the house is David Freeman, who, although not married to Sadie's mother, is accepted as Sadie's stepfather. He is a pleasant-looking, medium-brown man of about 30 years of age, with short, crisp hair, and an honest, independent, good-humored air. His education ended at about the third grade. Sadie's mother is darker, with unkempt hair, a hard face, and a surly manner. There is also a 10-year-old boy in the household, David Freeman's son by another woman at the time he was living with his first wife. The boy's mother gave the baby to David's first wife because the wife had no children and the mother had too many. An uncle and aunt of Sadie's also live in the home. The uncle is Sadie's father's brother, and the aunt is Sadie's mother' sister. The uncle assists on the farm and is an essential part of the economic unit of the household. The aunt, often ill and the victim of "spells," works when she can.

Sadie's lineage is complicated, but her mother explains it tonelessly and apparently without emotion. When the girl's grandmother married Randolph, her second husband, she already had a grown daughter by her first marriage and Randolph similarly had a grown son. These two became Sadie's parents although they never married because Sadie's mother did not like the man.

Working for a Negro Farmer

The stepfather is sharecropping with a Negro farmer who rents his land from a white man. He says:

> I'd rather work with my own color. They talk to you like you was a man. The white man talks to you like you was a boy. The colored boss don't cuss you out, neither. I make a better showing here than where I was before and get more out of my crop 'cause I'm working for a colored man.

Before he came to the present place he worked on a white man's plantation. It was, he said, "a one-man town, all owned by one white man, and too tough" for him.

Whatever Sadie decides to do as a career, the stepfather does not want his own son to follow him in farming, because "he would not get enough out of it." He would rather have him be a "carpenter or something mechanical." What is needed on a cotton farm is a large family, but his wife is emphatic about a small family. She says bluntly, "I don't like children much."

Daily Routine of a Girl on the Farm

Sadie's daily duties get her up at 4:30 in the morning. Her mother prepares breakfast—usually fried okra, salt pork, tomato gravy, and bread. The ailing aunt washes the dishes. By five o'clock they are all in the field. The blistering heat sends them in about eleven, and dinner is cooked—turnip greens, cornbread, salt pork, and sometimes pie. They lie around and rest until about 1:30, then return to the field until sundown. Supper consists of the left-overs from dinner.

Sadie walks to the local school, located four miles from her home, to attend the five-month school term. The school is an old, two-room, frame structure, with two teachers—the principal and his wife. The principal is also a house painter in his spare time. Sadie is in the eighth grade and likes her school work, such as it is, when she can attend. Her favorite subjects are arithmetic and spelling. English and arithmetic, she thinks, will be most important to her after school because "you always have to talk and to count."

Worries about Being "Saved"

She "got religion" when she was 8 years old but saw no "visions" or anything of the sort. "They don't have visions in the Church of

Christ," she said. Her main worry is whether she will be "saved." She is afraid of the devil and fire and brimstone, and she wants to go to heaven which, she says with conviction, is filled with milk and honey. The only complete books she has read are church books. She does not dance or go to the movies because her church forbids it. Her recreation is playing such simple games as "buzz seven," "minister's cat," and "eleven hands," at home or at church parties. However, there are times when she wishes she had never been born, for then she would not have to worry about school or being saved. The worst sin, she thinks, is having a baby before marriage. Then "I'd miss heaven and go to hell, and I'm working to go to heaven." The next worst sins in the order named are drinking, killing, and stealing.

Resentment Toward Stepfather

The last time she saw her real father was in 1926, when she was 6 years old. She wants very much to see him again and says that she loves him more than her stepfather, although the latter does more for her than her real father. But she would not like to live with her real father because "he drinks so much and stays drunk." She does not know his present "wife," but she knows that this woman takes care of him when he is drunk.

With a vagrant and consciously irrational vehemence she asserts, "I love my father 'cause if it hadn't been for him I wouldn't of been here," and adds, "I'd rather mamma to be married to him, and then I could have stayed with my father." When she visited her real father in 1926 he wanted to come back home with her, but her mother would not permit it. The resentment in Sadie's tone shows rather obvious jealousy toward her stepfather. She refers to her own father as "Daddy," sometimes "Father," and to her stepfather pointedly as her mother's husband, or her stepfather.

Attitude Toward Self

She is sensitive about color and prefers a light-brown complexion, but adds, "I like my color [dark-brown] but would like to have long hair." Her own hair is short. However, she thinks color is more important than hair, "because you can fix hair and make it look pretty, but you can't change color." She does not like white because "it wrinkles quick." Although she likes her own color, she recognizes that whites have more opportunities and that is the only reason she might like to be white. If she were white she would like to be a bookkeeper. Being what she is, she thinks she will probably sew and cook, or get married and not have to worry about a job.

Attitude Toward Whites

Sadie says "the poor white men are after the colored women on the streets. They ought to be after their own color if they're after anybody." She recalls walking down the street with a friend in Clarksdale on one occasion when two white men in a car stopped them and asked if they wanted to make a dollar. The girls did not reply. When the other girl's mother, who was walking behind, came up to them the men drove off. Sadie says:

> Whites are all right in their place and ought not to bother colored folks. I am scared of whites when they don't stay in their place. They like the colored women.

She says some whites are good and mentioned particularly a man whose office her mother cleaned. "He wasn't stingy, and he paid good," she said.

The mother says that she did not let Sadie play with white children after she was 8 or 9 years old. Before that age she thinks the white children do not know about color, but after that their parents teach them. Then they run to their parents with tales and there is danger of a fight in which the Negroes will inevitably suffer. They have as neighbors an Italian family. This farmer is a renter and lives across the road from Sadie's home. The stepfather says he is "good friends" with this family and often goes to their house and they come to his. He says that he eats with them "right in their own house." He likes them and "gets along fine" and the two little boys "play fine." But he will not allow his boy to go over to the Italian neighbor's house. It is all right for the Italian boy to come to his house, but not for his boy to go there.

> They treat us good so far, but we don't know what is to come. If the boy goes over to the Italian's house and something happens . . . maybe the Italian man might say something he didn't like. I'd know what to do . . . I'd come home, but the boy, he wouldn't know what to do.

Ambitions and Outlook

Sadie's chief ambition is to go to the Saints Industrial School near Lexington. This school is run by the Church of God in Christ and imposes a very rigid discipline on behavior. That is why she wants to go there and also why her mother prefers it; they have not been able, however, to save enough to cover the expenses of $4 a month. If her mother and stepfather cannot send her to the Industrial School, she hopes they will let her work her way through. This is her driving ambition at present and it overshadows every other interest. She does not plan to get married until late, but when she does she says she would prefer a husband a bit lighter than she is and would like to marry a doctor; she says, "Before I marry a farmer I wouldn't marry at all." Alter marriage she says she would like to have just one child because "then I could dress her like I want to."

The large number of families in which there are stepparents gives importance to Sadie's experience; her response to this fairly typical cultural situation is a neurotic one. From all present indications she will not be able to realize her ambition to get out of the farming class. This she has recognized to some extent and has taken refuge in religion.

Essie Mae Jones: Sister in a Tenant Family

Large families are necessary in the cotton economy, but this often means two or three incompatible sets of children in the household. The home of Essie Mae Jones is located about three miles from the little community of New Rising Star, in Macon County, Alabama. The one-story frame dwelling occupied by the family shows obvious signs of age and deterioration, but in spite of this its cleanliness and a fresh coat of whitewash make it appear attractive. Inside there is very little furniture. The two front rooms contain only beds, but these are neatly covered with white sheets. A large pallet is stretched across the floor. The crude furnishings are accentuated by the neatness. The floors have recently been scoured with a disinfectant, giving the place a sanitary, clean odor. There are no chairs in the house, but several small home-made benches are lined up on the porch. The yard and garden, like the house, have been made attractive. Flowers are growing and serve to relieve the gaunt and bare house. Despite the apparent poverty, it is obvious that the family takes pride in its home.

Essie Mae is 17 years old, tall and black. She wears a plaid dress patterned in intense shades of red, yellow, green, and pink. Her short, crinkly hair has been untwisted and combed free so that she appears to have a fringe around her head.

Her own mother died when she was 8 years old and her father has remarried, so with the new additions there are two sets of children in the household. Mrs. Lake Erie Jones, the wife, is a slender woman of dark-brown complexion who, possibly from work or lack of care and the rapid succession of child-births, or all of these, appears much older than her 28 years. She smiles frequently revealing teeth that are large and tobacco stained. The father is a small man of brown complexion, very pleasant and sincere. He is considerably older than his wife. Their interest in their children and their ambitions for them are manifest. The wife attempted to name the children in the household. She made two attempts to do so and finally gave up:

> Lord, we got so many of 'em here, seems like I can't keep 'em straight. Now I ain't the mother of these older children. Essie Mae, James, Lessie Belle, Liza Belle, and Thelma belong to Mr. Jones' first wife. She's dead. She died 'bout six or seven years ago. She was going to have another baby and taken fits the night the baby was born. Well, she and the baby both died 'fore we could get the doctor. I know, I was right here. See, she and me was first cousins so I was all the time right here with her. Then, Mr. Jones, he needed some woman to help him with all them little children, so he and me got married.

There are three sons of the husband who are almost as old as the wife, but they do not live at home. They are Essie Mae's full brothers. One of the boys is in Detroit and works in a barber shop. Will, Jr., is married and lives in Heflin, Alabama. Both of these boys write home and occasionally visit, but Tom, a third son who went to Atlanta several years ago, is completely out of touch with the family.

Stepmother Trouble

When the boys are on visits to the family they accept the wife and obey her mild orders. But Essie Mae is different, the stepmother says:

> Seems like since she's getting older she don't want to do what I tell her. Sometimes I don't understand that girl. As long as her father be 'round she do well. He makes 'em all mind me—his own and ourn; but Essie Mae kinda mean like. Reckon she don't mean no harm, but she's lazy. She won't do no work less I keep right behind her, and then she gets mad and declares I ain't her mother. Well, a stepmother's got as much say as a mother when a girl ain't got no mother. I never show no difference to her or my own, but seems like she kinda feels I love mine best and tries to be hard on me. Mine is just little and naturally we pets 'em. Essie Mae is a envious kind of girl. She be right proud of her father. Well, she gets "railed" [angry] when Will puts my children

first. She don't like that at all. Lessie Belle, Thelma—ain't none of the rest like that. I think Will always let Essie Mae have her own way, and now she just showing herself. I never has no trouble with her and the boys—nothing like that. She's just envious and jealous like, and I tell her that's dangerous. Folks get to killing and get in trouble when they get all worked up like that. I likes her fine myself. I tries to be just like a mother to her, but she ain't 'preciative. She be right good to these children. She plumb in love with this baby boy, Roosevelt. This is my knee baby. Ludie, my lap baby be sleeping.

Alma, the 5-year-old child, came out on the porch carrying Ludie, the baby. The wife exclaimed:

Lord a'mighty—the cat's got the kitty [she hurries to rescue the baby]. Alma's just crazy 'bout this baby. I have to watch her or she's carry him everywheres. You know she'll drop that baby and make him lose his good sense.

Conflict among the Children

Essie Mae and Lessie Belle sleep together in one room. Mr. and Mrs. Jones, Clarence, Roosevelt, and Ludie sleep in another room which has two double beds in it. James, the older son, has a cot in the third bedroom, and the double bed is occupied by Thelma, Liza Belle, and Alma. The family always sits down at the table together for meals.

It is obvious that Essie Mae is acutely aware of the brother and sister relationships in the home and emphasizes a preference for her own sisters and brothers. She says decisively:

I like papa best of all. He does what I tell him to do, and he don't make me do nothing I don't want to do. If I want anything all I got to do is ask papa and he will give it to me. Next I like my mother best. I don't mean that one out there. She ain't my real mother. She's only my stepmother. She's nice, I guess, but I don't like her like I do mama. She was kind and liked us all the same. My stepmother likes the little children better than she loves us because them is her children. Papa loves us best. Sometimes my stepmother tries to make it hard on us. She tells papa we don't behave and tries to make him punish us, but he don't. When she scolds Liza Belle I get mad and try to fight her. Liza Belle is the baby and I have to see to her.

She does not recognize the youngest child in the family as the baby.

That's my stepmother's baby, but it ain't my mother's baby. I'm talking 'bout my own mother. Liza Belle is my own mother's baby and my real sister. I tell Thelma and Lessie Belle and Liza Belle that ain't our real mother and just to talk to papa 'bout things we want. James is my real brother but he stays away most the time. This mother is kind to me, but I just can't like her like I did mama.

Liza Belle is Essie Mae's favorite sister, because she is "the baby" and James is her favorite brother "because he is my only real brother." Essie Mae is, nevertheless, very fond of her stepsisters and stepbrothers, and although she places them after her "real" ones in her affection, she fails to show the same resentment toward them that she shows toward her stepmother. This resentment grows stronger as Essie Mae grows older, and there is real jealousy for her father's affection. A neighbor said:

> I been knowing Essie Mae for a long time. That child won't leave her papa. I declare she is just crazy about her papa. Mr. Jones is a fine man, too. I ain't seen many men as kind and good to his children as that man. He just loves every one of them. 'Cose, I think Essie Mae is his favorite. When the mama died Essie Mae comforted him so much and, little as she was, she'd cook and do 'round for him. You can't get her far away from him. Now, Lake Erie Jones she be fine to all them children. Don't make no difference at all between them. Essie Mae's a little headstrong and wants things her way. I reckon her papa's made her selfish. He gives her nice clothes and spending money for school, but Lake Erie Jones do just what a mother would for them.

Tensions based upon jealousies sometimes arise where there are different sets of children in the family. The majority of rural Negro households are in some degree mixed. Thus, in the youth's earliest and most intimate group the sense of emotional security is qualified by problems of family organization.

Color as a Social Problem

Essie Mae has rationalized her color. She says:

> Black is the best color. I'd rather be black than anything. All Negroes belong to the African race and if you are black you look more like an African, and people can tell you got pure blood. I'm glad I'm darkskinned. I think colored people what look white is the worst. It shows they are mixed and been with white men. They call them people bad names. I don't like to say it but the children says white colored people is all bastards, and I believe it because if you belong to the black race you should be black. I like some light-skinned people, but it just don't look good to me.

Her best friends are of very dark complexion. She says she prefers going with dark-skinned girls because "when they get mad at you they don't call you 'black.'" Tangerine Smith, a close girl friend, is dark. They play together and like to go to church and Sunday school "and don't fight."

Family Income and Educational Opportunity

The father went as far as the fourth grade in school, and his wife as far as the sixth grade. They both had to leave school early to help on the farm and never went back. They want their children to get all the education they can, at least to go through high school. Essie Mae wants to go to Selma University. The father wants her to go, but times continue to be hard. He said:

> Farming ain't like it once was. Things is pretty tight now. There was a time when a man made a right smart living on crops, but now we work just as hard and long and don't have much to show for it. I rent this place and pay $80 a year for that and the house. 'Cose, I ain't got more than 30 acres under cultivation. Last year I raised eight bales of cotton. We got two prices on that. My best cotton brought 'bout 12 cents a pound. Reckon I raised just about four bales of that. Then I got 'bout 8 cents for the rest. I take mine and get the best price I could, so I don't get nothing more. I used 'round about two and a half tons of fertilizer. That cost me $70. That was just for cotton. I paid $15 for fertilizer for corn.

He has no idea as to the amount of money he cleared last year. According to his figures it would have been about $330 for cotton. The corn is used for the stock and for food at home; he also has a fine garden. His wife cans vegetables and fruits, which reduces the food bill. The family raises its own meat.

> Well, you see [explained the father] we trades up our food bill at the store. Then at the end of the season I pay it out in cotton. That takes plenty, and we got to pay $80 for our rent. That don't leave much. The rest we usually spend for clothes, and getting the children in school. Right now we spends just about $9 a week for food. All our meat is out, and we won't kill the hogs till late fall.

The Negro Community

The community in which Essie Mae lives provides few recreational facilities. All social gatherings are held at the church. Essie Mae likes to dance but knows it is frowned upon by the community.

> Folks here say if you dance, you dance to the devil. The most I do for fun is go to town sometimes, fish, and, when I'm in school, play volleyball.

She reads the *Country Home* magazine sometimes, and the newspaper every day, but she has gone to the movies only once in her life, and she did not like it.

> I don't like to sit still and look at fighting and things like they have in the movies, so I wouldn't go even if we had one out here.

She has never traveled. Once she visited Montgomery for a few hours, but she can remember nothing about the visit except that she went to a woman's house, ate dinner, and kept wishing she was back home. She insists she never wants to go away from home unless it is to go to Selma to school.

Relations with Whites

The pattern of the white community is accepted by the father, but not by Essie Mae. The father says:

> White folks are all right long as a man stays in his place. Down here in the South a Negro ain't much better off than he was in slavery times. We work all the time but don't get nothing for it 'cept a place to live and a plenty to eat. Some can't get that. Now you asked me 'bout voting. I'm willing to cooperate and go to vote, but white folks don't want that. They don't think much of Negroes voting. I ain't got nothin' 'gainst white people, but they won't give Negroes a chance. We all equal and ought to have a equal chance, but we can't get it here. In this settlement there ain't no white folks. You won't find a white family between here and Red Gap—that's up the road six or seven miles—so we don't have no trouble. Folks live peaceably here and tend to their own business so I consider it a good place to be. I don't know any place else I'd rather be. This suits me fine. I was born in Montgomery County but was raised here in Macon County. Reckon I was 'bout 5 years old when I come into this county, and I've stayed right here.

Essie Mae avoids all contact with white people. She says:

> I don't like them. I don't know why. There ain't no reason except they think they are better than colored and try to keep colored people down. Maybe all white people ain't alike, but I don't like none of them.

Willie Brayboy: Child of a Farm Hand

Farm hands are the lowest class of agricultural workers, and escape, even through education, is difficult for the children. Willie Brayboy is the type of youth who can be seen any day ambling aimlessly along the highways that wind through the great cotton estates. He is 15 years old, is in the third grade, and is one of a family of seven children. They are farm hands and they live in Bolivar County, Mississippi. William is about 5 feet tall and weighs about 125 pounds. His hair is harsh and set in tight spirals and is, apparently, never combed. His complexion is dark and rusty from want of bathing. His bare feet are caked with dirt and tough as leather. But he has sparkling, mischievous eyes and a wide playful grin which discloses decaying yellow teeth and coral-pink gums. He is dressed in a soiled and ragged polo shirt and blue denim overalls.

Willie is a dreamer, and his conversation is filled with fantastic accounts of travel, of people, and of escape.

> Yestiddy I went to New York. . . . Yes, sir, I went to New York in an automobile. No, it war'nt; it was a airplane I went to New York in. I saw the President, but he didn't see me. Yes, sir, he knows me. . . . I been to his house. . . . I didn't shake hands with him 'cause he was busy. I saw lotta other people, but they didn't see me. . . . I just walked around, and saw things and come back last night. . . . I come back 'bout two o'clock and took my airplane home. I don't know whether or no I'm going again.

Social Insecurity at School

Willie avoids school whenever he can. The children do not play with him. He knows them all, but has not been to their homes. He plays only with his brothers. "I don't hardly know none of the girls," he says. He adds, "I know some of them, though; but I ain't never kissed nair one of them." He feels the snubs of the boys directed at his very lowly social status, and finds some escape from the humiliation in fantasy and day-dreams.

> None of these ole boys'll fight with me, 'cause they know I can beat 'em. I don't like none of 'em, and most of 'em don't like me.

The reason why he does not want to go to school is made very clear in a sudden burst of enraged self-pity.

> Everybody round here pokes fun at me. Everybody says why don't I comb my hair, 'n why don't I wash up. My mother don't got no comb for me to be usin'.

He wants to be an electrician some day, and likes to tinker with wires. He actually repaired a lamp for Mrs. Miller, one of the few kindly women who do not "make him feel bad."

> Yes, suh, if I could go to school and learn how to be a 'lectrician, I'd go every day.

The Dreary Refuge that is Home

Willie's home is a two-room dilapidated cabin. It leans perilously to one side and seems about to collapse at any moment. There are two cots, one bed, and two chairs in the house. The boys sleep on the floor in the kitchen. A pile of freshly picked cotton is in a corner of one room. The walls are bare, and the sunlight streaks in like yellow blades from great cracks in the roof and sides.

The mother is a well-built and muscular woman. Her hair sticks out from a handerchief tied around her head. Her teeth are snuff stained. She wears a soiled and worn white dress, and shoes with so much of the tops cut off that almost her entire foot is exposed. On her legs are large pellagra scabs the size of a half dollar. She talks earnestly and sadly about her children, for their poverty is complicated by the father's vices of desperation.

> I want them children to get education and behave theyselves, I honest do. But it's just like this—they father take up all the money he make and gamble it away and drink it up. When I send them to school they learn or they won't go at all. Last year I just didn't have money to send 'em at all. You know yourself if you ain't got no shoes to wear and can't dress like the other children, and all the other children making fun of you, you wouldn't go neither.

Without comfort, security, or prospect of a better future, the ambitions of the youth of this level are diverted to empty dreams of escape.

Stanley Byrd: Mulatto Youth

There are relatively few mulatto youth on the plantations, and they are proud of their color. Stanley Byrd is a Coahoma County youth of 19, tall, muscular, and well-built. His complexion and hair are a light terra-cotta brown which Negroes sometimes call "meriny." He is lively and prankish, and frequently gets into trivial arguments but rarely fights. He walks with a slow shuffling gait that gives one the impression that he is always tired, and his habit of keeping his head lowered heightens this effect. He is, on the contrary, quite active and energetic when he is engaged in some sport. His heavy brows, full lips, and pug nose highlight his yellowish complexion. Long arms hang heavy and low from his shoulders, and his hands and joints are large and thick. His feet are of exceptional size. He wears misshapen, cut away old shoes that exaggerate the size of his enormous flat feet. Stanley's usual dress consists of a much worn and faded green flowered shirt, blue denim overalls with shoulder straps, and a sweat-stained and discolored collegiate felt hat that originally was white. When Stanley is dressed up he wears a white shirt, open at the collar and with the sleeves rolled up, white washable slacks, and white shoes. He always wears the discolored felt hat. He wears socks only when he is "dressed up," and they are usually white.

He began farming—slopping hogs—at the age of 7. Then he learned to cut wood for the stove, and later to milk the cows and feed the mules. At 12 his father and older brother taught him how to plow, but he was 15 before he had full responsibility as a plow hand. The family lived at first on a farm "in the hills," and at 6 he started to school in that community.

He stopped school when he was in the seventh grade. His oldest brother was sickly and could do very little work around the farm. Another brother was headstrong and unreliable, and usually went his own way. Stanley, the most dependable one, finally quit school after being interrupted so often in his schooling that he became discouraged. He has been out three years and talks vaguely of going back at some time, but actually never expects to return.

His mother is a deeply religious woman who reads the Bible regularly to the children, prays constantly, and sincerely laments the fact that the father, a normally genial parent while he lived, was a sinner. She is the moral strength of the household. She would say, "Turn favors if people do something for you, and don't run over folks or take advantage of them." She has taught them that lying and stealing are sins. Stanley says, "Mamma said God hates a liar and you has less chance to get into heaven if you is a liar."

Behavior Problems

There is an interesting ambivalence in Stanley's attitudes on sex relations. He would not marry a girl "if she had something to do with other fellows." However, at 19 he has a son 4 years old. He says:

> I see him often, and his mother too, but I don't have nothing to do with her no more. She just told me about it, but didn't try to make me marry her. I didn't want to marry her because she was too dark. I wasn't thinking about marrying, and would of tried to get out of it if she had wanted me. Lots of people know it's my kid. Her oldest sister often gets after me about it. but doesn't do nothing. People 'round don't make no difference, though some don't have too much to do with the girl. They never act like they think I ought to marry her though.

The attitude of the community toward certain types of behavior is not well defined. There is a general feeling of objection to drinking and gambling, but unless the offenders run afoul of the law and are put in jail not much control is exercised because both are rather common. Stanley says:

> There even was a little old preacher around that wasn't doing much at preaching, and he took to rolling dice. He said he could make more money gambling than he could preaching. Nobody did anything about it either. They didn't run him off or nothing. Some of the people won't have no more to do with him, but lots of 'em do.

Absence of Guides to Behavior

According to Stanley, there are no leaders among the young people in his community.

> Young folks don't travel much together, and each one does about as he wants to. There ain't no clubs and such things for anyone to head up. The only place they get together is at the church, and the old folks practically run that.
>
> There ain't much amusement either 'ceptin' dances or ball games. There is a little ball team that plays some. Fact, there ain't much to do. See, we live about half way between Lyons and Jonestown, and neither one is much. We even have to come into Clarksville to go to the show.

The only place that he has ever gone is Memphis, Tennessee.

> I went up there one time to see my aunt when she was sick. I like it pretty good. I didn't get to go around much 'cause I didn't stay very long, but what I saw was all right. I'd like to go and see some more places, like New York.

All the Boys Quit School

Stanley's father died five years ago of heart trouble. Since his father's death his mother has been running the farm, and is afraid to marry again because a stepfather might not be kind to the children. She had ambitions to have all the children go to college; but one quit because he did not like rural schools, another because he was not interested in anything, and Stanley quit because he had to work.

Color Troubles

He is conscious of his color difference from most of the boys of his acquaintance, and has adopted a pronounced attitude on the matter. "Dark people," he says "are hard to get along with." He goes with a dark girl, but does not take her out publicly. He says, "Most dark people are dumb and don't know nothing, and I'd rather not be fooling with them." Once while he was tossing fruit from an orchard to some of his companions, a peach struck the hen house and broke and a part of it struck a dark boy. Stanley apologized and forgot it promptly. A little later while they were standing near each other, the boy picked up a croquet mallet and asked him challengingly why Stanley had hit him. Thinking that the boy was playing, he laughed it off and apologized again. The dark boy struck Stanley on the temple, knocked out a tooth, and fractured his jawbone. He was rendered unconscious and "laid up" for several days.

> He had no cause to hit me and I wasn't expecting it, but black niggers are just mean that way. I ain't never goin' to fool with one no more. People used to tell me black was evil, but I didn't pay it no mind. I sure believe it now. Some black niggers are just naturally mean—like that boy that hit me.

Empty Future

Stanley has no plans for the future; he has never thought of being anything except, perhaps, a house painter. He recognizes that education probably plays an important part in getting a good job, but he says:

> Color makes a lot of difference too. You notice that they put all white on the good jobs and give niggers no 'count jobs like working on the highway or doing hard and dirty work that white folks ain't particular about doing.

His general lack of foresight also applies to his child. He says:

> I ain't never give it a thought. Her mamma and her people will take care of him. I might help it some day, but I hadn't never thought about it.

Juanita and Clint: Married

Early marriages are frequently unfortunate, socially and economically. Juanita Sawyer is 17 and her husband of three months is 19; they have a baby one week old. Young couples have a difficult time because there are not enough hands available for work in the fields to support them as sharecroppers. The worn-out land is too poor to offer a living unless there are many members to work the crop. For this reason young people usually remain with one or the other of their parents, or defer marriage until they can fit more comfortably into an economic unit. Young girls frequently marry men very much older than themselves, and are most fortunate when they can get a widower with children.

Juanita is a large girl of dark-brown complexion, with a broad face and a wide mouth. Her white and even teeth are small for her face. She looks weary and spent. The two-room cabin in which she lives with her husband and child, in an isolated section of Macon County, Alabama, is dilapidated and musty with age and long use. The roof over the bedroom hangs low and has some holes in it. She sits by the window helplessly indifferent to the decay around her. She and her husband have begun to try to get a foothold as a cropper family.

Her husband, Clint Sawyer, is of slight build, youthful and sophisticated in a rural sense, and a bit shifty. He was introduced to Juanita while she was in school by a girl friend at whose home he had lived. He had been a beau of this girl friend but she preferred not to get married.

Juanita's Family Background

Juanita's parents have been separated for five years, and the father has remarried and lives in Detroit. There is a little brother, born to her mother two years after her husband left. Juanita does not know the father of her youngest brother.

The school which she attended is sixteen miles from her parents' home, and she was sent to board in the home of a friend of the family nearer the school. Here she met her husband, and their marriage was as accidental as their meeting. When the principal of the school discovered that Juanita was pregnant, he let her complete her grade and take her examination; he insisted, however, that she should get married, and Clint agreed. She said, "I spec he didn't mind or he wouldn't of married me."

At home with her mother she had been unhappy. Her mother was a quarrelsome woman. Juanita said, "I think if my mother wasn't always quarreling and fussing my father would of stayed at home; but she treated him so bad he just left." She had wanted to run away but had no place to go. Now she is married. Marriage meant escape of a sort, but it also brought new responsibilities and a new definition of her economic role. She said:

> When you marry you suppose to live where your husband live, and he found this home. Some of his folks give him a bed and table and

the white man he work for give him a stove. Mamma give me the chairs. I reckon we'll get along all right.

Founding a Cropper Family

There is a well-born iron bed on one side of the room which is covered with a clean quilt. There is a slight hump in the center of the bed. Juanita rises slowly, as if in a daze, goes to the bed, pulls back the quilt and sheet, and reveals a tiny five-pound baby, who has been completely covered in spite of the humid heat. The baby's color is an unnatural red. She picks it up gently and gazes at it and sighs, "It's so little." The baby's eyes are filled with a thick yellow secretion. Juanita says casually, "Seem like something the matter with her eyes, I have to keep wiping out pus." She takes a corner of her dress and mops out the child's eyes. It cries feebly. Juanita looks puzzled, replaces the child on the bed, and draws the covers again.

> I just have to keep her covered up, these flies so bad they jest worry her so she can't sleep.

Clint has had trouble getting a good contract because he does not have enough hands to work the cotton. When he married he found a side job helping a white man who runs a café on the highway; he gets $2 a week and such food as he can occasionally "get away with." The baby is a burden. The young mother complained:

> Once I liked babies. I likes other folks' children, but seem like I just can't like this baby. I been trying, but I just don't love it. I don't think it's cute. She is ugly—I be very kind to her but it just look like I can't love her like I do other people's children. I don't never want no more.

Juanita's life pattern is set in terms of the dominant Negro community. She joined the Mt. Canaan Baptist Church after an operation for appendicitis when she was frightened at the thought of dying before her "soul had been saved." She does not want her husband to work for Negroes "cause they are all poor just like us, and after he works they may not pay him." She prefers white people, "They be fine. They give us a living." The wife of her husband's employer gave the baby all the clothes it has, a box of baby powder, and some oil.

In school Juanita was about like the average simple plantation girl—heavy, placid, and uninspired in school work, but well enough behaved to be permitted to complete her work even after her condition was so noticeable that it was the object of good-natured joking by her classmates. The principal said with bored resignation, "I've seen it happen too much. She'll have a baby every year and struggle along somehow."

David Hilman: Migratory Youth

David Hilman was born just across the creek from his present home in Greene County, Georgia. His family has been highly mobile; during his 17 years he has covered by truck, with his parents and their essential stock and household property, most of the hopeful spots of three southern states. Now he is back home again.

When he was about 3 years old the family migrated to Birmingham, Alabama. David does not know how his father ever heard about "out there." The boll weevil had struck in Greene County and left black havoc.

> Colored people couldn't furnish themselves and white people wouldn't let them have any money 'cause they didn't believe they could make good crops.

In the delta area larger capital might have taken a chance, but not in the impoverished old South where white owners were also poor. After three years in Birmingham they returned, partly because his mother was ill and partly because his father had a temperament less adjustable to the power plants in which he was working than to the soil. The stay was long enough to permit the oldest son to break away from the family and seek a career. He found a job in a barber shop in North Carolina and got married.

Trek to North Carolina

David's family remained on the farm six years, and when hard times struck again they packed their belongings and left for North Carolina.

> The crops we were making weren't much and the landlord couldn't help us. And then the house was in a awful condition. My brother was living in North Carolina. I don't know how he got up there. He said they were making good crops there and he wrote my father about it.

There were eleven members in the family party that set out for North Carolina. A sister's husband and a brother's wife were members of the economic household. They left in two trucks—one carrying the family, the other a mule, a cow, and some furniture. David was ill on the trip, and the party stopped in Hartford, Georgia. It was cold. The women folks went to look up a first cousin who was a preacher, but he was in the throes of a revival and could not see them. David stayed in the truck and in the early morning a policeman investigating the strange truck heard his groans and carried him to the jail to warm him up. The next morning they set out again and got as far as Greenville, South Carolina. The sickening fumes from the old truck nauseated the whole party, but it was David again who became really ill. Then the motor stopped running. They flagged a passing car and were dismayed to find it driven by a white woman. To their surprise she offered to take one of the brothers to the nearest town for help.

A New Home and New People

On the long North Carolina trip David got a deep fright. His father, who was an ardent reader of the Negro papers, had read aloud to the party the story of a white woman who had gotten a Negro to strike a white relative of hers over the head and kill him for his insurance. Listening to his father's vehement discussion of this case, David received his first dramatic introduction to the white world. His father had been angered because a mob wanted to kill the Negro, completely ignoring the white woman's responsibility. David developed a morbid fear of white people and fancied thereafter that he saw the white woman dogging him through the fields to bait him for a mob.

When they finally reached North Carolina the whole party of eleven moved into a two-room house. Nine of them slept in the two beds and two on the floor. David's father began sharecropping on halves. The location of their home was especially fascinating to David. Trucks came out from town regularly to dump garbage and trash. The boys from all around came to watch the trucks unload. They were mostly white boys, and one of their games was throwing bottles at the colored children to see them run.

> One time one of my little brothers lost his shoes, he was running so fast. His shoes were old and cut out, and they just come off while he was running.

When they got home on this occasion an older brother got his gun and went back to find the white boys but they had gone.

> My brother-in-law told my brother he shouldn't have carried a gun over there 'cause he might of got in some trouble. We were afraid to go over there after that, and we just stayed around the house, or went to the field.

Once a white boy who was a neighbor met him in the field and walked home with him. In the back yard they stumbled upon a leather strap, and David picked it up. The white boy said, "Give me that strap!" and tried to take it; he said his grandmother had been promising him a strap for his school books and he needed it. David said, "No," and ran with the strap. For days he hid, in a sweat of fear, expecting the white boy's grandmother to have him punished, perhaps killed. When nothing happened his fears abated and he regained confidence in himself.

School Problems

The children did not attend school in North Carolina because they did not have presentable clothes. They were already retarded because their father had withdrawn them for a year from the Georgia school when the principal had wanted them to "act monkey" for the white superintendent at a "concert."

Trouble with Whites

Their biggest problem in North Carolina was trouble with lower-class white people. Impoverished white neighbors removed the tires from their trucks and sold them, and stole their hunting dogs, but nothing could be done about it. In North Carolina the father was free to sell his cotton anywhere—a respite from plantation discipline, but all mills were alike. Always the white man would figure himself into a large share in the cotton. David recounted one incident:

> The white man figured how much my father owed him for ginning. He cross figured and all like that, and got my father all mixed up. He beat my father out of $100 or more. The white man's father-in-law come out and started raring around too. He said they'd never had a nigger come up there to a white man's house to settle up, 'cause they always stayed on the place and took what he give them. My father stayed down there and tried to get a settlement, and every time the white man come down there he would figure it up real fast and say he was in a hurry and had to go, so my father got tired of that and went over to his house for settlement.

The landlord thought David's father was a blustering novice and counted him out for the next year. When the crops came in good order, he saw his mistake and tried to get him to stay. But being defrauded of $100 and getting the worst mules and the last use of the wagons, discouraged him. His father said "he wouldn't stay if he gave him the whole plantation."

Trek Back to Georgia

So they went back to Georgia. On the return trip the mule and the cow were in the truck with the family and the furniture, because they could afford only one truck on this trip. They found their old place neglected and surrounded by weeds. The new owner lived in New York and came down only once a year. When the credit merchants refused an advance to the family, they managed to borrow money from a bank.

David welcomed the return home. In North Carolina they could not go to school, could not hunt without a license, and could not make cotton baskets from anything except dead trees.

David is now a full grown farm hand, getting up at four o'clock to feed the stock and, since his mother fell through the floor and injured herself, he helps with preparation of breakfast. He walks three miles to the highway to catch the school bus every time it runs. When the families cannot pay the driver's charge of $1.00 a month for each child, the driver cannot buy gas to run it. After school David helps his father in the field, and in winter cuts wood enough to keep fires going all day and night.

Family Links

David's family is linked with interesting characters and events in the history of the county. His mother's father was white.

> I used to hear my sisters say "I got some white blood in me," but I didn't know it was true until I went up and got my grandmother the other week. On the way back she told me how her father was white too.

He has a cousin who killed a man and escaped to Alabama. Another "cut up" a man and escaped. Two female cousins had children before they married. The sister who went farthest in school is now a stenographer in Detroit. "I guess we most proud of her," he said. The local preacher is an uncle who owns large parcels of land which he bought up as people fled before the boll weevil. This preacher was illiterate until a few years ago. It was an unsuccessful romance that goaded him into literacy. He wanted to marry one of the local girls who had graduated from school, and since he could not write he asked David's sister to write the proposal. The sister disliked the girl and wrote an insulting letter instead of a proposal of marriage, and shattered Uncle Wilbur's romance beyond possibility of repair. He decided to learn to do his own writing.

Conflict with the Community

The family is in a constant struggle with both the Negro and white communities. The Negroes dislike the father because he is a renter and the whites because he asserts himself when he believes he is right. David said:

> Colored people don't like my father because he is a renter, and a lot of them is just hands. So they tell the white man a lot of things about my father. They said he would steal things. Some of them is my kin people, and some of them knew him all his life.

The neighbors could blame their smaller crops for the landlord on the depredations of the Hilman hogs. Once the hogs actually broke out of their pens during a rain storm and got into a white man's corn. The white man sent for David's father and angrily accused him of letting his hogs run wild all the year. When his father disputed him another white man shouted. "Nigger, you know you called a white man a liar!" A fight started and David's father neither apologized nor ran. He was a strong man and could handle them both so long as they were without their guns.

The family now behaves with great caution, knowing well that they are a marked group and that the next time any white man starts something he is going to take the precaution of supporting his status with his gun and his white neighbors.

Madge Hickman: A Successful Farmer's Daughter

Diversified farming areas permit more independence, greater freedom of ownership, and securer subsistence, and these bring new responsibilities. Johnston County in North Carolina is outside the plantation area and its farmers do not depend wholly upon any one crop. They raise their own food and may even give some of their time to nonagricultural pursuits. Along with subsistence crops they raise some cotton and tobacco, which are essentially cash crops. Over 90 percent of the Negroes of the county are rural and over 70 percent of them live on farms. The Negro families in the county have a comparatively high tenancy rate, but this is not so likely to be a matter of fixed status as in the plantation counties, for it is more often possible to do other work along with farming.

Home Setting

Madge Hickman lives on her parents' 102-acre farm, about six miles out from a small town in Johnston County, in what is called the Good Samaritan section, because of the presence there of the Good Samaritan Baptist Church. Her grandmother owns an adjoining farm of 140 acres, and both produce cotton, tobacco, grain, and food stuffs.

The five-room house is well furnished. The living room is a mixture of old and new furnishings, reflecting at the same time respect for modern conveniences and a sentimental regard for the battered treasures from earlier days and generations. The basic furniture is an overstuffed suite consisting of a davenport and two chairs, upholstered in deep blue mohair, an end table, and a large console radio. Beside the radio is an old cane-bottomed armchair, painted blue to match the furniture. Across the room is a huge dresser, also old, and an elaborate hatrack. On the tiny center table is a very old kerosene lamp which supports a new and modern parchment shade. A pale green and yellow straw rug partially covers the floor. On the walls are pictures in aging hand-carved wooden frames or in tortoise shell frames which are cracked and curled with age; there is one large gilt frame holding a collection of recent pictures. The center art piece is a vivid, curiously fanciful tapestry representing George Washington apparently leaving a group of soldiers and riding toward the Statue of Liberty. On the mantel and table are a thick array of bric-a-brac, colored paper flowers, artificial oranges, animals blown from glass, and a collection of white elephants.

Madge's mother is a large, friendly, brown woman who is dressed neatly in a well-fitting blue and white cotton print dress. In her rapid, lisping speech are marks of schooling and some urban influence. The father, Mack Hickman, is a brown man with slightly wavy hair and a serious face. In the household also are a cousin, Pensy, who is 15 years old and named for her maternal grandmother, Pensacola, and the grandmother herself, a proud old woman of about 65. The pictures on the walls are an important link with the past. The hand-carved and tortoise shell picture frames belonged to Mack Hickman's mother, and her mother and grandmother had them before her.

In one frame is a picture of Mr. Hickman's mother, who has been dead about five years. She has the physical traits of an Indian. In another frame is a picture of Mr. Hickman, rigid and severe with his high collar and handle-bar mustache. There is another picture of two white men, dressed in military uniform and holding rifles. They are relatives of Mr. Hickman's, a generation removed. The canebottomed chair belonged to Mr. Hickman's great-grandmother.

Madge is 17 years old, tall and thin, with a nut-brown complexion, large brown eyes, and brownish hair that has been straightened and bobbed. Her manner is mild and childishly immature for her age. She has been humored from birth by her grandmothers and her father. She calls her parents by their first names and her grandmother "mamma."

Family Training

Madge describes some of the incidents of her childhood as follows:

> When I was about seven years old I went to a funeral, Lil [her mother] had just bought me a great big doll, she paid $8.50 for it; and it came in a big box. Well, we children decided to have a big funeral. Two of my cousins helped me. The boy was the preacher. The girl and I cried and cried and brought piles of flowers. We had a big funeral and buried the doll. Lil kept asking me where the doll was, but I told her I didn't know. I thought the doll was dead and I didn't want to dig it up. Then one day Mack [her father] was plowing and plowed up this doll and brought it to the house. He said "Lil, here's that doll you paid $8.50 for." It was all streaked and cracked, almost eaten up. Lil wanted to whip me, but my grandma took me in her apron and run off with me.

> I didn't start to school until I was 8 years old. Once the teacher whipped me because I didn't know my alphabet. She didn't have to whip me but once. I came home and I learned them. After that I always learned enough to get promoted. I stayed in the seventh grade two years, but that's the only grade I ever got left in. I couldn't pass the state examination for the seventh grade, so I had to take the seventh grade work over. The next time I was sick at examination time and one of the teachers gave me the examinations, and I passed.

> When I was little, Mack built me a playhouse and I tried to get Lil to let me have the victrola out in my house, but she wouldn't. Then one day she went away and I took the victrola out in my house, It rained and the records got wet and the machine too. It got so wet the spring broke, and after that I had to put my finger in it to make it run. Lil certainly was mad when she saw it, but Mack wouldn't let her whip me. He happened to be there when she saw it.

Daily Routine

Madge describes her day as follows:

In the winter I get up about 6 or 6:30. I sleep in the room with my grandma and Pence. Grandma sleeps in her bed and Pence and me sleep together. Pence helps me to clean up the bedroom. Then we eat breakfast. We have bacon and eggs, cornflakes, and biscuits. Some mornings I cook breakfast, usually on Wednesday morning. I like to give Lil a rest from cooking sometimes, so I cook. Then I dress; I take a sponge bath every morning and a bath in the tub twice a week. I don't want to smell. After that I dress.

I leave here at 7:45 every morning and drive to school. I get there at 8:30. I stay in school from 8:30 until 12:30, when we have lunch. Every day I spend about 25 cents for lunch. I buy apples and drinks and cakes or peanuts—just trash. Sometimes I buy so much I can't eat it all during lunch hour, and I eat in class afterwards. Once or twice the teacher has sent me out to finish eating. I hate that. But I like to eat in school; it tastes so much better.

We stay in school until 3. In the afternoon I play basketball. I play on the school team—forward. I play fairly well. In games last year I made 64 goals. In one game I made 15 out of 21 scores. I take typing too, some afternoons.

I like arithmetic best. I can understand that, but some of those other subjects, I just don't like—like history and English. I don't like either one.

Well, I leave school at 3. As soon as I get home I eat a boiled dinner—collards, home-made meat, bread, and something sweet. Then usually I have to go off somewhere for Mack. He just saves the things for me to do. Most of the time I'm back home by 6. Then I drink a pint of milk and study. Nobody helps me. I study each subject about 30 minutes, but I don't have any regular plan. I study awhile then walk around with Pence, and go back. I study sorter haphazard. I never study English unless we're going to have a test. I hate it. If we're going to have a test, I'll study it for 45 minutes. I go to bed at 9:30.

Flowers are my hobby. All those in the yard out there, I planted them. I just love flowers. I like to play all kinds of games—baseball, basketball, football, and soft ball. We play out here every Saturday. We have a girls' soft ball team out here, and some team plays every Saturday. Lots of people come and watch the game. Next Saturday we're going to Piney Grove to play the girls there. We do that just when school's out in the summer time. I like to swim and play cards too. I don't like to read. Sometimes I read western stories and *True Story*, but not often. Usually I read the newspapers.

I spend lots of time doing things for Mack [her father]. I get his money and pay his men. I keep up with the money for him. One time they sent him too little money and I counted it before I started paying the men. I told Mack and went back and asked for the rest. The man gave it to me, and said he was sorry he made a mistake. But I notice that when he makes mistakes it's always in his favor. I count it first every time. I take out about $5 or $10 a week for myself, and I've got $140 in the bank.

Ambitions and Personality

Madge's school principal says that she is very neat, is very spoiled as a result of family indulgence, and is never rude. "She never admits anything about herself, even things that are nice." She is ambitious and she says she wants to have a career, but this is not convincing. She seldom gets angry, and when a boy once said something very mean to her she just looked at him and laughed tolerantly. She is timid and quiet but likes a good time, and is the most popular girl in school.

Sam Calloway: Small Farmer's Son

Rural areas within the influence of large cities attract the city's vices along with its advantages. Davidson County, Tennessee, has more urban than rural dwellers, for the city of Nashville is located in it. The rural Negro population tends to concentrate on the periphery of the city and just outside the borders, and usually in settlements. A few of these settlements, however, are ten to fifteen miles from the city, far enough to continue as self-contained communities, but close enough to the city to be accessible to its influences.

Sam Calloway lives in one of these settlements with his mother, father, and a sister 12 years old. Their house is a one-and-a-half story structure of four rooms, very much in need of paint, wall paper, and general repairs. The family owns this house and another equally defective one nearby. Inside, the furniture has been shifted to escape the water which comes in through holes in the roof. Sam's father works in a lumber yard and leaves the farming to the family. The mother is large and genial; the father tall, awkward, and casual in his movements. There are two older sons who are now away from home; all the children were born where the family now lives.

Sam is 15 years old, but weighs 165 pounds and looks 17 or 18. He dresses in blue overalls, and walks with a heavy, slow tread which again belies his youth. His brown face is chiseled sharply and his eyes show dark rings. Farm labor has made him muscular. He works about as a laborer on farms, especially during harvesting time, doing anything the farmers will give him to do. Now at 15 he is considering leaving school when he finishes the eighth grade. In the first place, he feels that he is too large to be sitting in class with students so much smaller. Then, the money he can earn means more to him than what he is getting from school.

> What I'd really like to do is to go to an engineering school. I sure wish there was one around here, then I'd want to go to school. If I had the money I'd go up North to one. They don't care up North if you're colored.

Recreation and Religion

What worries his mother just now are his coughing spells and his companions. When he was 12 years old the doctors said he had tuberculosis, but she thinks "it's all gone now." Nevertheless she says:

> I don't think it would be good for him to set in class all day, with that cough he have now. When he's out in the open air I feels a lot better about him.

The other problem involves the whole community. There are three "taverns" which accommodate the local people as well as the people out from the city for a lark. The nickel-in-the-slot phonographs play "hot numbers" and cheap bootleg whisky can be bought. Sam says:

> We go to the taverns and joints around here. We drink beer, smoke, and dance with the girls. I don't like beer much; I just drink because the other guys drink it. We dance with the girls and play around with them. Ain't nothing else to do but that. The folks out here don't say nothing about us fellows and gals going to the taverns. Most of them do the same thing under cover. You can get a gal there and proposition her if you want to.

Some of the girls are hardened tavern habitués. One of them has a reputation for having "cut up" three men at different times in her romantic career. The community does not provide organized recreation for its youth. During the school term the children play baseball and football, but these are very largely spectator sports.

Sam seldom goes to church, and when he does it is to meet his girl friend. "Old people make too much fuss over religion," he thinks. Moreover, he does not have very high regard for the ministry.

> It ain't just the people in the church that don't do the way the preacher says they ought to do, but the preacher don't move quite right himself

sometimes. If you look around long enough you'll set the preachers making plenty "creeps" [trysts]. I know one who makes them every week.

Attitude towards Whites

He is not uncomfortably aware of the white community.

> White folks don't worry me. I just don't bother them and they never bothered me. The white folks live down the highway mostly.

Ambitions

Sam goes on dreaming of becoming an engineer, or perhaps the owner of a car factory, or even a car salesman, because "you know a lot about cars then and can drive all you want to." He does not want too much education.

> I think too much schooling, like going to college, does a lot of people harm. You can make money doing what I want to do.

But he cannot get away to begin his engineering study, and so he thinks he will just give it up.

> When I read in the mechanic books sometimes about the places where they train engineers, I feel kinda bad. If I was white I could go to Vanderbilt or some other place right here in the state.

Hylan Lewis' essay gives an overview of cultural life in a small southern town. Charles Johnson offers ten pictures of Negro youths who lived in or near such a place. In both selections, repeated references were made to the attractions of the North. There, it was said, life would be different. In many ways it was and is.

Here Claude Brown, author of Manchild in the Promised Land, *gives a brief self-portrait of what it is like to grow up in Harlem, the biggest black community in the country Comparing this essay to the two previous ones, the contrast between life down South and up North is strikingly presented.*

14

Harlem, My Harlem

Claude Brown

At the age of nine I had already acquired the reputation of being the worst boy in the neighborhood. And in my neighborhood this was no easy accomplishment. My frequent appearance in juvenile court was beginning to bother the judges. By spring of 1946 I had been placed in four juvenile detention centers by the Manhattan Domestic Relations Court. However, during my travels through New York City while truant from school, I had become exceptionally well acquainted with the city subways. As a result, I was usually back on the streets of Harlem within two days, from wherever the court had placed me. A year earlier, I had acquired the habit of staying away from home for several days and nights which occasionally lengthened into weeks. Due to my skill at living in the streets, it would sometimes be many days before my parents learned of my unofficial departure from the places to which I had been confined by the courts.

While roaming the streets at night with one or two other boys

From *Dissent*, 8 (Summer 1961) 378–382.

who were also afraid to go home or disgusted with home life, I was often arrested for breaking into stores and stealing. I only stole items that I could sell to my private customers or to one of the neighborhood "fences." And I knew a large number of the latter. Among my many customers and associates were prostitutes, pimps, dope peddlers, stick-up artists, professional thieves, and other petty criminals with great ambitions.

My favorite fence was Miss Eileen. She was not the highest paying fence; in fact, there is no such thing. Any thief will tell you, they are all a bunch of crooks. But Miss Eileen had such a nice way of robbing me. She would put her arm around me and beg me in a very sexy tone while she played with my ears. I thought she was the prettiest lady in the world. I think she was the first woman I ever knew who had red hair. Miss Eileen was also something more than a fence, and I would have discovered this much sooner had it not been for my youth. Many times when I came to her house at night she would be in her slip and a new husband would be there. As time went on I heard the older fellows talking about selling Miss Eileen something for a "piece of loving." I too began to dream of the day when I could sell her something for a piece of loving, but to my regret I never got the chance. A year later Miss Eileen went to jail for three years, and when she came out she wasn't as pretty as she used to be. As a result, she changed her "game" to selling drugs. For three years she was very successful in the "horse trade," but gave it up and did seven years for her troubles at the insistence of the Narcotics Bureau. The last time I saw her she was profitably engaged in one of Harlem's more legal vices; the "numbers" racket.

These were the people I admired and wanted to be accepted by. People like Miss Eileen and my other teachers from the streets of Harlem.

By June, 1946 I had been expelled from not less than six public schools in New York City, and refused acceptance by as many others. The Board of Education would tolerate my numerous absences from school, and even my fighting with teachers. But they refused to have a boy in the school system who had attempted to push another boy out of a five-story window.

Following a thirty-day psychiatric observation period in Bellevue Hospital, I was ordered out of the state by a juvenile court judge. After enduring what seemed at the time a miserable year on a small farm in South Carolina, I returned to New York. When I arrived in Harlem on August 10, 1947, I was also returning to a familiar way of life. Less than two months later I was standing before Judge Bolyn diligently trying to look pathetic. She appeared to be a woman devoid of any emotions, especially pity. From Judge Bolyn, to whom I am deeply indebted today, I received my first sentence.

My first court sentence was actually not a sentence at all, but a commitment to Wiltwyck School for Boys for an indefinite time.

Wiltwyck is an interracial institution which accepts delinquent boys from eight to twelve, committed by the courts of New York or by social agencies. Only children are considered who can profit by its program of individualized treatment in the regulated and planned environment of a children's community.

Following a two and a half years' stay at Wiltwyck, I returned to my dear old Harlem. I was then thirteen. In a few weeks I became uncomfortably aware of not being able to fit in anymore. There were many new vices to learn, but somehow I just could not pick up where I had left off. Having no alternative, however, I set out to reestablish myself in the old community.

Things were somewhat different now. The dope fad had hit New York, and all of my old gang were using heroin. I wanted nothing to do with drugs, but the problem was very disturbing. Either I could continue my relationship with my old cohorts or get in with a younger gang of delinquents, my own age. The younger group was stealing and making much less money than my former partners. I would have chosen my old friends, but I was handicapped by parental restrictions. So I became leader of a gang of fellows mostly my own age. There were many things I could teach them, such as how to pick locks, how to rob a subway slot machine, how to pick a woman's pocketbook, how to bargain with the "fence," and how to roll "pot." Also, I knew how to organize a gang fight and hold a gang together.

I didn't have to steal for money, because Butch, Kidd, and Danny were doing good, "pushing horse," and money was mine for the asking. I think they preferred that I steal it from them. So, that's how I usually got it. Butch, Kidd, and Danny were all at least four years older than I was, and for many years we had all lived in the same tenement building. These guys whom I considered to be "big time," were like older brothers to me. They fought the bigger guys who tried to bully me. It was they who had taught me how to steal, how to live in the streets of Harlem. It was Danny who had taught me most of the street ways. He taught me by cheating me, taking me along on "scores," and showing me my mistakes whenever I lost a fight.

Whenever I lost a fight Danny would always say you should have stabbed that punk. To Danny, everybody was a punk. It was Danny who had first taught me how to use a knife in a street fight. I remember him showing me how to get the knife out of my belt without my opponent seeing it. Danny would say, "A cat should never know that you have a knife until he has been cut or stabbed." And this is usually the way it was when he stabbed a guy.

Butch was the most loyal guy I knew, and also the best thief. Butch had taught me how to hitch rides on street cars and buses. He also taught me not to run when I stole something. Butch would never admit that he was the best thief in the neighborhood. He would always say that Sol was the best because Sol had taught him many things about stealing. Sol was much older than Butch and had been stealing much longer, but he had been caught while Butch had not yet been "busted." In my opinion that made Butch the better thief.

Kidd had taught me how to play hookey from school. I was about six years old when I first heard about "hookey" and I pleaded with Kidd to teach me the game. He promised me he would teach me on the first day I went to school. This promise had to wait until the second day, because on the first day my mother took me to get me registered. Once I learned how to play hookey, I seldom went to school, and this often led to staying away from home. I would look in the mailbox and could always tell if there was a card from the school. The yellow truancy card in the mailbox meant that if I went home that night, the razor strop awaited me. When I played hookey I would either go on a stealing tour of the city or sneak into a movie. Kidd had also taught me how to sneak into a movie.

Stealing had become a part of me and I became very adept at this art. After Wiltwyck I felt lost whenever I was not stealing or "rumbling." Perhaps that's why I began to spend more time with my new gang and less time with my old cohorts.

Less than three months after my release, I was arrested for gang fighting, but was released in my mother's custody. Three weeks later I was in a backyard stealing some sheets off a clothes line. Turk, a member of my new gang whom I had become "tight" with, was with me. At my house there were festivities taking place because mama had hit the number. I had to get away from it and when I reached the street, the first person I saw was Turk. He was always ready to do whatever I suggested. Turk's favorite words were "Sonny, what are we gonna do?" That cold night in December, when I said to Turk, let's go steal some sheets, he seemed to be waiting for the suggestion.

When we had been in the backyard for about fifteen minutes, Turk shouted, "Foot it, Sonny!" I stood there waiting to see what he wanted to run from. I didn't see anybody, but after the first shot was fired I decided to run. By the time I reached the top of the stairs leading from the backyard I was feeling unusually tired. But I kept running even after I felt the blood streaming down my leg and realized I had been shot. I panicked and started yelling, "Turk! Turk! I'm shot." I ran into a fish-and-chip joint where I collapsed. As I lay on the floor of the dirty joint, my fear of dying began slowly to diminish.

I found myself wishing that mama would stop jumping up while she cried, because she was shaking the shabby floor and it made me feel the bullet more. I never gave a second thought to Turk's question when he bent over me as I fell to the floor, and asked me if I were going to tell the cops that he was with me. This was all very normal in Harlem where somebody was always getting shot, stabbed, or his throat cut. However, I found it disturbing to have it happen to me. As the pain began to ease up, I starting thinking how lucky I was to die this way. I thought about the boy whom I had watched two members of my old gang throw from the roof of a six-story building. I recalled how frightened he looked when they grabbed him, and I recalled his terrified screams as he went over. Yeah, compared to him I was really lucky.

While I lay on the rolling stretcher in Harlem Hospital emergency ward, I thought the police would never stop questioning me. Danny, Butch, and Kidd arrived shortly after I did. First Butch would beg me to tell him who had shot me, then Danny would start while Kidd threatened to kill Turk if I died. They all had their "pieces" and were ready and anxious to shoot somebody. Fortunately, I had not seen whoever it was that shot me, and could tell them no more than I had told the police.

Three weeks after my two-week stay in Harlem Hospital, and while the surgeon who had operated on me was still marveling at what he and God had done, I was sent to New York State Training School for Boys at Warwick, New York. I stayed at Warwick for nine months. When I returned to Harlem, I had learned many news ways of crimes. I had also become well acquainted with many of New York City's teen-age criminals.

Upon my return to Harlem I no longer cared to steal or partake in gang fights, but I had to steal a few things to show my gang that getting shot had not unnerved me. Two days after I came home, I received my first real pistol, as a coming home gift. After pulling enough scores to get up one hundred dollars, I bought a half pound of pot and went into business. Within two weeks, the word had gotten around that I had the best pot in town. For the next three months—at the end of which I got "busted"—I did a pretty good job of emulating a Harlem "hustler" who was doing good. This included wearing thirty-dollar shoes and giving frequent handouts to old friends who had become junkies. Danny, one of my favorite old tutors in the ways of the street, had now become my favorite junkie; I would always give him a "nickel bill" to get a fix.

Following two more trips to Warwick, I moved out of Harlem and got a job. Most of my spare time was spent in Harlem, taking the ribbing and laughing that my attending evening high school evoked from my old street corner cronies. They laughed for three years. When I entered college there were no more laughs.

Some interesting changes have occurred in Harlem during the past few years. It seems that many of the people who I once thought were merely waiting for something to happen to them, have made things happen. The last time I saw Danny, I could not help but admire him. Danny is making money by the fists full. There is nothing remarkable about a guy making lots of money selling drugs. But in Danny's case the admirable feat was his being able to kick an eight-year drug habit, and then make the stuff work for him. Danny is the only reformed junkie I have ever known to stay reformed for any length of time. And his presence in Harlem is most encouraging to other junkies who dream of kicking their habit and becoming pushers in turn.

I saw Turk yesterday and we talked of his next fight. It was an inspiring experience for me to hear Turk, who has become one of the world's leading heavyweight fighters, explain how he would beat his next opponent. It seems like only yesterday when I was explaining to him the strategy of our next "rumble."

The big changes in Harlem are in the people I know who have changed my sympathy to respect and admiration. If you've ever known a junkie for any length of time you'll understand the struggle he has to go through to get off the poison kick. He can't leave the world entirely, so for him to become master and dispenser of the thing that had ruled him for so long and so destructively is a great achievement. Harlem still has a much greater number of the miserable than any place else I know. This is inspiring also. Where else can one find so many people in such pain and so few crying about it?

While much early writing about black Americans concentrated on life in the South (and most communities researched by sociologists were located there), there have been exceptions. Such studies as St. Clair Drake and Horace Cayton's Black Metropolis, *autobiographies like Claude Brown's* Manchild in the Promised Land, *and novels such as Ralph Ellison's* Invisible Man *offered in-depth insights into the big city scene. Indeed, these works have become required reading in most courses on the black experience.*

To be added to the list is the recent volume Urban Blues, *by Charles Keil. As seen in those sections reprinted below, Keil is particularly concerned with projecting those aspects of urban Negro culture that even the best-known specialists have tended to overlook or underplay: the roots of "soul" and its auditory and tactile expression.*

15

Urban Blues

Charles Keil

I am primarily concerned with an expressive male role within urban lower-class Negro culture—that of the contemporary bluesman.

The terminology of this statement of purpose needs some clarification, for what an anthropologist calls his "conceptual vocabulary" is sometimes labeled "unnecessary jargon" by anyone who is not a social scientist, and might well be considered just plain "signifying" or "off-the-wall jive" by the people I'm writing about. Since I share the points of view of the latter more often than not, my definitions of these terms and others like them that appear in these pages tend to be simple and can usually be taken at face value. For example, urban lower-class people, as far as I am concerned, are those who live in big cities and have very little money.[1]

The term "role" is used here in the conventional theatrical sense for the most part—a person playing the role of Hamlet is supposed to act like Hamlet; a man who calls himself a father, a friend, or a

From Charles Keil, *Urban Blues*, 1966, pp. 1–29, by permission of The University of Chicago Press. Copyright © 1966 by The University of Chicago Press.

blues singer is expected to act the part or parts. These expectations define each role. An expressive role obligates the person who fills it to express something—the prayer of the priest, the joke of the comedian, the composition of an artist. What does the Negro audience expect of a bluesman today, and what does he express for them in his performance?

My attempts to answer these questions in the following pages have forced a confrontation with two problematic fundamentals: Negro culture, and the Negro male. It is the exploration of these components in my statement of purpose and the issues they raise that I would like to emphasize in this introduction.

There are fancier definitions, but essentially a culture is a way of life. In this sense, every individual is a cultured individual. Every child rapidly acquires the language, the eating habits, the religious beliefs, the gestures, the technology, the notions of common sense, the attitudes toward sex, the concepts of beauty and justice, the responses to pleasure and pain, of the people who raise him. These general guidelines for living vary remarkably from culture to culture. What seems pleasurable or just to an Eskimo may seem painful or criminal to me; but once a person has acquired a particular framework of values, beliefs, and attitudes, it is devilishly difficult to modify and impossible to erase entirely. Individuals come and go; cultures remain. To be sure, cultures change—sometimes rapidly—but the process is usually measured, if at all, in generations and centuries.

A basic axiom that underlies anthropological thought is that culture is always learned and never inherited. Anthropologists have long recognized this clear distinction between race and culture. But, judging by the current vocabulary of "race relations," the distinction is still not generally understood. I cannot think of a single respected or self-respecting anthropologist or geneticist who will seriously question its validity. Yet there has been no mass conversion to this principle, no general understanding of its implications; those who have accepted the distinction intellectually sometimes find it difficult to do so emotionally.

The facts on "race" are readily available elsewhere and need not be summarized extensively here. Scientists use the term to denote a shared gene pool—that is, any group of people who breed (exchange genes) with each other more often than they breed with outsiders. Americans, Hawaiians, hillbillies, Asians, Navahos, Negroes, the inhabitants of most small towns, Catholics, Brooklyn Jews are examples of such groups. Since people who share the same culture or locale are more likely to intermarry, the American race (or any other national gene pool which is in the process of formation) contains a great many genetic puddles and streams. Insofar as we can speak intelligently of a Negro race at all, it is something rather vague and, like the American can race of which it is a part, only beginning to take recognizable genetic shape. The scientist's flexible classifications are based upon measurable genetic factors, usually discrete blood and plasma characteristics, since racial classifications based upon appearances have been found to be extremely unreliable. Racists of course employ the latter criteria when they designate groups of people who "look different and act different" as races. This designation reveals a double or compound ignorance for it brings together dubious appearance criteria and totally irrelevant cultural factors—"acting different." This compound ignorance has given firm support to slavery, genocide, imperialism, and all the most hideous crimes of the past few centuries.

I, for one, would like to see the term "race" abandoned altogether and with it the pernicious rhetoric of race relations, racial conflict, race riot, struggle for racial equality, *ad nauseam.* Can a shared gene pool riot? No. Can it relate in any meaningful way to another bunch of genes? No. Nor can races conflict; but cultures can, and in this shrinking world they clash with increasing frequency. Racial equality is an established fact; the struggle is for cultural pluralism.

What are we to make of the "so-called Negro"? The Black Muslim phrase is particularly apropos, for the man called Negro is apparently three men: a genetic man, a cultural man, and a colored man. "Spelled with a capital 'N' by most publications (one of the important early victories of my own people in their fight for self-definition) the term describes a people whose origin began with the introduction of African slaves to the American colonies in 1619."[2] The capital "N" may represent a pyrrhic victory, however, for by insisting upon equality with Caucasians (another highly ambiguous category) proponents of the upper case would seem to have further obscured the crucial distinction between race and culture, to the detriment of the latter, as we shall see. There is still a third definition of "Negro" to contend with—the infamous social definition. A man may not fit a geneticist's definition of "Negro"; he may not participate in Negro culture, in fact he may have blue eyes, fair complexion, and a fully developed set of white American middle-class values. Yet American society will still label him "colored" or "Negro" if he has or is rumored to have an African ancestor or two—the proverbial touch of the tarbrush. I don't think it would be pedantic or petty at this point to insist that in the interests of rational discussion we begin to use three different terms in place of the indiscriminate (and therefore discriminatory) category "Negro." Perhaps "Negro" best fits the genetic definition, "negro" could be used for the irrational social concept, and in the cultural context "Afro-American" might be considered more appropriate. Since I am writing almost exclusively about cultural matters, I see no reason to force this terminology upon the reader. I would, however, like it to be perfectly clear that I use the term "Negro" in connection with a way of life, a culture, and in no other sense. Note that this usage allows me to include a few so-called white Negroes in my discussion if I care to, while excluding a number of black Americans who identify with the majority culture.

The social definition of the Negro—the fact that he is colored and an outcast—has almost hidden the fact that Negroes have a culture. Twenty-five years ago Melville Herskovits did a rather thorough job of debunking the American myth that "the Negro is a man without a past."[3] Although this myth is still prevalent, a much more dangerous revision of it current today is that the Negro has no culture or at least no viable culture worthy of attention. Yesterday's rural Negro may have had something like a folk culture, so the myth goes, but today's urban Negro can be found only in a set of sociological statistics on crime, unemployment, illegitimacy, desertion, and welfare payments. The social scientists would have us believe that the Negro is psychologically maladjusted, socially disorganized and culturally deprived. Others tell us that any Negro way of life that may exist is nothing more than a product of poverty and fear.[4] From an initial assumption that the Negro is only an American, a long string of insults and injuries inevitably flows. Remove the assumption, recognize a Negro culture, and many of the alleged pathologies disappear while others become subject to new and difficult verification.

Nat Hentoff writes:

> Not one of the many book reviews I read of Nathan Glazer's and Daniel Moynihan's *Beyond the Melting Pot* took exception to their over-whelmingly ignorant assertion that "the Negro is only an American and nothing else. He has no values and culture to guard and protect." That two such sophisticated social scientists were able to be so myopic is a measure, of course, of how ignorant most of us continue to be about what Ralph Ellison called the Negro American style, or rather, styles. As Ellison persistently points out, the complexity and sub-tlety of Negro experience in America have produced infinitely more diverse individualities among Negroes than their friends, enemies, and attending sociologists and psychologists have ever recognized.[5]

Ellison's magnificent novel *Invisible Man* and his recent collection of essays *Shadow and Act* establish him in my estimation as one of the most perceptive analysts of Negro culture writing today. Unlike most of the authors considered here, he is well aware of his heritage and the intricate strategies developed by Negroes in an effort to cope with America. Yet even Ellison shies away from Negro culture per se and prefers to speak of "an American Negro sub-culture" or "American Negro styles" with the accent on "American," "styles" and "subculture." Some statements from an Ellison essay written in 1958 illustrate this emphasis.

> Thus, since most so-called "Negro cultures" outside Africa are necessarily amalgams, it would seem more profitable to stress the term "culture" and leave the term "Negro" out of the discussion.

> Nor should the existence of a specifically "Negro" idiom in any way be confused with the vague racist terms "white culture" or "black culture"; rather it is a matter of diversity within unity.

> Culturally this people represents one of the many sub-cultures which make up that great amalgam of European and native American sub-cultures which is the culture of the United States.[6]

If Negroes are not the least amalgamated of all Americans, then what is the current struggle all about? The melting-pot tone of Ellison's remarks would lead us to believe that Negro culture is only one minor variation among many on the major American theme. I disagree.

There is an important sense, discussed below, in which the Negro is the most American of all Americans, but I must take strong exception to Ellison's statement that

> Its [the Negro people's] spiritual outlook is basically Protestant, its system of kinship is Western, its time and historical sense are American (United States), and its secular values are those professed, ideally at least, by all of the people of the United States.[7]

These generalizations may have validity when applied to the "black bourgeoisie"[8] and to a cluster of Negro intellectuals, but have little or nothing to do with the vast majority of Negroes living in the Northern ghettos and rural South.

Speaking in tongues, prophecy, healing, trance, "possession," a staff of nurses to assist those "filled with the Holy Ghost," frenzied dancing, hand clapping, tambourine playing, instrumental groups, fluctuating musical styles, singing-screaming sermons, constant audience participation—these and many other features of Negro church services are completely foreign to the prevailing conception of Protestantism. White Holy Roller churches still exist in many parts of the country, Southern snake-handling cults are occasionally reported,[9] and a few Yale Divinity School students have been dabbling in "glossolaly" recently. But ecstatic communion with "the living God" as practiced in the Negro store-front churches of Chicago is clearly far removed from the staid and stolid Puritanism that has dominated the American Protestant tradition. Significantly, it is only the Black Muslims (approximately twenty thousand in number) and a few other tiny sects who adhere faithfully to the Protestant ethic, and the Muslims are explicitly opposed to all manifestations of traditional American Negro culture (probably the principal reason that their membership isn't closer to the two hundred thousand they claim). The values usually associated with Protestantism—thrift, sobriety, "inner-directedness," strictly codified sexual behavior (better to marry than to burn), and a strong insistence on respectability—tend to be reversed in the Negro cultural framework. Preachers and elderly Negro women love to give these values lip service, but that's usually as far as conventional Protestantism goes.

To say that Negro kinship is Western, Ellison must overlook the most striking feature of Negro social structure—the battle of the sexes. Or, alternatively, he must disregard the essence of middle-class kinship in America—that is, the core concept of marital companionship and the primacy of the nuclear family over all other kinship ties. For the vast majority of Negroes, the battle of the sexes is no mere figure of speech. In the ghetto, men and women are considered to be separate and antagonistic species, and this division "overrides the minor distinctions of creed, class and color."[10] Men are "by nature" primarily interested in sexual satisfaction and independence (money will get you both); they are "strong sexually, and will take favors from anyone who will grant them. Women are said to be primarily interested in emotional support and their families (money is needed to keep the household intact); they are "weak" sexually, and tend to become attached to one or two men at a time. Men call women self-righteous, money-grabbing, treacherous, and domineering. Women simply say that all men are no good. Relationships between the sexes are usually governed by variations of the "finance-romance"[11] equation that appears in so many blues lyrics. This equation covers a gamut of ties ranging from May-December marriages for security (with a lover on the side for the May partner), through "getting help from my ol' man," to casual, semi-professional and professional prostitution.

The female forces on one side of the battle line consist of units like mother and daughter, sister and sister, niece and aunt, wife and mother-in-law, a matriarch with her daughters and grandchildren. Facing this formidable opposition is the independent Negro male who seeks allies where he can—in the gang, pool hall, blues bar, and barber shop. Moralizing types—Negro women in particular and

282

and white Americans generally—see him as lazy, shiftless, and irresponsible. White liberals see him as jobless and demoralized. Norman Mailer[12] portrays him as an existentialist stud, hedonistically at home in a world of violence, drugs, wine, women, and song. Apparently Ellison doesn't see him at all—an invisible man perhaps. However we characterize the anomalous position of the Negro male, he doesn't seem to fit gracefully into a conventional American or Western kinship system. Nor, for that matter, do the basic features of lower-class Negro kinship patterns match well with any non-Western kinship system that anthropologists have encountered. The battle of the sexes can of course be found raging in many slums around the world—for example, Athens, Mexico City, Liverpool, Johannesburg—but in most of these "cultures of poverty"[13] the battle tends to be resolved in terms of male authoritarianism rather than "mother-centeredness."[14] The study of lower-class culture (slum culture, culture of poverty, underculture, as you prefer) is in its infancy, and it is hazardous to make comparisons; but it would seem that the Negro male is on the whole farthest removed from both his family of origin—Mama excepted—and his family of procreation. The resultant kinship patterns are different in degree if not in kind from any others.

I do not want to leave the reader with the impression that every Negro is fatherless or that every Negro family is matrifocal, but the patterns sketched above are normative if not normal. That is, working-class or lower-class Negro couples who manage to stick together, as well as families in the emergent Negro middle class, define themselves and their ideals in contradistinction to these well-known ghetto conditions and are, in this antagonistic respect at least, a part of Negro culture. Finally, we can note that every urban culture of poverty is a product of Western industrialization or the beginnings of it, but I don't think that this is the point that Ellison has tried to make.

What about Ralph Waldo Ellison's contention that the Negro's "time and historical sense are American (United States)"? Again I must insist that Ellison speaks for himself but not for the man in the street. The writer-in-residence usually shows up for his literature classes on time. He writes cogent essays relating the past to the present and the future. And he knows that he has two historical traditions to draw upon in his work—the slavery and post-slavery experience of his immediate forebears, and the history in which his namesake Ralph Waldo Emerson played such a prominent part. The black man on the street corner, like most slum dwellers everywhere, lives for the present and tends to drift with events rather than show up for appointments, assuming that he has any. His historical perspective is epitomized in the adage "The white man's heaven is the black man's hell," lyricized so tenderly by the reformed calypsonian and Black Muslim minister Louis X The heavenly history found in high-school textbooks is mostly meaningless drivel to him, and what he knows of the history of hell he would just as soon forget. To plan for the future is probably futile; Emerson is unknown; and Negro History Week, promoted by middle-class strivers, is a bad joke. His history is American (United States) to be sure, but it is upside down.

The Negro's "secular values are those professed, ideally at least, by all of the people of the United States." The ironic shading of "ideally at least" suggests that the secular values Ellison has in mind are freedom, justice, and equality rather than wine, women, and song. The manner in which these two sets of values coexist and interpenetrate in Negro culture is given some attention in the present book, but I should like to pursue for a moment the notion of freedom, justice, and equality and the related view expressed by many leading authorities that the Negro is the most American of all Americans.

It is certainly true that the traditional American ideals have been given an urgently needed rehabilitation from time to time by a few black citizens audacious enough to blurt out some strong complaints concerning America's long-standing and pervasive hypocrisy. A very small minority within the minority legitimately qualify as most American, I think, when they not only cling to the ideals of the American Revolution but go so far as to act on those ideals in the face of an affluent, complacent populace that, by and large, couldn't care less—throw them a law, a crumb, a prize or something, just get them off the streets! If Negroes try to remind Americans of their spiritual heritage, they also offer an awful parody of the traditional American lust for material possessions. The American status-symbol quest becomes an obsession in the Negro community, where conspicuous consumption—the acquisition of the biggest cars and the flashiest clothes—sometimes takes precedence over adequate food and shelter. Like his fellow Americans, the Negro is addicted to TV, loves baseball, and to a certain extent he even loathes and fears the Negro.

Elkins[15] and many others, including Ellison, have noted the similarities between Negroes in America and the prisoners in a concentration camp who tend to adjust to the brainwashing cruelties and degradations of life there by identifying with the oppressor. They mimic their godlike guards in viewing each other as less than men, and act accordingly. To the extent that Negro culture is a concentration-camp culture—and I am not sure that the analogy is all that valid—the Negro is very American indeed. When so-called Negro spokesmen and white liberals speak of the Negro's Americanness, however, the concentration-camp analogy and ugly facts of slum life are often dispensed with in favor of the dangerous illusion that the Negro is an all-American boy at heart, with a pleasant Protestant outlook and a nice Western kinship system, upholding "our" secular values and sharing "our" sense of time and history.

Almost any Negro in the presence of a white or black bourgeois interviewer or social worker can recite a stream of conventional American values and beliefs without a hitch, halt, or second thought. Yet it is also true that these are rarely the cultural guidelines by which the person reciting them lives The art of the "put on" has of necessity been developed to an exceptionally high level in Negro culture,[16] and the researcher or leader who reports recited values at face value may be putting us all on twice over.

It is not at all easy to probe beneath the shucking and jiving of Negroes and Negro experts for an unclouded view of Negro culture and man's place in it. My rebuttal to Ellison's generalizations, for example, is only a preliminary outline of urban lower-class Negro culture and a slightly lopsided one at that. It could be classified, I suspect, with the grim reality genre of writing on the Negro problem as exemplified by Charles Silberman's socioeconomic study *Crisis in Black and White*[17] and by Kardiner and Ovesey's psychodynamic analysis *Mark of Oppression*.[18] These analysts fail to do what Ellison has done so well. Concerned primarily with the pathological side of Negro life—what whites have done to Negroes—they ignore or obscure what Negroes have done for themselves.

In the late 1940's Abram Kardiner and Lionel Ovesey compiled a thoroughly depressing assortment of psychoanalytic case histories based upon information given by twenty-five residents of Harlem. The individual histories themselves are certainly of value in assessing the impact of oppression upon Negroes in America, but the chapters preceding and following the personal stories are marred by false premises and ignorance of Negro survival techniques. A long concluding chapter on "The Expressions of Negro Personality" dwells on crime and broken homes, devotes a few paragraphs to Father Divine, and overlooks completely such essential forms of expression as jazz, blues, and comedy. The authors' passing comments on folklore, religion, and Negro culture as a whole are indicative:

> He had no culture, and he was quite green in his semi-acculturated state in the new one. He did not know his way about and had no intra-psychic defenses—no pride, no group solidarity, no tradition. This

was enough to cause panic. The marks of his previous status were still upon him—socially, psychologically and emotionally. *And from these he has never since freed himself* [emphasis added].[19]

We have seen little evidence of genuine religiosity among Negroes. They have invented no religion of their own.[20] The Br'er Rabbit and Uncle Remus tales are the only remnants of anything that can be called folklore.[21]

These Spirituals and folk tales do not belong to the contemporary scene, and hence, cannot be used in any way to supplement our study of the present-day Negro personality. Where, then, can we look for such expression?[22]

If the authors had left their offices and gone out into the Negro community, this question as well as a number of omissions and silly assertions might have been avoided.

Charles Silberman, probably the most candid and sensible white American to express himself on "the crisis" in recent years, feels there is little hope for American democracy unless Negroes obtain quality education (particularly at the pre-school and primary-school levels), strong community self-help organizations, and a viable identity. I agree wholeheartedly. Silberman's discussions of Martin Deutsch's revolutionary pre-school program and Saul Alinsky's equally radical self-helping organizational techniques are strong and to the point. But his chapter on "The Problem of Identification" is rather pessimistic and only partly successful, since he too denigrates Negro culture and seems largely unaware of the resources available to the Negro in shaping a positive identity:

> In contrast to European immigrants, who brought rich cultures and long histories with them, the Negro has been completely stripped of his past and severed from any culture save that of the United States.[23]
>
> Negroes are both more than an ethnic group and less; though their color makes them far more identifiable than any ethnic group, they lack the common history and cultural traditions which the other groups share. The Negro's central problem is to discover his identity, or to create an identity for himself. What history suggests is that when the Negro solves his problem of identity, he will have gone a long way towards finding the means of relating himself to every other American group.[24]

The central problem is not so much to discover or create a new identity as, first, to accept an identity that is already available and, second, to transform into working assets whatever crippling liabilities may be associated with that identity.

Silberman, Kardiner, Ovesey, and many others have neglected that special domain of Negro culture wherein black men have proved and preserved their humanity. This domain or sphere of interest may be broadly defined as entertainment from the white or public point of view and as ritual, drama, or dialectical catharsis from the Negro or theoretical standpoint. By this I mean only that certain Negro performances, called "entertaining" by Negroes and whites alike, have an added but usually unconscious ritual significance for Negroes. The ritualists I have in mind are singers, musicians, preachers, comedians, disc jockeys, some athletes,[25] and perhaps a few Negro novelists as well. These entertainers are the ablest representatives of a long cultural tradition—what might be called the soul tradition—and they are all identity experts, so to speak, specialists in changing the joke and slipping the yoke. An analysis of the Negro's situation in America today, if it is to be thorough and constructive, must take these strategic figures into account.[26]

The entertainment component of Negro culture is significant in at least four basic respects. First, it is the one area in Negro life that was clearly not stripped away or obliterated by slavery—the rituals I speak of have an indisputable West African foundation. Second, unlike the immigrant cultural traditions which have been either diluted or dissolved almost completely in the American context, this important cultural legacy linking American Negroes to Africa has not only survived but has thrived on adversity and grown stronger through the years. Third, it is now a full-fledged tradition in its own right. One does not have to be a specialist in African cultures ever on the alert for Africanisms or a psychologist of race relations studiously attuned to the marks of oppression in order to understand a performance by B. B. King, a sermon by the Reverend C. L. Franklin, a Moms Mabley comedy routine, or a John Coltrane saxophone solo. Familiarity (preferably intimate) with contemporary Negro culture and some sensitivity to the particular form of expression in question—music, rhetoric, choreography—are the only basic analytic prerequisites. Finally, and most important, the entertainers are masters of sound, movement, timing, the spoken word. One can therefore find in their performances the essentials and defining features—the very core in fact—of Negro culture as a whole.

The unique and full status of Negro culture is only partly dependent on the basic institutional elements, such as Church and family, that do not fit white American specifications. On another and perhaps more fundamental level, the shared sensibilities and common understandings of the Negro ghetto, its modes of perception and expression, its channels of communication, are predominantly auditory and tactile rather than visual and literate.[27] Sensibilities are of course matters of degree, and the sense ratio or "ratio-nality" of a particular culture can't be measured precisely. Nevertheless, the prominence of aural perception, oral expression, and kinesic codes or body movement in Negro life—its sound and feel—sharply demarcate the culture from the irrational white world outside the ghetto.[28] Negro and white Americans share the same general language (superficially a good argument for those who would relegate the Negro to a subcultural corner in homogenized America),[29] but their attitudes toward that language are polarized. In white America, the printed word—the literary tradition—and its attendant values, are revered. In the Negro community, more power resides in the spoken word and oral tradition—good talkers abound and the best gain power and prestige, but good writers are scarce.[30] It is no accident that much of America's slang is provided by Negro culture.[31] Nor is it strange that Negro music and dance have become America's music and dance. . . .

What I have found initially mysterious, however, is the almost universal disregard for the cultural framework that has fostered these forms of expression. Writers, including writers on Negro life, have a vested interest in literacy and the visual world view, to be sure, and some may simply be deaf to the pervasive aural-oral qualities of Negro culture. Then too, real rhetoric and ritual, the pattern and form, heart and soul of Negro expression, are largely unknown in white America.[32] Indeed, the words themselves have taken on decidedly negative connotations—rhetoric: bombastic oratory, trickery, meaningless word play; ritual: dry formality, perfunctory action, unthinking and meaningless behavior. In the literary or typographic world, the labels mere rhetoric and ritualistic are the kiss of death. From this perspective, Negro culture heroes must appear as entertainers at best or at worst as clowns. Finally, a substantial number of influential Americans (politicians, white liberals, the Negro middle class) see Negro culture as a threat, if they can see it at all, for it is bound to make a mockery of hastily legislated integration.[33]

At this point let us look again to the literature on the Negro.

Two studies of the urban Negro have appeared in paperback form recently: *Black Metropolis*, by Cayton and Drake,[34] and *The Eighth Generation Grows Up*, by Rohrer and Edmonson.[35] Both offer a great deal of information on ghetto life in Chicago and New Orleans that the reader may find useful in evaluating and contextualizing the chapters which follow. These studies place justifiably strong emphasis on the cultural difference between lower-, middle-, and upper-class Negroes. The analytic theme of *Black Metropolis* is socio-economic; *The Eighth Generation Grows Up*, following an earlier work, *Children of Bondage*,[36] uses culture and personality as frames of reference. The two studies complement each other closely. *Black Metropolis* contains an excellent chapter on "The World of the Lower Class" devoted almost entirely to religious activities and attendant values.[37] The case histories presented in *The Eighth Generation Grows Up*, aided by generational time depth and an inter-disciplinary approach, are much superior to those found in *Mark of Oppression*, particularly the biographies in which the ramifications of mother-centeredness are elaborated. Again, however, both books treat the entertainment world as peripheral. Drake and Cayton persistently talk about good-timing and pleasure-seeking in the Chicago Negro community, but view such behavior as escapist and nothing more. Rohrer and Edmonson include a ludicrous appendix reporting the statistical frequency of certain psychological variables in a sample of "authentically New Orleanian jazz songs" and "creole folk songs" (no further stylistic specification or sampling criteria given) that must rate as a small but classic example of sterile statistical significance in social science.[38] Nevertheless, these books are indispensable reading for those who want a more complete picture of the existence that nurtures the urban blues.

Rohrer and Edmonson make a sharp distinction between lower-class Negro culture[39] and two shadow cultures: the entertainment world and the underworld. Cayton and Drake are somewhat closer to reality, I think, when they distinguish three extensively overlapping groups within the Negro lower class: "a large group of disorganized and broken families"; "church folk" trying to be respectable; and "denizens of the underworld." "The lines separating these three basic groups are fluid and shifting, and a given household may incorporate individuals of all three types."[40] On the basis of my own limited research into lower-class life, I would go further, suggesting that the hustler (or underworld denizen) and the entertainer are ideal types representing two important value orientations for the lower-class Negro and need not be distinguished from the lower class as a whole. Both the hustler and the entertainer are seen as men who are clever and talented enough to be financially well off without working. In this sense, a good preacher can be both a hustler and an entertainer in the eyes of his parishioners and the Negro community at large.

Most ways of making good money without working are illegal, and Henry Williamson has explored many of these ways in *The Hustler*.[41] The most striking thing about his autobiography is not the thoroughly criminal character of his life, from the white American point of view, but that within his culture he is very well adapted, successful (when out of jail), and even enjoys "doin' wrong." Most important, perhaps, "Henry's account is surprisingly free of any signs of racial strife. He wears his Negro image comfortably—neither disgruntled nor proud."[42] Aside from hustlers, entertainers, and rare individuals like Malcolm X (who began his career as hustler) or Reinhardt (the archetypal preacher-hustler in Ellison's *Invisible Man*), few Negroes wear their image in real comfort. Those black men who are comfortable in this sense become logical career models for those who aren't. If we are ever to understand what urban Negro culture is all about, we had best view entertainers and hustlers as culture heroes—integral parts of the whole—rather than as deviants or shadow figures.

Roger Abrahams' aims and techniques in studying Negro folklore are similar to my own in approaching the blues, and, as might be expected, I admire his work immensely.[43] He has managed to specify many of the cultural pressures and personal needs that illuminate a limited range of stylized speech forms in a specific community, in this case a Negro neighborhood in Philadelphia. This is a rare achievement and a definite break from the dry and crusty tradition of folklore scholarship. Abrahams persists in yanking texts out of their social context and compiling them, but he for the most part abjures the dissection of archaic forms, and he does concentrate upon cultural processes in his discussion chapters. He lived in the neighborhood, and this fact alone accounts for many of the book's rare qualities.

Abrahams interprets most of the lore he has gathered in terms of the matrifocal complex, the battle of the sexes, and the plight of the disadvantaged, dispossessed Negro male.[44] He argues convincingly that verbal contest skills, good-talking, and word control in general enable a man to play out some of his aggressions and "achieve a kind of precarious masculine identity for himself and his group in a basically hostile environment."[45] Since manhood and the related themes of sex, aggression, control, and identity are basic to any consideration of the blues, the notion of "a kind of precarious masculine identity" and the reasoning behind it deserve close scrutiny.

Much Freudian and neo-Freudian psychological theory has been applied to the predicament of the Negro male. I feel that these applications have suffered from oversimplification and ethnocentrism. Although I do not have much new data to contribute or a full alternative theory with which to subvert the prevailing interpretation of Negro masculinity, I would like to question some of the basic tenets of this interpretation.

Parts of Abrahams' exposition are fairly typical:

> Growing up in this matrifocal system, the boys receive little guidance from older males. There are few figures about during childhood through which the boys can achieve any sort of positive ego identity. Thus their ideas of masculinity are slow to appear under the tutelage of their mothers, and sometimes never do emerge.[46]
>
> Women, then, are not only the dispensers of love and care but also of discipline and authority.[47]
>
> He might, and does to some degree, react against his mother as the authority. But he is emotionally attached to his mother as the source of love and security. This attraction-repulsion paradox is further complicated by the fact that the trauma of rejection is persistently re-enacted for him. He sees his mother sharing herself not only with other children, but also often with numerous men. Finally, rejection comes completely when the boy begins to become the man, and the mother rejects him as a member of that other group.[48]
>
> Having been denied a natural development of his sense of manness, he must constantly prove to himself that he is a man. Throughout most of the rest of his life this will be his major preoccupation, his "fixation."[49]
>
> The spirit of contest . . . is exhibited in nearly every visible facet of the life of the Negro, from gang play to interplay between the sexes to clothes and choice of employment. And through it all the contests are self-defeating because they are never able to give the men a sense of their own identity. They remain throughout most of their lives men *manqué*.[50]

These observations have a certain logical coherence and theoretical validity. Absent or disreputable fathers and loving but authoritarian mothers would seem to foster a formidable set of Oedipal and identity complexities. Indeed, Abrahams' statements are easily related to the aggression and adolescent sexuality that percolate through much of the folklore he gathered.[51] But I take strong exception to the view that lower-class Negro life style and its characteristic rituals and expressive roles are the products of overcompensation for masculine self-doubt. This is simply not true.

To begin with, it is entirely possible that "the Oedipal problem of managing and diverting aggression against the father"[52] may be easily resolved, mitigated, or avoided altogether in families in which the father is absent or weak and where a number of mothering women (grandmothers, aunts) are in or near the household. Even a large set of siblings and a string of visiting "uncles" do not compete for a mother's attention as a potent and omnipresent father might. The "uncles" and other males in the vicinity certainly offer some identity models to a young man growing up, but his sexual development is relatively unimpeded by them.

There is also some evidence which suggests that many Negro mothers do an excellent job of inculcating a strong masculine identity in their little boys at an early age. Esther Newton reports that mothers frequently vilify all those "no-good men" and conclude their indictment with the assertion that they are saving all their love and affection for "my little man right here, he's going to grow up and be a real lady killer," in other words, a no-good man.[53] Will Mama reject him when he attains that status, as Abrahams insists? I doubt it. Rather, she will take vicarious satisfaction from the fact that he exploits and mistreats the girls while retaining a basic loyalty to Mama.

The hustling career of "Edward Dodge: Nameless Con," chronicled with wonder and consternation by Rohrer and Edmonson in The *Eighth Generation Grows Up*[54] undermines the logic and theory of those who worry excessively about Negro masculinity. I would like to include the whole case history here, but a brief summary and a few excerpts must suffice. Edward grew up under classic matrifocal conditions; his mother was on her sixth official husband—a traveling preacher—at the time of the study. She seems to have loved, neglected, and disciplined Edward in random fashion during his formative years. He ran with a gang, spent time in reform school. "At 13 he was having sexual relations 'often' with little girls at school. He started 'doing it,' he says, when he was eight." At maturity, he is a typical hustler, pushing narcotics and apparently using them off and on, in and out of jail, separated from his wife, still living at his mother's flat, leading the fast life.

The authors find him a hopeless case, manifesting masculine insecurity in the worst way:

> Edward has fears about his manliness that seem to be altogether unconscious. Crude defensive methods, such as his beard and the tattoo of a girl's bosom on his chest, are evidences of his conflict about this.
>
> . . . he sees himself unconsciously as weak and defenseless. He never admits this to himself; rather he idealizes himself as a powerful but misunderstood and mistreated man. He thinks he is a great lover, and even a proper family man, and he maintains this rationalization despite overwhelming evidence to the contrary.
>
> His morality is external. If he can get away with it, he does it. He is a hedonistic, impulsive man in conflict with a depriving world. He does not understand why this world should not grant him his infantile wishes for a stable of women, a fancy car, and a hundred suits.
>
> Despite his bravado and assertive masculinity, Edward has never been able to leave his mother, and he has long since internalized her

ambivalence towards crime. . . . In his heart of hearts, Edward knows himself to be a failure—weak, nameless, and criminal, and he is unhappy.

Edward's mother, however, sees things very differently:

> Mrs. Burton blames Edward's trouble on bad company and women, explaining that he had to obtain lots of money to be able to entertain his girl friends. She thinks of herself as an exceptionally fine mother, and claims to be proud of her son, but her pride is inconsistent. She praises Edward's accomplishments as a swimmer and boxer, as well as his abilities at outwitting the police, but . . . comments that "jail is just what he needs to straighten him out. . . ." Despite her conviction that women are the cause of Edward's troubles, his mother is exceedingly proud of his prowess as a lover, and delights in pointing out the number of good-looking girls he has had.
>
> The extent of his promiscuous activities can be gauged by the frequent references made to them by his mother and by the pictures of numerous girls in his mother's house. His expensive shirts and suits were proudly displayed to one interviewer by Mrs. Burton. . . .
>
> Edward's mother assures us that he has spent vast sums on whiskey and dope and good times. She is very proud of the fact that he was greatly sought after by the young men and women in his community. Men thought of him as a leader: women were proud to be seen with him.

One incident in particular gives the game away:

> His relation to his current girl friend is similarly structured, and similarly obscure. She also is a nurse, and also proved loyal to him when he was jailed. To some extent, in fact, this girl was able to enlist the cooperation of both Edward's wife and mother in her efforts on his behalf, and remarkably she and his wife shared his attention on visiting days at the jail more or less amicably. Edward expressed no emotion about this girl in any of his interviews, and indicated that he had no expectation that she would be faithful to him during his prison term. Yet he clearly has some genuine success with women. An even more casual girl friend who worked as a barmaid near his mother's home also tried to help raise money to get him out on bail before his trial.

I don't think there can be any reasonable doubt that Edward's mother, wife, mistress, and assorted girl friends feel that he is a man, and a fairly impressive man at that. Edward thinks so too. Some white middle-class social scientists, enchanted with psychoanalytic theory, disagree. Whose word are we to believe on the matter? Clearly, lower-class Negro culture includes a concept of manhood that differs in kind from the white middle-class definition of a man as a head of a household, who holds down a steady job and sends his kids to college. Measured against this standard, Edward may well be a pathological, amoral deviant with profound psychological problems; but as far as he and his women are concerned, he spends his money freely, dresses well, and is great in bed. That's just the way he is—*a man*—and they like him that way, despite the fact that he's obviously "no good."

Abrahams, like Rohrer and Edmonson, conveniently ignores the culture, and is led to equally disastrous conclusions by the same theory of "masculine self-doubt and ambivalence."

> The love-hate ambivalence [toward mother and women generally], on the other hand, is undoubtedly responsible for many of the apparent effeminate traits of this otherwise masculine group. "Don Juanism," the method of hair grooming reminiscent of the handkerchief tying of Southern "Mammies," the importance of falsetto voices in quartet singing, the high prevalence of lisping, the whole "dandy" feeling of dress and walk—all are explicable because of this ambivalence. The "ego ideal" of these men is a confused one; though rejecting women they have accepted unconsciously certain symbols and actions of females.[55]

All "the apparent effeminate traits" that Abrahams notes are largely figments of his psychoanalytic imagination.

My impression is that those entertainers and hustlers who might be described as Don Juans are simply using their cash and prestige to enjoy a wide variety of women. Although most bluesmen of my acquaintance don't qualify for the supposedly monogamous middle class, they have formed lasting attachments and relationships with their wives; they like to "play around" whenever they can, but are hardly the victims of an insatiable desire to conquer every woman in sight.

The hair-processing techniques that Abrahams finds "reminiscent of the handkerchief tying of Southern Mammies" are designed to heighten masculinity. Backstage at the Regal Theatre in Chicago "process rags" are everywhere in evidence among the male performers, the same performers who put the women in the audience into states that border on the ecstatic. Prettiness (wavy hair, manicured nails, frilly shirts, flashy jackets) plus strength, tender but tough—this is the style that many Negro women find irresistible. A blues singer is not unconsciously mimicking Elvis Presley's hairdo (the opposite may be true) or Aunt Jemima's when he straightens his hair and keeps it in place with a kerchief. He is enhancing his sex appeal—nothing more.

Falsetto singing comes directly from Africa, where it is considered to be the very essence of masculine expression. The smallest and highest-pitched drum in a West African percussion ensemble or "family" is designated the male drum because its tone is piercing and the role it plays is colorful, dynamic, and dominant. The falsetto techniques of a West African cabaret singer are sometimes indistinguishable from those employed so effectively by Ray Charles, B. B. King, or the lead voice in a gospel quartet.[56]

I have seen no evidence whatever for a "high prevalence of lisping" but "the whole 'dandy' feeling of dress and walk" is again more easily explained in terms of a distinctive masculine style, culturally defined. I see no reason for attributing such behavior to an underlying love-hate ambivalence toward women, even if this ambivalence can be shown to be an important factor in other areas of Negro life. Any sound analysis of Negro masculinity should first deal with the statements and responses of Negro women, the conscious motives of the men themselves, and the Negro cultural tradition. Applied in this setting, psychological theory may then be able to provide important new insights in place of basic and unfortunate distortions.

This is not to say that there are no ambivalent men in the Negro community or that Negro homosexuality shouldn't be studied [57]—quite the contrary. But there is an even more pressing need for a thorough, extensive, and intimate study of "normal" lower-class Negroes in a typical slum neighborhood. Most studies have focused upon abnormal Negroes out of context: those who found their way to the analyst's couch, or those who were willing to cooperate with inquisitive social scientists, most of whom were white. It is significant in this regard that Rohrer, Edmonson, and a large Negro and white staff found it extremely difficult to get any information from Edward Dodge, and most of his women and all his male cronies remained completely inaccessible. James Baldwin's *Go Tell It on the Mountain*[58] reminds us that some families are male-authoritarian rather than matrifocal, and undoubtedly many lower-class households do not fit easily into either category. The monumental works of Frazier[59] and Myrdal[60] (which need updating) and certain vivid slices of slum life included in *Black Metropolis* and *The Eighth Generation Grows Up* give further indications that the full range, variety, and complexity of day-to-day existence in America's black belts have yet to be fully revealed. It is only when more comprehensive studies of urban lower classes in other countries become available that we will be able to establish more effectively the parts that class, caste, urbanism, and ethnicity have played in shaping Negro culture and the diversity of individuals who are struggling to find identities within it.

Regardless of the forces which have shaped Negro culture, it exists, and within this culture a number of individuals have already found viable identities as men and women. In this respect, the entertainers in general and today's bluesmen in particular are outstanding—they take a firm stance at the center of contemporary Negro culture. If black Americans are to be free and if white Americans are to learn something essential concerning themselves from the Negro's effort to identify himself, a good beginning can be made by attempting to find out what the urban blues are all about.

Notes

1. Some of the implications of urbanism and poverty are spelled out by Louis Wirth, "Urbanism as a Way of Life," *American Journal of Sociology* XLIV (1938), and by Michael Harrington, *The Other America* (New York, 1963).
2. Ralph Ellison, *Shadow and Act* (New York, 1964), p. 262.
3. Melville J. Herskovits, *The Myth of the Negro Past* (Boston, 1958), p. 2. Much of the myopic ignorance concerning Negro culture and styles that Nat Hentoff and I find so lamentable derives from the premature resolution of a debate between E. Franklin Frazier and Melville J. Herskovits (*The Negro in the United States*, rev. ed., New York, 1957). In his book, Herskovits attempted a thorough comparative study of African-derived cultures in the New World for the insights such a study might provide *vis-à-vis* "the American dilemma." Unfortunately, Herskovits overstated his case in the area of social organization when he insisted that the matrifocal family, economic independence of women, sexual attitudes, extended kinship patterns, and so on that are found in both contemporary West African cultures and American Negro communties can be seen as evidence of a tenacious, if somewhat generalized, set of familial values that were retained despite slavery. Frazier disagreed completely with this interpretation of the data, and I agree with him in this particular dispute. Slavery, as practiced in the United States at least, obliterated all but the faintest traces of African political, economic, and familial institutions. These aspects of life were rigidly controlled by the white slave masters. On the other hand, basic African predispositions governing religion and esthetics not only survived slavery, but were reshaped, nurtured, and magnified in response to slavery and post-slavery conditions. The facts that support this statement are available in abundance to anyone who will read *The Myth of the Negro Past.* Journalists and social scientists writing about the Negro in the past decade or so have invariably accepted Frazier's refutation of Herskovits' familial theories and have then proceeded to dismiss the rest of Herskovits' painstaking scholarship as well. Therefore, many writers have not even bothered to consult Herskovits' book before labeling the Negro traditionless, cultureless, and made in America.
4. No one can deny these two brute facts of ghetto life, but it is possible to show how a few Negroes have managed to survive and transcend them. I would also like to suggest that affluent white America suffers from spiritual impoverishment and that the suburban child is just as culturally deprived as his urban counterpart. Considering the white anxieties triggered by those unpredictable black forces penned up in the centers of American cities, contemplating the fifty billion dollars poured annually into that monument

to terror, the Pentagon, and noting with alarm the growing generation of snipers, bombers, Minute Men, Birchers, and Klansmen, it also seems clear where the designation "culture of fear" belongs.

5. *The Village Voice*, January 7, 1965, pp. 5, 16.

6. *Shadow and Act*, p. 263.

7. *Ibid.*, p. 262.

8. The Negro middle and upper classes form a special and rather "sick" American subculture according to two highly critical "participant observers." E. Franklin Frazier's *Black Bourgeoisie* (Glencoe, 1957) and Nathan Hare's recent vendetta *The Black Anglo-Saxons* (New York, 1965) do little more than ridicule the middle class as hopelessly trapped and deluded. A more sympathetic and constructive analysis of the difficulties faced by "newly arrived" Negroes, leavened perhaps with some humor, would be helpful and most refreshing at this point, it seems to me.

9. Weston LaBarre, *They Shall Take Up Serpents* (Minneapolis, 1962).

10. John H. Rohrer and Munro S. Edmonson, eds., *The Eighth Generation Grows Up* (New York, 1960), p. 129.

11. For a full and excellent discussion of sex role definitions and finance-romance relationships in the Negro community, see Esther Newton's "Men, Women and Status in the Negro Family" (unpublished Master's thesis, University of Chicago, 1964).

12. *Advertisements for Myself* (New York, l960), pp. 302–21.

13. Oscar Lewis, *The Children of Sanchez* (New York, 1963).

14. Compare Lewis' account of the Sanchez family in Mexico with the picture of Rio de Janeiro slums given in *Child of the Dark: The Diary of Carolina María de Jesús* (New York, 1962).

15. Stanley M. Elkins, *Slavery: A Problem in American Institutional and Intellectual Life* (Chicago, 1959).

16. The problem of distinguishing the skillful "put-on" from sincere "wishful thinking" is as important as it is complicated. In either, recited values often conflict with actual behavior. Do the reciters wish to be acceptable citizens, or do they want to push off (put on) agents of welfare colonialism and the white status quo so as to maintain their own way of life undisturbed? I suspect that most urban Negroes have both goals—white acceptance and Negro identity—dimly in view. Question: are these goals incompatible or complementary?

17. Silberman, *Crisis in Black and White* (New York: Random House, 1964).

18. *The Mark of Oppression* by Abram Kardiner and Lionel Ovesey (Cleveland and New York, 1951).

19. *Ibid.*, p. 384.

20. *Ibid.*, p. 385.

21. *Ibid.*, p. 340.

22. *Ibid.*, p. 341.

23. Silberman, *op. cit.*, p. 109.

24. *Ibid.*, p. 166.

25. I would not contest the usual argument that entertainment channels, broadly speaking, have been the only ones consistently open to Negroes in American society. It is important to note, however, that these ritualized forms developed within Negro culture and were only secondarily, if at all, patronized and

appropriated by the American majority. Even when Negroes have contributed to established white American entertainment forms (sports, for example), a distinctively Negro style often shapes or accompanies that contribution. The nothing ball and sucker ball as pitched by Satchel Paige, the base as stolen by Maury Wills, the basket catches of Willie Mays, the antics of the Harlem Globetrotters, the beautiful ritualization of an ugly sport by Sonny Liston and Mohammad Ali—a full list of the symbolic transformations accomplished by Negro magicians in the sporting world would be most impressive.

26. This entertainment-ritual tradition probably does not provide, in itself, a satisfactory solution to the identity problem, and Silberman is quite correct in stressing the impact of emerging Africa on the Negro's self esteem. But identification with contemporary Africa and the African past must be consciously sought, indeed, created for the most part, whereas the soul tradition is home-grown (with African seeds), already created, and ready to be used. A mixture of indigenous soul and restored ties to West African cultural and historical traditions may ultimately resolve the identity confusion. . . .

27. To appreciate the many ramifications and implications of this statement, see Marshall McLuhan's fascinating study of print technology's impact on the Western world, *The Gutenberg Galaxy.* If McLuhan's thesis is correct, the electronic or post-literate age and its high powered auditory forces that are now upon us ought to give Negro culture a big technological boost.

28. An essay I have written, "Motion and Feeling through Music," *Journal of Aesthetics* (Spring, 1966), considers the kinesic aspect of music and adds a few pieces to McLuhan's "simultaneous mosaic."

29. Englishmen and Americans use the same language, yet references to the American subculture are rare, even in the English anthropological literature.

30. The two writers who have merited most acclaim both served sound apprenticeships: James Baldwin as a preacher, Ralph Ellison as a musician.

31. Approximately 90 percent of the words that appear in the Sunday supplement slang glossaries can be traced to Negro culture. See also the dialogue in Clayton Riley's "Now That Henry Is Gone," *Liberator* V (July, 1965).

32. A thorough revamping of slum schools along ritualized and rhetorical lines (using the Lancasterian system as a starting point) would do far more to increase student motivation than all the Negro history, Negro contribution, and higher horizon courses combined. What is being taught to Negro children is certainly demoralizing enough, but the typographic manner in which it is being taught is even more destructive. A high degree of literacy should be one goal among many.

33. For the humor involved, listen to Moms Mabley's "Little Cindy Ella" monologue. Moms' recorded works (at least eight albums) are a singularly rich reservoir of Negro oral expression. When folklorists finally wake up to the fact that the electronic media are making folk of us all, I'm sure this repository of lore will receive the volumes of analysis it deserves.

34. Rev. ed., Vols. I and II (New York, 1962).

35. New York, 1964.

36. Allison Davis and John Dollard (Washington, 1940).

37. The quality of this chapter was an important factor in my decision not to explore the intimate relationship between sacred and secular roles in greater detail.

38. For a book-length classic in the same vein, see Neil Leonard's *Jazz and the White Americans* (Chicago, 1962).

39. Within the lower-class culture they articulate very clearly the opposing value orientations of the matriarchy and the gang.

40 *Op. cit.*, p. 600.

41. This is the autobiography of Henry Williamson, edited by R. Lincoln Kaiser, with a commentary by Paul Bohannan (New York, 1965).

42. Bohannan, *ibid.*, p. 215.

43. Roger D. Abrahams, *Deep Down in the Jungle . . . Negro Narrative Folklore from the streets of philadelphia* (Hatboro, Pa.: Folklore Associates, 1964).

44. I might add that all the materials were collected from a few men, since the author found the barrier between men and women and the boundaries of alien neighborhoods insurmountable.

45. *Ibid.*, p. 63.

46. *Ibid.*, p. 31.

47. *Ibid.*

48. *Ibid.*, p. 32.

49. *Ibid.*, p. 34.

50. *Ibid.*, p. 38.

51. And most of the lore seems to have been gathered from adolescents.

52. Erik Erikson, "Ego Development and Historical Change" in *Psychological Issues*, George S. Klein, ed. (New York, 1959), p. 29.

53. Personal communication.

54. All the following citations are from pp. 168–85.

55. Abrahams, *op. cit.*, p. 33.

56. I should like to stress again, however, that an Africanism argument may be both relevant and interesting, but it is not necessary to establish this point. If Negro women jump and shout when B. B. King cuts loose with a high falsetto, that is really all we need to know.

57. The nature of Negro homosexuality is a problem that needs to be explored in depth. A typology of faggots and Lesbians, coupled with the types of familial organization that tend to promote deviance, might go far in clearing the haze of illusion and controversy that surrounds Negro sexuality. I suspect that a surprising number of lower-class Negro men and women are ambisexual, homo- or hetero- according to circumstances. I might add that I have noticed a high tolerance of sexual deviancy in some Chicago blues bars. I would also agree with Gershon Legman (in Abrahams, *op. cit.*, p. 29) that matrifocality probably produces more deviancy among daughters than sons. But all these issues need further study before suspicions will give way to reasonable interpretations.

58. New York, 1953.

59. E. Franklin Frazier, *The Negro Family in the United States* (Chicago, 1939).

60. Gunnar Myrdal, *An American Dilemma: The Negro Problem and Modern Democracy* (New York, 1944).

Ulf Hannerz, a Swedish anthropologist, recently spent a year in Washington, DC., examining one aspect of lower-class Negro life: the phenomenon called "soul." Unlike Charles Keil, Hannerz did not conclude that "soul" is something unique to the black American. Rather, he viewed it as a crutch on which Negroes have come to lean in an uncertain era when, he says, it is becoming easier to enter the mainstream of American life.

While Hannerz's interpretation has already been subjected to much criticism, there are those who describe the emergence of "Black Alliances" on the campus in very similar terms, viewing the "rhetoric of soul" in instrumental rather than expressive terms.

16

The Rhetoric of Soul

Ulf Hannerz

I

The last few years have witnessed the emergence of a concept of "soul" as signifying what is "essentially Negro" in the black ghettos of the large cities of the Northern United States. In this paper, I will attempt to place this concept of "soul" in its social and cultural matrix, in particular with respect to tendencies of social change as experienced by ghetto inhabitants. In doing so, I will emphasize what I believe to be the dominant purpose of a "soul" vocabulary among its users. There will be clear points of convergence between my view of "soul" and that stated by Charles Keil in his book *Urban Blues.*[1] However, I believe that Keil's personal evaluation of some of the features of black ghetto culture tends to obscure the issue in some

From Ulf Hannerz, "The Rhetoric of Soul: Identification in Negro Society," *Race: A Journal of Race and Group Relations,* 9(April 1968), 453–465. Published by The Institute of Race Relations, London.

ways, and I also feel that a clearer picture of the essential social-structural and social-psychological features may be achieved.

This paper is based on field work in a lower-class Negro neighborhood in Washington, D.C. The field site seems to be in many ways typical of Negro slums in Northern American cities. It is situated at the edge of a large, ethnically homogeneous area. Its inhabitants share the common characteristics of America's lower-class urban Negroes: poverty, a high rate of unemployment, a considerable amount of crime, including juvenile delinquency, and widely varying family role-structures according to which it is relatively common that the adult woman dominates the family while the male is either absent or only temporarily attached—even when he is a permanent member of the household his participation in household affairs may be quite limited. (It should be noted that this is not said to be true of all households—it is only pointed out that unstable family relationships and female dominance are much more common among lower-class Negroes than among the American people in general.) Of the adults at the field site—a block-long street lined by two- or three-story row houses—a minority was born in Washington, D.C. The majority are immigrants from the South, particularly from Virginia, North Carolina, and South Carolina. Apart from conducting field work in this area by means of participant observation in the traditional sense, I have paid attention to those impersonal media which have a significant part in ghetto life; these are particularly important in the context of this study. I refer here to media which are specifically intended for a lower-class Negro audience: radio (three stations in Washington, D.C., are clearly aimed at Negroes), the recording industry, and stage shows featuring Negro rock-and-roll artists and comedians. (The term "rhythm and blues" used by whites to denote Negro rock-and-roll is now only infrequently used by the Negroes themselves.) These media have played a prominent part in promoting the vocabulary of "soul." (It may be added, on the other hand, that both the local Negro press such as the Washington *Afro-American*, and the national Negro publications, for example the monthly *Ebony*, are largely middle-class oriented and thus of limited value in the understanding of life in the ghetto where few read them.)

II

What, then, is "soul"? As the concept has come to be used in urban ghettos over the last number of years, it stands for what is "the essence of Negroness" and, it should be added, this "Negroness" refers to the kind of Negro with which the urban slum dweller is most familiar—people like himself. The question whether a middle-class, white-collar suburban Negro also has "soul" is often met with consternation. In fact, "soul "seems to be a folk conception of the lower-class urban Negro's own "national character." Modes of action, personal attributes, and certain artifacts are given the "soul" label. Typically, in conversations, one hears statements such as, "Man, he got a lot of soul." This appreciative opinion may be given concerning anybody in the ghetto, but more often by younger adults or adolescents about others of their own categories. In particular, speaking in terms of "soul" is common among younger men. This sex differentiation of the use of "soul" conceptions, I will suggest below, may be quite important in the understanding of the basis of the use of the "soul" concept.

The choice of the term "soul" for this "Negroness" is in itself note-worthy. First of all, it shows the influence of religion on lower-class Negroes, even those who are not themselves active church members—expressions of religious derivation, such as "God, have mercy!" are frequent in everyday speech among lower-class Negroes of all age and sex categories, and in all contexts. A very great number of people, of course, have been regular church goers at some point or other, at least at the time when they attended Sunday school, and many are actively involved in church activities, perhaps in one of the large Baptist churches but at least as often in small spiritualist storefront churches. Although the people who use the "soul" vocabulary in which we are interested here are seldom themselves regular church-goers, they have certainly been fully (although sometimes indirectly) exposed to the religious idiom; including such phrases as "a soul-stirring revival meeting."

Furthermore, the choice of a term which in church usage has a connotation of "the essentially human" to refer to "the essentially Negro," as the new concept of "soul" does, certainly has strong implications of ethnocentrism. If "soul" is Negro, the non-Negro is "non-soul," and, it appears, somewhat less human. Although I have never heard such a point of view spelled out, it would seem to me that it is implicitly accepted as part of an incipient "soul" ideology. It is very clear that what is "soul" is not only different from what is not "soul" (particularly what is mainstream middle-class American); it is also superior. "Soul" is an appraisive as well as dcsignative concept.[2] If one asks a young man what a "soul brother" is, the answer is usually something like "someone who's hip, someone who knows what he's doing." It may be added here that although both "soul brother" and "soul sister" are used for "soul" personified, the former is more common. Like "soul," "soul brother" and "soul sister" are terms used particularly by younger males.

Let us now note a few fields that are particularly "soul." One area is that of music (where the concept may have originated—see the article on the "soul" movement among jazz musicians by Szwed),[3] particularly the field of progressive jazz and rock-and-roll. This has been seized upon by those actively engaged in these fields. James Brown, a leading rock-and-roll singer, is often referred to as "Soul Brother Number One"; two of the largest record stores in Washington, D.C., with practically only Negro customers, are the "Soul Shack" and the "Soul City." Recently a new magazine named "Soul" appeared; its main outlet seems to be these *de facto* segregated record stores. It contains stories on rock-and-roll artists, disc jockeys, and the like. Excellence in musical expression is indeed a part of the lower-class Negro self-conception, and white rock-and-roll is often viewed with scorn as a poor imitation of the Negro genius. Resentment is frequently aimed at the Beatles who stand as typical of white intrusion into a Negro field. (Occasionally, a Beatle melody has become a hit in the Negro ghetto as well, but only when performed in a local version by a Negro group, such as the recordings of "Day Tripper" by the Vontastics. In such a case, there is little or no mention of its Beatles origin.)

The commercial side of Negro entertainment is, of course, directly tied to "soul" music. With counterparts in other large Negro ghettos in the United States, the Howard Theater in Washington stages shows of touring rock-and-roll groups and individual performers—each show usually runs a week, with four or five performances every day. Larger shows also make one-night only appearances at the Washington Coliseum. Occasionally, a comedian also takes part; Moms Mabley, Pigmeat Markham, or Redd Foxx are among those who draw large Negro audiences but few whites.

The "emcees" of these shows are often celebrities in their own right—some, such as "King" Coleman and "Georgeous George," tour regularly with the shows, others are local disc jockeys from the Negro radio stations. In Washington, such disc jockeys as "The Nighthawk" (Bob Terry), and "Soulfinger" (Fred Correy), make highly appreciated appearances at the Howard. Their station is WOL "Soul Radio" : it is clear that the commercial establishments with a vested interest in a separate Negro audience have seized upon the "soul" vocabulary, using it to further their own interests as well as supporting its use among the audience. Thus there is also for instance a WWRL "soul brother radio" in New York. However, one should not view the "soul" vocabulary solely as a commercial creation. It existed before it was commercialized, and the fact that it seems so profitable for commercial establishments to fly the banner of "soul" also indicates that whatever part these establishments have had in promoting it, it has fallen into fertile ground.

A second area of widespread "soul" symbolism is that of food. The dishes that are now "soul food" were once—and still are to some extent—referred to simply as "Southern cooking"; but in the Northern ghettos they increasingly come to stand for race rather than religion. In the center of the Washington Negro area, for instance, there is a "Little Harlem Restaurant" advertising "soul food." There are a number of such foods; some of those which are most frequently mentioned as "soul foods" are chitterlings (a part of the intestine of the pig), hog maw (pig tripe), black-eyed peas, collard greens, corn bread, and grits (a kind of porridge). Typically, they were the poor man's food in the rural South—in the urban North, they may still be so to some extent, but in the face of the diversity of the urban environment, they also come to stand as signs of ethnicity. (Thus in some Northern cities there are "soul food" restaurants catering to curious whites, much in the same way as any exotic cuisine.) One may note that references to "soul food" occur frequently in "soul music"; two of the hits of the winter 1966–67 were "Grits and Corn-bread" by the Soul Runners and the Joe Cuba Sextet's "Bang! Bang!" with the refrain "corn bread, hog maw and chitterling." Sometimes, the names of "soul foods" may themselves be used as more or less synonymous with "soul"—Negro entertainers on stage, talking of their experiences while journeying between ghetto shows around the country, sometimes refer to it as "the chitterling circuit," and this figure of speech usually draws much favorable audience reaction.

What, then, is "soul" about "soul music" and "soul food?" It may be wise to be cautious here, since there is little intellectualizing and analyzing on the part of the ghetto's inhabitants on this subject. I believe that this comparative absence of defining activity may itself be significant, and I will return to this possibility below. Here, I will only point to a few basic characteristics of what is "soul" which I feel make it particularly "essentially Negro"—referring again, of course, to urban lower-class Negroes rather than to any other category of people.

There is, of course, the Southern origin. The "Down Country" connotations are particularly attached to "soul food"; however, although Negro music has changed more and the contemporary commercial rock-and-roll is an urban phenomenon, it is certainly seen as the latest stage of an unfolding musical heritage. Thus the things that are "soul," while taking on new significance in the urban environment, provide some common historical tradition for ghetto inhabitants. One might also speculate on the possibility that the early and from then on constant and intimate exposure to these foods and to this music—for radios and record players seem to belong to practically every poor ghetto home—may make them appear particularly basic to a "Negro way of life."

When it comes to "soul" music, there are a couple of themes in style and content which I would suggest are pervasive in ghetto life and which probably make them appear very close to the everyday experience of ghetto inhabitants.

One of these is the lack of control over the social environment. There is a very frequent attitude among "soul brothers"—that is, the ghetto's younger males—that one's environment is somewhat like a jungle where tough, smart people may survive and where a lot happens to make it worth while and enjoyable just to "watch the scene" if one does not have too high hopes of controlling it. Many of the reactions in listening to "progressive jazz" seem to connect to this view; "Oooh, man, there just ain't nothing you can do about it but sit there and feel it goin' all the way into you." Without being able to do much about proving it, I feel that exposure to experiences—desirable or undesirable—in which one can only passively perceive events without influencing them is an essential fact of ghetto life, for better or for worse; thus it is "soul."

Related to this is the experience of unstable personal relationships, in particular between the sexes. It is a well-known fact that among lower-class urban Negroes there are many "broken" families (households without a husband and father), many temporary common-law unions, and in general relatively little consensus on sex roles. Thus, it is not much of an exaggeration to speak of a constant "battle of the sexes," and the achievement of success with the opposite sex is a focal concern in lower-class Negro life. From this area come most of the lyrics of contemporary rock-and-roll music. It may be objected that this is true of white rock-and-roll as well; to this it may be answered that this is very much to the point. For white rock-and-roll is predominantly adolescent music, thus reaching people with similar problems of unstable personal relationships. In the case of lower-class urban Negroes, such relationships are characteristic of a much wider age-range, and music on this theme also reaches this wider range. Some titles of recent rock-and-roll hits may show this theme: "I'm losing you" (Temptations), "Are you lonely" (Freddie Scott), "Yours until tomorrow" (Dee Dee Warwick), "Keep me hangin' on" (Supremes). "Soul" stands for a bitter-sweet experience; this often arises from contacts with the other sex, although there are certainly also other sources. This bitter-sweetness, of course, was typical already of the blues.

Turning to style, a common element in everyday social interaction as well as among storefront church preachers, Negro comedians, and rock-and-roll singers is an alternation between aggressive, somewhat boasting behavior, and plaintive behavior from an implicit underdog position.

This may not be the place to give a more detailed account of this style of behavior. However, as I said, it occurs in many situations and may itself be related to the unstable personal relationships, and the concomitant unstable self-conception, which was mentioned above. In any case, it seems that this style is seen as having "soul"; without describing its elements, "soul brothers" tend to describe its occurrences in a variety of contexts.

As I noted above, I have hesitated to try to analyze and define "soul," because what seems to be important in the emergence of the present "soul" concept is the fact that there is felt to be *something* which is "soul" rather than *what* that something is. There is, of course, some logic to this; if "soul" is what is "essentially Negro," it should not be necessary for "soul brothers" to spend too much time analyzing it. Asking about "soul" one often receives answers such as "you know, we don't talk much about it, but we've all been through it, so we know what it is anyway." Probably, this is to some extent true. What the lack of pronounced definition points to, in that case, is that "soul" vocabulary is predominantly for in-group consumption. It is a symbol of solidarity among the people of the ghetto, but not in more than a weak and implicit sense of solidarity *against* anybody else. "Soul" is turned inward; and so everybody who is touched by it is supposed to know what it means. So far there has been little interference with the "soul" vocabulary by outsiders, at least in any way noticeable to the ghetto dwellers. There have been none of the fierce arguments about its meaning which have developed around "black power," a concept which did not really evolve in the ghetto but is largely the creation of white mass media. "Black power" is controversial, and so white people insist on a definition. (And many black people, also depending on white media for news, tend to accept the interpretations of these media.) "Soul" is not equally threatening, and so ghetto dwellers can keep its mystique to themselves.

We may note in this context that the few interpreters of "soul" to the outside world are, in fact, outsiders; a kind of cultural brokers who give interested members of the larger society the "inside stuff" on the ghetto. But serving as such brokers, they hardly affect the uses of "soul" within the ghetto community. LeRoi Jones, the author, a convert to ghetto life who like so many converts seems to have become more militantly partisan than the more authentic ghetto inhabitants, has moved from a position where he rather impartially noted the ethnocentric bias of "soul"[4] to one where he preaches for the complete destruction of the present American society,[5] an activist program which I am sure is far out of step with the immediate concerns of the average "soul brother." Bennett, an editor of the middle-class *Ebony* magazine, is not particularly interested in "the folk myth of soul" but explains what he feels that 'soul' really is.[6] I am not convinced that his conception is entirely correct; it is certainly not expressed in the idiom of the ghetto. Keil, an ethnomusicologist, probably comes closer to the folk conception than anyone else, by giving what amounts to a catalogue of those ghetto values and experiences which its inhabitants recognize as their own.[7] In doing so, of course, one does not get a short and comprehensive definition of "soul" that is acceptable to all and in every situation—one merely lists the fields in which a vocabulary of "soul" is particularly likely to be expressed. This, of course, is what has been done in a partial and parsimonious way above.

Here we end the exposition of the "soul" concept. Summing up what has been said so far, the vocabulary of "soul," which is a relatively recent phenomenon, is used among younger Negro ghetto dwellers, and particularly young men, to designate in a highly approving manner the experiences and characteristics which are "essentially Negro." As such it is not an activist vocabulary for use in inter-group relations but a vocabulary which is employed within the group, although it is clear that by discussing what is "typically Negro" one makes an implicit reference to the non-Negro society. We turn now to an interpretation of the emergence of such a vocabulary in this group at this point of Negro history.

III

For a long time, the social boundaries which have constituted barriers to educational, economic and other achievement by Negro Americans have been highly impermeable. Although lower-class Negroes have to a considerable degree accepted the values of mainstream American culture in those areas, the very obviousness of the impermeability of social boundaries has probably prevented a more complete commitment to the achievement of those goals which have been out of reach. Instead, there has been an adjustment to the lower-class situation in which goals and values more appropriate to the ascribed social position of the group have been added to, and to some extent substituted for, the mainstream norms. Whether these lower-class concerns, experiences, and values are direct responses to the situation or historically based patterns for which the lower-class niche provides space is not really important here. What is important is that the style of life of the lower class, in this case the Negro lower class, is different from that of the upper classes, and that the impermeability of group boundaries and the unequal distribution of resources between groups have long kept the behavioral characteristics of the groups relatively stable and distinct from one another, although to a great extent, one of the groups—the lower-class Negroes—would have preferred the style of life of the other group—the middle-class whites—had it been available to them. As it has been, they have only been able to do the best with what they have had. In a way, then, they have had two cultures, the mainstream culture with which they are relatively familiar, which has in many ways appeared superior and preferable, and which has been closed to them, and the ghetto culture which is a second choice and based on the circumstances of the ascribed social position. (I will not dwell here on the typical features of the two cultures and the relationship between them; articles by Miller[8] and Rodman[9] are enlightening discussions of these topics.)

This, of course, sounds to some extent like the position of what has often been called "the marginal man." Such a position may cause psychological problems. However, when the position is very clearly defined and where the same situation is shared by many, the situation is perhaps reasonably acceptable—there is a perfectly understandable reason for one's failure to reach one's goal. Nobody of one's own kind is allowed to reach that goal, and the basis of the condition is a social rule rather than a personal failure. There are indications that marginality is more severely felt if the barrier is not absolute but boundary permeability is possible although uncertain. According to Kerckhoff and McCormick,

> an absolute barrier between the two groups is less conducive to personality problems than "grudging, uncertain and unpredictable acceptance." The impact of the rejection on an individual's personality organization will depend to some extent upon the usual treatment accorded members of his group by the dominant group. If his group as a whole faces a rather permeable barrier and he meets with more serious rejection, the effect on him is likely to be more severe than the same treatment received by a more thoroughly rejected group (one facing an impermeable barrier).[10]

My thesis here is that recent changes in race relations in the United States have indeed made the social barriers to achievement at least seem less impermeable than before to the ghetto population. One often hears people in the ghetto expressing opinions such as, "Yeh, there are so many programs, job-training and things, going on, man, so if you got anything on the ball you can make it." On the other hand, there are also assertions about the impossibility of getting anywhere which contradict the first opinion. Obviously, the clear-cut exclusion from mainstream American culture is gradually being replaced by ambivalence about one's actual chances. This ambivalence, of course, seems to represent an accurate estimate of the situation; the lower-class Negro continues to be disadvantaged, although probably his chances of moving up and out are somewhat better than earlier—people do indeed trickle out of the ghetto.

It is in this situation that the ethnocentric vocabulary of "soul" has emerged, and I want to suggest that it is a response to the uncertainty of the ghetto dweller's situation. This uncertainty is particularly strong for the younger male, the "soul brother." While women have always been able to live closer to mainstream culture norms, as homemakers and possibly with a type of job keeping them in touch with the middle-class world, men have had less chance to become competent in mainstream culture as well as to practice it. Older men tend to feel that current social changes come too late for them but put higher expectations on the following generation. Thus the present generation of young men in the Negro ghettos of the United States are placed in a new situation to which it is making new responses, and much of the unrest in the ghettos today is perhaps the result of these emerging pressures.

I will suggest here that this new situation must be taken into account if we are to understand the basis of the emergence of the "soul" vocabulary. The increasing ambivalence in conceptions of one's opportunities in the changing social structure may be accompanied by doubts about one's own worth. Earlier, the lack of congruence between mainstream culture norms and the lower-class Negro's achievements could easily be explained by referring to the social barriers. Under-achievement with respect to mainstream norms was an ascribed characteristic of lower-class Negroes. However, when as at present the suspicion arises, which may very well be mistaken, that under-achievement is not ascribed but due to one's own failure, self-doubt may be the result. Such doubt can be reduced in different ways. Some, of course, are able to live up to mainstream norms of achievement, thereby reducing the strain on themselves (but at the same time increasing that on others). Higher self-esteem can also be arrived at by affirming that the boundaries are still impermeable. A third possibility is to set new standards for achievement, proclaiming one's own achievements to be the ideals. It is not necessary, of course, that the same way of reducing self-doubt is always applied. In the case of "soul," the method is that of idealizing one's own achievements, proclaiming one's own way of life to be superior. Yet the same "soul brother" may argue at other times that they are what they are because they are not allowed to become anything else.

In any case, "soul" is by native public definition "superior," and the motive of the "soul" vocabulary, I believe, is above all to reduce self-doubt by persuading "soul brothers" that they are successful. Being a "soul brother" is belonging to a select group instead of to a residual category of people who have not succeeded. Thus, the "soul" vocabulary is a device of rhetoric. By talking about people who have "soul," about "soul music" and about "soul food," the "soul brother" attempts to establish himself in an expert and connoisseur role; by talking to others of his group in these terms, he identifies with them and confers the same role on them. Using "soul" rhetoric is a way of convincing others of one's own worth and of their worth; it also serves to persuade the speaker himself. As Burke expresses it,

> A man can be his own audience, insofar as he, even in his secret thoughts, cultivates certain ideas or images for the effect he hopes they may have upon him; he is here what Mead would call "an 'I' addressing its 'me'"; and in this respect he is being rhetorical quite as though he were using pleasant imagery to influence an outside audience rather than one within.[11]

The "soul" vocabulary has thus emerged from the social basis of a number of individuals, in effective interaction with one another, with similar problems of adjustment to a new situation. The use of "soul" rhetoric is a way of meeting their needs as long as it occurs in situations where they can mutually support each other. Here is, of course, a clue to the confinement of the rhetoric to in-group situations. If "soul" talk were directed toward outsiders, they might not accept the claims for its excellence—it is not their "folk myth." Viewing "soul" as such a device of rhetoric, it is also easier to understand why it is advantageous for its purposes not to have made it the topic of too much intellectualizing. As Geertz makes clear in his paper on "Ideology as a Cultural System,"[12] by analyzing and defining activity, one achieves maximum intellectual clarity at the expense of emotional commitment. It is doubtful that "soul" rhetoric would thrive on too much intellectual clarity; rather, by expressing "soul" ideals in a circumspect manner in terms of emotionally charged symbols such as "soul food" and "soul music," one can avoid the rather sordid realities underlying these emotions. As I pointed out above, the shared lower-class Negro experiences which seem to be the bases of "soul" are hardly in themselves such as to bring out a surge of ethnicpride. That is a psychological reason for keeping the "soul" concept diffuse. There is also, I believe, a sociological basis for the diffuseness. The more exactly a "soul brother" would define "soul," the fewer others would probably agree upon the "essential Negroness" of his definition; and, as we have seen, a basic idea of the rhetoric of "soul" is to cast others into roles which satisfy them and at the same time support one's own position. If people are cast into a role of "soul brother" and then find that there has been a definition established for that role which they cannot accept, the result may be overt disagreement and denial of solidarity rather than mutual deference. As it is, "soul" can be an umbrella concept for a rather wide variety of definitions of one's situation, and the "soul brothers" who are most in need of the ethnocentric core conception can occasionally get at least fleeting allegiance to "soul" from others with whom in reality they share relatively little, for instance individuals who are clearly upwardly mobile. On one occasion I listened to a long conversation about "soul music" in a rather heterogeneous group of young Negro men who all agreed on the "soulfulness" of the singers whose records they were playing, and afterwards I asked one of the men who is clearly upwardly mobile of his conception of "soul." He answered that "soul" is earthy, "there is nothing specifically Negro about it." Yet the very individuals with whom he had just agreed on matters of "soul" had earlier given me the opposite answer—only Negroes have "soul." Thus by avoiding definitions, they had found together an area of agreement and satisfaction in "soul" by merely assuming that there was a shared basis of opinion.

IV

Summing up what has been said, "soul" is a relatively recent concept used in the urban Negro ghetto, in particular by young men, to express what is "essential Negroness" and to convey appreciation for it. The point of view which has been expressed here is that the need for such a concept has arisen at this point because of increasingly ambivalent conceptions of the opportunity structure. While earlier, lack of achievement according to American mainstream ideals could easily be explained in terms of impermeable social barriers, the impression is gaining ground in the ghetto that there are now ways out of the situation. The young men who come under particularly great strain if such a belief is accepted must either achieve some success (which many of them are obviously still unable to do, for

various reasons), explain that achievement is impossible (which is probably not as true as it has been), or explain that achievement according
to mainstream ideals is not necessarily achievement according to their
ideals. The emergence of "soul," it has been stated here, goes some way
toward meeting the need of stating alternative ideals and also provides
solidarity among those with such a need. In implying or stating explicitly
that ghetto culture has a superiority of its own, the users of the "soul"
vocabulary seem to take a step beyond devices of established usage
which are terms of solidarity but lack or at least have less clear cultural
references—for example the use of "brother" as a term of either reference or address for another Negro. That is, it is more in the cultural
than in the social dimension that "soul" is an innovation rather than
just one more term of a kind. Of course, the two are closely connected.
It is advantageous to maintain a diffuse conception of "soul," for if an
intellectually clear definition were established, "soul" would probably
be both less convincing and less uniting.

The view of "soul" taken here is one of a piecemeal rhetoric attempt
to establish a satisfactory self-conception. For the great majority of
"soul brothers" I am sure this is the major basis of "soul." It may be
added that for instance LeRoi Jones[13] and Charles Keil[14] tend to give
the impression of a more social-activist conception of "soul," although
Keil tends to make it a prophecy rather than an interpretation. At least
at present, I think that there is little basis for connecting the majority of
"soul brothers" with militant black nationalism—there is hardly a "soul
movement." "Soul" became publicly associated with black militancy
as the term "soul brother" made its way to international prominence
during recent ghetto uprisings—Negro businessmen posted "soul
brother" signs in their windows, it was noted by mass media all over
the world. However, it is worth noting that this was an internal appeal
to the ghetto moral community by black shopkeepers, not a sign of
defiance of the outside world by the participants. It may be said that
the outsiders merely caught a glimpse of an internal ghetto dialogue.
Yet organized black nationalism may be able to recruit followers by
using some kind of transformed "soul" vocabulary, and I think there
are obviously attempts on its side to make more of "soul" than it is now.
Certainly, there is seldom any hostility to black militants among the
wider groups of self-defined "soul brothers," although the vocabulary
of "soul" has not been extensively employed for political purposes. If
it is so used, however, it could possibly increase the ghetto dwellers'
identification with political nationalism. Thus, if at present it is not
possible to speak of more than a "rhetoric of soul," it may be that

in the future we will find a "soul movement." If that happens, of course, "soul" may become a more controversial concept, as "black power" is now.

Notes

1. Charles Keil, *Urban Blues* (Chicago, University of Chicago Press, 1966).
2. Charles Morris, *Signification and Significance* (Cambridge, Mass., The M.I.T. Press, 1964).
3. John F. Szwed, "Musical Style and Racial Conflict," *Phylon* (vol. 27, 1966), pp. 358–66.
4. LeRoi Jones, *Blues People* (New York, William Morrow & Co., 1963), p. 219.
5. LeRoi Jones, *Home: Social Essays* (New York, William Morrow & Co., 1966).
6. Lerone Bennett Jr., *The Negro Mood* (New York, Ballantine Books, 1965), p. 89.
7. Charles Keil, *op. cit.*, pp. 164 et seq.
8. Walter B. Miller, "Lower Class Culture as a Generating Milieu of Gang Delinquency," *Journal of Social Issues* (vol. 14, 1958), pp. 5–19.
9. Hyman Rodman, "The Lower-Class Value Stretch," *Social Forces* (vol. 42, 1963), pp. 205–15.
10. Alan C. Kerckhoff and Thomas C. McCormick, "Marginal Status and Marginal Personality," *Social Forces* (vol. 34, 1955), p. 51.
11. Kenneth Burke, *A Grammar of Motives and a Rhetoric of Motives* (Cleveland, Meridian Books, 1962), p. 562.
12. Clifford Geertz, "Ideology as a Cultural System," in David E. Apter (ed.), *Ideology and Discontent* (New York, The Free Press, 1964).
13. LeRoi Jones, *Home: Social Essays*.
14. Charles Keil, *op. cit.*

Suggested Readings

Dollard, John. *Caste and Class in a Southern Town.* Garden City: Doubleday, 1949.
A northern white psychologist's investigation of the social structure of a small southern community in the 1930's. Of particular note is an early chapter on the problem of "bias."

Drake, St. Clair, and Horace R. Cayton. *Black Metropolis.* New York: Harcourt, Brace, 1945.
One of the first extensive studies of an American ghetto. The setting is Chicago.

Ellison, Ralph. *Invisible Man.* New York: Random House, 1947.
This powerful novel deals with one black man's search for identity.

Frazier, E. Franklin. *Black Bourgeoisie.* New York: The Free Press, 1957.
A description of the rise of a black middle class in the United States.

Johnson, Charles S. *Patterns of Negro Segregation.* New York: Harper & Row, 1943.
This book, which deals with variations on the theme of segregation, is drawn from the famous Carnegie Studies. Other volumes include Gunnar Myrdal's *An American Dilemma* and Melville J. Herskovits' *The Myth of the Negro Past.*

Liebow, Elliot. *Tally's Corner.* Boston: Little, Brown, 1967.
An award-winning study of Negro street corner men in Washington, D.C.

Meier, August, and Elliott Rudwick. *From Plantation to Ghetto.* New York: Hill & Wang, 1966.
A social history of the black man in America.

Osofsky, Gilbert. *Harlem: The Making of a Ghetto.* New York: Harper & Row, 1966.
A study of the growth and life of Harlem from 1890–1930.

Rowan, Carl T. *South of Freedom.* New York: Alfred A. Knopf, 1952.
This is a Negro journalist's description of a trip from Minnesota "back home" in the late 1940's.

Wright, Richard. *Black Boy.* New York: Harper & Row, 1937.
Richard Wright's personal story of life in the south and in Chicago.

Community, Class, and Family Life

Any law that degrades human personality is unjust. All segregation statutes are unjust because segregation distorts the
soul and damages the personality. It gives the segregator a
false sense of superiority and the segregated a false sense of
inferiority. Segregation, to use the terminology of the Jewish
philosopher Martin Buber, substitutes an "I-it" relationship
for an "I-thou" relationship and ends up relegating persons
to the status of things.

Martin Luther King, Jr.

The first essay in this section begins by describing the difference between the assimilation and social mobility of black Americans and those to whom they are often compared—the European immigrants. As G. Franklin Edwards points out, blacks, who have been here as long as anyone except the Pilgrims (and, of course, the Indians), have never enjoyed opportunities afforded to even the poorest whites.

The main subject of this essay is the black man's response to the mutually debilitating forces of social and physical isolation. Special attention is paid to the structure of the family and other institutions of the black community and to what Edwards (a lifelong integrationist) sees as the obstacles for bringing Negroes into the mainstream of American life.

17

Community and Class Realities

G. Franklin Edwards

One of the paradoxes of American life is that though the Negro is an old-line American he is not yet fully American. His presence in this country antedates that of most immigrant groups, but his career and community life are greatly different from those of immigrants from northern and southern Europe. In terms of the basic socialization processes and the community contexts in which they occur, differences between the Negro and these immigrant groups, including the most recent large-scale arrivals, the Puerto Ricans, are apparent.

Immigrant groups from Europe have followed a somewhat typical process as they moved into the main stream of American life. Most members of these groups entered the work force at the bottom of the economic ladder, as small farmers and as unskilled, semiskilled,

From G. Franklin Edwards, "Community and Class Realities: The Ordeal of Change," in "The Negro American," *Daedalus* (Winter 1966), 1–23. Reprinted with permission of *Daedalus*, Journal of the American Academy of Arts and Sciences, Boston, Mass.

and service workers. They lived initially among fellow immigrants in small village communities or in poorer city neighborhoods in which communal institutions helped cushion the cultural shock induced by the differences between life in their countries of origin and life in the United States. Family, church, the foreign language press, and mutual aid organizations helped in the adjustment process. Members of the second and succeeding generations acquired increasing amounts of education and the skills necessary to take advantage of available opportunities; eventually the Americanization process was fairly complete. By and large, members of these groups have assimilated American values and today experience little physical and cultural isolation based upon ethnicity. Although individual members of these groups continue to experience discrimination in the areas of admission to educational institutions, job promotions in industry, and acceptance into voluntary associations, a consciousness of group rejection does not exist. In those instances where strong ingroup community life exists, it is owing more to the persistence of group cohesion than to restraints from without.

In contrast to the pattern of immigrant groups, the Negro has remained socially and morally isolated from the American society. At no time in the almost three and a half centuries of his history in this country has he been "counted in." His caste-like position is owing more to restraints from without than to any centripetal force serving to keep him separated from other groups. He has lived, according to E. Franklin Frazier's characterization, as "a nation within a nation."[1] Robin Williams recently has referred to the general Negro community as "a world in the shadow,"[2] and James Silver, in describing an extreme instance of a local community's exclusion of Negroes, has referred to the "closed society."[3]

One basic difference between the Negro and these immigrant groups is that the former served for nearly two centuries as slaves. Although succeeding generations of Negroes acquired increased amounts of education after the Emancipation, access to opportunities commensurate with formal training often was denied because of color. The failure to learn certain basic skills to qualify for jobs in the world of work placed serious limitations upon the horizontal and social mobility experienced by members of the group. As a matter of fact, the social mobility of Negroes up to the present has been determined more by conditions within the Negro community than by those of the broader society. The number and distribution of Negroes within the professions, for example, have been related more directly to the needs of the Negro community for certain types of services than to the demands of the broader society.[4] It is for this reason that clergymen and teachers, functionaries required by the segregated Negro community, have represented at least one-half of all Negro professional persons at any given period.

The segregation of Negroes from the main stream of American life has produced institutional patterns and behavior which have a bearing upon contemporary efforts to eliminate inequalities between the two major racial groups. The behaviors are expressed as deviations of Negroes from many normative patterns of American life and suggest something of the magnitude of the differentials which must be dealt with if reconciliation, rather than further alienation, is to be achieved.

The contrasts in background experiences between the Negro and immigrant groups raise the fundamental question of whether, given the promise of recent changes, the Negro will now be integrated into American society in much the same manner as have these other groups. Any strict analogy between the future course of the Negro's relationship to American society and the processes which occurred in the experiences of immigrant groups, however, is subject to serious limitations and error.

The long history of oppression has profoundly affected the Negro's self-esteem. The fears, suspicions and feelings of inadequacy generated in the Negro by his subordinate status are not duplicated in the experiences of immigrant groups. Moreover, color and other physical traits distinguish the Negro sharply from other groups in the society. In the past these characteristics were taken as physical stigmata which reinforced negative attitudes toward the Negro. Sharp physical differences were not present to complicate the relationships of immigrants to American society, although differences in this regard can be observed between the northern Europeans, on the one hand, and southern Europeans and Orientals, on the other.

The attitudes of the Negro toward himself are merely reciprocals of the attitudes of other groups toward him. There always have been serious reservations on the part of American whites regarding the Negro's capacity to live on a basis of equality with other Americans. Such reservations about the potentialities of immigrant groups for assimilation were not held in the same serious way.

Finally, it should be observed that significant advancement in the status of the Negro comes at a time when economic conditions are quite different from those faced by immigrant groups. The great influx of immigrants came at a time when there was a market for agricultural labor and unskilled work and mobility through these avenues was still possible. The Negro today has been displaced from the farm and must now compete for work in an urban market which requires a somewhat higher degree of education and technical skill than was the case a half century ago. Given the present educational and occupational inadequacies of a large segment of the Negro population, the task of overcoming these deficiencies is formidable.

While it is clear that further changes in the status of the Negro will occur in the years ahead, moving the Negro nearer to equality with other Americans, the processes by which this will be achieved are certain to be difficult and tortuous. The remainder of this essay is an elaboration of this viewpoint.

Foremost among the indicators of the social isolation of Negroes is the Negro ghetto. It represents at once the restrictions placed upon the living space of the Negro minority and, as Kenneth Clark recently has pointed out, a way of life with a peculiar institutional patterning and psychological consequences.[5] Unlike most immigrant ghettos, which show a tendency to break up, the Negro ghetto, especially in Northern cities, has become more dense.

Karl Taeuber and Alma Taeuber, on the basis of an examination of segregation indices in 109 American cities from 1940 to 1960, note that in 83 of the 109 cities the segregation index was higher in 1950 than in 1940. Between 1950 and 1960, only 45 of these cities showed an increase. But it was observed that cities with already high levels of segregation were prominent among those with increases. A most significant observation is that in recent years Southern cities have had the highest increases in the physical segregation of Negroes, and the South now has the highest index of any region.[6] This is important inasmuch as in earlier periods Negroes were less segregated in the older Southern cities than in cities located in other regions.[7]

The concentration of Negroes in the central cities of our metropolitan areas and within the inlying cores of these central cities is too well documented to warrant elaboration here. Our concern is with the fact that the areas inhabited by Negroes are inferior in terms of housing quality, recreational facilities, schools, and general welfare services, and that all of these deficiencies contribute to crime, delinquency, school dropouts, dependency, broken families, excessive deaths, and other conditions which represent the "pathology of the ghetto." The pathology is most evident in housing. In 1960, for example, 44 per cent of all dwelling units occupied by Negroes were substandard. Though nonwhites occupied only 10 per cent of all dwelling units, they occupied 27 per cent of those classed as substandard. Thirteen per cent of nonwhites lived in units which were seriously overcrowded, and there was an increase of 85,000 such units occupied by Negroes between 1950 and 1960.[8]

Efforts to break up the ghetto, and hence to ameliorate the pathological conditions generated by it, have not been productive. Attempts by Negroes to leave the ghetto run afoul of a most formidable network of relationships involving brokers, builders, bankers, realtors, and citizens' organizations serving to restrict Negroes to certain neighborhoods.[9] There is, indeed, a vast profit to be made from slum housing, and this accounts for much of the behavior of some realtors. One study demonstrates that a slum landlord receives fifteen dollars more monthly if a substandard unit is rented to a Negro family than if the same unit were rented to a white family.[10] Myths regarding neighborhood deterioration following Negro occupancy persist, despite empirical studies which expose their fallacious character.

By and large, our urban renewal programs, designed to revitalize the older, more dilapidated areas of our cities, have not succeeded in providing better accommodations in the renewal areas for most Negroes, the majority of the displacees. They have succeeded very largely in having Negroes move into public housing and blighted areas. While in many instances the physical accommodations to which displaced populations moved represent an improvement over their former dwellings,[11] segregation has not been lessened. In our metropolitan centers, for example, despite recent efforts to build small, scattered public housing units, most projects constructed under this program have been large in size and have contributed to segregation as they became either nearly all-white or nearly all-Negro.

It is clear that the Negro ghetto, unlike other ghettos, has had great external pressure to keep it "hemmed in." While some of the greater concentration of Negroes in the older areas of our cities stems from income differentials between Negroes and whites, the Taeubers, using data for the city of Chicago, found that income differentials accounted for only 14 percent of the observed racial segregation in housing in 1950 and 12 percent in 1960.[12] They further observed that "on every measure—the Puerto Rican population [of Chicago] is less well off—it is less educated, of lower income, more crowded, less likely to be homeowners, less well housed, and lives in older buildings, yet the index of residential segregation for Puerto Ricans is sixty-seven as compared to eighty-two for Negroes."[13] There is now considerable evidence, also, that after two generations of strong community solidarity Chinese and Japanese communities in our cities show a considerable dispersion.[14]

Although in recent years some moderation of the tight housing market has occurred within the central city—thus permitting Negroes to obtain housing left by the whites who moved to the suburbs—the proportion of the suburban population which is Negro has declined steadily since 1900. Negroes have become increasingly locked in the central city, giving rise to the observation that there is a white noose around our central cities. In 1960, Negroes were less than 5 percent of the population of metropolitan areas outside central cities, but they made up 17 percent of the central city population of these areas.[15]

There is some hope that Executive Order 11063, issued by President Kennedy on November 20, 1962, banning discrimination in housing insured by agencies of the federal government, will have a salutary effect in reducing the degree of concentration and segregation of the Negro population. But skeptics point out that the Order does not cover all home-mortgage insuring agencies of the federal government, the Home Loan Bank Board constituting an important exception, and in recent years a smaller proportion of new construction has been built with federal insurance. Most importantly, the Order is not retroactive, leaving unaffected the housing stock existing at the time of its issuance.

Access by Negroes to much of the newly constructed housing must depend upon the supplementation of the national Order against discrimination by state and local ordinances having the same objective. In recent years there has been an increase in the number of such ordinances. By and large, however, the basic approach of local communities is conciliation of disputes, and much depends upon the vigor with which these local ordinances are enforced if they are to have any significant effect in countering discrimination and reducing segregation.

But significant moderation of Negro concentration and segregation depends upon more than laws against discrimination, however important these may be. The attitudes of both Negroes and whites toward integrated community life are important determinants of the extent to which deconcentration will occur, given enforcement of even the most severe sanctions against discrimination. There is abundant evidence, as mentioned earlier, that myths exist regarding the lowering of housing values and the maintenance of community patterns following invasion by Negroes, and many whites are inclined to move, so that in time complete succession, or turnover of neighborhoods from white to Negro, occurs. On the other hand, there is some resistance on the part of Negroes to moving into areas, especially the suburbs, where few Negroes live. This is particularly characteristic of families with children who must attend school and are dependent on neighbors for play and other social experiences. The well-founded fear of rejection by white neighbors leads to a foregoing of economic advantages which purchases in white areas represent or, in the case of suburban purchases, of a style of living consistent with one's social and economic level. Though numerous white liberal groups, mainly in suburban communities, have organized to encourage Negroes to purchase homes in their neighborhoods, they are often disappointed with the responses to their sincerest solicitations. The centripetal forces tying Negroes to the Negro community are the products of fear and isolated living and are likely to discourage any large exodus of Negroes to suburban communities in the immediate future. Doubtless open-occupancy patterns will result in a significantly larger number of Negroes residing in mixed areas at some future period, but the pattern of increase is likely to be exponential rather than linear.

This continued physical separation of the major racial groups has an impact upon social relationships between them. It limits the number of intimate contacts and the possibilities for understanding which grow out of association. Robin Williams, on the basis of an examination of the patterns of interracial contact in a large number of communities, concludes that the presence of a Negro subcommunity limits Negro interaction with whites, and barriers to communication between the two groups lead to inadequate understanding and to a perception of the other group as hostile.[16] Duncan and Lieberson make the same point in a somewhat different way when they state that segregation is inversely related to assimilation.[17]

The growing awareness of the limitations of life in the ghetto, as a result of the influence of mass media, increased physical mobility, and better education, has played a vital part in precipitating the "Negro Revolution." The mass demonstrations for equality of treatment in places of public accommodations, for access to better quality schools, for equal employment opportunities and voting rights are thought of as efforts by Negroes to achieve first-class citizenship. In another sense, they are efforts to overcome the barriers which have isolated Negroes from aspects of American life.

The difficulty of overcoming the problems created by the physical fact of the ghetto is indicated by attempts to improve the quality of education of schools in slum areas. In our large metropolitan cities, because of the segregation in housing and the traditional neighborhood concept of school attendance, a disproportionate number of schools, particularly at the elementary level, becomes predominantly Negro or predominantly white, with the Negro schools being inferior. Opposing theories for dealing with this situation, generally regarded as undesirable, have generated serious community conflicts. There are those who feel that the efforts should be concentrated upon improving the quality of education in these depressed areas by larger allocations for plant improvement, remedial work, new curricula, and better trained teachers. Other students of the problem contend that substantial improvement of slum schools cannot be achieved until such schools lose their predominantly Negro or predominantly white character. It becomes necessary in the thinking of the protagonists of this latter view to develop methods for overcoming racial imbalances in

325

the schools. While a variety of techniques have been proposed, each has generated rather serious opposition. It is patent that this problem, one of the serious concerns of the leaders of the Negro Revolution largely because it is tied to segregation in housing, will not be easily solved.

As mentioned previously, the ghetto has not only restricted the interaction of Negroes with other members of the society, and hence symbolized the isolation under which Negroes have lived; but it has also been a primary force in the generation and persistence of atypical institutional patterns which are viewed as dysfunctional in any effort at reconciliation. Doubtless the foremost of these institutions is the Negro family which, because of historical circumstances connected with slavery and the isolated conditions under which Negroes have lived in both urban and rural areas, is characterized by rather significant variations from the dominant American family pattern. It is not so much the differences *per se*, or any mere deviation of Negro family characteristics from those of white middle-class families, but the variations in structural and interactional features known to be desirable in family living which become causes of concern.

The most salient feature of Negro family life which captures the attention of those concerned with integration of Negroes into American life is the degree of disorganization represented by structural breakdown. In only three-quarters of all Negro families, as compared with approximately nine-tenths of all white families, were both spouses present. One Negro family in five (21 percent) was headed by a female and 5 percent had only the male head present. Thus one Negro family in four, as compared with one white family in ten, was headed by a single parent. This differential in the percentage of families headed by one parent accounts in part for the fact that in 1960 only one-third of Negro children under eighteen years of age, as compared with one in ten white children of comparable age, lived in families in which only one parent was present.

The assumption underlying the desirability of family unity—the presence of both spouses—is that on balance the economic, social, and affectual roles may be best discharged when both mates are present in the home. Divorce, desertion, and separation follow the generation and expression of tensions which, even before rupture occurs, reduce the effectiveness with which the mates can discharge the duties and obligations of family life, as well as deny the satisfactions derived from the intimate sharing of experiences and attainment of goals. In essence, the organized and unified family becomes at once a matrix for the personal satisfaction of the marital partners and for the protection, proper socialization, and well-being of their children. This is not to deny that the basic goals of family life, regarding child-rearing and other functions, may not be achieved by the single-parent family. Given the complexities of modern urban life and the established normative values around which the modern family is organized, however, the discharge of family functions may best be achieved when the family is unified.

In analyzing the statistics on the Negro family one becomes aware that the instability of the Negro family unit is greater than is represented by statistics on the percentages of males and females enumerated as widowed or divorced. In 1960, 15 percent of all Negro males and 20 percent of all Negro females, though enumerated by the Census as married, were living apart from their mates. The percentage of Negro males separated from their mates is four times as large as the comparable percentage for white males, and for Negro females four and one-half times as large as for white females.

The instability of Negro family life is explained only in part by the historical conditioning of attitudes toward family life, beginning with slavery, when strong family ties were not encouraged and Negroes, as Elkins has suggested, were made dependent upon whites.[18] The phenomenon arises also from forces of contemporary American life which place limits upon the possibility of successful family organization. These are reflected in the statistics on characteristics of the heads of Negro families.

As reported by the last Census, approximately one-half, 48.5 percent, of the heads of nonwhite (mainly Negro) families had not finished elementary school. Even in urban areas where access to educational opportunities is somewhat greater and school-attendance laws somewhat better enforced than in rural farm and nonfarm areas, two out of five nonwhite family heads failed to reach the last year of elementary school. Of nonwhite heads living in rural nonfarm and rural farm areas, 70 and 80 percent, respectively, had failed to attain this level of schooling.[19] The low level of educational achievement for such a large proportion of nonwhite family heads has obvious implications for the cultural life to which the Negro child is exposed in the home and doubtless for the type of motivation the child receives for achievement in school. It also is related to the labor-force participation and income of nonwhites.

In an economy in which automation is rapidly introducing changes in the demand for certain types of labor, the heads of nonwhite families were disproportionately represented in those occupational categories in which fewer workers are required and monetary returns are small. Only 13 percent of all nonwhite family heads, as compared with 40 percent of white heads, were in professional, managerial, and clerical occupations for which labor demands are increasing. One in five white heads, but only one in ten among non-white, was a skilled worker. Thus, one in four nonwhite heads, as compared with three in five white, were white-collar and skilled workers.[20] The heavier identification with semiskilled and unskilled work accounts in part for the nonwhite employment rate being twice as large as the comparable rate of whites and for greater underemployment among nonwhites.

The type of job and both underemployment and unemployment influence the relatively low income of nonwhite family heads. The median nonwhite family income of $3,465 in 1963 was only approximately 53 percent of the white family income of $6,548. More than two-fifths of all nonwhite families (41 percent) earned less than $3,000 in 1963, which placed them at the poverty level, and only one in twenty earned $10,000 or more in the same year.[21] It is significant to note, in line with our previous discussion regarding the desirability of family closure— both parents in the home—that in 1959 families in which both husband and wife were present in the home had a median income of $3,633 as compared with a median of $1,734 for families having a female head.[22]

The problems of the Negro family, then, in terms of its instability and the associated phenomena of crime, delinquency, school dropouts, high morbidity and mortality are related to a complex of interwoven factors, of which level of educational attainment and income are important components. The President of the United States, in a historic speech at Howard University in June 1965, pointed to the complexity of the problem by stating that the provision of jobs, decent homes, welfare and social programs, care of the sick, and understanding attitudes are only partial answers to the conditions of the Negro family.[23] "The breakdown of the Negro family," he stated, "is related to centuries of oppression and persecution of the Negro man. It flows from long years of degradation and discrimination which have attacked his dignity and assaulted his ability to produce for his family."[24] The President added that though we know much about Negro family life, other answers are still to be found. For this reason he indicated he would call a White House Conference in the fall to explore the problem further.

A definitive study by Hylan Lewis of child-rearing practices among low-income Negro families in the District of Columbia reveals that there is, indeed, still much to be learned about the operating dynamics and underlying causes of disorganization among such units.[25] What often is accepted as knowledge about these families is in fact mythology. It is noted, in the first instance, that these families are not homogeneous as regards their organization, functioning, and ambitions for their children. In many of them considerable strength is to be noted, but the exigencies of daily living often deny the achievement of the parents' most ambitious plans. Though parents set training and discipline goals for their children, these are often undermined by influences beyond their power, and the actual control over their children may be lost as early as the fifth or sixth year.

Investigation reveals that many of these parents, particularly the mothers, are warm, human, and concerned individuals who, despite deprivation and trouble, are persistent in their desires to have their children become respectable and productive citizens and in their willingness to sacrifice for them. The picture contrasts with the common belief that in an overwhelming majority of low-income families parents reject their children and are hostile to them.

Lewis' study raises questions regarding assigned reasons for alleged male irresponsibility toward family obligations and the degree of family concern with pregnancy out of wedlock and illegitimate births. There does appear to be a greater degree of concern by the male regarding his responsibilities and by family members regarding the sexual behavior of their offspring than is commonly recognized. What in fact emerges is that the behavior of these lower-income families is a practical response to untoward circumstances which undermine the well-intentioned, but often unattainable, goals of these units.

The major problems of the Negro family are experienced in urban areas where more than 70 percent of such families now live. There has been a heavy migration during the past twenty-five years from farms and small towns to large metropolitan areas. The limited extent to which many of these families can cope with the demands of urban life, given the low educational level and obsolescent skills of the adults, raises serious questions for the American society as well as for the families themselves. The War on Poverty, youth opportunity programs, medicare and other changes in our social security program are certain to exercise some influences in ameliorating existing conditions. But the deep-seated nature of many of those conditions and the personality damage they have produced, as expressed in feelings of powerlessness, hopelessness, and forms of anti-social conduct, give rise to the prediction that no easy solution to problems of the Negro family may be found. This is especially true of those "hard core" or multi-problem families in many of which at least two generations have been dependent on public assistance programs. Present efforts to focus upon the young, as evidenced in Project Head Start and programs for youth, on the assumption that this population is most amenable to change, are based upon sound theory. There remains, however, the complex problem of improving the skills and enhancing the self-esteem of the adult members whose personalities are crystallized and whose levels of expectation have been shaped under an entirely different set of conditions. What is apparent is that the problems of the Negro family are intimately tied to those of the larger community.

The elimination of many of these difficulties depends upon a commitment to invest a great deal more of our resources in improving educational and social services, including more effective family limitation programs. What is indicated is that by opening the opportunity structure and providing both formal and informal education on a more extensive scale through diverse programs, key figures in many Negro problem families will be enabled over time to develop self-esteem and a "rational" approach to urban life, which many students regard as indispensable for successful adjustment to the urban environment. This can hardly occur as long as the present constraints and limitations continue to operate against a large segment of the Negro population or, to put it differently, as long as the isolation of the Negro is continued.

The difficulty of changing existing patterns is evident in a number of current efforts. The Manpower Retraining Program, for example, has encountered difficulty in working with enrollees with less than an eighth-grade education, which would exclude large numbers of Negro males from successful participation. Of all projects started under the Manpower Development and Retaining Act in 1963, 3 percent of the enrollees had less than eight years of schooling, while 36 percent had between eight and eleven years. Fifty-one percent were high-school graduates, and another 10 percent had gone beyond the high-school level.[26] Educational levels must be raised considerably before some of the disadvantaged can benefit from available training opportunities.

The problems of developing motivation, rather than supplying specific job skills, appear to be even harder to overcome. Charles Silberman, among others, has pointed out that the effort to eliminate poverty must involve the poor in action programs if the motivation to improve their lot is to be realized. Recent controversies over involvement of the poor in strikes, boycotts, and pickets and the use of other techniques to dramatize their condition and counteract feelings of apathy and cynicism have been sharply criticized by local citizens, especially those in the power structure.[27]

Finally, the bold program advanced by Whitney Young, Executive Director of the National Urban League, calling for a "Marshall Plan" for Negroes as a means of upgrading the competency and wellbeing of the Negro family, encounters serious opposition.[28] The charge of preferential treatment is raised, and this runs counter to the ideology of equal treatment. What is more important is that the practical operation of such a program would encounter difficulty from institutionalized patterns. To request preferential treatment for Negroes in apprentice programs and preferential hiring after completion of training, for example, cross-cuts seniority and other established principles of union organization and practice.

All of the above are mere illustrations of the complications involved in any effort to strengthen the Negro family in particular and to upgrade Negro life in general. They should serve to introduce some caution into the thinking of those sanguine persons who are persuaded that broad-scale and rapid changes are likely to occur in a short period of time. (The position taken here is not an apology for the gradualist position regarding race relations changes. It is, indeed, understandable that civil rights groups must inveigh continuously against the gradualist perspective as a matter of strategy. Our concern is with traditional and countervailing influences which have the effect of slowing the pace at which change might occur.)

The disabilities of the Negro family discussed in the preceding paragraphs are most characteristic of low-income units. Not all Negro families are affected by inadequate income, education, and employment opportunities, and many of them do not lack strong family traditions. There is a considerable differentiation within the Negro community in terms of status groups and social classes.

E. Franklin Frazier observed that as late as World War I the Negro middle class was composed "principally of teachers, doctors, preachers, trusted persons in personal service, government employees, and a few business men."[29] He stated further that:

> This group was distinguished from the rest of the Negro population not so much by economic factors as by social factors. Family affiliation and education to a less degree were as important as income. Moreover, while it exhibited many middle-class features such as its emphasis on morality, it also possessed characteristics of an upper class or aristocracy.[30]

The urbanization of the Negro population, beginning with World War I and continuing to the present, resulted in the formation of large ghettos in Northern and Southern cities and provided the condition for greater occupational differentiation within the Negro community. The differentiation was more pronounced in Northern communities where Negroes had a substantially greater opportunity to enter clerical and technical occupations than was true in Southern cities, and where the large population base provided economic support for a sizeable corps of professional functionaries. Education and income became more important than social distinctions in determining class membership.

The Negro middle class today includes a still relatively small, but expanding, number of persons. If occupation is used as a criterion for determining membership and those in professional and technical, clerical, sales, and skilled occupations are included, only approximately 26 percent of all nonwhite workers belong to the middle class. White workers in these above-mentioned categories represent 64 percent of all whites in the labor force.[31] The contrast between the two occupational structures is further indicated by the fact that the percentage of white workers, taken as a proportion of all white workers, is twice as large as the comparable percentage of nonwhite workers in professional and kindred occupations, and in clerical and skilled work; four times as large in managerial occupations; and three times as large in the sales category.

In none of the specific occupational categories associated with the middle class did nonwhite male workers achieve parity with white males in median income. The nearest approximation to parity in 1959 was in clerical and kindred occupations in which the nonwhite male median earnings of $4,072 was approximately 85 percent of the white male median of $4,785. In none of the other categories did nonwhite male workers receive so much as 70 percent of the median income of white males in the category.[32]

The expansion of the Negro middle class has been most marked by accretion of persons in professional, technical, clerical, and sales occupations. This expansion by approximately 300 000 persons since 1940 has been influenced in part by government policy which prohibits those business firms holding contracts with the federal government from discriminating against workers on the basis of race, religion, creed, or national origin. In engineering, architecture, and the natural sciences, occupations oriented to the wider world of work rather than to the Negro community, the increases among Negroes, though small in absolute numbers, have been rather dramatic. Between 1950 and 1960, there was a three-fold increase in the number of Negro engineers. The number of Negro architects increased by 72 percent, and the number of natural scientists by 77 percent.[33] This expansion comes at the end of a half century in which Negroes could hardly expect to earn a living in these fields and thus were not encouraged to prepare for entering them.

The number of Negroes in medicine, dentistry, and law, whose services traditionally have been oriented to the Negro community, has begun to increase rather significantly. During the 1950's, physicians increased by 14 percent, dentists by 31 percent, and lawyers by 43 percent.[34] More substantial fellowship and scholarship aid, ability to pay for professional education, as well as the opening of the segregated professional schools in the Southern states, have contributed to this result.

It is not only the increase in number of these professionals which

deserves attention; the improved opportunities for advanced training and learning experiences are also of importance. On the basis of
increased opportunities for internships and residency training, the number of Negro physicians who became diplomates of medical specialty
boards increased from 92 in 1947 to 377 in 1959.[35] Negro physicians,
lawyers, and dentists are admitted today to membership in local societies
of national professional organizations in larger numbers and enjoy the
privileges these societies provide for continued professional growth.

It should be remembered, however, that these gains, while significant in
terms of what has occurred in Negro life heretofore, are relatively small. The
ratios of the actual to expected numbers of Negroes in middle-class occupations, as measured by the total labor force distribution, are extremely small.[36]

The differences between Negro and white community life cannot be
measured solely by variations in income, occupation, education, and
other objective indicators. In assessing the differences, it is important to
recognize that the Negro class structure and institutions have emerged
in response to segregation and represent adjustments to the isolation
under which Negroes have lived. The meaning of relationships within
the community and the values placed upon them must be considered.

Frazier has observed, for example, that in the absence of a true upper
class based upon old family ties and wealth, the Negro middle class
simulates the behavior of the white upper class without possessing
the fundamental bases upon which such behavior rests.[37] Moreover,
segregation has provided a monopoly for many Negroes in business
and the professions and has introduced, in many cases, differential
standards of performance. This has important consequences for any
consideration of desegregation, for those who enjoy a vested interest
in the segregated community are not likely to welcome competition
from the broader community. The Negro church represents an extreme
instance of vested interest in the Negro community and, at the same
time, is the most important institution giving expression to the Negro
masses. For this reason no degree of acceptance of Negroes by white
churches is likely to bring about the dissolution of Negro churches.[38]

The Negro community doubtless will be the source of social life of
Negroes for some time into the future. Sororities, fraternities, clubs,
and other organizations will continue to serve a meaningful function.
The acceptance by whites of Negroes as fellow workers often bears little
relationship to their willingness to share social experiences with them
outside the plant or office or to have them as neighbors.

The importance of the Negro community as a source of social

life is indicated by the fact that, though the majority of the members of a Negro professional society felt that its members should identify with the local chapter of the national organization representing the profession when the opportunity became available, one-quarter had some reservation about joining and another 5 percent were opposed to joining. The underlying reasons for reservations to becoming members of the formerly white organization were that, though Negroes may be accepted as professional colleagues, they would not be treated as social equals and that opportunities for leadership roles would be lost if the Negro association were dissolved.[39] What is patently indicated is that most members thought they should have the *right* to membership in the local chapter of the national organization, but they should retain their own association for social and professional reasons.

Despite the effort to conserve the conceived advantages of the Negro community, the larger social forces are introducing changes. Already the small Negro entrepreneurial group is threatened by these forces. Speaking to a group of Negro businessmen in Detroit, the Assistant Secretary of Commerce for Economic Affairs referred to the disappearance of the monopoly Negroes formerly held in certain businesses.[40] The impact of desegregation is being felt, he said, in The Negro market, for, as the income of Negro consumers expands, white businessmen become more conscious of the Negro's purchasing power. To this end they have added a cadre of professional Negro salesmen to their payrolls for the specific purpose of developing the Negro market. The success of this undertaking is indicated by the fact that many of the employed Negroes have risen to top executive posts in these organizations. Moreover, Negroes have begun to buy in increasing amounts from shopping centers serving the Negro community and have begun to patronize places of public accommodations other than those traditionally operated by Negroes. This change in consumer behavior represents a steady and gradual erosion of the position of the Negro businessman. The cruelest blow of all, the Assistant Secretary stated, is that "the large life insurance companies serving the market at large are bidding away Negro life insurance salesmen at an increasing rate."[41] These and other changes are certain to influence the structure of the Negro community.

The Ordeal of Change

From observing current developments in race relations and the operation of the larger social forces in our society, it is evident that several basic conditions operate to influence the pattern and pace at which change is occurring. These provide some insight into what may be expected in the future in regard to the general status of the Negro minority; they document the theory of slow and gradual change for some time to come in most areas and somewhat more rapid change in others.

A first consideration, not prominently mentioned heretofore, is the opposition to change by segments of the white community. Beginning with the school desegregation decision, there has been a mobilization of white community efforts to prevent the attainment of desegregation in many aspects of community life. This opposition has taken a variety of forms: the closing of schools, violence visited upon Negroes, intimidation of Negroes and threats to their job security, the rise of some hate groups—such as Citizens' Councils and Night Riders—and the strengthening of others—such as the Ku Klux Klan—the resurrection of racial ideologies having the purpose of establishing the inferiority of the Negro, and a variety of other techniques designed to slow the desegregation process.[42]

What is important in this connection is that many of the organizations connected with the opposition have had the support, if not the leadership, of prominent persons in the power structure; many governors, mayors, legislators, and prominent businessmen have all given support to the resistance efforts, owing to political and economic expediency, if not to personal sentiment. Moreover, persons with some claim to scientific respectability in the academic community have contributed to the questioning of whether differentials between Negroes and whites stem from the former's disadvantaged community life or from the Negro's innate biological inferiority.[43]

There is no doubt that these forces have served to slow the process of desegregation. As late as December 1964, only 2 percent of Negro pupils in eleven Southern states formerly having segregated school systems were attending schools with whites. If the six Border states where desegregation did not encounter the same serious opposition as in the other eleven states are included in the count, only 11 percent of Negro pupils attend schools having a mixed population.[44] This has led to one student's referring to developments in this area as "ten years of prelude," suggesting that the pace may be somewhat more rapid in the future.[45]

There does appear to be a lessening of the opposition in many areas as a result of several important factors. These include self-interest on the part of prominent businessmen, many of whom have spoken out against violence and have used their influence otherwise. The passage of important legislation within the past year—the Civil Rights Act of 1964 and the Voting Rights Act of 1965—are certain to have an influence in softening open resistance. But doubtless resistance to change will continue in subtle ways, perhaps under a blanket of legitimacy, as in the instance of the large-scale discharge of Negro teachers in Southern states in recent months following the necessity of having to comply with the Commissioner of Education's "Statement of Policies" for enforcement of Title VI of the Civil Rights Act, by which Southern school systems are expected to make a substantial start toward complete desegregation by September 1965 and to complete the process by the fall of 1967.

A second important force affecting change is inherent in the nature of the phenomenon itself, especially the contribution made by the accumulated disabilities of the Negro family, and in individuals in terms of inadequate education, job skills, housing, patterns of dependency, and low self-esteem. The advancement toward a more equalitarian society depends upon how fully these disabilities can be overcome or eliminated. Any analysis must consider the generational problem, for the extent to which the education and job skills of many adult family heads—those over forty-five, for example—can be improved is problematic.

A stronger basis of hope rests with the generation which begins school under improved educational conditions and whose levels of aspiration will be shaped by a social context which varies considerably from that of the past half century, and may be expected to vary even more in the future. But even under the most favorable circumstances, the improvement of educational qualifications of Negroes to a position of parity with those of whites, an essential factor for job equality, may not be easily achieved. One prominent sociologist on the basis of statistical calculations concluded:

> Whatever the future may hold with respect to the on-coming cohorts of young Negroes, the performance to date, together with the postulate that educational attainment is a "background" characteristic [for employment], enables us to make a most important prediction: the disparity between white and nonwhite levels of education attainment in the general population can hardly disappear in less than three-quarters of a century. Even if Negroes in their teens were to begin immediately to match the educational attainment of white children, with this equalization persisting indefinitely, we shall have to wait fifty years for the last of the cohorts manifesting race differentials to reach retirement age.[46]

The achievement of educational and occupational equality is far more difficult to attain than equal treatment in public accommodations. Many civil rights leaders recognize this and, now that the public accommodations struggle has been successful, consider that the movement has entered a new and much tougher phase.

A third force affecting change is the attitudes held by certain

Negroes who either have a vested interest in segregation or are generally fearful of the deleterious consequences desegregation will bring. This has been discussed in an earlier section, and only a further example will be furnished here. As early as 1954 Negro teachers in South Carolina registered great fear over the possible untoward effects of desegregation of the public school system on their professional status as teachers. The chief fears expressed concerned the large amount of possible job displacement, new ways to evade the granting of equality in pay, employment, and benefits, greater demands for professional preparation, and the employment of fewer couples in the school system. Though most of these teachers were ideologically committed to desegregation, their fears regarding their jobs and community relationships with whites suggest that many of them, of necessity, were ambivalent toward desegregation.[47]

It is not likely that these attitudes strongly counteract tendencies to change. Their significance lies more in the manifest desire of Negroes to maintain social distance from whites in community relations as a result of their perception of the adverse use of power by whites.

The most significant influence in determining the pattern and pace of race relations changes is the federal government. The early court decisions, particularly in the area of public accommodations, orders by the executive, and recent legislation by the Congress have had salutary effects in altering disability-producing conditions. With more rigorous enforcement, they are likely to have an even more important influence in the future. The Civil Rights Act of 1964 provides a wedge for undermining, or at least neutralizing, much of the support for denying the constitutional rights of Negroes. The sanctions provided in Title VI of the Act, relating to nondiscrimination in federally assisted programs, is certain to produce a high measure of compliance. Under the Voting Rights Act of 1965, it is expected that between 50 and 70 percent of eligible Negro voters in the five Deep South states (Alabama, Georgia, Louisiana, Mississippi, and South Carolina) will be registered to vote by the time of the 1966 elections.[48] This result, along with the greater political consciousness of Negroes throughout the country, is certain to improve the power position of the group and result in the election of large numbers of Negroes to public office.[49]

The change in the position of the government in respect to the status of Negroes results from the altered position of this country in world affairs since the end of World War II and to a substantial shift in public opinion regarding the position of the Negro during that period. It is important, therefore, to view contemporary changes as a part of broader social movements toward improved welfare for the disadvantaged within the country and in the world. These broad forces tend to override resistances, but they are subject to challenges and counter pressures. If viewed in this broad perspective, it is clear that more significant changes which will bring the Negro greater opportunities for participation in our society lie ahead. When, in fact, basic equalities will be achieved cannot be predicted.

Notes

1. E. Franklin Frazier, *Black Bourgeoisie* (New York, 1957), p. 15.
2. Robin M. Williams, Jr., *Strangers Next Door* (New York, 1964), p. 252.
3. James W. Silver, *Mississippi: The Closed Society* (New York, 1963), p. 164.
4. G. Franklin Edwards, *The Negro Professional Class* (Chicago, 1959), pp. 23–26.
5. Kenneth Clark, *Dark Ghetto* (New York, 1965), pp. 63–80.
6. Karl Taeuber and Alma Taeuber, *Negroes in Cities* (Chicago, 1965), pp. 37–43.
7. *Ibid.*, pp. 43–53.
8. *Our Nonwhite Population and its Housing: The Changes between 1950 and 1960*, Office of the Administrator, Housing and Home Finance Agency (Washington, D.C., 1963), pp. 13, 15.
9. A discussion of the supports for housing segregation is given in the Report of the Commission on Race and Housing, *Where Shall We Live?* (Berkeley, Calif., 1958), pp. 22–34.
10. Beverly Duncan and Philip Hauser, *Housing a Metropolis* (Chicago, 1960), p. 208.
11. Statistics on improvements in the quality of housing received by relocated families is given in *The Housing of Relocated Families*, Office of the Administrator, Housing and Home Finance Agency (Washington, D.C., 1965).
12. Karl Taeuber and Alma Taeuber, "Recent Trends in Race and Ethnic Segregation in Chicago." *Proceedings of the Social Statistics Section, American Statistical Association* (Washington, D.C., 1962), p. 14.
13. *Ibid.*, p. 13.
14. *Where Shall We Live?, op. cit.,* p 248.
15. U.S. Bureau of the Census, *U.S. Census of Population: 1960.* Selected Area Reports, Standard Metropolitan Areas, Final Report PC (3)-ID (Washington, D.C., 1963), Table 1.
16. Robin M. Williams, Jr., *op. cit.*, p. 248.
17. Otis Dudley Duncan and Stanley Lieberson, "Ethnic Segregation and Assimilation," *American Journal of Sociology*, Vol. 64 (January 1959), p. 370.
18. Stanley Elkins, *Slavery* (Chicago, 1959), pp. 115–133.
19. The statistics in this section are taken from G. Franklin Edwards, "Marriage and Family Life Among Negroes," *The Journal of Negro Education*, Vol. 32 (Fall 1963), pp. 451–465.
20. *Ibid.*, p. 463.
21. Current Population Reports, "Income of Families and Persons in the United States; 1963," Series P-60, No. 43 (Washington, D.C., 1964), Table 1, p. 21.
22. *U.S. Census of Population: 1960, U.S. Summary*, Detailed Characteristics, Final Report PC (1)-ID (Washington, D.C., 1963), Tables 224 and 225, pp. 594–603.
23. *The Howard University Magazine*, Vol. 7, No. 4 (July 1965), p. 7.
24. *Ibid.*
25. Lewis' study, conducted over a period of five years, is now being prepared for publication. The references in this paper were taken from various reports which the investigator made available to the writer.

26. *Manpower Report of the President* (Washington, D.C., 1964), Table F-3, p. 253.
27. Charles E. Silberman, *Crisis in Black and White* (New York, 1964), pp. 309 ff.
28. Whitney Young, Jr., *To Be Equal* (New York, 1964), pp. 22–23.
29. E. Franklin Frazier, "The New Negro," in *The New Negro Thirty Years Afterward* (Washington, D.C., 1955), p. 26.
30. *Ibid.*
31. Computed from U.S. Bureau of the Census, *U.S. Census of Population: 1960, U.S. Summary,* Detailed Characteristics, Final Report PC (1)-ID, Table 208.
32. *Ibid.*
33. Computed from *U.S. Census of Population: 1940,* Vol. II. *Characteristics of the Population,* Part 1, U.S. Summary, Table 128, p. 278; and *U.S. Census of Population: 1960,* Vol. I, *Characteristics of the Population,* Part 1, *U.S. Summary,* Table 205, p. 544.
34. Ibid.
35. From data supplied the writer by Dr. W. Montague Cobb, editor of the *Journal of the National Medical Association.*
36. Ratios for many of these occupations are supplied in Leonard Broom and Norval Glenn, *Transformation of the Negro American* (New York, 1965), Table 5, pp. 112–113.
37. This is the thesis of E. Franklin Frazier, *Black Bourgeoisie* (Chicago, 1957). See, especially, pp. 195–212. See also Frazier, "Human, All too Human," *Survey Graphic:* twelfth Calling America Number (January 1947), pp. 74–75, 99–100.
38. E. Franklin Frazier, "Desegregation as a Social Process," in Arnold Rose (ed.), *Human Behavior and Social Processes* (Boston, 1962), p. 619.
39. Martha Coffee, "A Study of a Professional Association and Racial Integration," unpublished Master's thesis, Department of Sociology, Howard University, Washington, D.C., 1953.
40. "Desegregation and the Negro Middle Class," remarks of Dr. Andrew F. Brimmer, Assistant Secretary of Commerce for Economic Affairs. Detroit, Michigan, July 16, 1965.
41. *Ibid.,* p. 8.
42. A good discussion of these hate groups is given in James W. Vander Zanden, *Race Relations in Transition: The Segregation Crisis in the South* (New York, 1965), pp. 25–54. See also Arnold Forster and Benjamin Epstein, *Report on the Ku Klux Klan* (New York, 1965).
43.. See the following: Wesley C. George, *The Biology of the Race Problem* (A report prepared by commission of the Governor of Alabama, 1962); and Dwight J. Ingle, "Racial Differences and the Future," *Science,* Vol. 146 (October 16, 1964), pp. 375–379.
44. Figures from *Southern School News,* Vol. 11 (December 1964), p. 1.
45. Benjamin Muse, *Ten Years of Prelude: The Story of Integration Since the Supreme Court's 1954 Decision* (New York, 1964).
46. Otis Dudley Duncan, "Population Trends, Mobility and Social Change," a paper prepared for the Seminar on Dimensions of American Society, Committee on Social Studies, American Association of Colleges for Teacher Education, p. 52.
47. Hurley Doddy and G. Franklin Edwards, "Apprehension of Negro Teachers Concerning Desegregation in South Carolina," *Journal of Negro Education,* Vol. 24 (Winter 1955), Table 1, pp. 30–31.
48. *The Washington Post,* September 6, 1965, p. 1.
49. For a list of the growing number of Negro office holders, see Harold F. Gosnell and Robert E. Martin, "The Negro as Voter and Office Holder," *Journal of Negro Education,* Vol. 32 (Fall 1963), pp. 415–425.

Franklin Edwards focused upon the social barriers that have served to keep Negroes second-class in name and in fact. Here, Kenneth Clark examines the psychological defenses used to cope with the ever-present reminders of their ascribed status.

While both of these social scientists are aware of what others have called "black culture," they tend 3to see its norms and values as reactions to, or, better stated, as defenses against, discrimination. The implication in both essays is that most black Americans, if asked by whites what they really want, would say, "What you got."

18

The Psychology of the Ghetto

Kenneth B. Clark

It is now generally understood that chronic and remediable social injustices corrode and damage the human personality, thereby robbing it of its effectiveness, of its creativity, if not its actual humanity. No matter how desperately one seeks to deny it, this simple fact persists and intrudes itself. It is the fuel of protests and revolts. Racial segregation, like all other forms of cruelty and tyranny, debases all human beings—those who are its victims, those who victimize, and in quite subtle ways those who are merely accessories.

This human debasement can only be comprehended as a consequence of the society which spawns it. The victims of segregation do not initially desire to be segregated, they do not "prefer to be with their own people," in spite of the fact that this belief is commonly stated by those who are not themselves segregated. A most cruel and psychologically oppressive aspect and consequence of enforced segregation

---

is that its victims can be made to accommodate to their victimized status and under certain circumstances to state that it *is* their desire to be set apart, or to agree that subjugation is not really detrimental but beneficial. The fact remains that exclusion, rejection, and a Stigmatized status are not desired and are not voluntary states. Segregation is neither sought nor imposed by healthy or potentially healthy human beings.

Human beings who are forced to live under ghetto conditions and whose daily experience tells them that almost nowhere in society are they respected and granted the ordinary dignity and courtesy accorded to others will, as a matter of course, begin to doubt their own worth. Since every human being depends upon his cumulative experiences with others for clues as to how he should view and value himself, children who are consistently rejected understandably begin to question and doubt whether they, their family, and their group really deserve no more respect from the larger society than they receive. These doubts become the seeds of a pernicious self- and group-hatred, the Negro's complex and debilitating prejudice against himself.

The preoccupation of many Negroes with hair straighteners, skin bleachers, and the like illustrates this tragic aspect of American racial prejudice—Negroes have come to believe in their own inferiority. In recent years Negro men and women have rebelled against the constant struggle to become white and have given special emphasis to their "Negroid" features and hair textures in a self-conscious acceptance of "negritude"—a whole-hearted embracing of the African heritage. But whether a Negro woman uses hair straightener or whether she high-lights her natural hair texture by flaunting *au naturel* styles, whether a Negro man hides behind a neat Ivy League suit or wears blue jeans defiantly in the manner of the Student Non-violent Coordinating Committee (SNCC), each is still reacting primarily to the pervasive factor of race and still not free to take himself for granted or to judge himself by the usual standards of personal success and character. It is still the white man's society that governs the Negro's image of himself.

Fantasy Protections

Many Negroes live sporadically in a world of fantasy, and fantasy takes different forms at different ages. In childhood the delusion is a simple one—the child may pretend that he is really white. When Negro children as young as three years old are shown white- and Negro-appearing dolls or asked to color pictures of children to look like themselves, many of them tend to reject the dark-skinned dolls as "dirty" and "bad" or to color the picture of themselves a light color or a bizarre shade like purple. But the fantasy is not complete, for when asked to identify which doll is like themselves, some Negro children, particularly in the North, will refuse, burst into tears, and run away. By the age of seven most Negro children have accepted the reality that they are, after all, dark skinned. But the stigma remains; they have been forced to recognize themselves as inferior. Few if any Negroes ever fully lose that sense of shame and self-hatred.

To the Negro child the most serious injury seems to be in the concept of self-worth related directly to skin color itself. Because school is a central activity at this age, his sense of inferiority is revealed most acutely in his lack of confidence in himself as a student, lack of motivation to learn, and in problems of behavior—a gradual withdrawal or a growing rebellion. The effects of this early damage are difficult to overcome, for the child who never learns to read cannot become a success at a job or in a society where education and culture are necessary. In addition, there is the possibility that poor teaching, generally characteristic of the ghetto schools, tends to reinforce this sense of inferiority and to give it substance in the experience of inferior achievement. The cycle that leads to menial jobs and to broken homes has then begun; only the most drastic efforts at rehabilitation can break that cycle.

The obsession with whiteness continues past childhood and into adulthood. It stays with the Negro all his life. Haryou [Harlem Youth Opportunities Unlimited] recorded a conversation between teen-age boys about their hair styles that reflected this obsession.

> You know, if he go in there with his hair slick up like white, they might go for him better, you know.
> They might use him for a broom or a mop.
> Well, why do you wear "brushes?"
> Why do I wear "brushes?" It's a blind, a front. Are you saying that I'm ignorant?
> He's a playboy. He like to do his hair like that. He's ashamed of his own hair, you know. He feels bad that he's black and now he wants to be half and half. He wants to be a half-breed.
> When your great granmammy was taken advantage of in the fields, what was happening then? Have you ever seen a light-skinned African? Have you ever seen an African your color?
> No.
> All right then; two bird dogs don't make nothing but a bird dog.
> You don't have to go all the way, getting your hair slicked.
> I don't have to go all the way black either, do I?
> What are you going to do? You can't go all the way white.

Teen-age Negroes often cope with the ghetto's frustrations by retreating into fantasies related chiefly to their role in society. There is, for example, a fantasy employed by many marginal and antisocial teen-agers, to pretend to knowledge about illicit activities and to a sexual urbanity that they do not, really, have. They use as their models the petty criminals of the ghetto, whose colorful, swaggering style of cool bravado poses a peculiar fascination. Some pretend falsely to be pimps, some to have contacts with numbers runners. Their apparent admiration of these models is not total but reflects a curious combination of respect, of contempt, and, fundamentally, of despair. Social scientists who rely on questionnaires and superficial interviews must find a way to unravel this tangled web of pretense if their conclusions are to be relevant.

Among the young men observed at Haryou, fantasy played a major role. Many of these marginal, upward-striving teen-agers allowed others to believe that they were college students. One young man told his friends that he was a major in psychology. He had enrolled in the classes of a Negro professor with whom he identified, and he described those lectures in detail to his friends. The fact is that he was a dropout from high school. Others dressed like college students and went to college campuses where they walked among the students, attempting to feel a part of a life they longed for and could not attain. Some carried attaché cases wherever they went—often literally empty. One carried ordinary books camouflaged by college bookcovers and pretended to "study" in the presence of friends. Most of these young men were academically at the fifth-or sixth-grade reading level; none was in college. Another youngster who said he was in college planned to become a nuclear physicist. He spoke most convincingly about his physics and math courses and discussed the importance of Negroes' going into the field. Within a year, however, he had been dropped for non-attendance from the evening session of the municipal college at which he was enrolled. He had not taken even a first course in physics and had not been able to pass the elementary course in mathematics. He explained this failure in a complicated story and reported that he now intended to get a job. Later he described his new job in the executive training program of a high-status department store downtown. He was saving for college where he would continue with nuclear physics. He carried an attaché case to work each day. But the truth was that he was not in an executive training program at all; he had a job as a stock clerk. Yet the fantasy was one of performance; there was truth in his dreams, for if he had been caught in time he might have become a scientist. He did have the intellectual potential. But as a Negro, he had been damaged so early in the educational process that not even the surge of motivation and his basic intelligence could now make his dreams effective. His motivation was sporadic and largely verbal; his plans were in the realm of delusion. To some, this form of social schizophrenia might seem comic, but a more appropriate response is tears, not laughter.

Sex and Status

In Negro adults the sense of inadequate self-worth shows up in lack of motivation to rise in their jobs or fear of competition with whites; in a sense of impotence in civic affairs demonstrated in lethargy toward voting, or community participation, or responsibility for others; in family instability and the irresponsibility rooted in hopelessness.

But, because, in American life, sex is, like business advancement, a prime criterion of success and hence of personal worth, it is in sexual behavior that the damage to Negro adults shows up in especially poignant and tragic clarity. The inconsistency between the white society's view of the Negro as inferior and its sexual exploitation of Negroes has seemed to its victims a degrading hypocrisy. Negroes observe that ever since slavery white men have regarded Negroes as inferior and have condemned interracial marriage while considering illicit sexual relationships with Negro women appropriate to their own higher status. The white man in America has, historically, arranged to have both white and Negro women available to him; he has claimed sexual priority with both and, in the process, he has sought to emasculate Negro men. Negro males could not hold their women, nor could they defend them. The white male tried to justify this restriction of meaningful competition with the paradoxical claim that Negro males were animal-like and brutish in their appetites and hence to be feared and shunned by white women. The ironic fact has been that, given the inferiority of their racial status, Negro males have had to struggle simply to believe themselves men. It has long been an "inside" bit of bitter humor among Negroes to say that Negro men should bribe their wives to silence.

Certain Negro women of status who have married white men report that their choice was related to their discovery that the Negro men they knew were inferior in status, interests, and sophistication and hence unsuitable as partners. Many problems of race and sex seem to follow this principle of the self-fulfilling prophecy. The Negro woman of status may see the Negro male as undesirable as a sexual partner precisely because of his low status in the eyes of whites. Unlike a white female who may reassure herself that the lower the status of the male, the more satisfying he is as a sexual partner, the upper-class Negro female tends to tie sexual desirability to status and exclude many Negro males as undesirable just because their status is inferior. It is a real question whether this "discovery" is based on fact or whether these women are not accepting the white society's assumption of the low status of Negro men and therefore expecting them to be weak. On the other hand, frustrated, thrillseeking white males or females who have been told all their lives that Negroes are primitive and uninhibited may seek and find sexual fulfillment among the same Negroes who are cool, distant, or hostile in their relationship to other Negroes. In sexual matters it appears that those who expect weakness or gratification often find what they expect.

As Negro male self-esteem rises in the wake of the civil rights movement, one interesting incidental fact is that any Negro woman who is known to be the mistress of a white public official—and particularly any mistress of a segregationist—has been put under a growing pressure to break that relationship. In the past, Negroes tended to suppress their bitterness about such illicit relationships, accepting the white male's evaluation of himself and of them, and in a sense forgiving the Negro woman for submitting to the temptation of protection and economic gain. In the last decade, however, Negro mistresses of white officials are more openly rejected and are regarded as one of the "enemy."

White men were accustomed to possessing Negro women without marriage, but today the fact that a number of white men are married to Negro women of status, particularly those who are well known in the theatrical world, indicates that Negro women are placing higher value upon their own dignity than many other Negro women were permitted to in the past—and so are the white men who marry them. But, though a Negro woman may gain status by marrying into the white community, Negro men, even in the North, remain vulnerable if they seek to cross racial lines and to break this most fearsome of social taboos. When they have done so they have paid a tremendous price—lynching, murder, or a prison sentence in the South, social condemnation in the North—but, above all, the price of their own self-doubt and anxiety. The full complexity of social disapproval and personal doubt is difficult to resist psychologically even when the law allows and protects such nonconformist behavior.

The emerging, more affirmative sexual pride among Negro males may have as one of its consequences an increasing trend toward more open competition between white and Negro males for both white and Negro females. One of the further consequences would probably be an intensification of hostility of white males toward interracial couples and toward the white female participants, reflecting the desire on the part of the white male to preserve his own competitive advantage. One would expect him then to employ his economic and political power—without suspecting the fundamental basis of his antagonism—to maintain the inferior status of the Negro male for as long as possible. An important level of racial progress will have been reached when Negro and white men and women may marry anyone they choose, without punishment, ostracism, ridicule, or guilt.

The Negro Matriarchy and the Distorted Masculine Image

Sexual hierarchy has played a crucial role in the structure and pathology of the Negro family. Because of the system of slavery in which the Negro male was systematically used as a stud and the Negro female used primarily for purposes of breeding or for the gratification of the white male, the only source of family continuity was through the female, the dependence of the child on his mother. This pattern, together with the continued post-slavery relegation of the Negro male to menial and subservient status, has made the female the dominant person in the Negro family. Psychologically, the Negro male could not support his normal desire for dominance. For the most part he was not allowed to be a consistent wage earner; he could not present himself to his wife and children as a person who had the opportunity or the ability to compete successfully in politics, business, and industry. His doubts concerning his personal adequacy were therefore reinforced. He was compelled to base his self-esteem instead on a kind of behavior that tended to support a stereotyped picture of the Negro male—sexual impulsiveness, irresponsibility, verbal bombast, posturing, and compensatory achievement in entertainment and athletics, particularly in sports like boxing in which athletic prowess could be exploited for the gain of others. The Negro male was, therefore, driven to seek status in ways which seemed either antisocial, escapist, or socially irresponsible. The pressure to find relief from his intolerable psychological position seems directly related to the continued high incidence of desertions and broken homes in Negro ghettos.

The Negro woman has, in turn, been required to hold the family together; to set the goals, to stimulate, encourage, and to protect both boys and girls. Her compensatory strength tended to perpetuate the weaker role of the Negro male. Negro boys had the additional problem of finding no strong male father figure upon which to model their own behavior, perhaps one of the reasons for the prevalent idea among marginal Negroes that it is not masculine to sustain a stable father or husband relationship with a woman. Many young men establish temporary liaisons with a number of different women with no responsibility toward any. Among Negro teen-agers the cult of going steady has never had the vogue it seems to have among white teen-agers; security for Negroes is found not in a relationship modeled after a stable family—for they have seen little of this in their own lives—but upon the relationship they observed in their own home: unstable and temporary liaisons. The marginal young Negro male tends to identify his masculinity with the number of girls he can attract. The high incidence of illegitimacy among Negro young people reflects this pervasive fact. In this compensatory distortion of the male image, masculinity is, therefore, equated with alleged sexual prowess.

The middle-class white and Negro male often separates women into two categories, good women with whom he will go steady and marry, and others with whom he has and will continue to have sexual relations alone. The lower-class Negro is, in a way, more sophisticated than either in his refusal to make undemocratic distinctions between "good girls" and "others". The consistently higher illegitimacy rate among Negroes is not a reflection of less virtue or greater promiscuity, but rather of the fact that the middle-class teen-agers are taught the use of contraceptives and learn how to protect themselves from the hazards of premarital and illicit sexual contacts. The middle-class girl is able to resort to abortions, or she gives birth secretly, surrendering the child for adoption. In the case of marginal young people, or the upwardly mobile Negro, what contraceptive ideas he has are unreliable; and rarely does the girl participate in protection, in part because it is taken as a sign of masculinity for the male to supervise such matters. Illegitimacy among these groups, therefore, is a consequence, in large part, of poverty and ignorance.

Among Negro middle-class families the attitude toward sex is vastly different from that among marginal and lower-class Negro groups. The middle-class Negro fears he will be identified with the Negro masses from whom he has escaped or tried to escape, and sex is a focal point of anxiety. The middle-class girl is often so rigidly protected that normal sexual behavior is inhibited, or she learns to be sophisticated about the use of contraceptives. For her, as for white middle-class girls, sex is tied to status and aspirations. She wants to make a good marriage—marriage to a white man might even be available—and the motivation to avoid illegitimate pregnancy is great.

The marginal young people in the ghetto, through their tentative and sporadic relationships, are seeking love, affection, and acceptance perhaps more desperately than young people elsewhere. Person-to-person relationships are, for many, a compensation for society's rejection. They are, in a sense, forced to be quite elemental in their demands, and sex becomes more important for them than even they realize. They act in a cavalier fashion about their affairs, trying to seem casual and cool, but it is clear nonetheless that they are dominated by the complexity of their needs.

The girl, like the boy, has no illusions. Unlike the middle-class girl who believes—or demands—that each relationship should be forever, and who tries to hold on to the boy, the marginal Negro lower-class girl is realistic about the facts of the situation. Nor does she expect to hold the boy. Sex is important to her, but it is not, as in middle-class society, a symbol of status, to be used to rise into a better family or a higher income bracket. The marginal Negro female uses her sex, instead, to gain personal affirmation. She is desired, and that is almost enough. The relationship, whatever its social and psychological limitations, is pure in the same sense as innocence—that is, it is not contaminated by other goals. For her and for the boy, sex is time-contained, with its own intrinsic worth and value, not animal in its expression, but related to the urgent human need for acceptance; it is sophisticated, not primitive.

This innocent sophistication includes the total acceptance of the child if a child comes. In the ghetto, the meaning of the illegitimate child is not ultimate disgrace. There is not the demand for abortion or for surrender of the child that one finds in more privileged communities. In the middle class, the disgrace of illegitimacy is tied to personal and family aspirations. In lower-class families, on the other hand, the girl loses only some of her already limited options by having an illegitimate child; she is not going to make a "better marriage" or improve her economic and social status either way. On the contrary, a child is a symbol of the fact that she is a woman, and she may gain from having something of her own. Nor is the boy who fathers an illegitimate child going to lose, for where is he going? The path to any higher status seems closed to him in any case.

Illegitimacy in the ghetto cannot be understood or dealt with in terms of punitive hostility, as in the suggestion that unwed mothers be denied welfare if illegitimacy is repeated. Such approaches obscure, with empty and at times hypocritical moralizing, the desperate yearning of the young for acceptance and identity, the need to be meaningful to someone else even for a moment without implication of a pledge of undying fealty and foreverness. If, when the girl becomes pregnant, the boy deserts or refuses to marry her, it is often because neither can sustain an intimate relationship; both seem incapable of the tenderness that continues beyond immediate gratification. Both may have a realistic, if unconscious, acceptance of the fact that nothing else is possible; to expect—to ask—for more would be to open oneself to the inevitable rejections, hurts, and frustrations. The persistent experience of rejection spills over into the anticipation and acceptance of rejection in a love relationship. This lack of illusion stems from the fact that there can be no illusion in any other area of life. To expose oneself further to the chances of failure in a sustained and faithful relationship is too large to risk. The intrinsic value of the relationship is the only value because there can be no other.

Among most lower-class Negroes, competition in sex is predominantly heterosexual and free. In the Negro middle class sexual freedom and expression are often identified with lower-class status, and many men and women are therefore governed chiefly by their inhibitions and cannot act freely in matters of sex. The men may be impotent, the women frigid, and both afflicted with guilt. Some compensate for the restraints on sexual adequacy and fulfillment through fantasies and boasting about a false prowess. Other middle-class Negro men retreat into noncommittal peripheral relationships with women, avoiding all alternatives—homosexuality, heterosexuality, or verbal bombasts—as risks requiring more ego strength than their resources permit. Instead, a blank and apathetic sexlessness domiates their lives. They withdraw from all commitment to another person seeking refuge from the dangers of personal vulnerability.

Considering the depth and the complexity of the need, aggressive sexual behavior may, for many of the racially damaged, make the difference between personal stability and instability. Until the lower-class Negro is free to compete for and to win the socially acceptable rewards of middle-class society, the ghetto's pattern of venereal disease, illegitimacy, and family instability will remain unbroken. But when that time comes, no one can expect destructive sexual activity to cease abruptly. What is more likely is a shift to another, some would say "higher," level of behavior; then the Negro's sexual "misbehavior" will be indistinguishable in all respects from that of the respectables—with full participation in divorce, abortions, adultery, and the various forms of jaded and fashionable middle- and upper-class sexual explorations. There might even be the possibility of sexual fulfillment and health.

White Rationalizations

It is now rare even for the most ardent apologist for the *status quo* seriously to assert that the American pattern of segregation has beneficial consequences. Some do, however, continue to argue that the Negro's inferiority and inherent character defects demand that he be segregated. Others suggest that the chances of his developing those traits and characteristics which would make him more acceptable to the white community would be greater if he would function within his own community until he demonstrates that he is worthy of associating with others. Among the questions which remain unanswered by this type of argument are: Under what circumstances is the Negro ever adjudged worthy or deserving of association with others, and how can he be expected to develop these traits of "worthiness" under conditions which tend to perpetuate characteristics of unworthiness as described by the proponents of this position themselves? In the belief no doubt that this was a statement of compassion, one white opponent of New York's school integration plan said: "If I were God, what would I do to improve the lot of the Negro? If I were God, I'd make everybody white."[1] To sensitive Negroes, this betrays the ultimate condescension—the belief that to *be* Negro means irrevocable rejection.

Even this point of view is not logically consistent, since the same individuals who reject Negroes as offensive have no difficulty, as we have noted above, in accepting Negroes in close and at times intimate association and relationship, for example, as servants or menials or mistresses, as long as the inferior position of the Negro and the dominant position of the white is clearly perceived and accepted by both.

The answers to these questions cannot be found in any single devil—but must be sought in the compliant or accessory role of many in society. However, more privileged individuals understandably may need to shield themselves from the inevitable conflict and pain which would result from their acceptance of the fact that they *are* accessories to profound injustice. The tendency to discuss disturbing social issues such as racial discrimination, segregation, and economic exploitation in detached, legal, political, socio-economic, or psychological terms as if these persistent problems did not involve the suffering of actual human beings is so contrary to empirical evidence that it must be interpreted as a protective device. After World War II, the bulk of the German people *could not know* what was going on in the death camps. The people of Mississippi *had to believe* in 1964 that the disappearance and death of the three civil rights workers in that state was a diversionary strategy plotted by civil rights groups. Negroes generally expected that a grand jury in New York City *would have found* that it was justifiable homicide performed in the line of duty for a white policeman to kill a fifteen-year-old Negro boy who was "attacking him with a penknife." Insensitivity is a protective device. Among its more primitive examples are: The prevalent beliefs that the predicament of the masses of Negroes reflects their inherent racial inferiority; that the poor are to blame for the squalor and despair of the slums; that the victims of social injustice are somehow subhuman persons who cause and perpetuate their own difficulties; that the more responsible and superior people of the society not only have no obligation for the "irresponsibles" but must be vigilant to see that all of the power of government is used to protect them and their children from them; and that any contrary or compassionate interpretation of the plight of the poor or the rejected is merely the sentimental and naive expression of impractical do-gooders or "bleeding hearts."

More subtle and obscure forms of protection against facing the consequences of social injustice are to be found among those social scientists who cultivate that degree of academic detachment which blocks meaningful or insightful study of human affairs. The preoccupation with trivia—as if this were the ultimate scientific virtue and goal—leads to the irrelevance of much social science research. It is interesting to speculate on the significance of the fact that during the ten years after the U.S. Supreme Court school desegregation decision, an increasing number of social scientists have raised questions concerning the "scientific validity" of the psychological and sociological data cited by the Court as evidence of the damage which segregation inflicts upon personality. Not one of these critics had questioned these data and their interpretations prior to the Court's decision, although the studies on which they were based had been published and available for critical reactions for many years prior to their use in the historic decision.

Certain students of jurisprudence have also criticized the Court's decision on the grounds that the Brown decision, which ruled that state laws requiring or permitting racial segregation in public schools violated the equal protection clause of the Fourteenth Amendment, was based upon flimsy sociological and psychological data rather than upon more stable and heretofore determining legal grounds. This, too, is a purist approach rooted in the belief that detachment or enforced distance from the human consequences of persistent injustice is objectively desirable. It may rather be of service primarily as a subconscious protection against personal pain and direct involvement in moral controversies.

The language and the emphasis of the Court's decision made any such evasion of the human costs of racial segregation quite difficult. The Court insisted upon a simple and direct statement of the reality:

> To separate them from others of similar age and qualifications solely because of their race generates a feeling of inferiority as to their status in the community that may affect their hearts and minds in a way unlikely ever to be undone. The effect of this separation on their educational opportunities was well stated by a finding in the Kansas case by a court which nevertheless felt compelled to rule against the Negro plaintiffs: Segregation of white and colored children in public schools has a detrimental effect upon the colored children. The impact is greater when it has the sanction of the law: for the policy of separating the races is usually interpreted as denoting the inferiority of the Negro

group. A sense of inferiority affects the motivation of a child to learn. Segregation with the sanction of the law, therefore, has a tendency to retard the educational and mental development of Negro children and to deprive them of some of the benefits they would receive in a racially integrated school system.[2]

The obscuring function of legal technicalities and the equivocations of social science jargon were rejected and in their place was offered an understandable statement of the inevitable anguish of rejected and stigmatized human beings.

The pervasive need to turn one's back on any clear evidence of man's inhumanity to man exemplified in the cool objective approach is probably most clearly seen, though in a more subtle form, in the detached "professionalism" of many social workers and in the selective isolation of many psychiatrists and clinical psychologists. Some members of these "helping fields," too, have often defended as objectivity what, to the client, feels more like insensitivity. Furthermore, in their preoccupation with the problem of the individual and their insistence upon reducing him to a manageable system of assumptions, the disturbing and dehumanizing social realities behind his personal agony may be avoided. With the professional perspective which constricts social vision to the impulses, strengths, and weaknesses of the individual "client" as if these can be isolated from the injustices and pathologies of his life, these professionals need not confront the difficult problems of the nature and origin of the social injustices nor run the risks of conflict with the many vested interests which tend to perpetuate the problems of the poor and the rejected. This posture is built into the nature of their training and reinforced by their complex role as agents of the more privileged classes and the admitted and irrevocable fact of their identification with the middle classes. The professionals themselves would point out, also, that the routinizing pressure of bureaucratic procedures, and a heavy case load of human suffering dull the edge of concern and that the most sensitive among them feel, within the structure, uncertain and helpless as to how to address themselves to the problem of social change. It is not surprising, altogether, that compassion is usually sooner or later subordinated to accommodation; yet it is hard for many to understand why they are irrelevant to the root problems of the poor.

Some theorists and practitioners maintain that it is not within their power or training to attempt to help working-class and low-status people because the problems of these people are psychosocial and, since they cannot be "reached," are not amenable to the psychotherapeutic and casework techniques thought to be helpful in working with middle-class individuals. Some professionals tend to limit their role to that of models or interpreters of the middle-class norms of speech, behavior, dress, values, and ways of handling problems and feelings. In view of their status and psychological distance, the social workers concern to "relate to" the "client" seems pathetic in its failure of elemental empathy. The stated or unstated goal of this type of "therapeutic" relationship must then become that of helping the client "adjust" to his life realities, i.e., to keep him from "acting out" his rebellion in antisocial or self-destructive ways and thereby to function more effectively *within* the continuing pathology of his society. These goals are consistent with the *status quo* convenience of the middle class. They are consistent with the benign artificiality of response from these professionals which repels the members of the working class, for whom the immediate and pressing realities of their daily lives alone seem relevant. That middle-class individuals are not equally repelled may be an indication of the extent to which pretenses and protective detachment have become norms of middle-class adjustment—particularly in a society of accepted injustice. This is not to say that individual therapy is not needed and cannot be effective. It is to say that such procedures are not effective where social pathology is at the root of the individual's maladjustment. It is a real question whether adjustment or indifference to the reality of injustice is not the real neurosis, and rebellion the evidence of health.

Moral Objectivity

Objectivity, without question essential to the scientific perspective when it warns of the dangers of bias and prejudgment in interfering with the search for truth and in contaminating the understanding of truth, too often becomes a kind of a fetish which serves to block the view of truth itself, particularly when painful and difficult moral insights are involved. The question of the nature of objectivity in law, in science, in human relationships, is complex and cannot be resolved by attempts to make it synonymous with the exclusion of feeling and value. Objectivity that implies detachment or escape from psychological reality decreases understanding and can be used merely to avoid the problem. In the social sciences, the cult of objectivity seems often to be associated with "not taking sides." When carried to its extreme, this type of objectivity could be equated with ignorance. When the social psychology department of an outstanding Eastern university received a substantial grant to endow a chair in the field of race relations, the responsible officials of that department decided that, in order to obtain the most objective person, they should consider no one who had worked extensively in the field of race relations. Indeed, they decided to appoint someone who had

had no experience in this field at all, and chose a man whose major contribution to psychology was rather in the field of the experimental psychology of visual discrimination. Perhaps the guiding assumption was that the problem of American race relations was to be understood in the most fundamental terms of the capacity of the rods and cones of the human retina to differentiate color! Imagine, however, if a chair in nuclear science were to be filled in any university, how transparently absurd it would seem to choose a man with no experience in the field, on the grounds that he thereby would be more objective! The fact that this did not seem absurd to scholars in the case of race relations is a revealing commentary. It may be that where essential human psychological and moral issues are at stake, noninvolvement and noncommitment and the exclusion of feeling are neither sophisticated nor objective, but naive and violative of the scientific spirit at its best. Where human feelings are part of the evidence, they cannot be ignored. Where anger is the appropriate response, to exclude the recognition and acceptance of anger, and even to avoid the feeling itself as if it were an inevitable contamination, is to set boundaries upon truth itself. If a scholar who studied Nazi concentration camps did not feel revolted by the evidence no one would say he was unobjective, but rather fear for his sanity and moral sensitivity. Feeling may twist judgment, but the lack of feeling may twist it even more. And to insist on quantitative measurement and analysis of certain phenomena, of, for example, love or friendship, is to distort the nature of the phenomenon itself. It is not to enlarge truth, but to constrict it.

Even to pose an hypothesis is to move away from literal objectivity, *if* objectivity is to be defined as total openmindedness. Objectivity should play a role not in the refusal to make hypotheses, but in the rigorous assessment of the evidence accumulated for that hypothesis, so as to guard, as far as possible, against any distortion of these facts. When one cares deeply what the answer to a question is, one must exercise even greater care to examine the evidence than if the answer is of no personal consequence. To refuse science the right to deal with such phenomena is to set intolerable limits, for moral decisions, like all others, should be based on fact. Responsible objectivity includes the totality of reality, not a part alone.

Notes

1.   *New York Times Magazine*, September 20, 1964, p. 122.
2.   *Brown v. Board of Education*, 347 U.S. 483 (1954).

Originally written as a working paper for a White House Conference, "To Fulfill These Rights," Daniel P. Moynihan's report The Negro Family *rapidly became one of the most controversial and widely debated documents ever printed by the government.*

Here is the famous (some would say infamous) "Moynihan Report." It is reprinted here in its entirety (save for the appendices) to give the reader the opportunity to judge for himself the focus and content of Moynihan's argument and to weigh his often overlooked suggestions.

19

The Negro Family

Daniel P. Moynihan

I. The Negro American Revolution

The Negro American revolution is rightly regarded as the most important domestic event of the postwar period in the United States.

Nothing like it has occurred since the upheavals of the 1930's which led to the organization of the great industrial trade unions, and which in turn profoundly altered both the economy and the political scene. There have been few other events in our history—the American Revolution itself, the surge of Jacksonian Democracy in the 1830's, the Abolitionist movement, and the Populist movement of the late nineteenth century—comparable to the current Negro movement.

There has been none more important. The Negro American revolution holds forth the prospect that the American Republic, which

From Daniel P. Moynihan, *The Negro Family: The Case for National Action*, Washington D.C.: Office of Policy Planning and Research, U.S. Department of Labor, 1965.

at birth was flawed by the institution of Negro slavery, and which throughout its history has been marred by the unequal treatment of Negro citizens, will at last redeem the full promise of the Declaration of Independence.

Although the Negro leadership has conducted itself with the strictest propriety, acting always and only as American citizens asserting their rights within the framework of the American political system, it is no less clear that the movement has profound international implications.

It was in no way a matter of chance that the nonviolent tactics and philosophy of the movement, as it began in the South, were consciously adapted from the techniques by which the Congress Party undertook to free the Indian nation from British colonial rule. It was not a matter of chance that the Negro movement caught fire in America at just that moment when the nations of Africa were gaining their freedom. Nor is it merely incidental that the world should have fastened its attention on events in the United States at a time when the possibility that the nations of the world will divide along color lines seems suddenly not only possible, but even imminent.

(Such racist views have made progress within the Negro American community itself—which can hardly be expected to be immune to a virus that is endemic in the white community. The Black Muslim doctrines, based on total alienation from the white world, exert a powerful influence. On the far left, the attraction of Chinese Communism can no longer be ignored.)

It is clear that what happens in America is being taken as a sign of what can, or must, happen in the world at large. The course of world events will be profoundly affected by the success or failure of the Negro American revolution in seeking the peaceful assimilation of the races in the United States. The award of the Nobel Peace Prize to Dr. Martin Luther King was as much an expression of the hope for the future, as it was recognition for past achievement.

It is no less clear that carrying this revolution forward to a successful conclusion is a first priority confronting the Great Society.

The End of the Beginning

The major events of the onset of the Negro revolution are now behind us.

The *political events* were three: First, the Negroes themselves organized as a mass movement. Their organizations have been in some ways better disciplined and better led than any in our history. They have established an unprecedented alliance with religious groups throughout the nation and have maintained close ties with both political parties and with most segments of the trade union movement. Second, the Kennedy-Johnson Administration committed the Federal government to the cause of Negro equality. This had never happened before. Third, the 1964 Presidential election was practically a referendum on this commitment: if these were terms made by the opposition, they were in effect accepted by the President.

The overwhelming victory of President Johnson must be taken as emphatic popular endorsement of the unmistakable, and openly avowed course which the Federal government has pursued under his leadership.

The *administrative events* were threefold as well: First, beginning with the establishment of the President's Committee on Equal Employment Opportunity and on to the enactment of the Manpower Development and Training Act of 1962, the Federal government has launched a major national effort to redress the profound imbalance between the economic position of the Negro citizens and the rest of the nation that derives primarily from their unequal position in the labor market. Second, the Economic Opportunity Act of 1964 began a major national effort to abolish poverty, a condition in which almost half of Negro families are living. Third, the Civil Rights Act of 1964 marked the end of the era of legal and formal discrimination against Negroes and created important new machinery for combating covert discrimination and unequal treatment. (The Act does not guarantee an end to harassment in matters such as voter registration, but does make it more or less incumbent upon government to take further steps to thwart such efforts when they do occur.)

The *legal events* were no less specific. Beginning with *Brown* v. *Board of Education* in 1954, through the decade that culminated in the recent decisions upholding Title II of the Civil Rights Act, the Federal judiciary, led by the Supreme Court, has used every opportunity to combat unequal treatment of Negro citizens. It may be put as a general proposition that the laws of the United States now look upon any such treatment as obnoxious, and that the courts will strike it down wherever it appears.

The Demand for Equality

With these events behind us, the nation now faces a different set of challenges, which may prove more difficult to meet, if only because they cannot be cast as concrete propositions of right and wrong.

The fundamental problem here is that the Negro revolution, like the industrial upheaval of the 1930's, is a movement for equality as well as for liberty.

Liberty and Equality are the twin ideals of American democracy. But they are not the same thing. Nor, most importantly, are they equally attractive to all groups at any given time; nor yet are they always compatible, one with the other.

Many persons who would gladly die for liberty are appalled by equality. Many who are devoted to equality are puzzled and even troubled by liberty. Much of the political history of the American nation can be seen as a competition between these two ideals, as for example, the unending troubles between capital and labor.

By and large, liberty has been the ideal with the higher social prestige in America. It has been the middle class aspiration, par excellence. (Note the assertions of the conservative right that ours is a republic, not a democracy.) Equality, on the other hand, has enjoyed tolerance more than acceptance. Yet it has roots deep in Western civilization and "is at least coeval with, if not prior to, liberty in the history of Western political thought."[1]

American democracy has not always been successful in maintaining a balance between these two ideals, and notably so where the Negro American is concerned. "Lincoln freed the slaves," but they were given liberty, not equality. It was therefore possible in the century that followed to deprive their descendants of much of their liberty as well.

The ideal of equality does not ordain that all persons end up, as well as start out equal. In traditional terms, as put by Faulkner, "there is no such thing as equality *per se*, but only equality *to:* equal right and opportunity to make the best one can of one's life within one's capability, without fear of injustice or oppression or threat of violence."[2] But the evolution of American politics, with the distinct persistence of ethnic and religious groups, has added a profoundly significant new dimension to that egalitarian ideal. It is increasingly demanded that the distribution of success and failure within one group be roughly comparable to that within other groups. It is not enough that all individuals start out on even terms, if the members of one group almost invariably end up well to the fore, and those of another far to the rear. This is what ethnic politics are all about in America, and in the main the Negro American demands are being put forth in this now traditional and established framework.[3]

Here a point of semantics must be grasped. The demand for Equality of Opportunity has been generally perceived by white Americans as a demand for liberty, a demand not to be excluded from the competitions of life—at the polling place, in the scholarship examinations, at the personnel office, on the housing market. Liberty does, of course, demand that everyone be free to try his luck or test his skill in such matters. But these opportunities do not necessarily produce equality: on the contrary, to the extent that winners imply losers, equality of opportunity almost insures inequality of results.

The point of semantics is that equality of opportunity now has a different meaning for Negroes than it has for whites. It is not (or at least no longer) a demand for liberty alone, but also for equality—in terms of group results. In Bayard Rustin's terms, "It is now concerned not merely with removing the barriers to full *opportunity* but with achieving the fact of equality." [4] By equality Rustin means a distribution of achievements among Negroes roughly comparable to that among whites.

As Nathan Glazer has put it, "The demand for economic equality is now not the demand for equal opportunities for the equally qualified: it is now the demand for equality of economic results . . . The demand for equality in education . . . has also become a demand for equality of results, of outcomes." [5]

Some aspects of the new laws do guarantee results, in the sense that upon enactment and enforcement they bring about an objective that is an end in itself, e.g., the public accommodations title of the Civil Rights Act.

Other provisions are at once terminal and intermediary. The portions of the Civil Rights Act dealing with voting rights will achieve an objective that is an end in itself, but the exercise of those rights will no doubt lead to further enlargements of the freedom of the Negro American.

But by and large, the programs that have been enacted in the first phase of the Negro revolution—Manpower Retraining, the Job Corps, Community Action, et al.—only make opportunities available. They cannot insure the outcome.

The principal challenge of the next phase of the Negro revolution is to make certain that equality of results will now follow. If we do not, there will be no social peace in the United States for generations.

The Prospect for Equality

The time, therefore, is at hand for an unflinching look at the present potential of Negro Americans to move from where they now are to where they want, and ought to be.

There is no very satisfactory way, at present, to measure social health or social pathology within an ethnic, or religious, or geographical community. Data are few and uncertain, and conclusions drawn from them, including the conclusions that follow, are subject to the grossest error.* Nonetheless, the opportunities, no less than the dangers, of the present moment, demand that an assessment be made.

That being the case, it has to be said that there is a considerable body of evidence to support the conclusion that Negro social structure, in particular the Negro family, battered and harassed by discrimination, injustice, and uprooting, is in the deepest trouble. While many young Negroes are moving ahead to unprecedented levels of achievement, many more are falling further and further behind.

After an intensive study of the life of central Harlem, the board of directors of Harlem Youth Opportunities Unlimited, Inc. summed up their findings in one statement: "Massive deterioration of the fabric of society and its institutions. . ."[6]

It is the conclusion of this survey of the available national data, that what is true of central Harlem, can be said to be true of the Negro American world in general.

If this is so, it is the single most important social fact of the United States today.

II. The Negro American Family

At the heart of the deterioration of the fabric of Negro society is the deterioration of the Negro family.

It is the fundamental source of the weakness of the Negro community at the present time.

There is probably no single fact of Negro American life so little understood by whites. The Negro situation is commonly perceived by whites in terms of the visible manifestations of discrimination

---

*As much as possible, the statistics used in this paper refer to Negroes. However, certain data series are available only in terms of the white and nonwhite population. Where this is the case, the nonwhite data have been used as if they referred only to Negroes. This necessarily introduces some inaccuracies, but it does not appear to produce any significant distortions. In 1960, Negroes were 92.1 percent of all nonwhites. The remaining 7.9 percent is made up largely of Indians, Japanese, and Chinese. The combined male unemployment rates of these groups is lower than that of Negroes. In matters relating to family stability, the smaller groups are probably more stable. Thus 21 percent of Negro women who have ever married are separated, divorced, or their husbands are absent for other reasons. The comparable figure for Indians is 14 percent; Japanese, 7 percent; Chinese 6 percent. Therefore, the statistics on nonwhites generally understate the degree of disorganization of the Negro family and underemployment of Negro men.

and poverty, in part because Negro protest is directed against such obstacles, and in part, no doubt, because these are facts which involve the actions and attitudes of the white community as well. It is more difficult, however, for whites to perceive the effect that three centuries of exploitation have had on the fabric of Negro society itself. Here the consequences of the historic injustices done to Negro Americans are silent and hidden from view. But here is where the true injury has occurred: unless this damage is repaired, all the effort to end discrimination and poverty and injustice will come to little.

The role of the family in shaping character and ability is so pervasive as to be easily overlooked. The family is the basic social unit of American life; it is the basic socializing unit. By and large, adult conduct in society is learned as a child.

A fundamental insight of psychoanalytic theory, for example, is that the child learns a way of looking at life in his early years through which all later experience is viewed and which profoundly shapes his adult conduct.

It may be hazarded that the reason family structure does not loom larger in public discussion of social issues is that people tend to assume that the nature of family life is about the same throughout American society. The mass media and the development of suburbia have created an image of the American family as a highly standardized phenomenon. It is therefore easy to assume that whatever it is that makes for differences among individuals or groups of individuals, it is not a different family structure.

There is much truth to this; as with any other nation, Americans are producing a recognizable family system. But that process is not completed by any means. There are still, for example, important differences in family patterns surviving from the age of the great European migration to the United States, and these variations account for notable differences in the progress and assimilation of various ethnic and religious groups.[7] A number of immigrant groups were characterized by unusually strong family bonds; these groups have characteristically progressed more rapidly than others.

But there is one truly great discontinuity in family structure in the United States at the present time: that between the white world in general and that of the Negro American.

The white family has achieved a high degree of stability and is maintaining that stability.

By contrast, the family structure of lower class Negroes is highly unstable, and in many urban centers is approaching complete breakdown.

N.B. There is considerable evidence that the Negro community is in fact dividing between a stable middle-class group that is steadily growing stronger and more successful, and an increasingly disorganized and disadvantaged lower-class group. There are indications, for example, that the middle-class Negro family puts a higher premium on family stability and the conserving of family resources than does the white middle-class family.[8] The discussion of this paper is not, obviously, directed to the first group excepting as it is affected by the experiences of the second—an important exception. (See Section IV, The Tangle of Pathology.)

There are two points to be noted in this context.

First, the emergence and increasing visibility of a Negro middle-class may beguile the nation into supposing that the circumstances of the remainder of the Negro community are equally prosperous, whereas just the opposite is true at present, and is likely to continue so.

Second, the lumping of all Negroes together in one statistical measurement very probably conceals the extent of the disorganization among the lower-class group. If conditions are improving for one and deteriorating for the other, the resultant statistical averages might show no change. Further, the statistics on the Negro family and most other subjects treated in this paper refer only to a specific point in time. They are a vertical measure of the situation at a given moment. They do not measure the experience of individuals over time. Thus the average monthly unemployment rate for Negro males for 1964 is recorded as 9 percent. But *during* 1964, some 29 percent of Negro males were unemployed at one time or another. Similarly, for example, if 36 percent of Negro children are living in broken homes *at any specific moment*, it is likely that a far higher proportion of Negro children find themselves in that situation *at one time or another* in their lives.

Nearly a Quarter of Urban Negro Marriages are Dissolved

Nearly a quarter of Negro women living in cities who have ever married are divorced, separated, or are living apart from their husbands.

The rates are highest in the urban Northeast where 26 percent of Negro women ever married are either divorced, separated, or have their husbands absent.

On the urban frontier, the proportion of husbands absent is even higher. In New York City in 1960, it was 30.2 percent, *not* including divorces.

Percent Distribution of Ever-Married Females with Husbands Absent or Divorced, Rural-Urban, 1960

	Urban		Rural Nonfarm		Rural Farm	
	Nonwhite	*White*	*Nonwhite*	*White*	*Nonwhite*	*White*
Total, husbands absent or divorced	22.9	7.9	14.7	5.7	9.6	3.0
Total, husbands absent	17.3	3.9	12.6	3.6	8.6	2.0
Separated	12.7	1.8	7.8	1.2	5.6	0.5
Husbands absent for other reasons	4.6	2.1	4.8	2.4	3.0	1.5
Total, divorced	5.6	4.0	2.1	2.1	1.0	1.0

SOURCE: *U.S. Census of Population, 1960, Nonwhite Population by Race*, PC (2) 1c, table 9, pp. 9–10.

Among ever-married nonwhite women in the nation, the proportion with husbands present *declined* in *every* age group over the decade 1950–60, as follows:

Age	Percent With Husbands Present	
	1950	*1960*
15–19 years	77.8	72.5
20–24 years	76.7	74.2
25–29 years	76.1	73.4
30–34 years	74.9	72.0
35–39 years	73.1	70.7
40–44 years	68.9	68.2

Although similar declines occurred among white females, the proportion of white husbands present never dropped below 90 percent except for the first and last age group.[9]

Nearly One-Quarter of Negro Births are Now Illegitimate

Both white and Negro illegitimacy rates have been increasing, although from dramatically different bases. The white rate was 2 percent in 1940; it was 3.07 percent in 1963. In that period, the Negro rate went from 16.8 percent to 23.6 percent.

The number of illegitimate children per 1,000 live births increased by 11 among whites in the period 1940–63, but by 68 among nonwhites. There are, of course, limits to the dependability of these

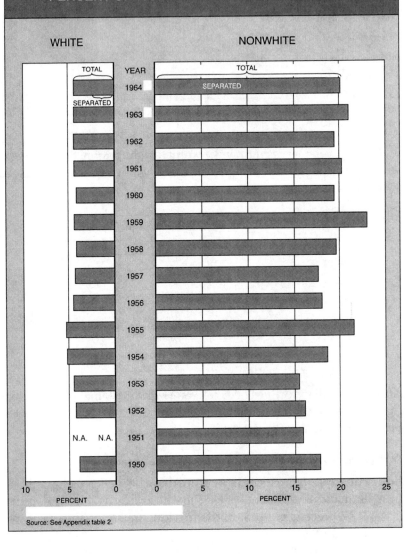

PERCENT OF WOMEN WITH HUSBANDS ABSENT

Source: See Appendix table 2.

statistics. There are almost certainly a considerable number of Negro children who, although technically illegitimate, are in fact the offspring of stable unions. On the other hand, it may be assumed that many births that are in fact illegitimate are recorded otherwise. Probably the two opposite effects cancel each other out.

Percent Distribution of Ever-Married Negro Females with Husbands Absent or Divorced, in Urban Areas, by Region, 1960

	North East	North Central	South	West
Total, husbands absent or divorced	25.6	22.6	21.5	24.7
Divorced	3.9	7.3	4.8	9.9
Separated	16.0	11.7	11.9	10.7
Husbands absent for other reasons	5.7	3.6	4.8	4.1

SOURCE: *U.S. Census of Population, 1960, Nonwhite Population by Race*, PC (2) 1c, table 9, pp. 9–10.

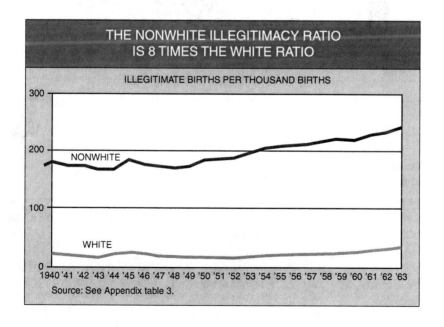

THE NONWHITE ILLEGITIMACY RATIO IS 8 TIMES THE WHITE RATIO

ILLEGITIMATE BIRTHS PER THOUSAND BIRTHS

NONWHITE

WHITE

1940 '41 '42 '43 '44 '45 '46 '47 '48 '49 '50 '51 '52 '53 '54 '55 '56 '57 '58 '59 '60 '61 '62 '63

Source: See Appendix table 3.

On the urban frontier, the nonwhite illegitimacy rates are usually higher than the national average, and the increase of late has been drastic.

In the District of Columbia, the illegitimacy rate for nonwhites grew from 21.8 percent in 1950, to 29.5 percent in 1964.

A similar picture of disintegrating Negro marriages emerges from the divorce statistics. Divorces have increased of late for both whites and nonwhites, but at a much greater rate for the latter. In 1940 both groups had a divorce rate of 2.2 percent. By 1964 the white rate had risen to 3.6 percent, but the nonwhite rate had reached 5.1 percent—40 percent greater than the formerly equal white rate.

Almost One-Fourth of Negro Families are Headed by Females

As a direct result of this high rate of divorce, separation, and desertion, a very large percent of Negro families are headed by females. While the percentage of such families among whites has been dropping since 1940, it has been rising among Negroes.

The percent of nonwhite families headed by a female is more than double the percent for whites. Fatherless nonwhite families increased by a sixth between 1950 and 1960, but held constant for white families.

It has been estimated that only a minority of Negro children reach the age of 18 having lived all their lives with both their parents.

Percent Distribution of White and Nonwhite Families in the United States, by Type of Family 1950 and 1960

Type of Family	1960			1950		
	White	*Non-White*	*Difference*	*White*	*Non-white*	*Difference*
All families	100	100		100	100	
Husband-wife	88	74	14	87	78	9
Other male head	3	5	—2	4	4	0
Female head	9	21	—12	9	18	—9

SOURCE: *U.S. Census of Population, 1960, U.S. Summary (Detailed characteristics)*, table 186, p. 464.

Once again, this measure of family disorganization is found to be diminishing among white families and increasing among Negro families.

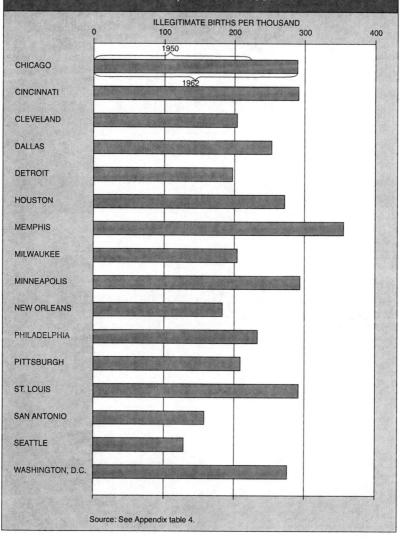

ILLEGITIMACY RATIOS PER 1,000 NONWHITE BIRTHS, BY CITY, 1950 AND 1962

ILLEGITIMATE BIRTHS PER THOUSAND

Source: See Appendix table 4.

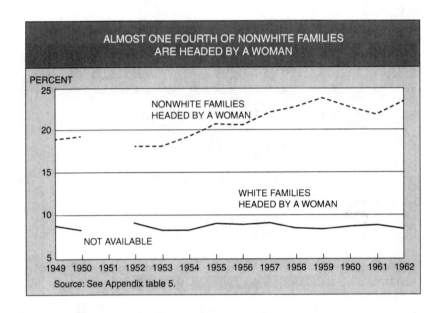

ALMOST ONE FOURTH OF NONWHITE FAMILIES
ARE HEADED BY A WOMAN

PERCENT

NONWHITE FAMILIES
HEADED BY A WOMAN

WHITE FAMILIES
HEADED BY A WOMAN

NOT AVAILABLE

1949 1950 1951 1952 1953 1954 1955 1956 1957 1958 1959 1960 1961 1962

Source: See Appendix table 5.

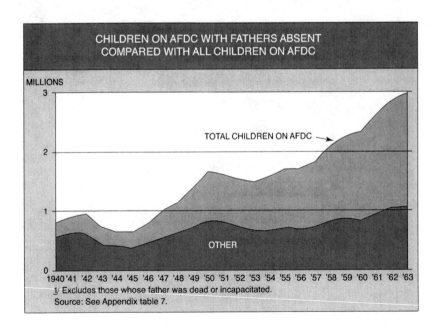

CHILDREN ON AFDC WITH FATHERS ABSENT
COMPARED WITH ALL CHILDREN ON AFDC

MILLIONS

TOTAL CHILDREN ON AFDC

OTHER

1940 '41 '42 '43 '44 '45 '46 '47 '48 '49 '50 '51 '52 '53 '54 '55 '56 '57 '58 '59 '60 '61 '62 '63

1/ Excludes those whose father was dead or incapacitated.

Source: See Appendix table 7.

The Breakdown of the Negro Family has Led to a Startling Increase in Welfare Dependency

The majority of Negro children receive public assistance under the AFDC program at one point or another in their childhood.

At present, 14 percent of Negro children are receiving AFDC assistance, as against 2 percent of white children. Eight percent of white children receive such assistance at some time, as against 56 percent of nonwhites, according to an extrapolation based on HEW data. (Let it be noted, however, that out of a total of 1.8 million nonwhite illegitimate children in the nation in 1961, 1.3 million were *not* receiving aid under the AFDC program, although a substantial number have, or will, receive aid at some time in their lives.)

Again, the situation may be said to be worsening. The AFDC program, deriving from the long established Mothers' Aid programs, was established in 1935 principally to care for widows and orphans, although the legislation covered all children in homes deprived of parental support because one or both of their parents are absent or incapacitated.

In the beginning, the number of AFDC families in which the father was absent because of desertion was less than a third of the total. Today it is two-thirds. HEW estimates "that between two-thirds and three-fourths of the 50 percent increase from 1948 to 1955 in the number of absent-father families receiving ADC may be explained by an increase in broken homes in the population."[10]

A 1960 study of Aid to Dependent Children in Cook County, Ill. stated:

> The "typical" ADC mother in Cook County was married and had children by her husband, who deserted; his whereabouts are unknown, and he does not contribute to the support of his children. She is not free to remarry and has had an illegitimate child since her husband left. (Almost 90 percent of the ADC families are Negro.)[11]

The steady expansion of this welfare program, as of public assistance programs in general, can be taken as a measure of the steady disintegration of the Negro family structure over the past generation in the United States.

III. The Roots of the Problem

Slavery

The most perplexing question about American slavery, which has never been altogether explained, and which indeed most Americans

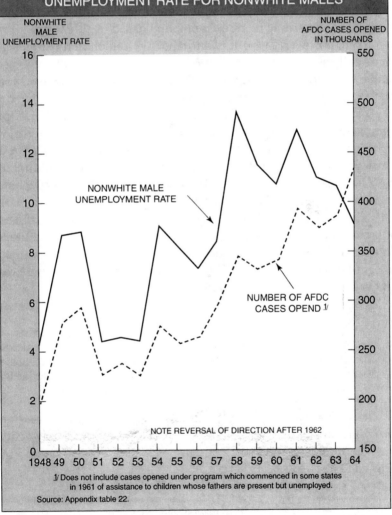

CASES OPENED UNDER AFDC COMPARED WITH UNEMPLOYMENT RATE FOR NONWHITE MALES

NONWHITE
MALE
UNEMPLOYMENT RATE

NUMBER OF
AFDC CASES OPENED
IN THOUSANDS

NONWHITE MALE
UNEMPLOYMENT RATE

NUMBER OF AFDC
CASES OPEND 1/

NOTE REVERSAL OF DIRECTION AFTER 1962

1948 49 50 51 52 53 54 55 56 57 58 59 60 61 62 63 64

1/ Does not include cases opened under program which commenced in some states
in 1961 of assistance to children whose fathers are present but unemployed.

Source: Appendix table 22.

hardly know exists, has been stated by Nathan Glazer as follows: "Why was American slavery the most awful the world has ever known?"[12] The only thing that can be said with certainty is that this is true: it was.

American slavery was profoundly different from, and in its lasting effects on individuals and their children, indescribably worse than, any recorded servitude, ancient or modern. The peculiar nature of American slavery was noted by Alexis de Tocqueville and others, but it was not until 1948 that Frank Tannenbaum, a South American specialist, pointed to the striking differences between Brazilian and American slavery. The feudal, Catholic society of Brazil had a legal and religious tradition which accorded the slave a place as a human being in the hierarchy of society—a luckless, miserable place, to be sure, but a place withal. In contrast, there was nothing in the tradition of English law or Protestant theology which could accommodate to the fact of human bondage—the slaves were therefore reduced to the status of chattels—often, no doubt, well cared for, even privileged chattels, but chattels nevertheless.

Glazer, also focusing on the Brazil-United States comparison, continues.

> In Brazil, the slave had many more rights than in the United States: he could legally marry, he could, indeed had to, be baptized and become a member of the Catholic Church, his family could not be broken up for sale, and he had many days on which he could either rest or earn money to buy his freedom. The Government encouraged manumission, and the freedom of infants could often be purchased for a small sum at the baptismal font. In short: the Brazilian slave knew he was a man, and that he differed in degree, not in kind, from his master.[13]
>
> [In the United States,] the slave was totally removed from the protection of organized society (compare the elaborate provisions for the protection of slaves in the Bible), his existence as a human being was given no recognition by any religious or secular agency, he was totally ignorant of and completely cut off from his past, and he was offered absolutely no hope for the future. His children could be sold, his marriage was not recognized, his wife could be violated or sold (there was something comic about calling the woman with whom the master permitted him to live a "wife"), and he could also be subject, without redress, to frightful barbarities—there were presumably as many sadists among slaveowners, men and women, as there are in other groups. The slave could not, by law, be taught to read or write; he could not practice any religion without the permission of his master, and could never meet with his fellows, for religious or any other purposes, except in the presence of a white; and finally, if a master wished to free him,

every legal obstacle was used to thwart such action. This was not what slavery meant in the ancient world, in medieval and early modern Europe, or in Brazil and the West Indies.

More important, American slavery was also awful in its effects. If we compared the present situation of the American Negro with that of, let us say, Brazilian Negroes (who were slaves 20 years longer), we begin to suspect that the differences are the result of very different patterns of slavery. Today the Brazilian Negroes are Brazilians; though most are poor and do the hard and dirty work of the country, as Negroes do in the United States, they are not cut off from society. They reach into its highest strata, merging there—in smaller and smaller numbers, it is true, but with complete acceptance—with other Brazilians of all kinds. The relations between Negroes and whites in Brazil show nothing of the mass irrationality that prevails in this country.[14]

Stanley M. Elkins, drawing on the aberrant behavior of the prisoners in Nazi concentration camps, drew an elaborate parallel between the two institutions. This thesis has been summarized as follows by Thomas F. Pettigrew:

Both were closed systems, with little chance of manumission, emphasis on survival, and a single, omnipresent authority. The profound personality change created by Nazi internment, as independently reported by a number of psychologists and psychiatrists who survived, was toward childishness and total acceptance of the SS guards as father-figures—a syndrome strikingly similar to the "Sambo" caricature of the Southern slave. Nineteenth-century racists readily believed that the "Sambo" personality was simply an inborn racial type. Yet no African anthropological data have ever shown any personality type resembling Sambo; and the concentration camps molded the equivalent personality pattern in a wide variety of Caucasian prisoners. Nor was Sambo merely a product of "slavery" in the abstract, for the less devastating Latin American system never developed such a type.

Extending this line of reasoning, psychologists point out that slavery in all its forms sharply lowered the need for achievement in slaves. . . . Negroes in bondage, stripped of their African heritage, were placed in a completely dependent role. All of their rewards came, not from individual initiative and enterprise, but from absolute obedience—a situation that severely depresses the need for achievement among all peoples. Most important of all, slavery vitiated family life. . . . Since many slave-owners neither fostered Christian marriage among their slave couples nor hesitated to separate them on the auction block, the slave household often developed a fatherless matrifocal (mother-centered) pattern.[15]

The Reconstruction

With the emancipation of the slaves, the Negro American family began to form in the United States on a widespread scale. But it did so in an atmosphere markedly different from that which has produced the white American family.

The Negro was given liberty, but not equality. Life remained hazardous and marginal. Of the greatest importance, the Negro male, particularly in the South, became an object of intense hostility, an attitude unquestionably based in some measure on fear.

When Jim Crow made its appearance towards the end of the 19th century, it may be speculated that it was the Negro male who was most humiliated thereby; the male was more likely to use public facilities, which rapidly became segregated once the process began, and just as important, segregation, and the submissiveness it exacts, is surely more destructive to the male than to the female personality. Keeping the Negro "in his place" can be translated as keeping the Negro male in his place: the female was not a threat to anyone.

Unquestionably, these events worked against the emergence of a strong father figure. The very essence of the male animal, from the bantam rooster to the four-star general, is to strut. Indeed, in 19th century America, a particular type of exaggerated male boastfulness became almost a national style. Not for the Negro male. The "sassy nigger" was lynched.

In this situation, the Negro family made but little progress toward the middle-class pattern of the present time. Margaret Mead has pointed out that while "In every known human society, everywhere in the world, the young male learns that when he grows up one of the things which he must do in order to be a full member of society is to provide food for some female and her young."[16] This pattern is not immutable, however: it can be broken, even though it has always eventually reasserted itself.

> Within the family, each new generation of young males learn the appropriate nurturing behavior and superimpose upon their biologically given maleness this learned parental role. When the family breaks down—as it does under slavery, under certain forms of indentured labor and serfdom, in periods of extreme social unrest during wars, revolutions, famines, and epidemics, or in periods of abrupt transition from one type of economy to another—this delicate line of transmission is broken. Men may flounder badly in these periods, during which the primary unit may again become mother and child, the biologically given, and the special conditions under which man has held his social traditions in trust are violated and distorted.[17]

E. Franklin Frazier makes clear that at the time of emancipation Negro women were already "accustomed to playing the dominant role in family and marriage relations" and that this role persisted in the decades of rural life that followed.

Urbanization

Country life and city life are profoundly different. The gradual shift of American society from a rural to an urban basis over the past century and a half has caused abundant strains, many of which are still much in evidence. When this shift occurs suddenly, drastically, in one or two generations, the effect is immensely disruptive of traditional social patterns.

It was this abrupt transition that produced the wild Irish slums of the 19th Century Northeast. Drunkenness, crime, corruption, discrimination, family disorganization, juvenile delinquency were the routine of that era. In our own time, the same sudden transition has produced the Negro slum—different from, but hardly better than its predecessors, and fundamentally the result of the same process.

Negroes are now more urbanized than whites.

Urban Population as Percent of Total, by Color, by Region, 1960

Region	White	Negro
United States	69.5	73.2
Northeast	79.1	95.7
North Central	66.8	95.7
South	58.6	58.4
West	77.6	92.6

SOURCE: *U.S. Census of Population, PC* (1) ID, 1960, *U.S. Summary,* table 155 and 233; PC (2)-1C, *Nonwhite Population by Race,* table 1.

Negro families in the cities are more frequently headed by a woman than those in the country. The difference between the while and Negro proportions of families headed by a woman is greater in the city than in the country.

Percent of Negro Families with Female Head, by Region and Area, 1960

Region	Urban	Rural Nonfarm	Rural Farm
United States	23.1	19.5	11.1
Northeast	24.2	14.1	4.3
North Central	20.8	14.7	8.4
South	24.2	20.0	11.2
West	20.7	9.4	5.5

SOURCE: *U.S. Census of Population, 1960, Nonwhite Population by Race,* PC (2) 1C, table 9, pp. 9–10.

The promise of the city has so far been denied the majority of the Negro migrants, and most particularly the Negro family.

In 1939, E. Franklin Frazier described its plight movingly in that part of *The Negro Family* entitled "In the City of Destruction":

> The impact of hundreds of thousands of rural southern Negroes upon northern metropolitan communities presents a bewildering spectacle. Striking contrasts in levels of civilization and economic well-being among these newcomers to modern civilization seem to baffle any attempt to discover order and direction in their mode of life.[18]
>
> In many cases, of course, the dissolution of the simple family organization has begun before the family reaches the northern city. But, if these families have managed to preserve their integrity until they reach the northern city, poverty, ignorance, and color force them to seek homes in deteriorated slum areas from which practically all institutional life has disappeared. Hence, at the same time that these simple rural families are losing their internal cohesion, they are being freed from the controlling force of public opinion and communal institutions. Family desertion among Negroes in cities appears, then, to be one of the inevitable consequences of the impact of urban life on the simple family organization and folk culture which the Negro has evolved in the rural South. The distribution of desertions in relation to the general economic and cultural organization of Negro communities that have grown up in our American cities shows in a striking manner the influence of selective factors in the process of adjustment to the urban environment.[19]

Frazier concluded his classic study, *The Negro Family*, with the prophesy that the "travail of civilization is not yet ended."

> First, it appears that the family which evolved within the isolated world of the Negro folk will become increasingly disorganized. Modern means of communication will break down the isolation of the world of the black folk, and, as long as the bankrupt system of southern agriculture exists, Negro families will continue to seek a living in the towns and cities of the country. They will crowd the slum areas of southern cities or make their way to northern cities where their family life will become disrupted and their poverty will force them to depend upon charity.[20]

In every index of family pathology—divorce, separation, and desertion, female family head, children in broken homes, and illegitimacy—the contrast between the urban and rural environment for Negro families is unmistakable.

Harlem, into which Negroes began to move early in this century, is the center and symbol of the urban life of the Negro American. Conditions in Harlem are not worse, they are probably better than in most Negro ghettos. The social disorganization of central Harlem,

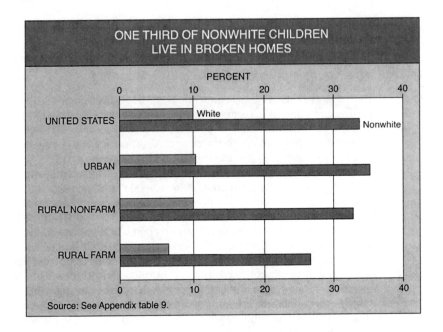

ONE THIRD OF NONWHITE CHILDREN
LIVE IN BROKEN HOMES

PERCENT

Source: See Appendix table 9.

Estimated Illegitimacy Ratios Per 1,000 Livebirths for Nonwhites in Central Harlem by Health Area, 1963

Health Area [1]	Nonwhite
Total	434.1
No. 8	367.6
No. 10	488.9
No. 12	410.1
No. 13	422.5
No. 15	455.1
No. 16	449.4
No. 19	465.2
No. 24	424.8
No. 85.10	412.3
No. 85.20	430.8

[1] Statistics are reported by geopgraphical areas designatd "Health Areas."
SOURCE: Department of Health, New York City.

comprising ten health areas, was thoroughly documented by the HARYOU report, save for the illegitimacy rates. These have now been made available to the Labor Department by the New York City Department of Health. There could hardly be a more dramatic demonstration of the crumbling—the breaking—of the family structure on the urban frontier.

Unemployment and Poverty

The impact of unemployment on the Negro family, and particularly on the Negro male, is the least understood of all the developments that have contributed to the present crisis. There is little analysis because there has been almost no inquiry. Unemployment, for whites and nonwhites alike, has on the whole been treated as an economic phenomenon, with almost no attention paid for at least a quarter-century to social and personal consequences.

In 1940, Edward Wight Bakke described the effects of unemployment on family structure in terms of six stages of adjustment.[21] Although the families studied were white, the pattern would clearly seem to be a general one, and apply to Negro families as well.

The first two stages end with the exhaustion of credit and the entry of the wife into the labor force. The father is no longer the provider and the elder children become resentful.

The third stage is the critical one of commencing a new day-to-day existence. At this point two women are in charge:

> Consider the fact that relief investigators or case workers are normally women and deal with the housewife. Already suffering a loss in prestige and authority in the family because of his failure to be the chief bread winner, the male head of the family feels deeply this obvious transfer of planning for the family's well-being to two women, one of them an outsider. His role is reduced to that of errand boy to and from the relief office.[22]

If the family makes it through this stage Bakke finds that it is likely to survive, and the rest of the process is one of adjustment. *The critical element of adjustment was not welfare payments, but work.*

> Having observed our families under conditions of unemployment with no public help, or with that help coming from direct [sic] and from work relief, we are convinced that after the exhaustion of self-produced resources, work relief is the only type of assistance which can restore the strained bonds of family relationship in a way which promises the continued functioning of that family in meeting the responsibilities imposed upon it by our culture.[23]

Work is precisely the one thing the Negro family head in such circumstances has not received over the past generation.*

The fundamental, overwhelming fact is that *Negro unemployment,*
with the exception of a few years during World War II and the Korean
War, *has continued at disaster levels for 35 years.*

Once again, this is particularly the case in the northern urban areas
to which the Negro population has been moving.

The 1930 Census (taken in the spring, before the depression was in
full swing) showed Negro unemployment at 6.1 percent, as against 6.6
percent for whites. But taking out the South reversed the relationship:
white 7.4 percent, nonwhite 11.5 percent.

By 1940, the 2 to 1 white-Negro unemployment relationship that
persists to this day had clearly emerged. Taking out the South again,
whites were 14.8 percent, nonwhites 29.7 percent.

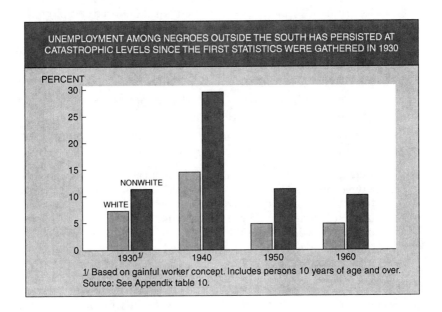

UNEMPLOYMENT AMONG NEGROES OUTSIDE THE SOUTH HAS PERSISTED AT CATASTROPHIC LEVELS SINCE THE FIRST STATISTICS WERE GATHERED IN 1930

1/ Based on gainful worker concept. Includes persons 10 years of age and over.
Source: See Appendix table 10.

Since 1929, the Negro worker has been tremendously affected by
the movements of the business cycle and of employment. He has been
hit worse by declines than whites, and proportionately helped more
by recoveries.

---

* An exception is the rather small impact of the ADC-U program since 1961, now expanded by
Title V of the Economic Opportunity Act.

From 1951 to 1963, the level of Negro male unemployment was on a long-run rising trend, while at the same time following the short-run ups and downs of the business cycle. During the same period, the number of broken families in the Negro world was also on a long-run rise, with intermediate ups and downs.

A glance at the chart on page 382 reveals that the series move in the same directions—up and down together, with a long-run rising trend—but that the peaks and troughs are 1 year out of phase. Thus unemployment peaks 1 year before broken families, and so on. By plotting these series in terms of deviation from trend, and moving the unemployment curve *1 year ahead*, we see the clear relation of the two otherwise seemingly unrelated series of events; the cyclical swings in unemployment have their counterpart in increases and decreases in separations.

The effect of recession unemployment on divorces further illustrates the economic roots of the problem. The nonwhite divorce rates dipped slightly in high unemployment years like 1954–55, 1958, and 1961–62.

Divorce is expensive: those without money resort to separation or desertion. While divorce is not a desirable goal for a society, it recognizes the importance of marriage and family, and for children some family continuity and support is more likely when the institution of the family has been so recognized.

The conclusion from these and similar data is difficult to avoid: During times when jobs were reasonably plentiful (although at no time during this period, save perhaps the first 2 years, did the unemployment rate for Negro males drop to anything like a reasonable level) the Negro family became stronger and more stable. As jobs became more and more difficult to find, the stability of the family became more and more difficult to maintain.

This relation is clearly seen in terms of the illegitimacy rates of census tracts in the District of Columbia compared with male unemployment rates in the same neighborhoods.

In 1963, a prosperous year, 29.2 percent of all Negro men in the labor force were unemployed at some time during the year. Almost half of these men were out of work 15 weeks or more.

The impact of poverty on Negro family structure is no less obvious, although again it may not be widely acknowledged. There would seem to be an American tradition, agrarian in its origins but reinforced by attitudes of urban immigrant groups, to the effect that family morality and stability decline as income and social position rise. Over the years this may have provided some consolation to the poor, but there is little evidence that it is true. On the contrary, higher family incomes are unmistakably associated with greater

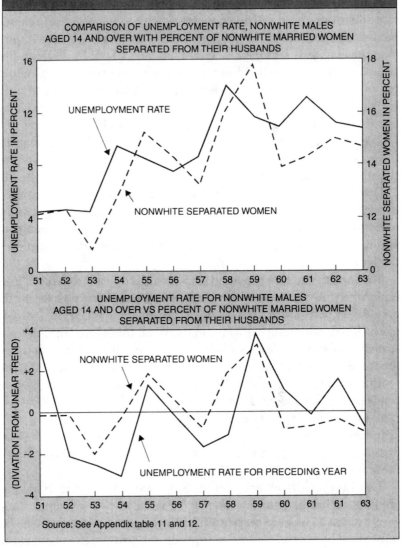

COMPARISON OF UNEMPLOYMENT RATE, NONWHITE MALES AGED 14 AND OVER WITH PERCENT OF NONWHITE MARRIED WOMEN SEPARATED FROM THEIR HUSBANDS

UNEMPLOYMENT RATE IN PERCENT

NONWHITE SEPARATED WOMEN IN PERCENT

UNEMPLOYMENT RATE

NONWHITE SEPARATED WOMEN

UNEMPLOYMENT RATE FOR NONWHITE MALES AGED 14 AND OVER VS PERCENT OF NONWHITE MARRIED WOMEN SEPARATED FROM THEIR HUSBANDS

(DIVIATION FROM LINEAR TREND)

NONWHITE SEPARATED WOMEN

UNEMPLOYMENT RATE FOR PRECEDING YEAR

Source: See Appendix table 11 and 12.

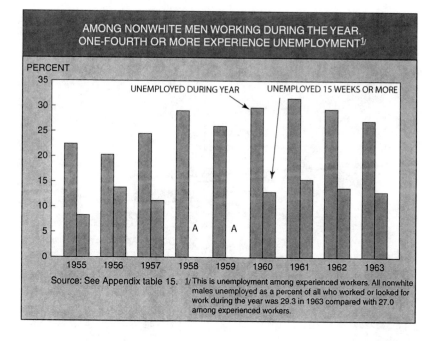

AMONG NONWHITE MEN WORKING DURING THE YEAR,
ONE-FOURTH OR MORE EXPERIENCE UNEMPLOYMENT[1]

PERCENT

UNEMPLOYED DURING YEAR   UNEMPLOYED 15 WEEKS OR MORE

Source: See Appendix table 15. 1/ This is unemployment among experienced workers. All nonwhite males unemployed as a percent of all who worked or looked for work during the year was 29.3 in 1963 compared with 27.0 among experienced workers.

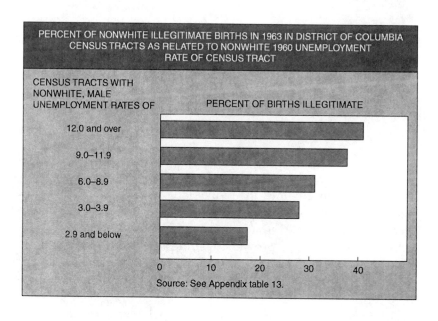

PERCENT OF NONWHITE ILLEGITIMATE BIRTHS IN 1963 IN DISTRICT OF COLUMBIA
CENSUS TRACTS AS RELATED TO NONWHITE 1960 UNEMPLOYMENT
RATE OF CENSUS TRACT

CENSUS TRACTS WITH
NONWHITE, MALE
UNEMPLOYMENT RATES OF   PERCENT OF BIRTHS ILLEGITIMATE

12.0 and over

9.0–11.9

6.0–8.9

3.0–3.9

2.9 and below

Source: See Appendix table 13.

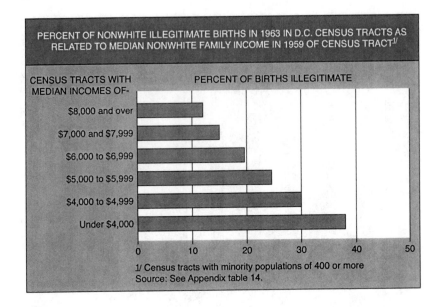

PERCENT OF NONWHITE ILLEGITIMATE BIRTHS IN 1963 IN D.C. CENSUS TRACTS AS RELATED TO MEDIAN NONWHITE FAMILY INCOME IN 1959 OF CENSUS TRACT[1/]

CENSUS TRACTS WITH MEDIAN INCOMES OF-

PERCENT OF BIRTHS ILLEGITIMATE

1/ Census tracts with minority populations of 400 or more
Source: See Appendix table 14.

family stability—which comes first may be a matter for conjecture, but the conjunction of the two characteristics is unmistakable.

The Negro family is no exception. In the District of Columbia, for example, census tracts with median incomes over $8,000 had an illegitimacy rate one-third that of tracts in the category under $4,000.

The Wage System

The American wage system is conspicuous in the degree to which it provides high incomes for individuals, but is rarely adjusted to insure that family as well as individual needs are met. Almost without exception, the social welfare and social insurance systems of other industrial democracies provide for some adjustment or supplement of a worker's income to provide for the extra expenses of those with families. American arrangements do not, save for income tax deductions.

The Federal minimum wage of $1.25 per hour provides a basic income for an individual, but an income well below the poverty line for a couple, much less a family with children.

The 1965 Economic Report of the President revised the data on the number of persons living in poverty in the United States to take account of the varying needs of families of different sizes, rather than using a flat cut off at the $3,000 income level. The resulting revision illustrates the significance of family size. Using these criteria, the number of poor families is smaller, but the number of large families who are poor increases, and the number of children in poverty rises by more than one-third—from 11 million to 15 million. This means that one-fourth of the Nation's children live in families that are poor.[24]

A third of these children belong to families in which the father was not only present, but was employed the year round. In overall terms, median family income is lower for large families than for small families. Families of six or more children have median incomes 24 percent below families with three. (It may be added that 47 percent of young men who fail the Selective Service education test come from families of six or more.)

During the 1950–60 decade of heavy Negro migration to the cities of the North and West, the ratio of nonwhite to white family income in cities increased from 57 to 63 percent. Corresponding declines in the ratio in the rural nonfarm and farm areas kept the national ratio virtually unchanged. But between 1960 and 1963, median nonwhite family income slipped from 55 percent to 53 percent of white income. The drop occurred in three regions, with only the South, where a larger proportion of Negro families have more than one earner, showing a slight improvement.

Ratio of Nonwhite to White Family Median Income, United States and Regions, 1960–63

Region	1960	1961	1962	1963
United States	55	53	53	53
Northeast	68	67	66	65
North Central	74	72	68	73
South	43	43	47	45
West	81	87	73	76

SOURCE: U.S. Department of Commerce. Bureau of the Census, Current Population Reports, Series P-60, *Income of Families and Persons in the United States,* No. 37 (1960), No. 39 (1961), No. 41 (1962), No. 43 (1963). Data by region, table 11 in P-60, No. 41, for 1962, table 13 in P-60, No. 43, for 1963 and, for 1960 and 1961, unpublished tabulations from the Current Population Survey.

Because in general terms Negro families have the largest number of children and the lowest incomes, many Negro fathers literally cannot support their families. Because the father is either not present, is unemployed, or makes such a low wage, the Negro woman goes to work. Fifty-six percent of Negro women, age 25 to 64, are in the work force, against 42 percent of white women. This dependence on the mother's income undermines the position of the father and deprives the children of the kind of attention, particularly in school matters, which is now a standard feature of middle-class upbringing.

The Dimensions grow

The dimensions of the problems of Negro Americans are compounded by the present extraordinary growth in Negro population. At the founding of the nation, and into the first decade of the 19th century, 1 American in 5 was a Negro. The proportion declined steadily until it was only 1 in 10 by 1920, where it held until the 1950's, when it began to rise. Since 1950, the Negro population has grown at a rate of 2.4 percent per year compared with 1.7 percent for the total population. If this rate continues, in seven years 1 American in 8 will be nonwhite.

These changes are the result of a declining Negro death rate, now approaching that of the nation generally, and a fertility rate that grew steadily during the postwar period. By 1959, the ratio of white to nonwhite fertility rates reached 1:1.42. Both the white and nonwhite fertility rates have declined since 1959, but the differential has not narrowed.

Family size increased among nonwhite families between 1950 and 1960—as much for those without fathers as for those with fathers. Average family size changed little among white families, with a slight increase in the size of husband-wife families balanced by a decline in the size of families without fathers.

Average Number of Family Members by Type of Family and Color, Conterminous United States, 1960 and 1950

Type of Family	1950 White	1950 Nonwhite	1960 White	1960 Nonwhite
All families	3.54	4.07	3.58	4.30
Husband-wife	3.61	4.16	3.66	4.41
Other male head	3.05	3.63	2.82	3.56
Female head	3.06	3.82	2.93	4.04

Source: *U.S. Census of Population, 1960, U.S. Summary (Detailed Characteristics),* table 187, p. 469.

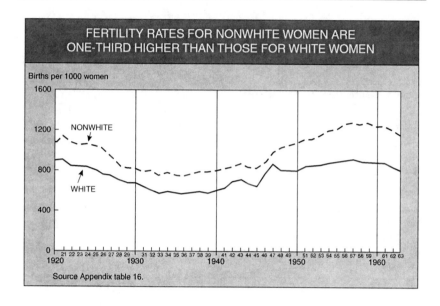

FERTILITY RATES FOR NONWHITE WOMEN ARE ONE-THIRD HIGHER THAN THOSE FOR WHITE WOMEN

Births per 1000 women

Source Appendix table 16.

Negro women not only have more children, but have them earlier. Thus in 1960, there were 1,247 children ever born per thousand ever-married nonwhite women 15 to 19 years of age, as against only 725 among white women, a ratio of 1.7:1. The Negro fertility rate overall is now 1.4 times the white, but what might be called the generation rate is 1.7 times the white.

This population growth must inevitably lead to an unconcealable crisis in Negro unemployment. The most conspicuous failure of the American social system in the past 10 years has been its inadequacy in providing jobs for Negro youth. Thus, in January 1965 the unemployment rate for Negro teenagers stood at 29 percent. This problem will now become steadily more serious.

During the rest of the 1960's the nonwhite civilian population 14 years of age and over will increase by 20 percent—more than double the white rate. The nonwhite labor force will correspondingly increase 20 per cent in the next 6 years, double the rate of increase in the nonwhite labor force of the past decade.

As with the population as a whole, there is much evidence that children are being born most rapidly in those Negro families with the least financial resources. This is an ancient pattern, but because

Population and Labor Force Projections, by Color

	Percent Increase	
	Actual	*Projected·*
	1954–64	*1964–70*
Civilian population age 14 and over		
White	15.6	9.7
Nonwhite	23.9	19.9
Civilian labor force		
White	14.6	10.8
Nonwhite	19.3	20.0

· Population and labor force projections by color were made by the Bureau of Labor Statistics. They have not been revised since the total population and labor force were re-estimated, but are considered accurate measures of the relative magnitudes of increase.

SOURCE: Bureau of Labor Statistics.

Family Income in 1959	Number of Children Per Nonwhite Mother Age 35–39, 1960
Under $2,000	5.3
$2,000 to $3,999	4.3
$4,000 to $4,999	4.0
$5,000 to $5,999	3.8
$6,000 to $6,999	3.5
$7,000 to $9,999	3.2
$10,000 to $14,999	2.9
$15,000 and over	2.9

SOURCE: 1960 Census, *Women by Number of Children Ever Born*, PC (2) 3A, table 38 p. 188.

the needs of children are greater today it is very possible that the education and opportunity gap between the offspring of these families and those of stable middle-class unions is not closing, but is growing wider.

A cycle is at work; too many children too early make it most difficult for the parents to finish school. (In February, 1963, 38 percent of the white girls who dropped out of school did so because of marriage or pregnancy, as against 49 percent of nonwhite girls.)[25] An Urban League study in New York reported that 44 percent of girl dropouts left school because of pregnancy.[26]

Low education levels in turn produce low income levels, which deprive children of many opportunities, and so the cycle repeats itself.

IV. The Tangle of Pathology

That the Negro American has survived at all is extraordinary—a lesser people might simply have died out, as indeed others have. That the Negro community has not only survived, but in this political generation has entered national affairs as a moderate, humane, and constructive national force is the highest testament to the healing powers of the democratic ideal and the creative vitality of the Negro people.

But it may not be supposed that the Negro American community has not paid a fearful price for the incredible mistreatment to which it has been subjected over the past three centuries.

In essence, the Negro community has been forced into a matriarchal structure which, because it is so out of line with the rest of the American society, seriously retards the progress of the group as a whole, and imposes a crushing burden on the Negro male and, in consequence, on a great many Negro women as well.

There is, presumably, no special reason why a society in which males are dominant in family relationships is to be preferred to a matriarchal arrangement. However, it is clearly a disadvantage for a minority group to be operating on one principle, while the great majority of the population, and the one with the most advantages to begin with, is operating on another. This is the present situation of the Negro. Ours is a society which presumes male leadership in private and public affairs. The arrangements of society facilitate such leadership and reward it. A subculture, such as that of the Negro American, in which this is not the pattern, is placed at a distinct disadvantage.

Here an earlier word of caution should be repeated. There is much evidence that a considerable number of Negro families have managed to break out of the tangle of pathology and to establish themselves as stable, effective units, living according to patterns of American society in general. E. Franklin Frazier has suggested that the middle-class Negro American family is, if anything, more patriarchal and protective of its children than the general run of such families.[27] Given equal opportunities, the children of these families will perform as well or better than their white peers. They need no help from anyone, and ask none.

While this phenomenon is not easily measured, one index is that middle-class Negroes have even fewer children than middle-class whites, indicating a desire to conserve the advances they have made and to insure that their children do as well or better. Negro women who marry early to uneducated laborers have more children than white women in the same situation; Negro women who marry at the common age for the middle class to educated men doing technical or professional work have only four-fifths as many children as their white counterparts.

It might be estimated that as much as half of the Negro community falls into the middle class. However, the remaining half is in desperate and deteriorating circumstances. Moreover, because of housing segregation it is immensely difficult for the stable half to escape from the cultural influences of the unstable one. The children of middle-class Negroes often as not must grow up in, or next to the slums, an experience almost unknown to white middle-class children. They are therefore constantly exposed to the pathology of the disturbed group and constantly in danger of being drawn into it. It is for this reason that the propositions put forth in this study may be thought of as having a more or less general application.

Children Born per Woman Age 35 to 44: Wives of Uneducated Laborers who Married Young, Compared with Wives of Educated Professional Workers who Married After Age 21, White and Nonwhite, 1960 [1]

	Children Per Woman	
	White	*Nonwhite*
Wives married at age 14 to 21 to husbands who are laborers and did not go to high school	3.8	4.7
Wives married at age 22 or over to husbands who are professional or technical workers and have completed 1 year or more of college	2.4	1.9

[1] Wives married only once, with husbands present.

SOURCE: 1960 Census, *Women by Number of Children ever Born*, PC (2) 3A, table 39 and 40, pp. 199–238.

In a word, most Negro youth are in *danger* of being caught up in the tangle of pathology that affects their world, and probably a majority are so entrapped. Many of those who escape do so for one generation only: as things now are, their children may have to run the gauntlet all over again. That is not the least vicious aspect of the world that white America has made for the Negro.

Obviously, not every instance of social pathology afflicting the Negro community can be traced to the weakness of family structure.

If, for example, organized crime in the Negro community were not largely controlled by whites, there would be more capital accumulation among Negroes, and therefore probably more Negro business enterprises. If it were not for the hostility and fear many whites exhibit towards Negroes, they in turn would be less afflicted by hostility and fear and so on. There is no one Negro community. There is no one Negro problem. There is no one solution. Nonetheless, at the center of the tangle of pathology is the weakness of the family structure. Once or twice removed, it will be found to be the principal source of most of the aberrant, inadequate, or antisocial behavior that did not establish, but now serves to perpetuate the cycle of poverty and deprivation.

It was by destroying the Negro family under slavery that white America broke the will of the Negro people. Although that will has reasserted itself in our time, it is a resurgence doomed to frustration unless the viability of the Negro family is restored.

Matriarchy

A fundamental fact of Negro American family life is the often reversed roles of husband and wife.

Robert O. Blood, Jr., and Donald M. Wolfe, in a study of Detroit families, note that "Negro husbands have unusually low power."[28] and while this is characteristic of all low income families, the pattern pervades the Negro social structure: "the cumulative result of discrimination in jobs . . . , the segregated housing, and the poor schooling of Negro men."[29] In 44 percent of the Negro families studied, the wife was dominant, as against 20 percent of white wives. "Whereas the majority of white families are equalitarian, the largest percentage of Negro families are dominated by the wife."[30]

The matriarchal pattern of so many Negro families reinforces itself over the generations. This process begins with education. Although the gap appears to be closing at the moment, for a long while, Negro females were better educated than Negro males, and this remains true today for the Negro population as a whole.

The difference in educational attainment between nonwhite men and women in the labor force is even greater; men lag 1.1 years behind women.

The disparity in educational attainment of male and female youth age 16 to 21 who were out of school in February 1963, is striking. Among the nonwhite males, 66.3 percent were not high school graduates, compared with 55.0 percent of the females. A similar difference

Educational Attainment of the Civilian Noninstitutional Population 18 Years of Age and Over, March 1964

Color and Sex	Median School Years Completed
White	
Male	12.1
Female	12.1
Nonwhite	
Male	9.2
Female	10.0

SOURCE: Bureau of Labor Statistics, unpublished data.

existed at the college level, with 4.5 percent of the males having completed 1 to 3 years of college compared with 7.3 percent of the females.

The poorer performance of the male in school exists from the very beginning, and the magnitude of the difference was documented by the 1960 Census in statistics on the number of children who have fallen one or more grades below the typical grade for children of the same age. The boys have more frequently fallen behind at every age level. (White boys also lag behind white girls, but at a differential of 1 to 6 percentage points.)

Percent of Nonwhite Youth Enrolled in School Who are 1 or More Grades Below Mode for Age, by Sex, 1960

Age	Male	Female
7 to 9 years old	7.8	5.8
10 to 13 years old	25.0	17.1
14 and 15 years old	35.5	24.8
16 and 17 years old	39.4	27.2
18 and 19 years old	57.3	46.0

SOURCE: 1960 Census, *School Enrollment*, PC (2) 5A, table 3, p. 24.

In 1960, 39 percent of all white persons 25 years of age and over who had completed 4 or more years of college were women. Fifty-three percent of the nonwhites who had attained this level were women.

However, the gap is closing. By October 1963, there were slightly more Negro men in college than women. Among whites there were almost twice as many men as women enrolled.

There is much evidence that Negro females are better students than their male counterparts.

Daniel Thompson of Dillard University, in a private communication on January 9, 1965, writes:

> As low as is the aspirational level among lower class Negro girls, it is considerably higher than among the boys. For example, I have examined the honor rolls in Negro high schools for about 10 years. As a rule, from 75 to 90 percent of all Negro honor students are girls.

Fall Enrollment of Civilian Noninstitutional Population in College, by Color and Sex—October 1963 (in thousands)

Color And Sex	Population, Age 14–34, Oct. 1, 1963	Number Enrolled	Percent of Youth, Age 14–34
Nonwhite			
Male	2,884	149	5.2
Female	3,372	137	4.1
White			
Male	21,700	2,599	12.0
Female	20,613	1,451	7.0

SOURCE: U.S. Bureau of the Census, *Current Population Reports*, Series P-20, No. 129, July 24, 1964, tables 1, 5.

Dr. Thompson reports that 70 percent of all applications for the National Achievement Scholarship Program financed by the Ford Foundation for outstanding Negro high school graduates are girls, despite special efforts by high school principals to submit the names of boys.

The finalists for this new program for outstanding Negro students were recently announced. Based on an inspection of the names, only about 43 percent of all the 639 finalists were male. (However, in the regular National Merit Scholarship program, males received 67 percent of the 1964 scholarship awards.)

Inevitably, these disparities have carried over to the area of employment and income.

In 1 out of 4 Negro families where the husband is present, is an earner, and someone else in the family works, the husband is not the principal earner. The comparable figure for whites is 18 percent.

More important, it is clear that Negro females have established a strong position for themselves in white collar and professional employment, precisely the areas of the economy which are growing most rapidly, and to which the highest prestige is accorded.

The President's Committee on Equal Employment Opportunity,

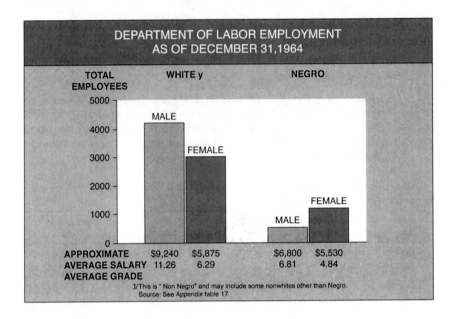

DEPARTMENT OF LABOR EMPLOYMENT
AS OF DECEMBER 31,1964

1/This is " Non Negro" and may include some nonwhites other than Negro.
Source: See Appendix table 17.

making a preliminary report on employment in 1964 of over 16,000 companies with nearly 5 million employees, revealed this pattern with dramatic emphasis.

> In this work force, Negro males outnumber Negro females by a ratio of 4 to 1. Yet Negro males represent only 1.2 percent of all males in white collar occupations, while Negro females represent 3.1 percent of the total female white collar work force. Negro males represent 1.1 percent of all male professionals, whereas Negro females represent roughly 6 percent of all female professionals. Again, in technician occupations, Negro males represent 2.1 percent of all male technicians while Negro females represent roughly 10 percent of all female technicians. It would appear therefore that there are proportionately 4 times as many Negro females in significant white collar jobs than Negro males.
> Although it is evident that office and clerical jobs account for approximately 50 percent of all Negro female white collar workers, it is significant that 6 out of every 100 Negro females are in professional jobs. This is substantially similar to the rate of all females in such jobs. Approximately 7 out of every 100 Negro females are in technician jobs. This exceeds the proportion of all females in technician jobs— approximately 5 out of every 100.

Negro females in skilled jobs are almost the same as that of all females in such jobs. Nine out of every 100 Negro males are in skilled occupations while 21 out of 100 of all males are in such jobs.[31]

This pattern is to be seen in the Federal government, where special efforts have been made recently to insure equal employment opportunity for Negroes. These efforts have been notably successful in Departments such as Labor, where some 19 percent of employees are now Negro. (A not disproportionate percentage, given the composition of the work force in the areas where the Main Department offices are located.) However, it may well be that these efforts have redounded mostly to the benefit of Negro women, and may even have accentuated the comparative disadvantage of Negro men. Seventy percent of the Negro employees of the Department of Labor are women, as contrasted with only 42 percent of the white employees.

Among nonprofessional Labor Department employees—where the most employment opportunities exist for all groups—Negro women outnumber Negro men 4 to 1, and average almost one grade higher in classification.

The testimony to the effects of these patterns in Negro family structure is widespread, and hardly to be doubted.

Whitney Young: Historically, in the matriarchal Negro society, mothers made sure that if one of their children had a chance for higher education the daughter was the one to pursue it.[32]

The effect on family functioning and role performance of this historical experience [economic deprivation] is what you might predict. Both as a husband and as a father the Negro male is made to feel inadequate, not because he is unlovable or unaffectionate, lacks intelligence or even a gray flannel suit. But in a society that measures a man by the size of his pay check, he doesn't stand very tall in a comparison with his white counterpart. To this situation he may react with withdrawal, bitterness toward society, aggression both within the family and racial group, self-hatred, or crime. Or he may escape through a number of avenues that help him to lose himself in fantasy or to compensate for his low status through a variety of exploits.[33]

Thomas Pettigrew: The Negro wife in this situation can easily become disgusted with her financially dependent husband, and her rejection of him further alienates the male from family life. Embittered by their experiences with men, many Negro mothers often act to perpetuate the mother-centered pattern by taking a greater interest in their daughters than their sons.[34]

Deton Brooks: In a matriarchal structure, the women are transmitting the culture.[35]

Dorothy Height: If the Negro woman has a major underlying concern, it is the status of the Negro man and his position in the community and his need for feeling himself an important person, free and able to make his contribution in the whole society in order that he may strengthen his home.[36]

Duncan M. MacIntyre: The Negro illegitimacy rate always has been high—about eight times the white rate in 1940 and somewhat higher today even though the white illegitimacy rate also is climbing. The Negro statistics are symptomatic of some old socioeconomic problems, not the least of which are underemployment among Negro men and compensating higher labor force propensity among Negro women. Both operate to enlarge the mother's role, undercutting the status of the male and making many Negro families essentially matriarchal. The Negro man's uncertain employment prospects, matriarchy, and the high cost of divorces combine to encourage desertion (the poor man's divorce), increases the number of couples not married, and thereby also increases the Negro illegitimacy rate. In the meantime, higher Negro birth rates are increasing the nonwhite population, while migration into cities like Detroit, New York, Philadelphia, and Washington, D.C. is making the public assistance rolls in such cities heavily, even predominantly, Negro.[37]

Robin M. Williams, Jr., in a study of Elmira, New York: Only 57 percent of Negro adults reported themselves as married—spouse present, as compared with 78 percent of native white American gentiles, 91 percent of Italian-American, and 96 percent of Jewish informants. Of the 93 unmarried Negro youths interviewed, 22 percent did not have their mother living in the home with them, and 42 percent reported that their father was not living in their home. One-third of the youths did not know their father's present occupation, and two-thirds of a sample of 150 Negro adults did not know what the occupation of their father's father had been. Forty percent of the youths said that they had brothers and sisters living in other communities: another 40 percent reported relatives living in their home who were not parents, siblings, or grandparents.[38]

The Failure of Youth

Williams' account of Negro youth growing up with little knowledge of their fathers, less of their fathers' occupations, still less of family occupational traditions, is in sharp contrast to the experience of the white child. The white family, despite many variants, remains a powerful agency not only for transmitting property from one generation to the next, but also for transmitting no less valuable contracts with the world of education and work. In an earlier age, the Carpenters, Wainwrights, Weavers, Mercers, Farmers, Smiths acquired their names as well as their trades from their fathers and grandfathers. Children today still learn the patterns of work from their fathers even though they may no longer go into the same jobs.

White children without fathers at least perceive all about them the pattern of men working.

Negro children without fathers flounder—and fail.

Not always, to be sure. The Negro community produces its share, very possibly more than its share, of young people who have the something extra that carries them over the worst obstacles, But such persons are always a minority. The common run of young people in a group facing serious obstacles to success do not succeed.

A prime index of the disadvantage of Negro youth in the United States is their consistently poor performance on the mental tests that are a standard means of measuring ability and performance in the present generation.

There is absolutely no question of any genetic differential: Intelligence potential is distributed among Negro infants in the same proportion and pattern as among Icelanders or Chinese or any other group. American society, however, impairs the Negro potential. The statement of the HARYOU report that "there is no basic disagreement over the fact that central Harlem students are performing poorly in school"[39] may be taken as true of Negro slum children throughout the United States.

Eighth grade children in central Harlem have a median IQ of 87.7, which means that perhaps a third of the children are scoring at levels perilously near to those of retardation. IQ *declines* in the first decade of life, rising only slightly thereafter.

The effect of broken families on the performance of Negro youth has not been extensively measured, but studies that have been made show an unmistakable influence.

Martin Deutsch and Bert Brown, investigating intelligence test differences between Negro and white 1st and 5th graders of different social classes, found that there is a direct relationship between social class and IQ. As the one rises so does the other: but more for whites than Negroes. This is surely a result of housing segregation, referred to earlier, which makes it difficult for middle-class Negro families to escape the slums.

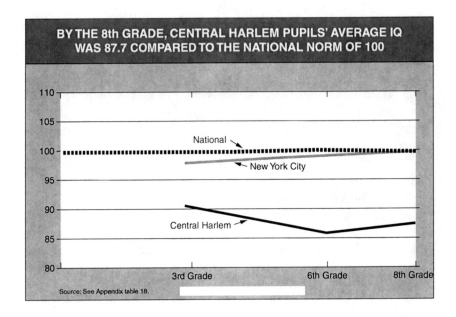

BY THE 8th GRADE, CENTRAL HARLEM PUPILS' AVERAGE IQ WAS 87.7 COMPARED TO THE NATIONAL NORM OF 100

Source: See Appendix table 18.

The authors explain that "it is much more difficult for the Negro to attain identical middle- or upper-middle-class status with whites, and the social class gradations are less marked for Negroes because Negro life in a caste society is considerably more homogeneous than is life for the majority group."[40]

Mean Intelligence Scores of Negro Children by School, Grade, Social Class, and by Presence of Father

Social Class and School Grade	Father Present	Father Absent
Lowest social class level		
Grade 1	95.2	87.8
Grade 5	92.7	85.7
Middle social class level		
Grade 1	98.7	92.8
Grade 5	92.9	92.0

(Adapted from authors' table.)

Therefore, the authors look for background variables other than social class which might explain the difference: "One of the most striking differences between the Negro and white groups is the consistently higher frequency of broken homes and resulting family disorganization in the Negro group."[41]

Father Absent from the Home

Lowest Social Class Level		Middle Social Class Level		Highest Social Class Level	
White	Negro	White	Negro	White	Negro
15.4%	43.9%	10.3%	27.9%	0.0%	13.7%

(Adapted from authors' table.)

Further, they found that children from homes where fathers are present have significantly higher scores than children in homes without fathers.

	Mean Intelligence Scores
Father Present	97.83
Father Absent	90.79

The influence of the father's presence was then tested *within* the social classes and school grades for Negroes alone. They found that "a consistent trend within both grades at the lower SES [social class] level appears, and in no case is there a reversal of this trend: for males, females, and the combined group, the IQ's of children with fathers in the home are always higher than those who have no father in the home."[42]

Percent of Nonwhite Males Enrolled in School, by Age and Presence of Parents, 1960

Age	Both Parents Present	One Parent Present	Neither Parent Present
5 years	41.7	44.2	34.3
6 years	79.3	78.7	73.8
7 to 9 years	96.1	95.3	93.9
10 to 13 years	96.2	95.5	93.0
14 and 15 years	91.8	89.9	85.0
16 and 17 years	78.0	72.7	63.2
18 and 19 years	46.5	40.0	32.3

SOURCE: 1960 Census, *School Enrollment*, PC (2) 5A, table 3, p. 24.

The authors say that broken homes "may also account for some of the differences between Negro and white intelligence scores."[43]

The scores of fifth graders with fathers absent were lower than the scores of first graders with fathers absent, and while the authors point out that it is cross sectional data and does not reveal the duration of the fathers' absence, "What we might be tapping is the cumulative effect of fatherless years."[44]

This difference in ability to perform has its counterpart in statistics on actual school performance. Nonwhite boys from families with both parents present are more likely to be going to school than boys with only one parent present, and enrollment rates are even lower when neither parent is present.

When the boys from broken homes are in school, they do not do as well as the boys from whole families. Grade retardation is higher when only one parent is present, and highest when neither parent is present.

The loneliness of the Negro youth in making fundamental decisions about education is shown in a 1959 study of Negro and white dropouts in Connecticut high schools.

Only 29 percent of the Negro male dropouts discussed their decision to drop out of school with their fathers, compared with 65 percent of the white males (38 percent of the Negro males were from broken homes). In fact, 26 percent of the Negro males did not discuss this major decision in their lives with anyone at all, compared with only 8 percent of white males.

A study of Negro apprenticeship by the New York State Commission Against Discrimination in 1960 concluded:

> Negro youth are seldom exposed to influences which can lead to apprenticeship. Negroes are not apt to have relatives, friends, or neighbors in skilled occupations. Nor are they likely to be in secondary schools where they receive encouragement and direction from alternate role models. Within the minority community, skilled Negro 'models' after whom the Negro youth might pattern himself are rare, while substitute sources which could provide the direction, encouragement, resources, and information needed to achieve skilled craft standing are nonexistent.[45]

Percent of Nonwhite Males Enrolled in School Who are 1 or More Grades Below Mode for Age, by Age Group and Presence of Parents, 1960

Age Group	Both Parents Present	One Parent Present	Neither Parent Present
7–9 years	7.5	7.7	9.6
10–13 years	23.8	25.8	30.6
14–15 years	34.0	36.3	40.9
16–17 years	37.6	40.9	44.1
18–19 years	60.6	65.9	46.1

SOURCE: 1960 Census, *School Enrollment*, PC (2) 5A, table 3, p. 24

Delinquency and Crime

The combined impact of poverty, failure, and isolation among Negro youth has had the predictable outcome in a disastrous delinquency and crime rate.

In a typical pattern of discrimination, Negro children in all public and private orphanages are a smaller proportion of all children than their proportion of the population although their needs are clearly greater.

On the other hand Negroes represent a third of all youth in training schools for juvenile delinquents.

Children in Homes for Dependent and Neglected Children, 1960

	Number	Percent
White	64,807	88.4
Negro	6,140	8.4
Other races	2,359	3.2
All races	73,306	100.0

SOURCE: 1960 Census, *Inmates of Institutions*, PC (2) 3A, table 31, p. 44.

It is probable that at present, a majority of the crimes against the person, such as rape, murder, and aggravated assault are committed by Negroes. There is, of course, no absolute evidence; inference can only be made from arrest and prison population statistics. The data that follow unquestionably are biased against Negroes, who are arraigned much more casually than are whites, but it may be doubted that the bias is great enough to affect the general proportions.

	Number of Arrests in 1963	
	White	*Negro*
Offenses charged total	31,988	38,549
Murder and nonnegligent manslaughter	2,288	2,948
Forcible rape	4,402	3,935
Aggravated assault	25,298	31,666

SOURCE: *Crime in the United States* (Federal Bureau of Investigation, 1963) table 25, p. 111.

Again on the urban frontier the ratio is worse: 3 out of every 5 arrests for these crimes were of Negroes.

In Chicago in 1963, three-quarters of the persons arrested for such crimes were Negro; in Detroit, the same proportions held.

In 1960, 37 percent of all persons in Federal and State prisons were Negro. In that year, 56 percent of the homicide and 57 percent of the assault offenders committed to State institutions were Negro.

	Number of City Arrests in 1963[1]	
	White	*Negro*
Offenses charged total	24,805	35,520
Murder and nonnegligent manslaughter	1,662	2,593
Forcible rape	3,199	3,570
Aggravated assault	19,944	29,357

[1] In 2,892 cities with population over 2,500.

SOURCE: *Crime in the United States* (Federal Bureau of Investigation, 1963) table 31, p. 117.

The overwhelming number of offenses committed by Negroes are directed toward other Negroes: the cost of crime to the Negro community is a combination of that to the criminal and to the victim.

Some of the research on the effects of broken homes on delinquent behavior recently surveyed by Thomas F. Pettigrew in *A Profile of the Negro American* is summarized below, along with several other studies of the question.

Mary Diggs found that three-fourths—twice the expected ratio—of Philadelphia's Negro delinquents who came before the law during 1948 did not live with both their natural parents.[46]

In predicting juvenile crime, Eleanor and Sheldon Glueck also found that a higher proportion of delinquent than nondelinquent boys came from broken homes. They identified five critical factors in the home environment that made a difference in whether boys would become delinquents: discipline of boy by father, supervision of boy by mother, affection of father for boy, affection of mother for boy, and cohesiveness of family.

In 1952, when the New York City Youth Board set out to test the validity of these five factors as predictors of delinquency, a problem quickly emerged. The Glueck sample consisted of white boys of mainly Irish, Italian, Lithuanian, and English descent. However, the Youth Board group was 44 percent Negro and 14 percent Puerto Rican, and the frequency of broken homes within these groups was out of proportion to the total number of delinquents in the population.[47]

> In the majority of these cases, the father was usually never in the home at all, absent for the major proportion of the boy's life, or was present only on occasion.

(The final prediction table was reduced to three factors: supervision of boy by mother, discipline of boy by mother, and family cohesiveness within what family, in fact, existed, but was, nonetheless, 85 percent accurate in predicting delinquents and 96 percent accurate in predicting nondelinquents.)

Researchers who have focussed upon the "good" boy in high delinquency neighborhoods noted that they typically come from exceptionally stable, intact families.[48]

Recent psychological research demonstrates the personality effects of being reared in a disorganized home without a father. One study showed that children from fatherless homes seek immediate gratification of their desires far more than children with fathers present.[49] Others revealed that children who hunger for immediate gratification are more prone to delinquency, along with other less social behavior.[50] Two psychologists, Pettigrew says, maintain that inability to delay gratification is a critical factor in immature, criminal, and neurotic behavior.[51]

Finally, Pettigrew discussed the evidence that a stable home is a crucial factor in counteracting the effects of racism upon Negro personality.

> A warm, supportive home can effectively compensate for many of the restrictions the Negro child faces outside of the ghetto; consequently, the type of home life a Negro enjoys as a child may be far more crucial for governing the influence of segregation upon his personality than the form the segregation takes—legal or informal, Southern or Northern.[52]

A Yale University study of youth in the lowest socioeconomic class in New Haven in 1950 whose behavior was followed through their 18th year revealed that among the delinquents in the group, 38 percent came from broken homes, compared with 24 percent of nondelinquents.[53]

The President's Task Fore on Manpower Conservation in 1963 found that of young men rejected for the draft for failure to pass the mental tests, 42 percent of those with a court record came from broken homes, compared with 30 percent of those without a court record. Half of all the nonwhite rejectees in the study with a court record came from broken homes.

An examination of the family background of 44,448 delinquency cases in Philadelphia between 1949 and 1954 documents the frequency of broken homes among delinquents. Sixty-two percent of the Negro delinquents and 36 percent of white delinquents were not living with both parents. In 1950, 33 percent of nonwhite children and 7 percent of white children in Philadelphia were living in homes without both parents. Repeaters were even more likely to be from broken homes than first offenders.[54]

Juvenile Delinquents—Philadelphia by Presence of Parents, 1949–54

	White			Negro		
	All Court cases	First Offenders	Recidivists	All Court cases	First Offenders	Recidivists
Number of cases	20,691	13,220	4,612	22,695	11,442	6,641
Number not living with both parents	7,422	4,125	2,047	13,980	6,586	4,298
Percent not living with both parents	35.9	31.2	44.4	61.6	57.6	64.7

SOURCE: Adapted from table 1, p. 255, "Family Status and the Delinquent Child," Thomas P. Monahan, *Social Forces*, March 1957.

The Armed Forces

The ultimate mark of inadequate preparation for life is the failure rate on the Armed Forces mental test. The Armed Forces Qualification Test is not quite a mental test, nor yet an education test. It is a test of ability to perform at an acceptable level of competence. It roughly measures ability that ought to be found in an average 7th or

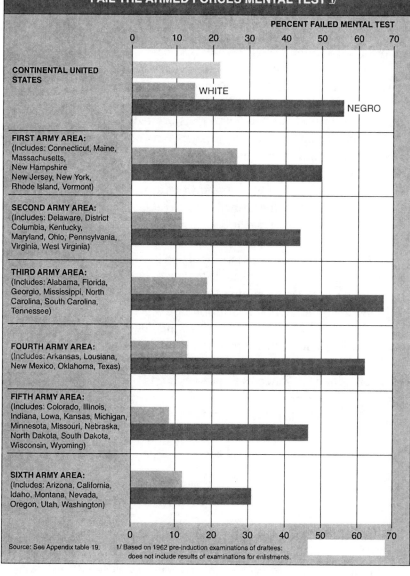

ALMOST FOUR TIMES AS MANY NEGROES AS WHITES FAIL THE ARMED FORCES MENTAL TEST 1/

PERCENT FAILED MENTAL TEST

CONTINENTAL UNITED STATES

WHITE
NEGRO

FIRST ARMY AREA:
(Includes: Connecticut, Maine, Massachusetts, New Hampshire New Jersey, New York, Rhode Island, Vermont)

SECOND ARMY AREA:
(Includes: Delaware, District Columbia, Kentucky, Maryland, Ohio, Pennsylvania, Virginia, West Virginia)

THIRD ARMY AREA:
(Includes: Alabama, Florida, Georgio, Mississippi, North Carolina, South Carolina, Tennessee)

FOURTH ARMY AREA:
(Includes: Arkansas, Lousiana, New Mexico, Oklahoma, Texas)

FIFTH ARMY AREA:
(Includes: Colorado, Illinois, Indiana, Lowa, Kansas, Michigan, Minnesota, Missouri, Nebraska, North Dakota, South Dakota, Wisconsin, Wyoming)

SIXTH ARMY AREA:
(Includes: Arizona, California, Idaho, Montana, Nevada, Oregon, Utah, Washington)

Source: See Appendix table 19.   1/ Based on 1962 pre-induction examinations of draftees; does not include results of examinations for enlistments.

8th grade student. A grown young man who cannot pass this test is in trouble.

Fifty-six percent of Negroes fail it.

This is a rate almost four times that of the whites.

The Army, Navy, Air Force, and Marines conduct by far the largest and most important education and training activities of the Federal Government, as well as provide the largest single source of employment in the nation.

Military service is disruptive in some respects. For those comparatively few who are killed or wounded in combat, or otherwise, the personal sacrifice is inestimable. But on balance service in the Armed Forces over the past quarter-century has worked greatly to the advantage of those involved. The training and experience of military duty itself is unique; the advantages that have generally followed in the form of the G.I. Bill, mortgage guarantees, Federal life insurance, Civil Service preference, veterans hospitals, and veterans pensions are singular, to say the least.

Although service in the Armed Forces is at least nominally a duty of all male citizens coming of age, it is clear that the present system does not enable Negroes to serve in anything like their proportionate numbers. This is not a question of discrimination. Induction into the Armed Forces is based on a variety of objective tests and standards, but these tests nonetheless have the effect of keeping the number of Negroes disproportionately small.

In 1963 the United States Commission on Civil Rights reported that "A decade ago, Negroes constituted 8 percent of the Armed Forces. Today . . . they continue to constitute 8 percent of the Armed Forces."[55]

In 1964 Negroes constituted 11.8 percent of the population, but probably remain at 8 percent of the Armed Forces.

Enlisted Men	Percent Negro
Army	12.2
Navy	5.2
Air Force	9.1
Marine Corps	7.6
OFFICERS	
Army	3.2
Navy	.2
Air Force	1.2
Marine Corps	.2

The significance of Negro under-representation in the Armed Forces is greater than might at first be supposed. If Negroes were represented in the same proportions in the military as they are in the population, they would number 300,000 plus. This would be over 100,000 more than at present (using 1964 strength figures). If the more than 100,000 unemployed Negro men were to have gone into the military the Negro male unemployment rate would have been 7.0 percent in 1964 instead of 9.1 percent.

In 1963 the Civil Rights Commission commented on the occupational aspect of military service for Negroes. "Negro enlisted men enjoy relatively better opportunities in the Armed Forces than in the civilian economy in every clerical, technical, and skilled field for which the data permit comparison."[56]

There is, however, an even more important issue involved in military service for Negroes. Service in the United States Armed Forces is the *only* experience open to the Negro American in which he is truly treated as an equal: not as a Negro equal to a white, but as one man equal to any other man in a world where the category "Negro" and "white" do not exist. If this is a statement of the ideal rather than reality, it is an ideal that is close to realization. In food, dress, housing, pay, work—the Negro in the Armed Forces *is* equal and is treated that way.

There is another special quality about military service for Negro men: it is an utterly masculine world. Given the strains of the disorganized and matrifocal family life in which so many Negro youth come of age, the Armed Forces are a dramatic and desperately needed change: a world away from women, a world run by strong men of unquestioned authority, where discipline, if harsh, is nonetheless orderly and predictable, and where rewards, if limited, are granted on the basis of performance.

The theme of a current Army recruiting message states it as clearly as can be: "In the U.S. Army you get to know what it means to feel like a man."

At the recent Civil Rights Commission hearings in Mississippi a witness testified that his Army service was in fact "the only time I ever felt like a man."

Yet a majority of Negro youth (and probably three-quarters of Mississippi Negroes) fail the Selective Service education test and are rejected. Negro participation in the Armed Forces would be less than it is, were it not for a proportionally larger share of voluntary enlistments and reenlistments. (Thus 16.3 percent of Army sergeants are Negro.)

Alienation

The term alienation may by now have been used in too many ways to retain a clear meaning, but it will serve to sum up the equally numerous ways in which large numbers of Negro youth appear to be withdrawing from American society.

One startling way in which this occurs is that the men are just not there when the Census enumerator comes around.

According to Bureau of Census population estimates for 1963, there are only 87 nonwhite males for every 100 females in the 30-to-34-year age group. The ratio does not exceed 90 to 100 throughout the 25-to-44-year age bracket. In the urban Northeast, there are only 76 males per 100 females 20-to-24-years of age, and males as a percent of females are below 90 percent throughout all ages after 14.

There are not really fewer men than women in the 20-to-40 age bracket. What obviously is involved is an error in counting: the surveyors simply do not find the Negro man. Donald J. Bogue and his associates, who have studied the Federal count of the Negro man, place the error as high as 19.8 percent at age 28; a typical error of around 15 percent is estimated from age 19 through 43.[57] Preliminary research in the Bureau of the Census on the 1960 enumeration has resulted in similar conclusions, although not necessarily the same estimates of the extent of the error. The Negro male *can* be found at age 17 and 18. On the basis of birth records and mortality records, the conclusion must be that he is there at age 19 as well.

Ratio of Males per 100 Females in the Population, by Color, July 1, 1963

	Males Per 100 Females	
Age	*White*	*Nonwhite*
Under 5	104.4	100.4
5–9 years	103.9	100.0
10–14 years	104.0	100.0
15–19 years	103.2	99.5
20–24 years	101. 2	95.1
25–29 years	100.1	89.1
30–34 years	99.2	86.6
35–39 years	97.5	86.8
40–44 years	96.2	89.9
45–49 years	96.5	90.6

SOURCE: *Current Population Reports*, Series P-25, No. 276, table 1 (Total Population Including Armed Forces Abroad).

When the enumerators do find him, his answers to the standard questions asked in the monthly unemployment survey often result in counting him as "not in the labor force." In other words, Negro male unemployment may in truth be somewhat greater than reported.

The labor force participation rates of nonwhite men have been falling since the beginning of the century and for the past decade have been lower than the rates for white men. In 1964, the participation rates were 78.0 percent for white men and 75.8 percent for nonwhite men. Almost one percentage point of this difference was due to a higher proportion of nonwhite men unable to work because of long-term physical or mental illness; it seems reasonable to assume that the rest of the difference is due to discouragement about finding a job.

If nonwhite male labor force participation rates were as high as the white rates, there would have been 140,000 more nonwhite males in the labor force in 1964. If we further assume that the 140,000 would have been unemployed, the unemployment rate for nonwhite men would have been 11.5 percent instead of the recorded rate of 9 percent, and the ratio between the nonwhite rate and the white rate would have jumped from 2:1 to 2.4:1.

Understated or not, the official unemployment rates for Negroes are almost unbelievable.

The unemployment statistics for Negro teenagers—29 percent in January 1965—reflect lack of training and opportunity in the greatest measure, but it may not be doubted that they also reflect a certain failure of nerve.

"Are you looking for a job?" Secretary of Labor Wirtz asked a young man on a Harlem street corner. "Why?" was the reply.

Richard A. Cloward and Robert Ontell have commented on this withdrawal in a discussion of the Mobilization for Youth project on the lower East Side of New York.

> What contemporary slum and minority youth probably lack that similar children in earlier periods possessed is not motivation but some minimal sense of competence.
>
> We are plagued, in work with these youth, by what appears to be a low tolerance for frustration. They are not able to absorb setbacks. Minor irritants and rebuffs are magnified out of all proportion to reality. Perhaps they react as they do because they are not equal to the world that confronts them, and they know it. And it is the knowing that is devastating. Had the occupational structure remained intact, or had the education provided to them kept pace with occupational changes, the situation would be a different one. But it is not, and that is what we and they have to contend with.[58]

Narcotic addiction is a characteristic form of withdrawal. In 1963, Negroes made up 54 percent of the addict population of the United

States. Although the Federal Bureau of Narcotics reports a decline in the Negro proportion of new addicts, HARYOU reports the addiction rate in central Harlem rose from 22.1 per 10,000 in 1955 to 40.4 in 1961.[59]

There is a larger fact about the alienation of Negro youth than the tangle of pathology described by these statistics. It is a fact particularly difficult to grasp by white persons who have in recent years shown increasing awareness of Negro problems.

The present generation of Negro youth growing up in the urban ghettos has probably less personal contact with the white world than any generation in the history of the Negro American.[60]

Until World War II it could be said that in general the Negro and white worlds lived, if not together, at least side by side. Certainly they did, and do, in the South.

Since World War II, however, the two worlds have drawn physically apart. The symbol of this development was the construction in the 1940's and 1950's of the vast white, middle- and lower-middle class suburbs around all of the Nation's cities. Increasingly the inner

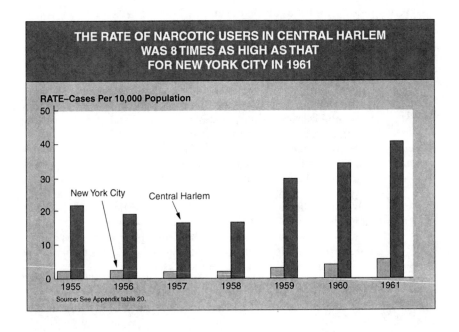

THE RATE OF NARCOTIC USERS IN CENTRAL HARLEM WAS 8 TIMES AS HIGH AS THAT FOR NEW YORK CITY IN 1961

RATE–Cases Per 10,000 Population

Source: See Appendix table 20.

cities have been left to Negroes—who now share almost no community life with whites.

In turn, because of this new housing pattern—most of which has been financially assisted by the Federal government—it is probable that the American school system has become *more*, rather than less segregated in the past two decades.

School integration has not occurred in the South, where a decade after *Brown v. Board of Education* only 1 Negro in 9 is attending school with white children.

And in the North, despite strenuous official efforts, neighborhoods and therefore schools are becoming more and more of one class and one color.

In New York City, in the school year 1957–58 there were 64 schools that were 90 percent or more Negro or Puerto Rican. Six years later there were 134 such schools.

Along with the diminution of white middle-class contacts for a large percentage of Negroes, observers report that the Negro churches have all but lost contact with men in the Northern cities as well. This may be a normal condition of urban life, but it is probably a changed condition for the Negro American and cannot be a socially desirable development.

The only religious movement that appears to have enlisted a considerable number of lower class Negro males in Northern cities of late is that of the Black Muslims: a movement based on total rejection of white society, even though it emulates whites more.

In a word: the tangle of pathology is tightening.

V. The Case for National Action

The object of this study has been to define a problem, rather than propose solutions to it. We have kept within these confines for three reasons.

First, there are many persons, within and without the Government, who do not feel the problem exists, at least in any serious degree. These persons feel that, with the legal obstacles to assimilation out of the way, matters will take care of themselves in the normal course of events. This is a fundamental issue, and requires a decision within the Government.

Second, it is our view that the problem is so inter-related, one thing with another, that any list of program proposals would necessarily be incomplete, and would distract attention from the main point of inter-relatedness. We have shown a clear relation between male employment, for example, and the number of welfare dependent children. Employment in turn reflects educational achievement, which depends in large part on family stability, which reflects employment. Where we should break into this cycle, and how, are the most difficult domestic questions facing the United States. We must first reach agreement on what the problem is, then we will know what questions must be answered.

Third, it is necessary to acknowledge the view, held by a number of responsible persons, that this problem may in fact be out of control. This is a view with which we emphatically and totally disagree, but the view must be acknowledged. The persistent rise in Negro educational achievement is probably the main trend that belies this thesis. On the other hand our study has produced some clear indications that the situation may indeed have begun to feed on itself. It may be noted, for example, that for most of the post-war period male Negro unemployment and the number of new AFDC cases rose and fell together as if connected by a chain from 1948 to 1962. The correlation between the two series of data was an astonishing .91. (This would mean that 83 percent of the rise and fall in AFDC cases can be statistically ascribed to the rise and fall in the unemployment rate.) In 1960, however, for the first time, unemployment declined, but the number of new AFDC cases rose. In 1963 this happened a second time. In 1964 a third. The possible implications of these and other data are serious enough that they, too, should be understood before program proposals are made.

However, the argument of this paper does lead to one central conclusion: Whatever the specific elements of a national effort designed to resolve this problem, those elements must be coordinated in terms of one general strategy.

What then is that problem? We feel the answer is clear enough. Three centuries of injustice have brought about deep-seated structural distortions in the life of the Negro American. At this point, the present tangle of pathology is capable of perpetuating itself without assistance from the white world. The cycle can be broken only if these distortions are set right.

In a word, a national effort towards the problems of Negro Americans must be directed towards the question of family structure. The object should be to strengthen the Negro family so as to enable it to raise and support its members as do other families. After that, how this group of Americans chooses to run its affairs, take advantage of its opportunities, or fail to do so, is none of the nation's business.

The fundamental importance and urgency of restoring the Negro

American Family structure has been evident for some time. E. Franklin Frazier put it most succinctly in 1950:

> As the result of family disorganization a large proportion of Negro children and youth have not undergone the socialization which only the family can provide. The disorganized families have failed to provide for their emotional needs and have not provided the discipline and habits which are necessary for personality development. Because the disorganized family has failed in its function as a socializing agency, it has handicapped the children in their relations to the institutions in the community. Moreover, family disorganization has been partially responsible for a large amount of juvenile delinquency and adult crime among Negroes. Since the widespread family disorganization among Negroes has resulted from the failure of the father to play the role in family life required by American society, the mitigation of this problem must await those changes in the Negro and American society which will enable the Negro father to play the role required of him.[61]

Nothing was done in response to Frazier's argument. Matters were left to take care of themselves, and as matters will, grew worse not better. The problem is now more serious, the obstacles greater. There is, however, a profound change for the better in one respect. The President has committed the nation to an all out effort to eliminate poverty wherever it exists, among whites or Negroes, and a militant, organized, and responsible Negro movement exists to join in that effort. Such a national effort could be stated thus:

> The policy of the United States is to bring the Negro American to full and equal sharing in the responsibilities and rewards of citizenship. To this end, the programs of the Federal government bearing on this objective shall be designed to have the effect, directly or indirectly, of enhancing the stability and resources of the Negro American family.

Notes

1. Robert Harris, *The Quest for Equality* (Baton Rouge, Louisiana State University Press, 1960), p. 4.
2. William Faulkner, in a speech before the Southern Historical Society in November 1955, quoted in *Mississippi: The Closed Society*, by James W. Silver (New York, Harcourt, Brace and World, Inc., 1964), p. xiii.
3. For a view that present Negro demands go beyond this traditional position see Nathan Glazer, "Negroes and Jews: The Challenge to Pluralism," *Commentary*, December 1964, pp. 29–34.
4. Bayard Rustin, "From Protest to Politics: The Future of the Civil Rights Movement," *Commentary*, February 1965, p. 27.
5. Nathan Glazer, *op. cit.*, p. 34.
6. *Youth in the Ghetto*, Harlem Youth Opportunities Unlimited, Inc., New York, 1964, p. xi.

7. Nathan Glazer and Daniel Patrick Moynihan, *Beyond the Melting Pot* (MIT Press and Harvard University Press, Cambridge, 1963), pp. 290–291.
8. E. Franklin Frazier, *Black Bourgeoisie* (New York, Collier Books, 1962).
9. Furnished by Dr. Margaret Bright, in a communication on January 20, 1965.
10. Maurine McKeany, *The Absent Father and Public Policy in the Program of Aid to Dependent Children* (Berkeley, University of California Press, 1960). P. 3.
11. "Facts, Fallacies and Future: A Study of the Aid to Dependent Children of Cook County, Illinois," (New York, Greenleigh Associates, Inc., 1960), p. 5.
12. Nathan Glazer, "Introduction," *Slavery*, Stanley M. Elkins (New York, Grosset & Dunlap, 1963), p. ix.
13. *Ibid.*, pp. xi–xii.
14. *Ibid.*, pp. ix–x.
15. Thomas F. Pettigrew, *A Profile of the Negro American* (Princeton, N.J., D. Van Nostrand Company, Inc., 1964), pp. 13–14.
16. Margaret Mead, *Male and Female* (New York, New American Library, 1962), p. 146.
17. *Ibid.*, p. 148.
18. E. Franklin Frazier, *The Negro Family in the United States* (Chicago, The University of Chicago Press, 1939), p. 298.
19. *Ibid.*, pp. 340–341.
20. *Ibid.*, p. 487.
21. Edward Wight Bakke, *Citizens Without Work* (New Haven, Yale University Press. 1940.)
22. *Ibid.*, p. 212.
23. *Ibid.*, p. 224.
24. Economic Report of the President, January 1965, p. 163.
25. Vera C. Perrella and Forrest A. Bogan, "Out of School Youth, February 1963," *Special Labor Force Report*, No. 46, Bureau of Labor Statistics, U.S. Department of Labor.
26. *Youth in the Ghetto, op. cit.*, p. 185.
27. E. Franklin Frazier, *Black Bourgeoisie* (New York, Collier Books, 1962.)
28. Robert O. Blood, Jr., and Donald M. Wolfe, *Husbands and Wives: The Dynamics of Married Living* (Illinois, The Free Press of Glencoe, 1960), p. 34.
29. *Ibid.*, p. 35.
30. *Ibid.*
31. Based on preliminary draft of a report by the President's Committee on Equal Employment Opportunity.
32. Whitney Young, *To Be Equal* (New York, McGraw-Hill Book Company, 1964), p. 25.
33. *Ibid.*, p. 175.
34. Thomas F. Pettigrew, *op. cit.*, p. 16.
35. Deton Brooks, quoted in *The New Improved American* by Bernard Asbell (New York, McGraw-Hill Book Company, 1965), p. 76.
36. Dorothy Height, in the Report of Consultation of Problems of Negro Women, President's Commission on the Status of Women, April 19, 1963, p. 35.
37. Duncan M. MacIntyre, *Public Assistance: Too Much or Too Little?* (New York, New York State School of Industrial Relations, Cornell University, Bulletin 53-1, December 1964), pp. 73–74.

38. Robin M. Williams, Jr., *Strangers Next Door* (Englewood Cliffs, N.J., Prentice-Hall, Inc., 1964), p. 240.

39. *Youth in the Ghetto, op. cit.,* p. 195.

40. Martin Deutsch and Bert Brown, "Social Influences in Negro-White Intelligence Differences," *Social Issues,* April 1964, p. 27.

41. *Ibid.,* p. 29.

42. *Ibid.*

43. *Ibid.,* p. 31.

44. *Ibid.*

45. "Negroes in Apprenticeship, New York State," *Monthly Labor Review,* September 1960, p. 955.

46. Mary H. Diggs, "Some Problems and Needs of Negro Children as Revealed by Comparative Delinquency and Crime Statistics," *Journal of Negro Education,* 1950, 19, pp. 290–297.

47. Maude M. Craig and Thelma J. Click, "Ten Years Experience with the Glueck Social Prediction Table," *Journal of Crime and Delinquency,* July 1963, p. 256.

48. F. R. Scarpitti, Ellen Murray, S. Dinitz and W. C. Reckless, "The 'Good' Boy in a High Delinquency Area: Four Years Later," *American Sociological Review,* 1960, 25, pp. 555–558.

49. W. Mischel, "Father-Absence and Delay of Gratification: Cross-Cultural Comparisons," *Journal of Abnormal and Social Psychology,* 1961, 63, pp. 116–124.

50. W. Mischel, "Preference for Delayed Reinforcement and Social Responsibility," *Journal of Social and Abnormal Psychology,* 1961, 62, pp. 1–7; "Delay of Gratification, Need for Achievement, and Acquiescence in Another Culture," *Journal of Abnormal and Social Psychology,* 1961, 62, pp. 543–552.

51. O. H. Mowrer and A. D. Ullman, "Time as a Determinant in Integrative Learning," *Psychological Review,* 1945, 52, pp. 61–90.

52. Thomas F. Pettigrew, *op. cit.,* p. 22.

53. Erdman Palmore, "Factors Associated with School Dropouts on Juvenile Delinquency Among Lower Class Children," *Social Security Bulletin,* October 1963, p. 6.

54. Thomas P. Monahan, "Family Status and the Delinquent Child," *Social Forces,* March 1957, p. 254.

55. Report of the U.S. Commission on Civil Rights, September 1963, p. 173.

56. *Ibid.,* p. 174.

57. Donald J. Bogue, Bhaskar D. Misra, and D. P. Dandekar, "A New Estimate of the Negro Population and Negro Vital Rates in the United States, 1930–1960," *Demography,* Vol. 1, No. 1, 1964, p. 350.

58. Richard A. Cloward and Robert Ontell, "Our Illusions about Training," *American Child,* January 1965, p. 7.

59. *Youth in the Ghetto, op. cit.,* p. 144.

60. Nathan Glazer and Daniel Patrick Moynihan, *op. cit.*

61. E. Franklin Frazier, "Problems and Needs of Negro Children and Youth Resulting from Family Disorganization," *Journal of Negro Education,* Summer 1950, pp. 276–277.

One of many critics of the "Moynihan Report," Laura Carper stresses the fact that "the Negro family is not the source of the 'tangle of pathology.' . . . It is the pathological relationship between white social institutions and the Negro community which has bred the statistics the report cites."

Using a unique ploy, the author characterizes the "pathology" of Irish, Puerto Rican, and, especially, Jewish families. She claims to use the same selective technique as that employed by Moynihan in his study of the Negro family. Underlying this critique is the provocative notion that what many call pathological responses may also be seen as healthy reactions to pathological situations

20

The Negro Family and the Moynihan Report

Laura Carper

MRS. BOYLE: We'll go. Come, Mary, an' we'll never come back here again. Let your father furrage for himself now; I've done all I could an' it was all no use—he'll be hopeless till the end of his days. I've got a little room in me sisther's where we'll stop till your throuble is over, and then we'll work together for the sake of the baby.

MARY; My poor little child that'll have no father!

MRS. BOYLE; It'll have what's far better—it'll have two mothers.

Juno and the Paycock, ACT III, SEAN O'CASEY.

The culmination of intensive efforts to codify the life of the hapless is a document published by the Department of Labor entitled *The Negro Family: The Case for National Action* and commonly referred to as "The Moynihan Report," after the reputed head of the investigation—the sociologist Daniel Moynihan. With the publication of this document a sociological theory which borders on an ideology has become a political weapon which we are all obliged to examine. In order to understand the theoretical framework within which this

From *Dissent,* 13 (March–April 1966), 133–140.

document was written, we must take a cursory look at sociological thought in the recent period.

In 1960, Dreger and Miller published in the *Psychological Bulletin* a critical evaluation of the "Comparative Psychological Studies of Negroes and Whites in the United States," which was an examination of the relevant contributions in the field between 1943 and 1958. They concluded that "in the areas of psychological functioning most closely related to the sociological, social class differences show up more clearly as a basis for differentiation between the two groups. Leadership, family life, child rearing practices, fertility and mate selection all seem to conform to social structure rather than to racial lines per se."

Dreger and Miller's conclusion reflected the intensive efforts of liberal sociological and psychological thought of the period. It was the culmination of a thoroughgoing examination of the corrosive effects of our peculiar social organization and value system on the Negro as compared to the white. They were unable to find a uniquely Negro personality or Negro psychology in any class. Their conclusion became a landmark in the field with which every investigator has been forced to contend.

In April 1964, however, *The Journal of Social Issues* published a collection of studies with an introduction by Thomas Pettigrew and Daniel C. Thompson and a lead article by Thomas Pettigrew which sought to delineate what Dreger and Miller were unable to locate—a Negro personality and a Negro psychology. Frankly admitting that in this effort social psychology was whistling in the dark since the Negro was notorious for his refusal to reveal his inner self to the social investigator and since it was virtually impossible to establish control groups of whites, Pettigrew nevertheless argued that past findings have "underestimated the corrosive effects on young children of impecunious ghetto living." This may indeed be true, but the theoretical basis of the issue is that due to the vicissitudes of his history and the brutality of white society, the Negro has developed a recognizable psychology and a recognizable personality which emerged under slavery, and that this psychology is self-sustaining and transmitted from generation to generation. The studies, together with the introduction, almost seem to argue for the existence of a racial unconscious.

The thinking here represents a powerful tendency in modern sociological thought; and it is this thinking, shorn of its somewhat hesitant and carefully hedged tone, which characterizes the ideological commitment of *The Report on the Negro Family* and the direction its authors feel national action should take.

The thesis of the Report is that Negro poor "confront the nation with a new kind of problem. Measures that have worked in the past, or would work for most groups in the present will not work here. A national effort is required that will give unity and purpose to the many activities of the Federal government in this area, directed to a new kind of national goal: the establishment of a stable Negro family structure." The presumption is that the Negro poor are no longer merely the victims of white institutional corruption but also, to an undetermined extent, of their corrosive family life; that despite the enactment of the voting rights bill, the creation of the "Manpower Retraining Program, The Job Corps, and Community Action—et al.," *fifty per cent* of the Negro population is incapable of profiting because of a psychological distemper.

The argument is supported with an array of statistics but without any effort to come to terms with the fact that variations in life style and social adjustment *within* the ghetto and between the Northern and Southern Negro poor are far more varied than between all of them and society at large. Fifty per cent of the Negro population is identified as reflecting the "social pathology" these statistics itemize, and the Negro family is recognized as its "source."

On page thirteen [page 372 here] there is a graph charting the nonwhite male unemployment rate and the number of AFDC (Aid to Families with Dependent Children) cases opened each year. This graph is the strongest argument the report offers to substantiate its thesis that the Negro poor have been so crippled by their situation and history that ordinary measures—which I suppose would be full employment, a radical revision of the ghetto school system, integrated education, decent housing, and a rigorously controlled police force—will no longer suffice; that what is now needed is a national effort not to alter our white social institutions but the way the Negro poor relate to each other on the primary personal level—the family.

The graph shows a direct correlation between the non-white male unemployment rate and AFDC cases opened each year between 1948 and 1961. As the unemployment rate drops, AFDC cases drop; as the unemployment rate rises, AFDC cases rise. But in 1962 a negative correlation begins to emerge; in 1963 the lines for each cross; in 1964 AFDC cases continue to rise as the unemployment rate continues to drop. Presumably, the negative correlation after 1962 shows or suggests that giving the Negro male a job will no longer insure or help insure family stability. The conclusion is that something more is needed.

I am not prepared to argue an economic determinist thesis. It is not my contention that the area of full employment is the only front on which we should fight. But I would like to attempt to explain the graph, particularly since the authors of the report direct the readers attention to the negative correlation and argue that no government program should be instituted which aims at relieving the plight of the Negro poor until the reasons for the reversal are understood.

The first consideration in evaluating statistics is to understand their relevance. *New* AFDC cases must therefore be compared with the unemployment rate of young Negroes. A little investigation shows that the unemployment rate for non-white males as a whole is not reflected in the unemployment rate of non-white youth. Non-white youth, male and female, show a radically different set of statistics; and it is of course the young and not the mature Negro woman who would be a new AFDC case. The unemployment rate for eighteen and nineteen year old non-white men rose from 23.9% in 1961 to 27.4% in 1963, and for eighteen and nineteen year old women who would be obliged to assist in the support of their families from 28.2% to 31.9%. Taken as a whole, the unemployment rate of non-white men between the ages of sixteen and twenty-four during the years in question fluctuates but shows little over-all change. In 1963, the year the lines for AFDC cases and the unemployment rate converged, the rates were especially high. Where the over-all non-white male unemployment rate went down in 1963, the unemployment rate for youth went up and then went down a little in 1964. The picture for young non-white women is comparable. Their rate showed a general tendency to increase.

These figures, although they radically temper the implications of the graph, do not account for the extent of the reversal. A complete explanation must include the famous 1962 change in the social security law. There is a remarkable correlation between AFDC figures and the date of the new law, which authorized greater social and case work service to the poor. In the state of Michigan at least (I choose Michigan arbitrarily, only because I live there and was in a position to discuss the graph with the welfare department), the department has interpreted this law as a directive to alter its standards. Prior to 1962, if an applicant was a poor housekeeper, mentally disturbed, or evidence of a male friend could be found, her application for AFDC was denied; after 1962 she was accepted if she showed need, regardless of her housekeeping practices, her mental health or her social life. Whereas between July 1960 and June 1961 33.4% of the applications were denied, only 28% were denied between July 1963 and June 1964. The strange graph in the Moynihan Report is the result of graphing the wrong things. The negative correlation is due to an inconsistency between youth unemployment rate and the unemployment rate of the non-white male population as a whole and to an important change in policy on the part of the welfare authorities. As a staff member of the department informed me, "it is our policy to give everyone a chance now." The thinking behind the new policy is that by accepting the "undeserving" poor as well as the "deserving" poor, case-work service is made available to those who need it most. It is inevitable that as news of this policy change spreads among the Negro poor and as each of the states slowly alters its policy to conform to this new view, AFDC cases will continue to rise.

The Negro family is not the source of the "tangle of pathology" which the report attributes to the Negro community. It is the pathological relationship between white social institutions and the Negro community which has bred the statistics the report cites—from low scholastic averages to drug addiction to arrest records to illegitimacy to unemployment rates. This is the reason the Black Muslims have chosen to withdraw, and this is the reason the civil rights movement has chosen to confront us.

The statistics I have tried to examine are the supportive evidence the report offers in defense of a social psychological theory. In brief the argument is that American slavery stripped the Negro of his culture and his most minimal human rights; and that the Negro, under continued oppression, developed a matriarchal family organization within which the male played an inadequate role, if any. The argument continues that since American family life is patriarchal, the matriarchal family formulation is pathological and is perpetuating a pathological Negro culture—as the statistics show. But I cannot help wonder with James Tobin, who published an interesting economic study in the Fall 1965 issue of *Daedalus*, why "personal attributes which doom(ed) a man to unemployment in 1932 or even 1954 or 1961 did not handicap him in 1944 or 1951 or 1956." Peter Townsend has pointed out that in 1930 many Englishmen estimated that as many as a million of their fellow-countrymen were unemployable because of their personal problems and only a decade later found that only 100,000 could be characterized in this way. There was a manpower shortage in 1940. What appears to be a social malformation in one period becomes the problem of isolated individuals in another.

The Negro poor are distinguished from the middle class primarily by the fact that they are poor. The father is haphazardly employed and at a very low wage. He is frequently absent from the family scene. He has either deserted or been thrown out by the mother. If he is present and works, he may squander his income. The children are raised by an extended family of adult women. This picture does not focus on fifty percent of the Negro families. But it does include a significant section of the Negro poor. Is it peculiar to them?

"Matriarchy" is a cultural formation common to many oppressed people throughout the history of western civilization—regardless of their own past history and regardless of the values they themselves held. A brilliant and moving characterization of how and why such a family constellation developed among the Irish poor can be found in Sean O'Casey's play *Juno and the Paycock*, from which I took the quotation which precedes this piece. The Irish matriarchal family formation is noteworthy because it existed in conflict with an Irish patriarchal ideal.

Both Patricia Sexton and Oscar Lewis have shown that the poor Puerto Rican family is beginning to move toward the same "pathology" as the Negro: illegitimacy and families with a woman at the helm.

The same can be said of Jewish family life in the *shtetl*. Although illegitimacy was not a problem (partly because divorce merely involved a witnessed statement placed in the hand of the wife; the father was frequently absent, either as a peddler on the road, as an immigrant in America, or as a permanent resident of the house of study who came home only to eat). Newly married couples usually moved into the home of the bride's parents. Among the Hassidic Jews (Hassidism was a movement initiated by the poor), it was common for the father to leave his wife and children without a kopek or a groshen in the house and depart for the Rebbe's court where he would dance and drink and spend all his money. As among the American poor, relations between husband and wife were cold and the roles of each clearly defined. The wife worked and assumed the main burden of supporting the family, and children became adults before they had ever had an opportunity to be children. The man either struggled desperately to make a living with little success or withdrew entirely into a private male society based on discourse or ecstasy and left the family to shift for itself. What the Jewish man succeeded in doing that the Negro man has failed to do is place a positive value on family desertion and personal withdrawal.

Since the Negro man does not rationalize his role as being a desirable religious achievement, it seems to me he would be easier to integrate into the surrounding culture than the Jew. After all, once integration became a viable possibility, even the *shtetl* Jew cast off what no longer served him. And the depth and extent to which oppression and poverty reduced the Jew can be measured by the disintegrative effects of the widespread Messianic movements, two of which emphasized orgiastic sexual practices as a means of insuring the coming of the Messiah.

I have chosen to detail the matriarchal organization of the Jewish family life not because it corresponds to the Negro family but because sociologists look upon Jewish family life as remarkably cohesive. Is the caricature I have drawn of the *shtetl* family accurate? Of course not. I have applied Mr. Moynihan's method of describing the Negro to a description of the Jew. I lumped a few hundred years of history together and failed to distinguish between people. Pathology is in the eye of the beholder. If one eliminates the positive social function of a cultural constellation, if one ignores the meaning personal relations have to the people involved, if one, in short, uses science to depersonalize, what emerges is always pathology. For health involves spontaneous human feelings of affection and tenderness which the Moynihan Report, like my deliberate caricature of Jewish family life, cannot encompass.

Let me also add that I am not trying to draw any direct analogies between the Irish poor, the Jewish poor, or even the Puerto Rican poor, and the Negro poor. I am seeking to show the "matriarchy" within the larger social context of what the report calls "patriarchy" is common to the way of life of poor people. And further, that people living under oppression always develop social formations which appear to the surrounding oppressive culture to be excessive or pathological. The form these so called excesses take varies from culture to culture and person to person within the culture—but no matter how extreme the nature of the adjustment, once the social pressure which created it is removed, a new adjustment develops. A people is not destroyed by its history. What destroys a people is physical annihilation or assimilation, not its family life.

The question the report raises is the direction a government program would take to insure family stability. What is the quality of the solutions Mr. Moynihan has in mind? The report includes a detailed description of the therapeutic effects of military service. Mr. Moynihan argues that the armed forces are educational and that they "provide the largest single source of employment in the nation." He admits that "for those comparatively few who are killed or wounded in combat, or otherwise, the personal sacrifice is inestimable. But on balance, service in the Armed Forces over the past quarter-century has worked greatly to the advantage of those involved. . . . Service in the United States Armed Forces is the *only* [author's italics] experience open to the Negro-American in which he is truly treated as an equal: not as a Negro equal to any white, but as one man equal to any man in a world where the category 'Negro' and 'white' do not exist." Mr. Moynihan further states that for the Negro "the armed forces are a dramatic and desperately needed change: a world away from women, a world run by strong men of unquestioned authority, where discipline, if harsh, is nonetheless orderly and predictable and where rewards, if limited, are granted on the basis of performance." This view of the desirability of army life is patently absurd. Underlying the Report's understanding of the problems of the Negro family is its author's concept of masculinity. According to the Report "the essence of the male animal, from the bantam rooster to the four-star general, is to strut."

I cannot here counterpose my taste in men or my concept of the good life against Mr. Moynihan's—but it seems clear to me that it is for the Negro male himself to determine his sexual and social style—whether strutting or not.

The challenge to the Negro community is political. It remains to be seen whether we can make room for the poor to acquire social and economic power. This is our social problem—and not the existence of a matriarchal family organization. What is more, Frank Riessman has found that involving emotionally disturbed people among the Negro poor in the civil rights movement can resolve their personal problems. What is destructive to the Negro man and woman is social impotence here and now, and what rehabilitates them is social power and the struggle for it. It is not new for a ruling elite to characterize its poor as incontinent and shiftless. It is the characteristic way in which those on top describe those on the bottom, even when sincerely trying to uplift them. My Negro landlady encountered a helpful woman who tried to tell her that Negro culture was rooted in the life style of slavery and fixed by history. In telling me about the conversation my landlady said, "That woman thinks that if she handed me a bail of cotton, I'd know how to make a dress out of it!" The Negro is not grappling with the social system under which he lived over a hundred years ago, or even with the social system under which he lived ten years ago. He is grappling with the social system under which he lives today.

In this second critique of The Negro Family, *Benjamin F. Payton is more concerned with the moral implications of what Moynihan says—and, presumably, stands for—than his interpretation of empirical data (though Payton has something to say about this as well). Perhaps the most significant example is Payton's concern over Moynihan's suggestion that "equality of group" must replace the traditional "equality of opportunity" argument.*

Here, curiously, Moynihan's sentiments (at least as viewed by his critic) are being echoed by militant young blacks who are demanding categorical rather than individual treatment. This represents the very sort of trend in civil rights that concerns the author of the following essay.

21

New Trends in Civil Rights

Benjamin F. Payton

An unusual kind of perplexity and frustration seems to have settled recently over segments of the civil rights movement. The phrase "an unusual kind" is used deliberately, for bewilderment and even failure have never been strangers to the leaders and participants of a movement that for decades skirted along the edges of political ostracism and social obloquy.

The peculiar character of the present quandary seems to be related to the very success of the movement in dealing with past frustrations; in overcoming the reluctance of Chief Executives to act on its behalf; in persuading the Supreme Court to protect its constitutional prerogatives; in prodding a fearful Congress to institute new laws to safeguard its constituents; and finally in shaming church and synagogue into affirming the moral majesty of its cause, in deed as well as in word, with bodies as well as with testaments.

Presently there are at least two schools of thought on how this

From *Christianity and Crisis*, 25 (December 13, 1965), 268–271; copyright by Christianity and Crisis, Inc., 1965.

perplexity can be explained. The first assumes that in the process of undoing the above-mentioned frustrations the major obstacles to the elimination of discrimination were also eradicated. It then goes on to view the present situation as a stage "beyond discrimination." According to this view, the trouble with the civil rights movement is that it does not understand that the central issue is no longer achieving "equality of opportunity" but is instead a matter of achieving "equal results." Because the debilitating conditions of slavery and the ensuing generations of deprivation have quite effectively disorganized the institutional structure of the Negro community, the power to reach the goal of "equal results" cannot be mobilized by Negro initiative in a relationship of equality with other groups. "Cultural deprivation" within the Negro community must, therefore, be overcome in order that "the newcomers" will be adequately socialized in the proper use of power.

In this view the next steps must be taken within the context of the Negro community itself by persons more qualified than Negroes to take them. The civil rights movement can form a sometimes useful adjunct to such efforts.

The second school of thought insists that America is far from reaching a "post-discrimination" stage. It holds that much of the bewilderment in the movement is a product of the rapid entrenchment of the "how-successful-we-have-been" view, particularly as expressed in the minds of persons who claim to be friendly to the movement. Exponents of this view insist that the undoing of *past* frustrations to the achievement of racial justice merely uncovered deeper resistances that continue in complex and often devious ways from the present into the future.

This school also believes that theories of "cultural deprivation," oddly tied to a goal more impossible than "equal opportunity," are but new masks for the old face of prejudice, new rationalizations for a persistent refusal to share power and position more equally with Negroes. Just as the next stage in the struggle may not be a battle strictly for *civil* rights, so the subject of the struggle is not only the underdevelopment of the Negro community but also the immaturity of the larger society, particularly its urban areas.

We will discuss the issues here under three headings: (1) "Equality," the Problem of Definition; (2) "Negro Family Stability" and the Problem of Power; and (3) "Metropolis" and the Problem of Context. Because of its immediacy and relevance, the report prepared early this year by the U.S. Department of Labor under the title *The Negro Family: The Case for National Action* will help shape the discussion. Written by Daniel P. Moynihan and Paul Barton when the former was Assistant Secretary of Labor, the document has come to be known as the "Moynihan Report."

"Equality," the Problem of Definition

According to some observers, the civil rights movement has pushed a new definition of "equality" to the fore of American politics. While the term tends to mean "equality of opportunity" in the minds of most white people, the report says that it "now has a different meaning for Negroes. . . . It is not (or at least no longer) a demand for liberty alone, but also for equality—in terms of group results. . . . It is increasingly demanded that the distribution of success and failure within one group be roughly comparable to that within other groups. It is not enough that all individuals start out on even terms, if the members of one group almost invariably end up well to the fore, and those of another far to the rear."

Now "equality" is the regulative principle for the whole notion of social justice. If this transformation from equality of opportunity to equality of group results has indeed occurred, then a major change in the meaning of an important moral concept has taken place, producing as it were an ideological chasm of vast proportions between Negroes and whites. For a real conflict between the ways in which Negroes and whites understand "equality" would further exacerbate relations between the two groups and make future agreements on the nature of the moral issue all but impossible. Since the evidence brought forth to support the point is so sketchy—two quotes, one from a sociologist and another from Bayard Rustin—one may be permitted the luxury of doubting the validity of the assertion.

In the event that Mr. Moynihan is proved correct, the problem ceases to be empirical and becomes a philosophical one. Is any group, whether white or Negro, morally justified in demanding "equal rights"? Can any group or person legitimately claim more than an "equal chance" to receive life's goods and services? I think not. The problem is that the "Moynihan Report" is not thoughtful enough about the nature of and the relationship between the moral concepts it uses.

A more assiduous process of concept-clarification would show that if the meaning of "equality of opportunity" has changed, it has become not a demand for "equal results" but a claim for intergroup relationships in which *equal chances* to achieve are a social reality and not just a legal theory. As R. H. Tawney has observed, authentic equality of opportunity "obtains insofar as . . . each member of a community, whatever his birth or occupation or social position, possesses in fact, and not merely in form, equal chances of using to the full his natural endowments of physique, of character and of intelligence." By imputing to Negroes the belief that "it is not enough that all individuals start out on even terms," the "Moynihan Report" assumes that Negroes do in fact enjoy equal life chances, but that for reasons rooted in historic past discriminations, the Negro community has been so traumatized that equal life chances are not enough.

Actually, of course, this point of view unintentionally falsifies the ethical problem and renders even more impossible the critical political problem. The goal of the civil rights movement is in the succinct title of Whitney Young's book, *To Be Equal.* But, as he says therein, "our basic definition of equal opportunity must include recognition of the need for special effort to overcome serious disabilities. . . ." Nevertheless, the claim for a "special effort" in behalf of the Negro is not a demand for equal results—an awkward and impossible goal. It is, again in Mr. Young's words, a demand "to provide the Negro citizen with the leadership, education, jobs, motivation, and opportunities that will permit him to help himself. It is not a plea to exempt him from the independence and initiative demanded by our free society. Just the opposite. It is a program crafted to transform the dependent man into the independent man."

The problem, therefore, is discrimination—in the present as well as in the past—not the failure to produce equal results under the assumed conditions of real equality of opportunity. A "special effort" is required precisely in order to produce equal life chances.

The Negro Family and the Problem of Power

The most serious mistakes of the "Moynihan Report" occur in the course of its analysis of the Negro family as "the fundamental source of the weakness of the Negro community at the present time." While acknowledging a relationship between the rate of unemployment and family stability, the burden of the report seeks to demonstrate that in 1960 "for the first time unemployment declined but the number of new Aid to Families with Dependent Children cases rose. In 1963 this happened a second time. In 1964 a third." Therefore, he arrives at "one central conclusion," namely that "the present tangle of pathology is capable of perpetuating itself without assistance from the white world." The point being that whereas under ordinary circumstances improvement in the broader socio-economic structures would produce positive changes in family life, the "tangle of pathology" in which the Negro family is involved prevents this from happening. Therefore, the report concludes, "a national effort toward the problems of Negro Americans must be directed toward the question of the family structure."

It should be said that the errors of the report are not rooted in any racial hostility on the part of its authors. Nevertheless, these errors have already produced quite damaging political consequences. They have led to facile "explanations" of the urban riots of 1964–65, and continue—clearly contrary to the intention of its authors—to provide ammunition to those who would deny to Negro citizens real equality of opportunity. (Southern newspapers have lifted large segments from the report and printed them.) Political consequences aside, the more important question relates to the validity of the report itself as a scientific piece of work. On this point some very glaring errors must be noted.

First, the report is much more optimistic about the employment situation among Negroes than are other observers. The crucial factor is income level, which Herman Miller, one of our most competent authorities on income statistics, believes is actually worsening rather than getting better among Negroes relative to whites.

Second, the method of analyzing family data by color instead of by income level results in an alarmist picture of differences between white and Negro family structures. Other more careful studies by Hylan Lewis at Howard University allow for income differential and reach much more sober conclusions.

Third, the analysis of illegitimacy rates among Negroes fails to analyze; it would have reached different conclusions if, rather than producing statistics without interpretation, it had taken into account these considerations: (1) the differential circumstances under which Negroes and whites report illegitimate births—the former mainly in *public* hospitals, the later mainly in *private* hospitals where concealment is much easier; (2) the approximately 2 million abortions that are performed each year in the United States, 95–99 per cent of them on white women; (3) unequal access to contraceptive devices and information; and (4) differential rates of adoption of Negro and white illegitimate children. Analysis of data by these factors reduces considerably the difference and removes entirely the alarmist overtones of the relationship between white and Negro family structures.

More important, careful analysis would show that however pathological or disorganized the Negro community might be, the student movement, the continued power of the Negro church and the tremendous "coping skills" generated by the Negro family itself are but a few of the factors that demonstrate the community's great reserves of untapped power and health. If these were harnessed under Negro leadership but with larger and more relevant national resources and co-operation, the remaining gap between Negroes and whites—a gap caused by continuing forms of discrimination—can be rapidly closed. If the focal point of the effort to mobilize our larger resources is not the Negro family, then neither is the main context the Negro community: it is, rather, Metropolis—its incoherences, its scarcities and its continuing discriminations.

Metropolis and the Problem of Context

In a University of Michigan commencement address, President Johnson summarized the goals of his Administration in his concept of the Great Society. Whatever else the term may mean, *sociologically* it refers to those broad changes under way in modern life that—initiated by large-scale industrial and technological innovations, sustained by the migration of masses of people from different backgrounds into urban areas and, more recently, out again into the suburbs—have transformed the relationships of small community life. In the process, they have complicated interminably the problem of ordering society in terms of such concepts as "justice" and "the common good."

The root problem is not, therefore, Negro "family breakdown" rooted in past injustices but "urbanization," its conflicts, inadequate resources and injustices. Urbanization raises the problem of civil rights to a new level, for it "means the creation of multi-ethnic metropolises." (Matthew Holden, Jr., *The Journal of Politics*, Vol. 26, No. 3, Aug. 1964, p. 637.) The problem that is really basic not only to the well-being of Negro citizens but to the health and security of the body politic is that "many central cities of the great metropolitan areas of the United States are fast becoming lower-class, largely Negro slums." The civil rights movement has forced us all to confront the fact that we must view not only the rural deltas of Mississippi but "the metropolitan area as a racial problem." (Morton Grodzins in *American Race Relations Today*, Raab, Ed., Double-day Anchor Book, p. 85.)

I have called the key problems raised acutely in this context "scarcity" and "discrimination." More accurately, they are abundant resources *scarcely used* and discrimination in Metropolis. Much of the bewilderment in the civil rights movement is rooted in the perception that even some friends find it impossible to see the issue this way.

But the facts show rather clearly that America is approaching a critical watershed in dealing with the civil rights issue. Welfare doles and social tinkering simply will not meet the crying, desperate needs heralded by the civil rights movement. A bold and imaginative statement of priorities needs to be set before the Federal Government, with a price tag attached. For municipal and state and private budgets simply do not have the resources to meet the developing crisis. The Federal Government must, therefore, make a bold entry into the whole arena of "metropolitics." . . .

If only they had listened!

This is the theme of Melvin M. Tumin's description of the failure of the American government to heed what social scientists have been telling them about race relations in this country for more than a quarter of a century. The author discusses and lists some eight empirically based generalizations emanating from a wide variety of basic research projects, all of which had (and have) important implications for social action. According to Tumin, "it was all there for the knowing, and it was all, or in large part, ignored. . . ."

Tumin goes further and describes two epochs: the earlier, basic research period and the recent time of government studies such as those by Moynihan, James Coleman, and the Civil Rights Commission. The findings of the former era were ignored by those who could have helped; the latter, he says, are being damned by those who could benefit most from their recommendations. Tumin suggests one fundamental reason why such a reaction has been forthcoming: "The Negroes, or at least many of them, simply no longer trust or believe in the efficacy of the slow workings of democracy. . . ."

22

Some Social Consequences of Research on Racial Relations

Melvin M. Tumin

Quite contrary to ordinary and widespread belief about scientific "ivory towers," there has been a serious and despairful lag between the time that scientists have published crucial research findings and the time, if at all, that public and private policy have moved toward any implementation of these findings. This, of course, renders preposterous the common allegations of ivory-tower escapism by academic scientists.

For there can be no doubt in the minds of anyone familiar with the social science research on race relations that today we would not have a history of recurring riots and civil disorders, nor a menacing threat of continued and unending riots and disorders, participated in by Negroes of all classes and educational levels, if, starting with the 1942 publication of the Myrdal volume on the situation of the American Negro, government and other agencies at federal, state and local levels had been at all responsive in any significant degree to

From The American Sociologist, 3 (May 1968), 117–123. Reprinted by permission of the American Sociological Association.

the obvious warnings and danger signs that social science research posted with much vigor and prominence.

One may say, in effect, that a major cause of the enormous foment of hate, anger, and despair in the Negro community today, and of the capacity of a small group of extreme militants to take legitimate leadership away (even if only temporarily) from the most serious, thoughtful, and concerned traditional leadership of the Negro community, has been the failure of the American government and public to respond to Negro needs in precisely the ways in which social science research since the 1940's, and even before, has indicated that these could and should be responded to, if we did not want to have what we have today by way of extraordinary intergroup conflict and hostility.

Consider, for instance, the fact that since 1940, and up through 1954 (when, for ten years, social science research on race relations was put into quietus by a shutdown in government and foundation sponsorship), we have had brilliant and detailed documentation of the plight of Negroes in every sector of their lives, political, economic, educational, residential, and in their family structures and in such life chances as infant mortality and early death and high rate of broken family. We had, also, in the 1940's, several major handbooks of methods and techniques for the reduction of prejudice and discrimination, as in the excellent inventories by Robin Williams (1947) and Arnold Rose (1948). In the 1940's, too, we had a masterful analysis of the web of government, and of intergroup relations within that web, conceived in terms of tensions and tension-reductions, by Robert MacIver, in his *The More Perfect Union* (1948). We had, too, the grave warnings regarding the weaknesses and cracks in American character and personality given to us by the studies in authoritarian personality. This is not to mention the more than prolific flow of articles and applied investigations documenting what Negroes felt and wanted and what the resistances were like in the white community.

So, too, if anyone was unclear as to what the nature of prejudice and the social sources of prejudice and discrimination might be, we had the fertile and seminal 1954 Allport volume on these topics, and a very valuable inventory of the best literature, compiled for the 1954 *Handbook of Social Psychology* by Harding, Kutner, Proshansky and Chein.

And if anyone wanted to know and cared about what was boiling up in Negroes under the pressure of increasingly denigrating and unacceptable circumstances of life, it was there for the reading and understanding in the terribly important and insightful *Mark of Oppression* (1950) by Kardiner and Ovesey.

Finally, and in some sense, firstly, we have had unending documentation since the 1930's of the insignificance and uselessness of skin color as a predictor of abilities and talents, and hence, the certain conclusion of the random interchangeability for all cultural functions of Negroes and whites. Here the works of Otto Klineberg and Ashley Montagu, among others, are outstanding.

One can say, then, with accuracy and exactness, that it was all there for the knowing, and it was all, or in large part, ignored, on three mistaken assumptions: (1) that slow and grudging minor concessions toward a far removed equality and first-class citizenship would suffice to handle things nicely because (2) after all, whites had the power and could dictate the terms and conditions and tempos and (3) after all, Negroes were docile, unorganized, and without leadership or the capacity for militant protest.

Not only were these assumptions wrong (and dangerously so), but, if stupidity is measured by the extent to which action is taken or not taken in spite of all evidence to the contrary, then these assumptions were stupidly mistaken as well.

That stupidity and that danger were compounded several times over by the failure to take advantage of the second chance that was given to the public and the government by the 1954 Brown *vs.* Topeka court decision regarding the inherently unequal character of segregated schools. Normally, history does not give such second chances, nor, except rarely, such third chances as the opportunities and warnings provided by the Montgomery bus strike and the early 1950 sit-ins by Negro college students. It should have been apparent when those Negroes with the best chances of "making it" in America took to civil disobedience that unless real change was initiated by white government and white society, Negroes would take the initiative.

I am not speaking here in the comfort of correct hindsight, like some Monday-morning quarterback. Those of us who have been working and writing and speaking in this field are on record with our researches and our warnings. We take no comfort in having seen and spoken of these things earlier than others. What comfort can there be in "speaking into the wind"? But, perhaps strong and urgent words now may contribute something to movement by government at all levels and by the lay public, quickly, deeply, and significantly enough to reduce some of the likelihood of widespread and ever more dangerous civil disorders that predictably face us from now on in.

Let us put the nonresponsiveness of government to social science research into historic perspective. When one does this, one sees two rather distinct periods.

If we date the effective beginnings of social science research on race relations from the Myrdal report (1944), we have a picture of a first period consisting of a decade of considerable activity from 1944 to 1954.

Then, starting in 1955, there is an apparent hiatus that lasts almost ten years, during which almost no major works in race relations appear. (A modest exception was my own study of readiness for and resistance to desegregation in a North Carolina city 1958).

Since 1964, however, we have had three major research publications on race: Daniel Moynihan's report on *The Negro Family* (1965); the 1966 Civil Rights Commission Report on *Racial Isolation*; and the extraordinarily provocative study by James Coleman and others in 1966 on *Equality of Educational Opportunity*.

It is important to distinguish between these two periods for several reasons. First, we are informed by these dates and facts that substantial research in the field is not much more than twenty years old, and that, of those twenty-two or twenty-three years since the Myrdal report, nearly half were prevented by political considerations from being significant.

Secondly, we are presented with a neat division between two different kinds of works. They differ, first, in the fact that all the important research work in the earlier period was financed either by universities or by foundations, or, in some cases, was done on shoestring budgets by individual scholars. In sharp contrast, the three major works of the last three years, on the Negro family, Negro isolation, and Negro education, were all sponsored and paid for and published by government agencies: the Department of Labor, the Civil Rights Commission, and the Office of Education.

From this first difference, we draw some inferences for an important second distinction between the two periods. The works of the earlier period seem largely to have arisen partly from the troubled consciences and partly from the scientifically immanent pressures in the academic community. By contrast, the latest documents of the second period seem to have been generated within the government bureaus themselves, as direct and surprisingly rapid responses by government to the tensions and pressures generated by social action in the Negro community (always remembering, of course, the presence in such bureaus of an increasing number of research people with academic histories or prospects).

These are not opposite tendencies that we are contrasting here. They differ, but they are not in direct contradiction. In the first case, the main feature seems to be one of relative detachment of research from policy, in either possible direction of flow of effects. In the second case, the flow of effects seems to go from social action in the streets to government concern about such action and then, from there, to the expression of that concern by government in the form of policy-related research; then, as we shall see soon, the movement is back to the streets again.

This is the picture we get of contrasting epochs and styles of research and of relationships between research and policy, if we focus alone on the three recent studies of family, isolation and education.

When one narrows his focus in that way, however, he tends to overlook the extraordinary richness of other basic research and policy-relevant documents prepared by individual scholars in the last four or five years. Consider, in this light, the 1964 book by Michael Harrington, *The Other America*, which can truly be said to have helped America and its government rediscover poverty in this country, after Galbraith had almost persuaded us not to give it a second thought. Can one doubt that the Harrington book made poverty respectable, both for public policy action and for social science research? And surely, Negro poverty and its consequences are central to race relations in this country.

Of equal importance, though in quite a different genre, is Samuel Bloom's 1964 book, *Stability and Change in Human Characteristics*. It was this book, more than any other, which alerted the academic, government, education, and lay communities to the dangers of early childhood, cultural, and intellectual deprivation, and documented the enduring consequences of such deprivation. We may worry much, as perhaps we should, about the ways in which Bloom's notion of early retardation has been dramatically and dangerously oversimplified. But we cannot deny the great care and scholarliness of Bloom's work and its significance for a vast array of both basic and applied researches. There may have been programs of higher horizons and cultural enrichment before Bloom's book. But the enthusiastic public support for the development and proliferation of such programs (albeit based on an untested assumption of their absolute indispensability to equality of education) can accurately be dated as coming after and because of this book and its dispersed messages.

Consider, too, the ingenious experimentation from 1962 on, by Robert Rosenthal at Harvard, on the subject of experimenter bias, which is easily translated into teacher bias. This research is outstanding for its demonstration of the types and intensities of distortion in testing outcomes that preconception about such outcomes can produce. Join this work with that of Harry Passow and Miriam Goldberg on homogeneous groupings and tracking, and we have the research matrix out of which vital policy implications for educational reform can and have been drawn. We see, for instance, from these works, how the self-confirming hypothesis and the self-verifying prejudice take on worlds of dangerous meanings when applied to the educational process and when related to early childhood deprivation.

I cite just these few works, two of them by outstanding academics and one by a social reformer and essayist, all of them apparently modest in dimension but decisively significant in their implications, so that I can now indicate that these works did not represent crash efforts, incited and impelled by the actions in the streets of dissident minorities; nor did they represent government responses to political pressures. But in many important senses they are as significant and consequential as the three major works sponsored by government bureaus. And surely of the Bloom and the Rosenthal works one can say that they represent basic rather than applied research, and primary research rather than secondary compilation. Further, whatever their political uses, they represent what the internal demands of developing bodies of scientific thought suggested were important next steps in research. The same remarks can be applied with almost equal force to the Myrdal volume and the earlier work by E. Franklin Frazier (1932) on the Negro family.

That these basic and primary scientific researches have had applied, secondary and political consequences is certain. One may also venture the judgment that if the political groundwork and setting had not been fertile and receptive to these studies, they would have remained recherché documents, treasured by various segments of the intellectual and academic community, but only occasionally, if at all, seeping into public view in today's mass market of information through the mysterious osmosis in which ladies' journals play a crucial part.

We are saying, in effect, that while these basic and primary researches had evident potential political vitality, that vitality was not expressed until the political ambiance was appropriate, and until, in a rather interesting and perhaps novel way, the implications of the basic research findings were put into politically usable and commanding form in the applied studies by Moynihan, Coleman, and the Civil Rights Commission, under the impulsion of the need of government to make a dramatic and sympathetic response to the agitation in the Negro community regarding the persisting plight of the Negro.

If it is fair to say that the applied researches by government bureaus gave political translation to the basic research materials, it is equally fair and important to note that the applied researches could hardly have been done with any success at all, and indeed might hardly have known what were the relevant questions to ask, if the basic researches had not already been on record. This is not to denigrate the quality of thought that went into the applied researches by the government bureaus, but rather to indicate the extent and quality of their interplay with the basic research materials which underlay them both theoretically and temporally.

If one now raises questions as to what these interrelations of basic and applied science and public policy and action indicate about scientific sensitivity to topical and pressing issues of the day, it is clear from the range of connections just cited that science can and does relate to policy in a variety of ways and that, judging by the dates of the research and applied documents, and by the political issues to which they were relevant, scientists have proven extraordinarily sensitive to what is going on "out there." If anything, they have been perhaps too sensitive and responsive. For, because of their urgent and full political relevance at the time of their appearance, these research materials have tended to get less of the basic scientific evaluation and criticism that all such documents need, and have tended too much to be judged in anti-scientific contexts and by irrelevant political criteria.

In any event, there is little point in debating whether scientists have been alert enough to the needs of the community. The research of the early period was way ahead of any public or governmental interest or action, even by the concerned victims themselves. In addition, the newer researches, though admittedly more applied than basic, could hardly have been more timely. Where then is the far-famed and deprecated "ivory tower"?

Perhaps most interesting and most curious and perhaps, too, most important of all, is the way in which the major findings of both the basic and applied researches have been greeted, responded to, and acted upon by the concerned public.

We can see this clearly by indicating first what the basic findings from those researches were, and then comparing the range of reactions expressed to them and actions taken upon them.

Here then are some of the major research findings:

1. Negroes and whites are, under conditions of equal opportunity and training, interchangeable at random for all cultural roles.

2. Desegregation and integration of Negroes and whites in all social contexts are indispensable to the achievement of equal opportunity and training for Negroes and for the achievement of stable political order for the society.

3. Negro social structures, especially Negro families and communities,

under prevailing ghetto conditions, require a fundamental reconstruction if they are to function effectively in the contributions our society expects such groups to make to the preparation of the child for adequate and satisfying functioning in the society.

4. Basic reconstruction of the economy, and the educational system and the polity are unavoidable if the Negro substructures are themselves to be able to be reconstructed adequately.

5. Until such reconstruction takes place, fundamental repair, compensatory and uplift work must be done to help Negro children over come the unavoidable disadvantages and deficiencies so many of them incur in their inadequate primary group training and support.

6. Wholesale reconstruction of the educational process, and reeducation and retraining of teachers are required to enable the schools to work adequately, and with something approaching equality, for underprivileged and deprived Negro children. Especially crucial here are those structures of relationships and of attitudes which tend to generate stereotypical preconceptions in teachers and other school officials regarding children's abilities or the lack of them and which function to create ceilings of limitations and restrictions on their possible growth.

7. The circles of miseducation, inadequate preparation, and poverty are interlocking and self-reinforcing. Especially in the economic sphere, the filtering-down effects that economists hope will ensue from a so-called tight labor market have not been very visible, insofar as the bottom twenty percent or so of income earners, where the Negroes are primarily located, seem to experience not more than a few droplets of the affluence circulating vigorously in the upper-half of the income brackets. Massive refurbishing of the economy appears, therefore, to be indispensable if the vicious cycle of self-reinforcing poverty is to be broken.

8. Close collaboration between Negroes and whites is vital to the development and enrichment of the democratic institutions and processes which are indispensable both to the improvement and uplift of the Negro community and to the general welfare of the entire society.

These, then, are some of the main policy implications which may be drawn from the researches. It is not, let us point out, that the researches say that Negroes *should* be made equal, uplifted, freed from poverty, and the like. But if they *are* to be freed from poverty, uplifted, and made equal, then the foregoing eight steps, among others, seem indispensable.

It is quite evident that these policy implications which have been drawn indirectly from the basic researches, and more directly and explicitly formulated and advocated in the applied documents put together by Moynihan, Coleman, and the Civil Rights Commission all were "on the side of the angels" insofar as that side is defined as being in favor of doing everything reasonable and conceivable, within the limits of democratic process, for the improvement of the situation of the Negroes.

It is most curious, indeed, in this light, to see the way in which the Moynihan thesis of the negative role of the often broken and misfunctioning Negro family in the development of Negro children has been seriously attacked by Negroes as a racist document, one, it is alleged, that seeks to displace the blame for the Negro situation onto the shoulders of the Negroes themselves and thus to divest the white community of its responsibility. Any simple reading of the Moynihan document will show that no such implications are to be found in the study. Yet this matter is still hotly debated. All these accusations, and the responses by Moynihan and others to them, and the responses of others to these responses, are documented at great length in the intriguing recent work by Lee Rainwater and William Yancey (1967). It is perfectly clear, from a reading of the ping-pong of controversy that this book recites, that this is one of those cases where one is sure to be damned by someone for something, no matter what he says.

In the same light, consider the recent fate of the Civil Rights Commission report on racial isolation. It has been attacked with great polemic elegance and even careful supplementary research by Joseph Alsop, of all people, on the grounds that it advocates an impossible, and hence dangerous, mandate to place desegregation of the schools first and foremost on the priority of required actions. This mandate was recently given legal force by Judge Skelly Wright's decision regarding the Washington schools, in which Wright ordered desegregation of the schools in the District, where over ninety percent of the students are Negro. Alsop argues persuasively, with supporting data, that this order is simply incapable of being implemented, and that any effort to do so, and thereby to delay focusing upon improving the quality of education without regard to desegregation of the facilities, is not only utopian but is dangerous and harmful to the Negro school child.

The exchanges in the *New Republic* between Alsop (1967) and social scientists (Schwartz et al., 1967), including one who served as chief consultant to the Civil Rights Commission in its study, have served to throw the connection between research and policy into a fearful muddle—or at least even more fearful a muddle than the one in which they already were embroiled. If Alsop's figures regarding likely Negro concentrations in major urban areas are correct, and they seem persuasively so at the moment, then, the whole point of the study of racial isolation, so far as its obviously intended demand for desegregation is concerned, is lost. So, too, the whole force of the Skelly Wright decision is emasculated, if indeed it was not already—even before it was written. Yet the Wright decision is surely the most liberal and far reaching implementation in formal law of the most soundly argued case for desegregation that social science research has been able to support.

How ironic, indeed, that such firmly based research and such courageously formulated law should find themselves arrayed in decisive battle against some of the persons in the interest of whose emancipation they were conceived and executed.

Nor does the case for the irony end there. For now the Coleman report is with us, and with it, the dissemination through the community of interested scholars and participants of the presumed finding that almost nothing about schools seems to make a significant difference in the intellectual functioning of the children who come to the schools. The exceptions are minor and almost trivial.

As with all scientific findings, one can go in quite opposite action directions with the very same data. Do the schools really not matter? Then forget about them, and especially about the efforts to desegregate them, since while "desegregation" may be somewhat more relevant than other factors, it is hardly worth mentioning itself.

Or, do the schools really not matter? Then, it must be that *as constructed* they do not matter, and what then can we do about reconstructing them so that they *will* matter in significant degree? Or, focusing alone on segregation *vs. desegregation*, if now the amount of desegregation seems to be trivially relevant to the intellectual performance of the children, then let us find out how and under what conditions desegregation might make a difference. Or, if segregation doesn't seem to be intellectually and otherwise any worse for Negro children, then forget about desegregation and try to build quality education in the ghetto schools.

But *will* quality education matter? The Coleman Report is in various quarters being interpreted as saying that even this is of little significance. Yet, in other quarters, the Coleman Report itself is being questioned; not its intent, or the worthiness of its having been accomplished, but rather its methodology and its sample and its instruments and its analysis. Perhaps, it is being suggested, the Report finds that the schools do not matter because the instruments used for testing the consequentially of differences in schools simply could not detect or grasp those dimensions of educational process and structure which might make very significant differences. And perhaps, too, others are urging, no repair work to the schools can possibly be effective that does not attack and destroy the basic conception of school as a process of competitive movement of differentiated cohorts through fixed curricula. Since the Coleman Report does not compare such drastically different alternative schools, perhaps that is why the schools, no matter how different, do not seem to make much of a difference.

We have, then, in these three most recent major works, instances of government responding to the pressure of events—riots, demonstrations, and the whole mess, by initiating and completing large-scale studies or surveys of the situation which could serve only to highlight with great effect the actual state of affairs. The intention could have been only to dramatize the situation enough to provoke further demand for effective government action and to disarm the likely opposition to such further welfare measures.

And they served their purposes—each of these studies did. They *did* highlight, and they *did* dramatize, and they *did* evoke the clamor for effective action, legislative and otherwise.

What neither they—nor anyone—expected, however, was the kind of Negro reactions they evoked—including most prominently, a reversal to a demand for separatism and grass roots community development and autonomy; in effect, for reinforced segregation. Had these demands been made by any but Negro militants, they would surely have been dubbed racist and white supremacist.

One can say, with some painful humor, that never has social research been so substantial, in the first instance, and so relevant in the second instance to matters of pressing moment, and *so quickly followed up with social action and policy that run directly against the major grain of the research.*

In using the phrase—the "major grain of the research"—I am appearing to imply that the research suggests a direction of social action. But this is not so. The research *per se*, indicates no direction at all and never does, in the nature of the thing called scientific research. The directionality is given, if at all, by the conditions under which the research is initiated and by the obvious intention of the initiators and supporters.

The report on the Negro family could never have been intended for any program other than social reconstruction of the Negro community, through massive intervention by government, to permit Negro families to play more positive functions.

The report on equality of opportunity in education could surely never have been meant to do anything other than to retestify to the persistence of segregated schooling and the attendant damages, especially in the education of Negroes, in spite of the 1954 Court decision and the implementing decisions and measures formulated since then.

How then can we account for the adverse and reverse reactions of some portions of the Negro community to these researches? Why, in effect, have some of the Negro leaders chosen to stand the researches upside down, and recommend Negro separatism? Why should the notion of cultural deprivation have come to be considered a slur? Why the emphasis on a so-called indigenous and rich Negro culture? Why the denial of the role of the Negro family and community in the production of deprived and under-privileged children? Why the attack by Negroes on their closest allies in the white communities, the so-called white liberals, and the promulgation of the curious doctrine that it is better to deal with a whole and open racist than with a person who struggles against his own prejudices to act fairly? (Nor will any reading of Kenneth Clark on this subject or any of the other Negroes who have addressed themselves to it, make this any clearer.) Why, too, the active denial and denunciation of the doctrines of competence and fitness as criteria of eligibility for employment, and the substitution, instead, of the demand for quotas of Negroes in this and that place, regardless of competence? Why, above all, the reemergence of color consciousness, anti-white racism, and the insistence on the primacy of color as a criterion of selection and eligibility?

All of these would seem to run directly contrary, not only to what the researches show is necessary to Negro freedom and equality in this country, but what is also indispensable to any chance for a pluralist democratic polity, inside of which the Negro, like all other minority groups, has surely the best chance for a decent chance at a decent life.

There is a clear-cut answer. The Negroes, or at least many of them, simply no longer trust or believe in the efficacy of the slow workings of democracy and its customary slow modes of social change. They are not impressed with the arguments that point to the character of our federal government and its relations to the federation of 50 states, with the implicit set of states rights as obstacles to full equality. Nor do they care how resistant Southern Congressmen or Northerners may be, and how much the political process requires bargaining. Nor do they believe that we can have an all-out domestic effort and, at the same time, a 25 billion dollar-a-year war. They know, now, as never before, that power is as power does and that as humble petitioners they are not likely in their life-times to secure that to which they were entitled three hundred years ago.

Are they wrong to react in these ways? Perhaps. But the government, itself, has appeared to prove that they are right. The government, in its three major recent researches, has in fact documented the correctness of the despair and the disbelief of Negroes in the adequacy of American democratic institutions to change their lives significantly.

What an irony indeed! The government pays for major researches which prove that it is really not very worthwhile, nor wise, to trust in that government. What else could Negroes deduce from the fact that the Moynihan Report proves beyond a doubt how enduringly injured and wounded Negro children have been and will be by the broken sub-structures and primary groups in which they grow, and in which the adults have few, if any, alternatives to the modes of life they conduct?

And how else can we read the study of racial isolation, except as a document that verifies beyond doubt how little has been done to reduce segregation in communities and schools? And can there be any doubt that whatever else the Coleman Report tells us (perhaps wrongly), it unmistakably tells us that the schools, at least as presently structured, simply won't make any real difference in helping Negro children to become first-class citizens of this country?

If, then, Negroes say, because they feel it and have heard it and can see it, that this society has not moved; that its laws have not worked; that its protections have not been provided; that its facilities have not been shared; if this is how it looks to them, and if the Harrington volume, and the isolation study, and the Moynihan and Coleman reports tell them with figures that this is so, can anyone fail to understand why the Negroes draw the inferences they do about the need to secure power, to shake up the society, to dramatize their plight, and, if need be to construct their own society within a society?

The explanation, then, for the reverse and negative interpretations by Negroes of the best and most reliable findings of scientific research initiated on their behalf, must therefore be sought in these politics of despair and anger. It is as though a challenge has been seen by the Negro community: a challenge to "make it in America," against all odds and all existing institutional obstacles to the contrary. From one point of view, this represents an extraordinarily courageous kind of stand. From another point of view, it represents, curiously, the acceptance by the Negro community of the most-hated of white conservative or reactionary demands, namely, "All other groups have made it by them-selves and through self-help, so why can't you?"

From still another point of view, the Negro response is a translation into social policy of the doctrine of grass-roots community development, as against the élite, tough-nosed economist model of a developed élite pulling the rest of the community up by its bootstraps.

Whichever way one views these Negro responses, and whatever reasons one sees for them, they are there. Against them, however, must be set the less spectacular reactions of the majority of the Negro community who still, from all available information, pursue their way slowly, painfully, against great odds, through the American maze, searching for some greater margin of political, economic, and educational rights than they have had before; struggling, in short, through the rank order of their demands in just about the way that Myrdal asserted they would and against the same kinds of rank-ordered oppositions that Myrdal predicted they would meet.

Yet, one dares not take comfort in the fact of the peacefulness of the majority of Negroes. For, it takes no more than a tiny minority of determined and embittered men to initiate and sustain widespread civil disorder. And if a significant portion of the leadership of Negro militants comes from the better-educated, middle-class Negro group, let us not forget that there is also a very substantial layer of hating and hated, alienated and impoverished, Negro slum youth and adults for whom the opportunity to attack and wound and destroy any and every symbol of the society that hates and fears them is welcomed with pleasure and glee. For, to destroy that society, or its symbols, is proof of their manhood as well as serving as a delicious ventilation of their anger, even when they destroy their own houses and stores and streets.

Two facts persist that we must pay attention to, then. First, if Negroes are going to "make it" in American society, they are going to make it within the framework of democratic institutions and through the normal modes of social and economic mobility.

But if they are to have the opportunity to do so, and if they are to be realistically hopeful that they can do so, white society has to be willing, far more willing than it has been, to open the doors of that system of opportunity to Negroes. Failure to do so now, immediately, hugely, and dramatically, will insure that more and more of the peaceful majority of Negroes will pass over to the violent minority and that the momentary unattractiveness and weakness of the legitimate and peaceful Negro leadership will become a quasipermanent fact.

The fact is that either white society responds appropriately and actively to legitimate Negro demands and needs, or be prepared to meet the certainty of ever-increasing violent insurgence. One way to meet such insurgence, of course, is to wage all-out war against the Negro community. The white community, would, of course, win such a pitched battle, but in the process it just as surely would destroy itself and everything it values.

And what will government do, government at the federal, state and local levels, if in fact, resentful white, ethnic minorities decide to respond to Negro violence with their own counter violent insurgence? Never mind that a majority of whites would not do this. Insurgency needs only small, determined minorities.

These are the warning signs that social science research and Negro political action have once again posted.

As for the future of scientific research in these fields, it is not unlikely that the next phase will find numerous investigators taking up deliberate postures of social action, "justifying" these in the name of scientific obligations, and taking their cues as to tactics from the leads provided by the more militant and anti-intellectual segments of the Negro community.

Indeed, this trend is already in motion. A number of social scientists have become openly avowed partisans of Negro separatism and violence, and are claiming both the scientific propriety and the research support for their orientations. Needless to say, these orientations are neither proper nor supported. But such considerations are not likely either to persuade or deter these new partisans. Nor, on the other hand, are their new directions of activity likely to add anything significant to reliable knowledge about race relations, except as other, more dispassionate, observers, come to study them as instances of interesting, relevant, and important social experiments.

I say all this because I do not believe that as scientists we do science or society any good at all by jumping on political bandwagons. If science, for instance, is to serve well its own internal needs as well as the political needs of the community in the period to come, it would seem far wiser for it to be concerned with serious careful study of the why's and wherefore's of the successes and failures of the predictable efforts at Negro self-help and indigenous community development. For, failures there will be—no question—and perhaps even some modest successes. But if we become partisans of this or that cause, we will destroy our credibility and our capacity to function effectively as scientists, in the analysis of these outcomes.

So, too, if it seems, as it does, that Higher Horizons and Head Start and More Effective Schools do not seem to serve fully or even partly the purposes for which they were intended, perhaps this finding may lead in the future to investigating why it is that these programs do not work and what kinds of programs will work. For the Bloom and Rosenthal findings, among others, tell us that *some* such programs must work. Their researches show how the opposite works when the opposite forces are put into play, even if only impersonally in a class and color conscious society. That is, degradation, destruction, and restriction of potential are very effective indeed under prevailing circumstances of delayed start, impoverished beginning, and early circumscribed horizons.

I argue for scientific "detachment," too, because the hopes and lives of the people involved in these matters are simply too precious to permit them to be tossed about recklessly by this and that partisan demand that take turns gaining regnancy, not by the persuasiveness of their logic or even the rectitude of their sentiments, but rather by their deliberate and painful indifference to what is politically salutary in a democratic society and to what is needed if genuine equality is ever to be gained for all citizens.

If I see in all this one line of hope and optimism regarding the relation of science to policy, it is in the extraordinary growth of relevance of science, both in fact, as government and social action now operate, and in sentiment and belief, as the public now conceives of the role of science. It would, indeed, be a sad day if in this flush of new-found meaning and acceptance, science were to foul itself and its possible services to democracy and equality by insisting on altering the crucial role it has heretofore played and which has helped secure it prominence and acceptance.

As scientists, we shall probably always be damned by someone, sometimes more loudly than at others. We do ourselves no good by being sensitive to such damnation. We have, after all, our own kind of internal and immanent damnation to deal with. We shall serve everyone, including ourselves, much more effectively if we stick to our own lasts and are guided by our own best lights. These lasts and lights have not failed in the last 25 years to point the way to resolutions of our problems for those who cared to hear it as it really is and to go where the action is.

Notes

Allport, Gordon (1954). *The Nature of Prejudice*. Cambridge, Mass.: Addison-Wesley.

Alsop, Joseph (1967a). "Ghetto education." *The New Republic* (November 18); (1967b). "No more nonsense about ghetto education." *The New Republic* (July 22).

Bloom, Samuel (1964). *Stability and Change in Human Characteristics*. New York: John Wiley.

Clark, Kenneth B. (no date cited). *"Delusions of the white liberal."* Mimeograph.

Coleman, James S. et al. (1966). *Equality of Educational Opportunity*. Office of Education, U.S. Department of Health, Education, and Welfare. Washington, D.C.: U.S. Government Printing Office (OE-38001).

Frazier, E. Franklin (1932). *The Negro Family in Chicago*, Chicago: University of Chicago Press.

Harding, J. et al. (1954). In Gardner Lindzey (ed.), *Handbook of Social Psychology*. Cambridge, Mass.: Addison-Wesley.

Harrington, Michael (1963). *The Other America*. New York: Macmillan.

Kardiner, Abram, and Ovesey, Lionel (1962). *The Mark of Oppression* Cleveland: World Publishing (Meridian Books).

Klineberg, Otto (1935). *Race Differences*. New York: Harper & Row.

MacIver, R. M. (1948). *The More Perfect Union*. New York: Macmillan.

Montagu, Ashley (1952). *Man's Most Dangerous Myth: The Fallacy of Race*. New York: Harper.

Moynihan, Daniel P. (1965). *The Negro Family: The Case for National Action*. Office of Policy Planning and Research, Department of Labor. Washington, D.C.: U.S. Government Printing Office.

Myrdal, Gunnar (1944). *An American Dilemma: The Negro Problem and Modern Democracy*. New York; Harper.

Rainwater, Lee, and Yancey, William L. (1967). *The Moynihan Report and the Politics of Controversy*. A Transaction Social Science and Public Policy Report. Cambridge, Mass.: Massachusetts Institute of Technology Press.

Suggested Readings

Clark, Kenneth. *Dark Ghetto*. New York: Harper & Row, 1965.
A penetrating commentary on contemporary life in the Harlems of America.

Frazier, E. Franklin. *The Negro Family*. Chicago: University of Chicago Press, 1949.
The best-known study of the Negro family (and one upon which Daniel Moynihan drew in preparing his now famous report).

Grier, William H., and Price M. Cobbs. *Black Rage*. New York: Basic Books, 1968.
Case histories of black patients by two psychiatrists.

Moon, Bucklin, editor. *Primer for White Folks*. Garden City: Doubleday, 1945.
A collection of essays and stories on the problems of living in the "twoness" of a segregated society.

Myrdal, Gunnar. *An American Dilemma*. New York: Harper & Row, 1944.
The alleged discrepancy between "creed and conduct" is the thesis of this monumental volume. Its chief contribution, however, lies in a careful examination of Negro life during the first third of this century.

Pettigrew, Thomas. *A Profile of the Negro American*. Princeton: Van Nostrand, 1964.
A social psychologist looks at the society, culture, and, especially, the personality of the Negro at mid-century.

Rose, Arnold M. *The Negro's Morale*. Minneapolis: University of Minnesota Press, 1949.
A study of the problem of group identification.

Woodward, C. Vann. *The Strange Career of Jim Crow*. New York: Oxford University Press, revised 1966.
A study of the emergence of discriminatory practices in the Southern United States after the Civil War.

Youth in the Ghetto: A Study of the Consequences of Powerlessness. New York: Harlem Youth Opportunities Unlimited, Inc., 1964.
The famous "HARYOU-ACT" report on Harlem.

Index

CPSIA information can be obtained
at www.ICGtesting.com
Printed in the USA
FFOW01n1353160516
24130FF